Sexual Sameness

Lesbian and gay theory is now one of the most provocative areas of enquiry into questions of sex, gender and sexuality. *Sexual Sameness* looks at the differing textual strategies men and women writers have developed to celebrate same-sex living and loving. Examining writings as diverse as those of E.M. Forster, James Baldwin, Sylvia Townsend Warner and Audre Lorde, this wide-ranging book demonstrates how literature has been one of the few cultural spaces in which sexual outsiders have been able to explore forbidden desires. From the humiliating trials of Oscar Wilde to the appalling stigmatization of people living with AIDS, *Sexual Sameness* reveals the persistent homophobia that has until recently almost completely inhibited our understanding of lesbian and gay writing. In opening up lesbian and gay writing to informed and unintimidated methods of reading, *Sexual Sameness* will be of interest to a large and diverse lesbian and gay readership as well as to students of gender studies, literary studies and the social sciences.

Joseph Bristow is Lecturer in the Department of English and Related Literature at the University of York. He previously taught at Sheffield City Polytechnic. His books include *Empire Boys: Adventures in a Man's World* (1991), *Robert Browning: New Readings* (1991) and an edition of Oscar Wilde's *The Importance of Being Earnest* (Routledge 1992).

Sexual Sameness

Textual differences in lesbian and gay writing

Edited by
Joseph Bristow

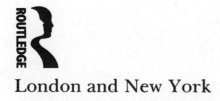

London and New York

First published 1992
by Routledge
11 New Fetter Lane, London EC4P 4EE

Simultaneously published in the USA and Canada
by Routledge
a division of Routledge, Chapman and Hall Inc.
29 West 35th Street, New York, NY 10001

Introduction and editorial material © 1992 Joseph Bristow

Typeset in 10 on 12 point Baskerville by
Florencetype Ltd, Kewstoke, Avon
Printed in Great Britain by
Butler and Tanner Ltd

British Library Cataloguing in Publication Data
Sexual Sameness: textual differences in lesbian and gay writing.
   I. Bristow, Joseph
   820.9920664

   ISBN 0-415-06936-X
   ISBN 0-415-06937-8   pbk

Library of Congress Cataloging in Publication Data
Sexual Sameness: textual differences in lesbian and gay writing/edited by Joseph
   Bristow.
        p.   cm.
   Includes bibliographical references and index.
   1. Gays' writings, English—History and criticism—Theory, etc.
   2. Lesbians' writings, English—History and criticism—Theory, etc.
   3. Lesbians' writings, American—History and criticism—Theory, etc.
   4. Gays' writings, American—History and criticism—Theory, etc.
   5. Homosexuality and literature.   6. Authorship—Sex differences.
   7. Lesbians in literature.   8. Gay men in literature.   I. Bristow, Joseph.
   PR120.G39S49   1992
   820.9'353—dc20   91–28659

   ISBN 0–415–06936–X   ISBN 0–415–06937–8 (pbk)

Contents

Contributors

David Bergman is the author of *Gaiety Transfigured: Gay Self-Representation in American Literature* (1991), and *Cracking the Code* (1985), which won the George Elliston Poetry Prize. He is Professor of English at Towson State University in Baltimore, Maryland.

Joseph Bristow is a lecturer in the Department of English and Related Literature at the University of York. He previously taught at Sheffield City Polytechnic. His books include *Empire Boys: Adventures in a Man's World* (1991), *Robert Browning: New Readings* (1991), and an edition of Oscar Wilde's *The Importance of Being Earnest* (Routledge English Texts, 1992).

Terry Castle, Professor of English at Stanford University, is the author of *Clarissa's Ciphers: Meaning and Disruption in Richardson's 'Clarissa'* (1982) and *Masquerade and Civilization: The Carnivalesque in Eighteenth-Century English Culture and Fiction* (1986). She is currently working on a book of essays on literary representations of lesbianism.

Diana Collecott teaches American and British literature at the Univeristy of Durham, England. Her doctorate is from the University of Bristol, and she has held research fellowships at Yale University for work in the manuscript collections there. She has contributed widely to journals and international symposia on modernism, feminist poetics and homosexuality, and is about to publish a full-length study of H.D.

Jonathan Dollimore is a reader in the School of English and American Studies at the University of Sussex. His previous writings include *Radical Tragedy: Religion, Ideology and Power in the Drama of Shakespeare and His Contemporaries* (1984, 2nd edn 1989), and *Political Shakespeare: New Essays in Cultural Materialism* (edited with Alan Sinfield, 1985). His most recent book is *Sexual Dissidence: Augustine to Wilde, Freud to Foucault* (1991).

John Fletcher, Lecturer in the Department of English and Comparative

Literature at the University of Warwick, is editor (with Andrew Benjamin) of *Abjection, Melancholia and Love: The Work of Julia Kristeva* (1990). He has published essays on psychoanalytic theory, homosexuality, film and literature. He is an Honorary Research Fellow at the Centre for Psychoanalytic Studies, University of Kent, a founding member of THERIP (the Higher Education Research and Information Network in Psychoanalysis), and a member of the Advisory Board of *Screen*.

Sherron E. Knopp is Professor of English at Williams College. She has published articles on a variety of classic and medieval topics – Catullus, Gottfried von Strassburg, *Le Roman de la Rose*, Chaucer and Arthurian romance – and is currently working on a book about Chaucer and medieval poetic theory, entitled *Chaucer and the Dilemmas of Fiction*. The essay on Virginia Woolf's *Orlando* won the Crompton-Noll Award of the Gay and Lesbian Caucus of the MLA in 1989.

Alan Sinfield's writings include *Political Shakespeare: New Essays in Cultural Materialism* (edited with Jonathan Dollimore, 1985), *Alfred Tennyson* (1986), *Literature, Politics and Culture in Post-War Britain* (1989), and *Faultlines: Cultural Materialism and the Politics of Dissident Reading* (1992). He teaches at the University of Sussex where he convenes the MA Programme in 'Sexual Dissidence and Cultural Change'. The essay in the present collection is part of a project on theatre and homosexuality from Wilde to Stonewall.

Clare Whatling is a graduate student on the Critical Theory Programme at the University of Nottingham.

Chris White is a lesbian Marxist who lives in Nottingham with her lover Elaine Hobby, two cats and a floating population of students. She is currently finishing her doctorate while teaching part-time at Loughborough University. She is editor (with Elaine Hobby) of a collection of lesbian literary criticism, *What Lesbians Do in Books* (1991).

Liz Yorke lectures part-time in English and women's writing at Manchester Polytechnic. She is the author of *Impertinent Voices: Subversive Strategies in Contemporary Women's Poetry* (1991), which examines the poetry of Adrienne Rich, H.D., Sylvia Plath, Olga Broumas, Audre Lorde and Susan Griffin in relation to French feminist theory.

Acknowledgements

Many people have greatly assisted in the making of this collection. First of all, my thanks must go to the editors of *Textual Practice*, particularly Terence Hawkes and Gillian Beer, for giving the project such encouragement at its earliest stages. Linda Anderson, Diana Collecott, and Judith Still offered important contacts which broadened the range of its contents. The Executive of the School of Cultural Studies at Sheffield City Polytechnic generously provided much-appreciated funds for my visit to the Third Annual Lesbian, Bisexual, and Gay Studies Conference at Harvard University in October 1990. Kate Flint gave me the opportunity to meet postgraduate students at the University of Oxford to discuss Wilde and *Dorian Gray*. Cath Cassy spent many hours converting Sherron Knopp's essay from its MLA format to the publisher's house style. Each of the contributors has been exceptionally patient with my numerous queries over the past twelve months. Finally, the indefatigable past and present editorial staff at Routledge – Jane Armstrong, Helena Reckitt, Talia Rodgers, and Julia Hall – were unfailing in their help.

Acknowledgements are made to the following for kindly granting permission to reprint these materials: the Editorial Board of *Textual Practice* for Chris White, ' "Poets and Lovers Evermore": The Poetry and Journals of Michael Field', Terry Castle, 'Sylvia Townsend Warner and the Counterplot of Lesbian Fiction', Diana Collecott, 'What is Not Said: A Study in Textual Inversion', and Alan Sinfield, 'Who Was Afraid of Joe Orton?'; the Modern Language Association for Sherron E. Knopp, ' "If I Saw You Would You Kiss Me": Sapphism and Subversiveness in Virginia Woolf's *Orlando*'; the Board of the Regents of the University of Wisconsin System for David Bergman, 'The African and the Pagan in Gay Black Literature'; GRM Associates, Inc., Agents for the Estate of Ida M. Cullen for 'Heritage' from the book *Color* by Countee Cullen © 1925 Harper & Brothers (copyright renewed 1953 by Ida M. Cullen); W.W. Norton & Co. for 'Love Poem', 'Dahomey', 'Litany for Survival', 'Letter for Jan', and 'Storybooks on a Kitchen Table' by Audre Lorde © 1975, 1978, 1982; W.W. Norton & Co. for 'The Phenomenology of Anger' and 'Splittings' by Adrienne Rich © 1974, 1978; McGraw-Hill Inc. for

extracts from 'Breaking Open' and 'Despisals' by Muriel Rukeyser ©
1982, reprinted by permission of William L. Rukeyser; to Carcanet Press
Ltd. and the New Directions Publishing Corporation for 'Hymen (1921)'
from H.D., *Collected Poems 1912–1944* © 1982 the Estate of Hilda
Doolittle; and King's College, Cambridge and the Society of Authors as
the literary representatives of the E.M. Forster Estate for permission to
reproduce the extracts from *Maurice* in Chapter 5. The photographs on
pp. 71, 86 and 89 are copyright of the Provost and Scholars of King's
College, Cambridge, and are located in King's College Library. The
photograph on p. 69 is reprinted by kind permission of the Director of
Sheffield Libraries and Information Services (Sheffield Archives,
Carpenter Collection Box 8/31a).

Every effort has been made to obtain permission to reproduce copyright
material. If any proper acknowledgement has not been made, or permission not received, we would invite copyright holders to inform us of
the oversight.

Joseph Bristow
School of Cultural Studies
Sheffield City Polytechnic
June 1991

1 Introduction

Joseph Bristow

Sexual Sameness brings together eleven representative essays by lesbian and gay literary critics working on both sides of the Atlantic. The focus is mainly on English and American literature, and the range of texts analysed here is reasonably wide – from the provocative fiction of Oscar Wilde to the controversial erotica of Joan Nestle. Practically all of these writings fall within a period of roughly one hundred years. Some of the authors under examination have been absorbed by the academy (Wilde, E.M. Forster, Virginia Woolf, James Baldwin), some are at present marginal to the canon (H.D., Sylvia Townsend Warner, Adrienne Rich, Audre Lorde), and others are in the process of being recovered (Michael Field, Langston Hughes, Countee Cullen). Their poems, plays, and novels shift to some extent across national and ethnic borders (Irish, English, white American, African-American). The collection maintains a more or less even balance between men and women writers. And the same may be said for the distribution of female and male contributors.

I wish to make the parameters of this volume of essays perfectly clear at the outset for a number of reasons. Although it is fairly obvious that each and every academic publication operates within particular institutional boundaries, and that the institutions in which we teach, read, and write about literary representation remain extremely powerful sites of cultural legitimation, these issues are especially pressing for those of us involved in researching lesbian and gay writing, since our field, in all its diversity, is only just coming into existence. The objects of our enquiry – literary works which disclose, articulate, even polemicize same-sex desires – have a peculiar standing within a discipline that has for many years placed an extraordinary emphasis on questions of value and discrimination, and therefore on marking out points of distinction between what is and is not worthy of serious analysis.

Over the past decade there have been several investigations into how and why English literary studies in Britain had at its inception to secure its place as a respectable field of study.[1] When it was established in the late nineteenth century, debates about the hazards of working-class literacy were particularly fraught, and proponents of English literature

1

in higher education laboured under considerable obligations to defend their work from charges of irresponsibility. As the educated classes looked despairingly at the ever-increasing sales of penny papers and other kinds of disreputable publication, there was certainly great pressure on advocates of English to make literary studies into a field of knowledge that had a clear moral purpose and a definite aesthetic value. Rather than pursue this point at length, all I need to add is that the aesthetic-moral axis around which the institutionalization of literature turned still has remarkable influence. To this day teachers frequently express concern about whether popular fiction, community drama, feminist writings, the narratives of soap operas – indeed, anything of dubious standing – ought to be allowed on the syllabus.

Yet considerable changes have indeed taken place in general academic awareness of what does and does not constitute 'literature'. Just as pedagogic methods for the transmission of skills in literary interpretation have shifted the centre of their authority away from the tutor more towards the student, so too have there been alterations in the scope of the texts we discuss in class, and the way we discuss them. Taught either by period or by genre (these are the prevailing models of text grouping on degree curricula), the works we consider in our seminars and lectures now include many more by women writers and Black writers. In this respect, publishing houses have both responded to and encouraged the redesigning of our literature programmes. And so it is fairly clear to see how canons of 'minority' writings – if we choose to call them that, and such labelling has its dangers – have been gradually forming since the 1970s and 1980s. These days we enjoy Virago Classics along with Penguin English Classics; and there is, to take a further example, the rich resource of the Schomburg Library of Nineteenth-Century Black American Women Writers, published by a company no less distinguished than Oxford University Press. But where do these disciplinary transformations leave lesbian and gay writing? And where, amid the residual moral-aestheticism of English studies, and the counter-cultural challenges of feminist and Black studies, might we locate lesbian and gay criticism?

Before proceeding to these important questions, let me first of all point out that lesbian and gay criticism does not comprise a coherent field. That, as I will argue, is its strength. Because of the alliance it endorses (the potentially controversial 'and' at its centre), it does not stand as one thing alone with fixed demarcations and singular methodological concerns. Indeed, it is vital to probe the co-ordinating conjunction – the 'and' – that yokes together the contributors, the academic practices, and the subject-matter involved in this book. By making connections between *sameness* and *difference* (and both terms have their complications), the title of this collection signals the overlapping concerns of discrete subcultures. *Lesbian* and *gay* designate entirely different desires, physical pleasures, oppressions, and visibilities. The mark of gender, given the cultural violence and the inequalities of power it sets in motion, is perhaps the most important distinction placed between lesbians and gay men. But both subordinated groups share parallel histories within a sexually prohibitive dominant culture, and these have inevitably brought us into the 'and' that both links and separates our sexual-political interests. Homosexuality is the word we are still too often made to share, even though it is clearly one one we have jointly learned to subvert and resist. This unhelpful and misleading sexual, legal, medical, and ultimately moral classification has for decades compounded our differences, and in its exceptionally inflexible implementation it has served to mask a great many confusions about sex, gender, and sexuality that saturate western culture. Its history, and the impact of that history on our own, need to be briefly examined here.

Emerging from late Victorian obsessions with sexual taxonomy (the precise origins of the term still remain open to debate: some say it came from developments in the fertilization of flowers, others from the work of a Hungarian sexual emancipationist), the category of the homosexual became a clinical definition that recognized for the first time, as Michel Foucault put it, a *type* of person, rather than a *sexual activity*, such as buggery.[2] The point I am making, however, is a simple one. No matter how we situate the modernity of this concept, homosexuality *denies the gendered difference* between men and women who desire their own sex. It produces sameness where there is not necessarily any at all. Only when modified by a sexual definition – male homosexuality or female homosexuality – can the distinction between lesbians and gay men be understood, and even then only within the severe limitations of an opposition between the sexes. This is an opposition that has served us very badly.

For a century at least, since Havelock Ellis theorized 'sexual inversion', the regulatory apparatuses of medicine, education, and the law have almost always seen us as two sides of the same coin. Images of lesbians and gay men frequently circulate in the popular imaginary as reflections of one another. Images of virile women and effeminate men preoccupy the popular press, if not more educated minds, and these keep reappearing on television, in the courts, and in books of literary criticism (to name just a few sites where this logic is in action) as versions of our apparently authentic selves. But, of course, the reality of our lives, not to say the literary representation of them, often speaks otherwise. None of us, either within our own gender or sexuality, conforms to one psychic, physiological, or political type – even if the idea of homosexuality would suggest that is the case. Desiring the same sex, we are not desiring the same things. Whatever our differences, then, we have historically been regarded, as it were, as twins. And since the law still insists on banishing our desires in almost the same breath – from public spaces, from school classrooms, from involvement in child custody, fostering and adoption, and so on – it is not so surprising that many of us have been led to make alliances with each other. Lesbian *and* gay criticism is one such outcome of the violence that has been done to us. And we are now seizing for the first time on the opportunity to consider openly how and why the dominant culture has silenced, excluded, and, sometimes in spite of itself, actually made spaces for, even produced, literary representations of same-sex desires by lesbian and gay writers. But in demonstrating that lesbian and gay male critics are prepared to appear between the covers of the same book, the structure of this collection should not be seen as a replication of how the dominant and heterosexually organized culture mistakes all the varying things we are. Nor should it be taken that the procedures adopted by these essays, juxtaposing a great range of desires, literary traditions and forms, and, importantly, concepts of sexuality are entirely compatible with one another.

If lesbian and gay studies is not a unified field (it refers outwards to two genders, and thus to two differing subcultures), it is none the less true that in the particular institutional history of literary studies lesbian and gay criticism has largely been enabled by more than twenty years of concerted feminist enquiry. Feminism has been its greatest intellectual resource. Yet the consequences of feminism in all its plurality have differing effects for lesbians and for gay men. Since lesbians have always played a prominent role within feminist campaigning since the 1960s, they have been instrumental in developing methods for investigating the cultural work of gender, the normative presuppositions of psycho-analysis, and the masculist biases of historiography, to name but a few of these achievements. There has, undeniably, been a strong presence of lesbian theory during what now adds up to more than two decades of feminist criticism. By comparison, gay men have worked from a much less advanced base of theory, and have had to learn a great many lessons from varieties of feminist scholarship.

This is an issue addressed by Eve Kosofsky Sedgwick in her introduction to *Epistemology of the Closet*, where the operative terms of sexual definition within lesbian and gay studies are treated with the utmost care and caution. Sedgwick frames her analysis of male–male sexual relations in this way:

> *Epistemology of the Closet* is a feminist book mainly in the sense that its analyses were produced by someone whose thought has been macro- and microscopically infused with feminism over a long period. At the many intersections where a distinctively feminist (i.e. gender-centred) and a distinctively antihomophobic (i.e. sexuality-centred) inquiry have seemed to diverge, however, this book has tried consistently to press on in the latter direction. I have made this choice largely because I see feminist analysis being considerably more developed than gay male or antihomophobic analysis at present – theoretically, politically, and institutionally.[3]

It is difficult to preface a collection of essays such as *Sexual Sameness* without mentioning Sedgwick's extraordinary work, since her investigations into male homosociality, or bonding between men, could be said at least to have established a theoretical framework, if not a disciplinary foundation, for gay male criticism. Sedgwick's highly innovative project is to explore how 'many of the major nodes of thought in twentieth-century western culture as a whole are structured . . . by a chronic, now endemic crisis of homo/heterosexual definition, indicatively male' (p.1), and, as the earlier passage from her book makes clear, she is acutely aware of the critical location of her writing. Her feminism, itself proceeding from an institutionally marginalized if not historically maligned position, has taken its increasingly sophisticated knowledge of gender to interrogate the precarious break between 'homo' and 'hetero' that dominant culture strives to keep as distinct as possible.

But in her powerful analyses of the manifold and crisis-inducing disruptions in social and sexual relations between men, Sedgwick has left some lesbian theorists wondering where their histories, their desires, and their representations remain within her feminist-orientated gay male criticism. Terry Castle's essay raises this question at some length (see pp. 128–47). Similarly, Sedgwick has been accused by one gay writer of misrepresenting gay male lives, on the ground, it would seem, of feminist intrusion.[4] These significant debates cannot be unpicked here. But what can be said is that Sedgwick's risk-taking work has both given the impetus to an intellectually vital arena of cultural debate, and has, by virtue of that, opened up a great many concerns about how feminists and gay men may or may not align their interests, how heterosexual feminists may or may not work together with lesbian critics, and how feminism is separate from but inevitably implicated in a field entitled lesbian and gay studies. Surrounding the co-ordinating 'and' between lesbians and gay men that has taken up much of my discussion so far are all sorts of anxieties about who has the right to speak for whom, about who is entitled to read and write about another's work, and about how we can, if we choose to do so, together create an area of knowledge about same-sex desires. At no point can we forget that lesbian and gay subcultures contain within them many discrete sexual-political groupings. Both have their separatist constituencies, just as they simultaneously include men and women who work from an understanding that we have more in common with each other than not.

There have been other responses to the emergence of lesbian and gay studies. One is a feminist-identified anxiety, very different in political direction from Sedgwick's. In *Feminist Literary Criticism: A Defence*, Janet Todd wonders whether, with the burgeoning of gay male criticism, 'feminism [will be thought to have] had its place in the liberal sun and should move over to leave the victim's space for a greater (male) victim, the homosexual'.[5] Todd would seem to be suggesting that there is at present an implicit competition between feminists and gay men about who possesses – or should possess – the most radical sexual politics, and who is therefore most deserving of serious attention. It strikes me that such a consideration will certainly prove a block to any progressive sexual politics that aims to bring an end to victimization within what remains a brutal gender/sexuality hierarchy. All types of feminist criticism need defending from neutralization within the academy but they do not require this kind of territorial defence, implying that there is only one exclusive space for a sexual victim – if that is how gay men and feminists are to see themselves.

Todd's troubled remark should, I feel, be viewed within the larger scope of current arguments about the increasing prominence of 'men's studies', with its primary emphasis on heterosexual masculinity. In literary criticism there is now a visible 'male feminism', and several studies and collections of essays explore its place in relation to, and difference from, the feminism it is trying variously to imitate, modify, and, some might argue, obliterate.[6] That feminism is now, if very slowly, being appropriated by radical men to discuss masculinity certainly prompts questions very similar to those active within lesbian and gay studies about who has the right to speak on another's behalf. Some will observe that male feminism is a contradiction in terms. (Does not the irreducibility of gender exclude men from feminism?) Others might say that heterosexual men may only be able to reconstruct their lives through feminist understanding. (What other discourses are currently available to change such men?) Given the proliferation of politically gendered positions in cultural theory, it is becoming more and more difficult to map out exactly how male feminists, straight-identified feminists, and lesbian and gay critics are currently relating to one another. Interwoven with each of these sexual-political types of criticism are voices that speak of connected forms of class and racial subordination. Perhaps by learning to respect and accept the meetings and partings of our concerns, those of us who inhabit counter-cultural spaces can develop our work along similar but not competing lines.

There have, of course, been other, much more familiar and altogether hostile responses to the appearance of lesbian and gay studies. In 1991 the University of Sussex launched an MA course in 'Sexual Dissidence and Cultural Change', enabling for the first time in Britain the formalized study of same-sex cultural practices. Organized, among others, by Jonathan Dollimore and Alan Sinfield (both contributors to the present collection), this master's degree met with the consternation of the press, a parliamentarian, and other dignitaries when publicity for applications was circulated. Both writers have been subject to attacks (as well as much praise) from the critical establishment for some time. Given the year-long cross-fire of opinions in the correspondence columns of the *London Review of Books* about Dollimore and Sinfield's work in 'cultural materialism' (April 1990–May 1991; the exchange of letters stems from continuing debates concerning their highly successful collection of essays *Political Shakespeare* (1985)), it is more than likely that their involvement in this postgraduate degree programme will result in even more assaults from so-called defenders of orthodox literary studies.

The traditional study of English and American literature finds itself in a paradoxical position if and when it denounces lesbian and gay criticism, since so many of the literary works within the canon have homosexuality, if not as their central, then as their displaced theme. Any reasonably conventional course in twentieth-century English writing might comprise a novel by Forster, one by Woolf, a volume of poems by W.H. Auden, and some of Joe Orton's dramas. But, given the constraints on most lesbians and gay men in being open about their sexualities even in the liberal academy, it was for many years nearly impossible to develop the critical vocabulary that would make sense of the relations between the emergence of a modern concept of homosexuality, and thereafter of lesbianism and gay maleness, and their articulation in literary forms. Literature in its purest and most high-flown sense has proved, for a century at least, to be one of the few cultural spaces in which same-sex love could find some expression – often obliquely (through, for example, the use of classical myth), sometimes explicitly (as in Forster's *Maurice*, although this novel was published posthumously, fifty-seven years after its completion). The work of lesbian and gay criticism, however, is not simply to reread canonical writings, and thereby come to an understanding of the historical, aesthetic, and political pressures under which homosexual representation has had to exist. It is equally, if not more so, engaged in the investigation of how and why modern sexualities have followed particular patterns, and how literary works – so frequently responsive to cultural transitions – mediate the making and breaking of these sexual behaviours. It is perhaps in its refusal to be complicit with the naturalizing tendencies of heterosexual analyses of gender and sexuality that lesbian and gay criticism has its greatest purchase. It speaks oppositionally from the sexually dissident margin to comprehend the heterosexually dominant centre, and in so doing aims to change it.

With such political transformations in mind, I want, finally, to go back to the title of this collection. Currently, discussions of gender and sexuality often revolve around the often loosely defined concept of difference – particularly sexual difference. As a term, sexual difference came into play in the 1970s when, as Mandy Merck has said, cultural theorists sought to 'semioticise subjectivity . . . to think its differences as the work of representation rather than some pre-existing social or biological reality'.[7] In the light of recent deconstructive and Lacanian thinking, one may well be led to believe that such a notion of difference involves the endless sliding of the desiring signifier, forever trying to reconstitute itself, forever at the mercy of deferral and delay. But, as Merck adds, despite this emphasis on the semiotic instability of meaning, desire, and representation, there is frequently a sense of dualism, if not heterosexism, in theories of sexual difference. By emphasizing *sameness*, lesbian and gay criticism works from an understanding that the notion of difference is not an infinitely elastic term. Its emphasis on sameness seeks to redress – if not reverse – such a notion of difference, drawing attention back to the particular interests – the same-sex desires – that theorizations of difference may occlude or disperse. There again, once the particularity of our concerns with sameness is accepted as a material fact – women with women; men with men – then the specific differences that inhabit the 'and' that brings us politically and critically together can be comprehended. All of the contributors to this collection examine the process of trying to write sexual sameness into literary form, of attempting to understand what it means to love someone of one's own sex, and of gaining knowledge about how and why the culture around us – so brutally in this era of AIDS – often seeks to forbid our existence.

2   The cultural politics of perversion: Augustine, Shakespeare, Freud, Foucault

Jonathan Dollimore

This chapter argues that perversion is not only a culturally central phenomenon, but, thereby, also a crucial category for cultural analysis.[1]

In Freud's theory of the sexual perversions the human infant begins life with a sexual disposition which is polymorphously perverse and innately bisexual. It is a precondition for the successful socialization and gendering of the individual – that is, the positioning of the subject within hetero/sexual difference – that the perversions be renounced, typically through repression and/or sublimation. In this way, not only is the appropriate human subject produced but so also is civilization reproduced. But the perversions do not thereby go away: repressed or sublimated, they help to constitute and maintain the very social order; this is one reason why that order requires their repression and sublimation. As such they remain intrinsic to normality and might be said to constitute the cement of culture, helping 'to constitute the social instincts' (11: 437–8)[2] and providing 'the energy for a great number of our cultural achievements' (8: 84). Sublimated perversions place 'extraordinarily large amounts of force at the disposal of civilized activity' because they are able to exchange their original aims (sexual) for other ones (social) without their intensity being diminished (8: 84; 12: 39, 41).

So one does not become a pervert but remains one (8: 84); it is sexual perversion, not sexual 'normality', which is the given in human nature. Indeed, sexual normality is precariously achieved and precariously maintained: the process whereby the perversions are sublimated can never be guaranteed to work; it has to be re-enacted in the case of each individual subject, and it is an arduous and conflictual process of psycho-sexual development from the polymorphous perverse to normality which is less a process of growth than one of restriction (7: 5). Sometimes it doesn't work; sometimes it appears to, only to fail at a later date. Civilization, says Freud, remains precarious and 'unstable' (1: 48), as a result.

The clear implication is that civilization actually depends upon that which is usually thought to be incompatible with it, a proposition which has been resisted inside psychoanalysis, and, even more, outside it. At its

9

worst, psychoanalysis has ignored Freud's theories and simply demo-
nized or pathologized the pervert, most notably the homosexual, in ways
exhaustively summarized in Kenneth Lewes's recent study.[3] Indeed, it is
ironically revealing that this idea of perversion as integral to culture is
today not so much associated with Freud's most influential psychoanalytic successors but with one of their most influential critics, Michel
Foucault. For Foucault, too, perversion is endemic to modern society,
though not in the Freudian sublimated form, nor because of a process of
desublimation or some other kind of breakdown in the mechanisms of
repression. It is one of the central arguments of Foucault's *History of
Sexuality* that perversion is not repressed at all; rather, culture actively
produces it. We are living through what he calls, in a chapter heading,
the 'perverse implantation'. Perversion is the product and the vehicle of
power, a construction which enables power to gain purchase within the
realm of the psychosexual: authority legitimizes itself by fastening upon
discursively constructed, sexually perverse, identities of its own making.[4]

So, though from opposed perspectives, Freud and Foucault discover
perversion to be not only central to culture but indispensably so, given
the present organization of culture. It is to make this point about the
centrality of perversion, and this point alone, that I've begun with Freud
and Foucault, and not because my project requires that I begin by
adjudicating between them. In fact, the place to begin is much further
back. I don't think we can assess either the psychoanalytic theory or its
Foucauldian critique until we've recovered the complex and revealing
history of perversion in some of its pre-Freudian meanings, which
necessarily include its non-sexual meanings. I begin, then, with the early
modern period in an attempt to replace the pathological sense of perversion with a political one. Far from wanting to psychoanalyse that period,
I want instead to use the Renaissance to help read psychoanalysis and,
simultaneously, to use psychoanalysis against its own conservative advocates. In short, I use history to read theory, but in a way enabled by
theory.

Pathology to Theology

> In the extreme, life is what is capable of error . . . error is at the
> root of what makes human thought and its history.[5]

Perversion is a concept signifying: (1) an erring, straying, or deviating
from (2) a path, destiny or objective which is (3) understood as natural or
right – right because natural (with the natural possibly having a yet
'higher' legitimation in divine law).

Immediately we encounter a paradox: why should the prima-facie
innocent activity of *departure* be so abhorrent? Why, for example, in this,
the first *OED* definition of 'perverse', is there the rapid slippage from

divergence to evil: 'turned away from the right way, or from what is right or good; perverted, wicked'? And – a related question – why should this deviation *from* something be seen also, instantly, as a wicked subversion *of* it? Part of the answer lies in the fact that perversion is regulated by the binary opposition between the natural and the unnatural. Again, it's those like Foucault who have theorized this view in relation to the modern period. But we find ample evidence of the same process in the earlier period. This, for example, is Francis Bacon from 1622: '[for] Women to govern men . . . [and] slaves freemen . . . [are] total violations and perversions of the laws of nature and nations'.[6] Binary opposites, as Derrida pointed out, and Bacon here confirms, are violent hierarchies. The natural/unnatural opposition has been one of the most violent of all hierarchies. Note how in the Bacon passage just quoted the violence of the hierarchy is displaced, through the concepts of violation and perversion, on to its subordinate terms – women and slaves. As we'll see, the attribution of perversion often involves this process, that is, a displacement of violence, contradiction, and crisis, from the dominant, wherein they are produced, on to the subordinate, especially the deviant.

The pervert deviates from 'the straight and narrow', the 'straight and true'; even such commonplace remarks as these bear the trace of western metaphysics, the epistemological, via metaphor, here picking up with the linear or the teleological. Somewhat over-schematically (and so provisionally) western metaphysics can be represented in terms of three related tenets: the one I've just referred to, teleology, together with essence and universality (these two being the source of essential truth and absolute truth respectively). One reason for recovering the linguistic histories of perversion is because they have often constituted a transgression of normative and prescriptive teleologies. Such transgression was especially feared in the Renaissance, an age obsessed with disordered and disordering movement, from planetary irregularity to social mobility, from the vagrant and masterless men roaming the state, to the womb which supposedly wandered the body of the 'hysterical' woman. All such phenomena contradicted the principles of metaphysical fixity as formulated in those three main categories – essence, universality and teleology – three categories which between them have profoundly fixed the social order in western culture. The charge of perversity was at once a demonizing and a disavowal of an aberrant movement that was seen to threaten the very basis of civilization; that is why time and again metaphysical fixity – fixed origin, nature, identity, development, and destiny – is invoked in the condemnation of that movement. Recall that Othello is described as an erring barbarian, the extravagant and wheeling stranger, and Desdemona as having erred from Nature. I return to *Othello* below.

Wayward Women and Religious Rebels

The sexological sense of perversion does not appear in the *OED* until its 1893 *Supplement*, and then only cautiously. However, in the numerous citations which the *OED* does give for the word and its cognate terms, two *other* kinds of pervert recur: the wayward, assertive woman – the woman on top – whom we've already glimpsed in that quotation from Bacon; and the religious heretic. At the beginning of Christian history, they went together. As Milton put it, justifying the ways of God to man, Satan created the perverted kingdom, and Eve was God's first convert. Or, rather, we should say that she was his first pervert. I'm trying to be precise rather than perverse: in theological discourse the term to describe the opposite of conversion is perversion, and it signifies that terrible deviation from the true religion to the false. It is this use which suggests a central paradox of the perverse, and another reason why perversion is so despised and feared. Perversion has its origins in, or exists in an intimate relation with, that which it subverts. I suppose this is really the case by definition: to err from the right way literally presupposes that one was once in the right place. But it goes deeper than that: in Burton's *Anatomy of Melancholy* (1622), it's not his discussion of what sexologists would later call the sexual perversions that produces the paradoxical sense of the word that interests me – although Burton *does* discuss these – but his discussion of what might be thought to be their opposite. Quite near the beginning of the *Anatomy*, Burton declares that it is not our bestial qualities that are potentially the most dangerous but our civilized ones: 'Reason, art [and] judgement,' properly employed, much avail us, 'but if otherwise perverted, they ruin and confound us'.[7] The 'shattering effect' of perversion – and I borrow this description from Leo Bersani[8] – is related to the fact that it originates internally to just those things it threatens. I call this the *perverse dynamic*.

Throughout western culture this paradox recurs: the most extreme threat to the true form of something comes not so much from its opposite or its direct negation, but in the form of its perversion. Somehow the perverse is inextricably rooted in the true and authentic, while being, in spite of (or rather because of) that connection, also the utter contradiction of it. This paradox begins to suggest why perversion, theological or sexual, is so often conceived as *at once utterly alien to, and yet mysteriously inherent within* the true and authentic. This is related to a further and equally disturbing paradox of the perverse, which suggests that we are created desiring that which is forbidden us. As John Norris put it in 1687: 'What strange perversity is this of Man! When 'twas a Crime to taste th' inlightning Tree, He could not then his hand refrain' (*OED*, 'perversity', p. 740). But long before this Augustine had indicated that Adam and Eve were already fallen before the definitive transgression of Eden: 'the evil act, the transgression of eating the forbidden fruit, was committed only when those who did it were already evil'

(XIV.13: 572).[9] The implication, here and elsewhere (e.g. XI, 13, 17, 18 and 20), is that both the angelic revolt in heaven and the human fall in Eden were predestined.

Privation and Perversion

Hence, of course, the so-called problem of evil in traditional theodicy: God's omnipotence has to be defended, while at the same time exonerating him from responsibility for evil. The impossibility of this task was nicely formulated by the philosopher David Hume paraphrasing Epicurus, as cited by Lactantius: 'Is he [God] willing to prevent evil, but not able? Then he is impotent. Is he able but not willing? Then he is malevolent. Is he both able and willing? When thence is evil?'[10]

Augustine's influential answer to the problem was the privative theory of evil: evil exists only as a lack, a privation, of good. This was in reaction against the Manichean heresy: to allow, as the Manicheans did, that evil was a real force coexistent with, and opposite to, good, compromised either God's omnipotence (he wasn't in complete control) or his goodness (he created evil). Augustine counters this heresy with the assertion that evil has no real existence. But the idea of evil simply as lack could never explain its destructive power. This is why *at the heart of Augustinian privation is perversion*. Perversion becomes a main criterion of evil, mediating between evil as lack and evil as agency. That is, perversion becomes something utterly inimical to authentic being, yet without authentic being itself.

For Augustine the most pernicious form of evil occurs when the human will deviates from good: 'when the will leaves the higher and turns to the lower, it becomes bad not because the thing to which it turns is bad, but because the turning is itself perverse [*perversa*]' (XII.6: 478).

Although such perversity is unnatural, against the order of nature, nothing actually in nature is evil: neither the nature to which the evil-doer turns nor, even, the evil-doer's own nature. Augustine adds, in an extraordinary passage, that 'not even the nature of the Devil himself is evil, in so far as it is a nature; it is perversion that makes it evil [*sed perversitas eam malet facit*]' (XIX.13: 87). We can begin to see then that for Augustine the perverse turning away from good (itself a perversion of the order of nature) is the essence of evil. Here is the beginning of a theory which will become the rationale for a history of untold violence: '*essentially*', *perversion becomes the negative agency within privation*.

In the words of theologians who have defined the privative theory of evil in our own time: 'the most radical opposition to which being can be subjected is not contrariety but privation'; 'evil is an inverted positivity'.[11] The power of evil is only the power of the good it perverts, and 'the more powerful this good is, the more powerful evil will be, not by virtue of itself, but by virtue of this good. This is why no evil is more powerful than that of the fallen angel.'[12]

The paranoiac potential of this theology is considerable. But if we read the fall narrative against the grain – that is, subject it to an aberrant decoding – without much effort we find the reason for the paranoia: after all, in the Christian scheme, evil not only erupts from within a divinely ordained order but, more telling still, it erupts from within the beings closest to God, *those who participate most intimately in divinity* – first the angels, then man, or rather woman – who make, according to another theologian, 'an inexplicably perverse misuse of their god-given freedom'.[13] That is to say, they allegedly pervert their most divine attribute, free will, which then becomes the primary, or for Augustine, the only, source of evil. Free will becomes an agency of privation.

In short, a negation/deviation erupts from *within* that which it negates (divinity) only to be then displaced on to the subordinate term of the God/man binary – and then further displaced on to the subordinate within man (i.e. woman). *Proximity, therefore, is the enabling condition of a displacement which in turn marks the 'same' as radically 'other'.*

It may seem strange that this study of perversion should go so far back into Christian history. I haven't space here to fill in many of the connections but let me simply suggest the way several popular notions of sexual perversion in our own time echo the Augustinian theory of evil:
(1) evil, says Augustine, is utterly inimical to true existence and yet itself lacks authentic existence (ontological or natural). Likewise with the sexual pervert *vis-à-vis* sexual normality;
(2) evil, says Augustine, is at once utterly alien to goodness and yet mysteriously inherent within it. Likewise sexual perversion is utterly alien to true sexuality yet mysteriously inherent within it, such that perversion must be rooted out by the ever vigilant;
(3) evil, says Augustine, has powers of perversion paradoxically the greater with the goodness and innocence of those being perverted. Likewise with sexual perversion: this being why, presumably, the young and the military are thought to be especially at risk. (I'm alluding to the fact that in the United Kingdom homosexuality in the military and for those under 21 is still illegal.) These echoes suggest a larger argument: as perversion has been retheorized in sexology and psychoanalysis, this earlier conceptual history has been largely obliterated but never entirely lost. In part, this history has been telescoped into a sexological and psychoanalytic narrative where it remains obscurely yet violently active.

Nature Erring from Itself

Augustine deploys and develops the concepts of perversion and deviation, making them definitive criteria of evil. At the same time, these concepts become lodged at the heart of those problems which haunt Christianity, and which ultimately sunder faith itself, most notably the realization (1) that we are created wicked; (2) that God himself bears 'the ultimate responsibility for evil' – the inevitable conclusion of theo-dicy;[14] and (3) that evil is intrinsic to good.

All three of these beliefs have the happy consequence of making the original pervert not Satan but God. But suppose for a moment we let God off the hook; let's concede that he, like successive US presidents in the face of illegal activities originating from the centre of their govern-ments, was innocent or at least ignorant, and that perversion actually originated with his one-time deputy, Satan, and that Eve was his first convert. (Or rather pervert.) This is the official line. It is a myth of origin which will help legitimize violence against women, and their subjection, for centuries to come:

> *Othello*: And yet, how nature erring from itself –
> *Iago*: Ay, there's the point, as (to be bold with you)
> Not to affect many proposèd matches
> Of her own clime, complexion, and degree,
> Whereto we see in all things nature tends –
> Foh! one may smell in such a will most rank,
> Foul disproportions, thoughts unnatural.
>
> (*Othello*, III, iii, 227–33)[15]

'Nature erring from itself': the perverse originates internally to, from within, the natural. Here Othello imagines, and Iago exploits, the para-doxical movement of the perverse: a *straying from* which is also a *contra-diction of*; a divergence which is imagined to subvert that from *which* it departs in the instant that it *does* depart. In short, from within that erring movement of the first line, a perverse divergence within nature, there erupts by the last line its opposite, the 'unnatural'. Additionally, in the accusation of perversion misogyny and xenophobia are rampant. And so too is racism: Iago demonizes Desdemona and Othello, she as the one who has degenerate desire, he as the object of that desire. Desire and object conjoin in the multiple meanings of 'will most rank' where 'will' might denote at once volition, sexual desire and sexual organ (cf. Sonnets 134–6), and 'rank' may mean lust, swollen, smelling, corrupt, and foul. All this in seven terrifying lines which effectively sign Desdemona's death warrant. It's a passage in which (among other things) the natural/unnatural binary is powerfully active. I've tried to represent it diagrammatically (see Figure 1).

The central vertical line represents the binary opposition between the natural and the unnatural: it is in the vertical to signify that the binary is also a violent hierarchy.

The erring/aberrant movement is marked as a deviation to the left; this is not arbitrary: psychoanalysis and, more significantly, anthro-pology confirm an intriguing cultural connection between deviation and left-sidedness. But our language has always confirmed as much: 'sinister' has, as one of its meanings, 'lying on or towards the left hand' (*Shorter OED*), while the Latin *sinister* has 'perverse' as one of its meanings (*Cassell's Latin Dictionary*).

The arcs, A_2 to D, represent the social and psychic processes inseparable from the opposition of the binary but which it cannot acknowledge in its legitimizing function. They are also what makes the perverse dynamic possible (though not in this case). Borrowing from Fredric Jameson, we can call them the political unconscious of the binary. The narrow arc (A_1), running between the natural and the perverse, simply represents the cultural marking or demonizing of difference. It is the identification of a threat which is also a differentiation of it from that which is threatened (the natural). That much wider arc (B), running between the unnatural and the perverse, is the field of displacement. That is, it marks the way in which, when the perverse is identified from the position of the natural, there occurs a simultaneous alignment of the perverse and the unnatural: the unnatural is folded up into, *thereby appearing as*, the perverse. It is this displacement which helps make possible the slippage from 'deviation from' to 'contradiction of' noted earlier in the *OED* definition. And what is marked on that other side of the diagram (C) is really what makes the displacement possible: the natural/unnatural binary is only ever a differential relation – that is, a difference which is always already one of intimate, though antagonistic, interdependence. What is constructed as absolutely other is in fact inextricably related. Hence the double arrow on C.

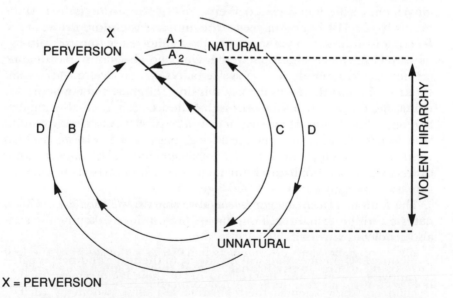

X = PERVERSION

Figure 1

B and C disclose the operation of A_2: the recognition of the perverse involves a mapping on to the deviation of one part of a split within the natural – 'nature erring from itself'; just as the unnatural is folded up into the perverse (B), so one part of the split natural is folded down into the perverse. This is marked by A_2. B and A_2 can be imagined as the two hands of a clock, each folding towards one another, and meeting across the axis of the perverse. And we should also remember that this double displacement may be mapped on to either an actual deviation or, as here, an imaginary one.

One might say that when the natural, especially in its guise as the normal (or normative), recognizes the perverse (A_1), it is only ever recognizing itself. But this is not to say that the two things are identical, or that one is simply a reflection of the other. In its splitting the natural produces the perverse as a disavowal of itself and as a displacement of an opposite (the unnatural) which, because of the binary interdependence of the two (the natural and the unnatural), is also an inextricable part of itself. This is represented by that clockwise continuum (D) – from the natural, through the unnatural, to the perverse.

The process of displacement (B) often figures in the construction of the perverse and the unnatural, and I want to explore it further, still with reference to the passage from *Othello*. It's extraordinary just how much treachery and insurrection Iago manages to attribute to Desdemona in just six lines. This is a play partly about impending war. Venetian civilization is at stake, at least to the extent that its military has moved to Cyprus to defend the island against the approaching Turks. In 1575 Thomas Newton declared of the Turks: 'They were (indeed) at the first very far off from our clime and region, and therefore the less to be feared, but now they are even at our doors and ready to come into our houses.'[16] It's been shown how the symbolic geography of the play creates just this effect of Cyprus as a beleaguered outpost,[17] while Richard Marienstras shows how, at this time, England's xenophobia was increasing in spite, or maybe because, of the fact that it was also embarking on colonization and expansion.[18] The result was a real conflict between, if you like, the centripetal tendencies of nationalism, and the centrifugal tendencies of colonialist expansion. One consequence of this conflict was a paranoid search for the internal counterparts of external threats.

The famous *Homily Against Disobedience and Wilfull Rebellion* (1571) is obsessed with internal rebellion, the enemy within, weakening the state and rendering it vulnerable to

> all outward enemies that will invade it, to the utter and perpetual captivity, slavery, and destruction of all their countrymen, their children, their friends, their kinsfolk left alive, whom by their wicked rebellion they procure to be delivered into the hands of foreign enemies.[19]

In this *Homily*, the sin of rebellion encompasses *all* other sins in one (pp. 609, 611–12). Racism plays its part: a Royal Edict of 1601 expresses discontent 'at the great number of "Negars" and "blackamoors" which are crept into the realm'; Queen Elizabeth wanted them transported out of the country. The ostensible reason was unemployment among the English, but the representation of Black people 'as satanic, sexual creatures, a threat to order and decency, and a danger to white womanhood' was also a factor.[20] Such considerations meant that, for many in early modern England, the implicit confrontation in *Othello* was between civilization and barbarism. (Although, as Martin Orkin reminds us in *Shakespeare against Apartheid*, the struggle for Cyprus was actually conducted between two imperialist powers.[21])

According to Iago, Desdemona's 'thoughts unnatural' involve a threefold transgression: of 'clime, complexion, and degree'; that is, of region, colour, and rank; or, in our terms, of country, race, and class – three of civilization's most jealously policed boundaries. Is it coincidence, then, that what Desdemona violates – country, race, and class – are all three at risk in the war with the Turks? Country, obviously; race, in the sense that that enemy is, in the terms of the play, racially and culturally inferior; class, or degree, in the sense that it is the indispensable basis both of the culture being defended and of the military doing the defending. So what we witness here is a classic instance of displacement: an external threat recast as an internal deviation; through imagined sexual transgression the perverse subject – the desiring woman – becomes a surrogate alien, a surrogate Turk. And, remarkably, yet in a way all too familiar, the internal deviation which allegedly replicated the external threat is located in the domestic realm, at the most protected central region of the patriarchal order, and at the furthest remove from its beleaguered borders. And it's located within one who is, by any substantial criteria, powerless.

By looking at two instances of the pervert – the religious heretic and the wayward woman – I've been trying to indicate how the pre-sexological and pre-Freudian history of the concept of perversion can be reconstructed as one of struggle and conflict between domination and insubordination, between desire and law, and between transgression and conformity. I have also attempted to demonstrate how this earlier history of perversion figured centrally in the language of paranoia and displacement, and how it could trigger the paradoxes inherent within, and so subvert, the orders which are defined over and against the pervert. Significantly, it is easier to trigger the paradoxes subversively in the case of religious heresy than with the wayward woman. Note how in the *Othello* passage the paradox – indeed contradiction – has almost surfaced ('nature erring from itself') but not quite. The instability produced by that almost-apparent contradiction is contained, or re-formed, by Iago into a violent hierarchy and its repression. Hence Desdemona's death. It is a powerful reminder that dominant social formations can and do reconstitute themselves around the selfsame contradictions that destabilize them. Through disavowal and displacement the same instability that destabilizes can become a force of repression much more than a force of liberation.

In the remainder of this chapter I consider the representation of sexual perversion in the modern period in the light of the concept's 'lost history'. I do not want to leave the Renaissance without remarking that there *were* instances of gender struggle at that time in which contradictions were successfully exploited by subordinate groups for subversive ends. (One of the most fascinating instances of all is the controversy in the period over female cross-dressing, which I've discussed elsewhere.[22])

Perversion and Psychoanalysis

In our own century the repressive deployment of psychiatry and psychoanalysis has been obvious and notorious, especially with regard to the so-called perversions, and one in particular: homosexuality. As an example I've chosen an essay by Sandor Feldman. He writes: 'As a practitioner, I have learned that, *essentially*, homosexuals want to mate with the opposite sex. In therapy my intention is to discover what kind of fear or distress *diverted* the patient from *the straight line* and made a *devious detour* necessary.' All homosexuals, he continues, started as heterosexuals. Moreover, 'the main part of the therapy . . . is to emphasize that the patient's original position is a healthy one, given as a precious gift by nature'. The analyst must:

> bear in mind always that his real goal is to bring up the patient to the biologically given heterosexual relationship which is not created by the therapy but liberated for use . . . The homosexual will, for a while at least, stubbornly insist that . . . homosexuality remains for him the only route to sexual gratification. This is all untrue. The more convinced the analyst is that an underlying natural personal relationship in sexual and in other ways is present, the more . . . the patient will come to the same conclusion as the analyst: that man is born for woman and woman is born for man.[23]

This is stunningly crass but not untypical in its assumptions. Feldman reproduces a familiar metaphysics of nature: essence/teleology/universality. An essential sexuality moves along a teleologically defined path of psychosexual development (Feldman's 'straight line' – already encoded in the biological origin) to the universal goal: heterosexual union. So in the first instance his theory should be understood not only as a crass appropriation of Freud but also as a containment of the perverse via the traditional metaphysical schema which Freud rejects. Let's be clear about this: Freud had used his account of perversion to *subvert* theories of sexuality growing from the same tradition that Feldman reinvokes in Freud's name. Freud rejects those theories by retaining and developing the paradoxes within the semantic field of perversion, especially that major paradox outlined earlier: the shattering effect of perversion arises from the fact that it is integral to just those things it threatens.

I sketch Freud's theory of the perversions with two aims in mind. Specifically, I want to explore the way he incorporates into his theory the paradoxical dynamic of perversion – what I've called the perverse dynamic. More generally, I simply want to outline a theory which is more challenging than most contemporary versions of psychoanalysis allow. The larger project from which this essay derives argues that the perverse dynamic begins to challenge key aspects of the psychoanalytic project itself, just as with Christianity before it.

Freud says: 'the abandonment of the reproductive function is the common feature of all perversion. We actually describe a sexual activity as perverse if it has given up the aim of reproduction and pursues the attainment of pleasure as an aim independent of it' (1: 358). On this account, especially since the arrival of the postmodern, we are presumably all perverts now, actual or aspiring. (I'm reminded of the postmodern anecdote about the foot fetishist who was in love with the foot but had to settle for the whole person.) A more specific definition is clearly required, and Freud provides it: perversions are sexual activities which involve *an extension, or transgression, of limit* with respect 'either to the part of the body concerned or to the sexual object chosen' (8: 83). In the first case (namely the part of the body), perversion would involve the lingering over the immediate relations to the sexual object – as might the foot fetishist just invoked – relations which 'should normally be traversed rapidly on the path towards the final sexual aim'. That is, reproduction via heterosexual genital intercourse (7: 62). In the second case (sexual object), it would involve the choosing of an 'inappropriate' object – for example, someone of the same sex.

As I indicated at the outset, in the formation of the socialized, gendered subject – that is, the production of the human subject within hetero/sexual difference – the perversions are necessarily repressed, sublimated, and renounced. Sublimated perversion remains intrinsic to normality and indeed provides, as it were, the cement of culture. As a consequence, 'some perverse trait or other is seldom absent from the sexual life of normal people' (1: 364). As regards homosexuality: *everyone* has made a homosexual object choice, says Freud, if only in their unconscious. In short: 'in addition to their manifest heterosexuality, a very considerable measure of latent or unconscious homosexuality can be detected in *all* normal people' (9: 399). Moreover, 'homosexual impulses are invariably discovered in every single neurotic'. Indeed, the repression of perverse desire actually generates neurosis – hence Freud's statement that neurosis is the negative of the perversions (7: 163).

Freud is unrelenting in finding perversion, especially homosexuality, in those places where it is conventionally thought to be *most* absent, and where this assumed absence actually constitutes identity. There is, for instance, the inextricable connection between perversion and childhood. It is not only that children are sexual beings but also that their sexuality is quintessentially – one might say, naturally – perverse (8: 352). All children, says Freud, may well be homosexuals (8: 268). Conversely, there is a quality of childlike innocence about the perversions themselves.

Relatedly, Freud insists on attributing to the perversions precisely the qualities usually thought to be possessed only by their opposite. For instance, far from being 'bestial' or 'degenerate', the perversions are intellectual and idealistic, involving 'an idealization of instinct'. He says of the Wolf Man, one of his most famous patients:

> The process has led to a victory for the faith of piety over the rebelliousness of critical research, and has had the repression of the homosexual attitude as its necessary condition. Lasting disadvantages resulted . . . His intellectual activity remained seriously impaired after the first great defeat. (9: 307)

He says too that love, far from being that which transcends perversion, is that which liberates it: 'Being in love . . . has the power to remove repressions and reinstate perversions' (11: 95). Further, the 'omnipotence of love is perhaps never more strongly proved than in such of its aberrations as these', i.e. the perversions. He continues: *'The highest and lowest are always closest to each other in the sphere of sexuality'* (7: 75; my emphasis). And further still, the satisfaction afforded by perverse desire is greater than that afforded by desire which has been socially tamed (12: 67).

I hope to have sketched enough for the destructive implications of Freud's theory to be apparent. At the very least, a range of central binary oppositions (spiritual/carnal; pure/degenerate; normal/abnormal) – oppositions upon which the social order depends – are either inverted removed or collapsed into a relational interdependence: a deep, mutual, antagonistic implication. But even more is at stake, and Freud is quite explicit about this: there is something chaotic and subversive about perversion. The persistence and ever-threatened re-emergence of perversion means that civilization has failed to secure its own reproduction. The repressive organization of sexuality which constitutes normality 'falls apart' (7: 156). The perversions, therefore, become a paradigm of the (in)subordinate displacing the dominant (for that read, heterosexual, reproductive, genital intercourse). In their 'multiplicity and strangeness' (1: 346), says Freud, the perversions constitute a threatening excess of difference originating from within the same. So Freud attributes to the perversions an extraordinary disruptive power: (1) they subvert the genital organization of sexuality, thereby sabotaging the whole process of normative psychosexual development (or subjection) upon which civilization depends; (2) they subvert sexual difference itself, whether it be biological (reproduction) or social (sublimation); and (3) perversion affords more pleasure than those forms of organized desire based on its repression (and this apart from the pleasure of transgression itself, which is a separate issue). Moreover, perversion may be produced by what is conventionally assumed to be at the furthest possible remove from it (that is, love). Finally, perversion cannot be eliminated. It persists in three principal ways: an active practice by some; the repressed constituent of neurosis; and the always unstably sublimated basis of civilization itself.

Polymorphous Perverse to the Perverse Dynamic

I oppose Freud's account of perversion to Feldman's work not in order to return to Freud – to uncover the authentic voice of psychoanalysis – but to follow further the complex history of perversion. As yet, little in my argument depends on the correctness or otherwise of Freud's views. However, via Freud, we can see that the concept of perversion always embodied what has now become a fundamental and crucial proposition – call it deconstructive, poststructuralist, postmodern, whatever. It is the proposition that what a culture designates as alien, utterly other and different, is never so. Culture exists in a relationship of difference with the alien, which is also a relationship of fundamental, antagonistic interdependence. What is constructed as absolutely other is, in fact, inextricably related – most obviously in terms of the binary opposition, Derrida's violent hierarchy. Freud goes further: civilization is not merely dependent upon perversion; the latter, via sublimation, is integral to the former since civilization is rooted in perversion. The binary is not merely transcended or dissolved. Rather, the different is inscribed within the selfsame. One doesn't become a pervert but remains one. Put another way, every inlaw was once, and in a crucial sense remains, an outlaw. It is because culture repeatedly disavows this fact that manifest perversion is made the focus of endless demonizing and displacement. In an article called 'Civilised Sexual Morality' (1908), Freud pushes the process even further, showing how civilization reaches a stage of development where it begins to produce the very perversion it needs to suppress. In Freud, then, there emerges a truly violent dialectic between repression and perversion, and it is one which suggests that the most terrifying fear may not be of the other but of the same, and that the social is marked by an interconnectedness so radical that it has to be disavowed in most existing forms of social organization.

Above all, Freud brilliantly identifies the psychic basis of what I've been describing; I am thinking especially of his concepts of resistance, disavowal, negation, and splitting. One of the most acute accounts is in his article on 'Repression' (1915):

[T]he objects to which men give most preference, their ideals, proceed from the same perceptions and experience as the objects which they most abhor, and . . . they were originally only distinguished from one another through slight modifications. . . . Indeed . . . it is possible for the original instinctual *representative* to be split in two, one part undergoing repression, while the remainder, *precisely on account of this intimate connection*, undergoes idealization. (11: 150; my emphasis)

Alongside this passage should be read his account of the way negation and disavowal always involve a simultaneous acknowledgement of what is being negated and disavowed (15: 438–40). Such are the processes which produce the perverse and which are in turn destabilized by the perverse dynamic. Freud offers a narrative whereby we begin to understand how and why the negation of homosexuality has been in direct proportion to its centrality; why the culturally marginal position of homosexuality has been in direct proportion to its cultural significance; and, ultimately, why homosexuality is so strangely integral to the selfsame heterosexual culture which so obsessively denounces it.

But – and it's a big but – Freud helped to telescope the perverse dynamic into a transhistorical psychosexual narrative, with the consequence that the history – the cultural dynamic of perversion briefly outlined in the first half of this essay – was lost. What that history reveals is a fundamentally different kind of displacement. It reveals not the endless Freudian displacement of sexuality into culture (e.g. via sublimation), but a displacement going the other way: the endless displacement of social crisis and conflict into sexuality. Moreover, this may well be the more important kind of displacement. That is why, increasingly, and as a matter of life and death for some, a crucial task for a radical sexual politics for the present is to expose this displacement of the political into the sexual. To expose this structure involves not the familiar task of *liberating* sexuality but rather this task of *taking sexuality apart and revealing the histories within it*, the displacements which constitute it.

Since Freud, the twentieth century has been faced not only with the crassness of Feldman's version of perversion but also, within more sophisticated varieties of psychoanalysis, the suppression of Freud's much more radical concept of the same. What makes both kinds of containment possible is not just the limitations of the psychoanalytic project itself but, as I've tried to show, a much longer metaphysical tradition privileging dominant social formations, sexual and otherwise, in terms of essence, nature, teleology, and universality. At the same time, the challenge of the perverse remains inscribed irreducibly within the same tradition, as it does within psychoanalysis.

I've been concerned to make visible a particular cultural dynamic with the aim of retrieving the concept of perversion as a category of cultural analysis. I started with the historically earlier semantic fields of perversion. The etymological histories are significant, partly for what they convey directly but more importantly for the cultural dynamic which the concept of perversion sought to control, repress, and disavow. So we need to go beyond such definitions and, in seeking to recover what is repressed and disavowed (the histories of perversion), to ensure that the concept itself is extended and developed. This procedure – first, attention to a formal definition leading to, second, an historical recovery, which in turn promotes, finally, a conceptual development – is analogous to what has already occurred with, say, the Bakhtinian notions of carnival, inversion, and the dialogic.[24]

I conclude with a word about perversion as a strategy of cultural resistance. In the period of post-war change, a radical sexual politics explored the idea that if we could desublimate the polymorphous perverse, we would not only liberate ourselves from repression, but also liberate an energy which could transform the entire social domain. I'm reminded of those heady days of liberation in the 1960s when one was urged not just to sit in front of the tanks, but to fuck there as well. This is John Rechy:

> Promiscuous homosexuals (outlaws with dual identities . . .) are the shock troops of the sexual revolution. The streets are the battleground, the revolution is the sexhunt, a radical statement is made each time a man has sex within another on a street . . .
>   Cum instead of blood. Satisfied bodies instead of dead ones. Death versus orgasm. Would they bust everyone? With cumsmeared tanks would they crush all?[25]

Times, of course, change, and sexualities with them. The challenge lies not in the polymorphous perverse but in what I call the paradoxical perverse or the perverse dynamic. It's this concept which I've begun to reconstruct in Augustine, in the Renaissance, and in Freud, that I'd like to see developed for a cultural politics. I've indicated elsewhere how writers like Wilde and Genet embrace the central paradoxes of the perverse, turning and using them against the normative orders which demonize the sexual deviant.[26] In the case of both Wilde and Genet, the perverse dynamic subverts the binaries of which the pervert is an effect, and does so internally. Additionally, the perverse dynamic suggests that we exist in terms of a radical interconnectedness which is not so much the *basis* of social organization, as what that organization must disavow to survive in its existing forms. This dynamic also suggests that if we fear the other we also fear the same, *especially sameness within the other* (homosexual congress constituted as the other of heterosexuality). Therefore, we see that the other is sometimes only feared because it is structured within an economy of the same. Discriminations like homophobia occur not in spite of, but because of, sameness.

Oscar Wilde knew only too well of, and brilliantly explored, the dynamic, subversive connection between perversity and paradox. He wrote: 'what the paradox was to me in the sphere of thought, perversity became to me in the sphere of passion'.[27] But he wrote that from prison. So, in affirming a politics of the perverse, we should never forget the cost: death, mutilation, and incarceration have been, and remain, the fate of the pervert.

3 'Poets and lovers evermore': the poetry and journals of Michael Field

Chris White

What's in a Name?

Katherine Bradley and Edith Cooper were poets and lovers from 1870 to 1913. They lived together, converted to Catholicism together, and together developed the joint poetic persona of Michael Field. As aunt and niece their love was socially structured and sanctioned. As Catholics and classicists they developed a language of love between women. As Michael and Henry their life together is recorded in the surviving manuscript journals. And as Michael Field they presented themselves to the world as Poets. (The capitalization, and the sense of the importance of this activity, is theirs.) But were they lesbians in any recognizable sense? This question relates to a developing orthodoxy of lesbian history and politics, in particular the influential thesis of Lillian Faderman in *Surpassing the Love of Men* where she discusses Michael Field, an analysis which I will attempt to interrogate in this chapter.[1] I want to make an intervention in the interpretative practice employed by Faderman, whereby all loving relationships between women before the 1920s are viewed as romantic friendships, and not as sexualized or erotic. Through connecting questions of homosexual history, politics, and desire, this chapter will offer readings of poems and journal entries that build up a picture of a specific instance of homosexual history.

In their relationship and their work, Katherine and Edith typify many of the difficulties in deciphering the meaning and nature of love between women. Faderman's comments are based only on published extracts (a slender volume concerned primarily with their lives as Catholics) from their extensive journals covering the years 1869–1914. The scale of this material is enormous: thirty-six foolscap volumes, with several others consisting of correspondence and notes.[2] It is a remarkable resource, but it is neither assimilable to a linear narrative nor capable of being easily represented here. (There is also the problem that some words and phrases are indecipherable.) It would be a mistake, however, to assume that these journals offer anything like a straightforward access to the 'truth' about the relationship or Katherine and

26

Edith's understanding of it, even given all the usual reservations about the mediated status of autobiography.[3] The journals were left with instructions that they might be opened at the end of 1929, and that the editors, T. and D.C. Sturge Moore, should publish from them as they saw fit. It hardly needs pointing out that at some point the journals became directed towards publication. When that was, or to whom the journals are addressed, is never clear. There is, I must assume, no truly 'private' record.

In the journals and the poetry there are copious references that may be read as lesbian. These texts are dotted with the words 'Sapphic', 'Beloved', 'Lover' and 'Lesbian'.[4] Yet it is not possible to infer that such terms indicate a same-sex sexual relationship, while Faderman argues that they are not at all sexual. I intend to demonstrate that these references are not simply definable as 'sexual' or 'non-sexual', but have their origins in more diverse sources. Any such analysis must be hedged around by considering the historically specific treatment of the Sapphic and the Lesbian.

Classical Greek literature and culture provided one way for nineteenth-century homosexual writers to talk about homosexuality as a positive social and emotional relationship. These authors appropriated the works of Plato and the myths of male love and comradeship to argue for social tolerance of same-sex love. For homosexual writers, a culture that was in the nineteenth century regarded as one of the highest points of civilization provided a precedent that was both respectable and sexual. This deployment of a Greek cultural precedent appears in Katherine and Edith's volume *Bellerophôn*, published under the pseudonyms Arran and Isla Leigh, in the poem 'Apollo's Written Grief', on the subject of Apollo and Hyacinth. This poem may be understood as a homo-political appeal for tolerance and an expression of the search for the right way of conducting a homosexual relationship:

> Men dream that thou wert smitten by the glow
> Of my too perilous love, not by the blow
> Of him who rivalled me.[5]

Apollo's love for his 'bright-eyed Ganymede' (p. 160) is presented as the best option for the boy, since he would otherwise have been consumed by Zephyrus or Zeus 'in greed' (p. 160). Apollo's love would not have proved dangerous to Hyacinth who, in 'panting for the light' (p. 159) of the sun-god, 'sufferedest the divine/Daring the dread delight' (p. 159). This poem, therefore, employs the already existing construction and terminology for homosexual love and desire. These myths remained available to readings as homoerotic archetypes or ideals.[6] This poem is not explicitly, or even obviously, a lesbian text. All of its characters are male. All the relationships are masculine relationships; between father and son, god and cup-bearer. The absence of women indicates an exclusively masculine world, where women are simply not relevant. One might imagine that alongside this world there exists another where women live together. But some of the language in which the poem speaks of homosexuality has metaphorical relationships to desire between women. The reference to 'the glow/Of my too perilous love' (III, 1, 2–3) is not like the more frequent, although usually embedded, phallic references. Where a whole canon of male–male bondings and loves exists, women had only one classical equivalent to draw upon for expressions and strategies of female–female love – the poetry of Sappho. Katherine and Edith as Michael Field, in using one of the male precedents, are taking up an available model in which to talk about same-sex desire. In order for them to use the lesbian precedent of Sappho, that classical antecedent must be recuperated from male appropriations, salaciousness or prurience.

Katherine and Edith wrote at a time when treatments of Sappho's verse were numerous and diverse. There are instances of deliberate suppression of the female pronouns, as in T.W. Higginson's translation published in 1871. In the novels of Alphonse Daudet, Théophile Gautier and Algernon Charles Swinburne, Sappho and Sapphic women were constructed as sadistic, predatory corruptors of innocent women. This emerged from male fantasies about masculine women with phallic sexualities, women who behaved like men with 'innocent' women, which does not threaten the proper balance of power between the sexes, but transplants it. It also participates in a fantasy about unnatural women who are brutalizing and corrupting of true, feminine women, thus marking off men as living in a proper relationship to femininity. And, predictably, there is the erotic value for the man in having two women on display. A standard work on Greek culture describes Sappho as 'a woman of generous disposition, affectionate heart, and independent spirit . . . [with] her own particular refinement of taste, exclusive of every approach to low excess or profligacy'.[7] Alternatively, another academic author declared that there was 'no good early evidence to show that the Lesbian standard was low'[8] (that is, sexual). In other versions, Sappho was portrayed as a woman falling in love with the fisherman Phaon, committing suicide when that love was unreciprocated.[9] The plurality of depictions and appropriations of Sappho indicates the extent to which she and her work became a cultural battleground, much more so than any male homosexual equivalent. Where some writers attempt to recuperate at all costs the great poet from accusations of lewdness, and others concede the love between women, but deny it as being passion of a base nature, Michael Field hold her up as a paragon among women, and put the passion back into the poet's community of women. Michael Field's 1889 volume *Long Ago*, a series of poems based on and completing Sappho's fragments, explores the heterosexual version of Sappho, alongside poems on passion between women. They explained, in a letter of 11 June 1889, the thinking behind *Long Ago*.

I feel I have hope that you will understand the spirit of my lyrics – you who have sympathy with attempts to reconcile the old and the new, to live as in continuation the beautiful life of Greece. . . . What I have aspired to do from Sappho's fragments may therefore somewhat appeal to your sense of survival in human things – to your interest in the shoots and offspring of older literature.[10]

The reconciliation of the old and the new – of classical Greek culture and literature and nineteenth-century remakings of those forms and ideas – forms an important part of the conceptualization of homosexual desire, and more significantly, of the place of homosexuals in a dominantly heterosexual society. In this letter, Michael Field appeal to Pater's own analyses and interpretations in his essays and lectures on Greek studies, art, and literature.[11] Greek culture is not perceived as being mere history, a dead past of interest only to scholars and classicists. It is, rather, a potent and valid model for nineteenth-century British culture, which, for many critics and poets, ought to be reflected in the organization and standards of their own society. In addition to the political and cultural virtues of the Greek precedent, many writers, Michael Field among them, found images, texts, and authors that provided a positive framework in which to speak about desire between two men or two women, and this framework did not require the writers to begin from a point of self-justification or to address the dominant cultural ideas about sin and unnatural sexual practices. Greek culture was perceived as a young culture, and the associated discourses that connected youth with purity and innocence preserved Greek culture from accusations of adult vice and knowledge.[12]

Long Ago contains no references to sin or corruption. Relations between women are taken as a given. The forms of those relationships are complex and in a state of negotiation. There are fickle lovers, women who would rather marry men, quarrels between lovers, reconciliations and erotic interludes among the poems about the public making of poetry:

Come, Gorgo, put the rug in place,
  And passionate recline;
I love to see thee in thy grace,
  Dark, virulent, divine. . . .

Those fairest hands – dost thou forget
  Their power to thrill and cling?[13]

This is no sexless romance between friends, but an exotic eroticism. The loved/desired woman in the act of lying down is passionate and divine. There is the reference to the pleasure that can be given with hands between women.

If this is one version of Sappho, there are at least two other Sapphos in

Long Ago. One is a woman at the centre of a loving community of women, a community which she must keep safe from the intrusions of men. In poem LIV, 'Adown the Lesbian Vales', Sappho is in possession of a 'passionate unsated sense' which her maids seek to satisfy. The relationship between Sappho and her maids is premised upon a need to keep the women away from marriage: 'No girls let fall/Their maiden zone/At Hymen's call' (p. 96). The third Sappho is the heterosexual lover of Phaon:

> If I could win him from the sea,
> Then subtly I would draw him down
> 'Mid the bright vetches; in a crown
> My art should teach him to entwine
> Their thievish rings and keep him mine.[14]

This seems to be a possessive heterosexual desire, springing from a manipulative battle to win him in a destructive competition with the fisherman's work at sea. But the imagery is also quite sexy. The drawing down echoes the 'passionate recline' of the previous extract. Yet, where the focus in the latter is on Gorgo, here the focus is as much on the vetches as on the fisherman. The supposed erotic object does not stand centre stage. Instead it is the 'I' of Sappho who dominates, shaping the desire, which means annihilating the loved object. Even the seemingly heterosexual Sappho is not, in Michael Field's poetry, shown to be a truly feminine figure existing in a proper relationship to what ought instead to serve as the focus of all their desires, the masculine.

Masculinity in itself is not valued. In poem LXVI, Sappho prays to Apollo about Phaon:

> Apollo, thou alone cans't bring
>   To Phaon's feeble breast
> The fire unquenchable, the sting,
>   Love's agony, Love's zest.
> Thou needs't not curse him, nor transform;
> Give him the poet's heart of storm
> To suffer as I suffer, thus
> Abandoned, vengeful, covetous.[15]

I think this is a very funny poem. OK, Apollo, you don't need to turn him into something or someone else, and maybe you shouldn't curse him, although you could, and I did consider it for a while; just make Phaon like me. As he is, he's feeble and emotionally a bit inadequate, and if you make him like me, a poet, with a poet's emotional turbulence, he'd be much improved. And then I'll probably abandon him, and leave him to stew. Love with a man untransformed by a god just isn't worth the hassle.

The second and third versions of Sappho come into conflict over the issue of virginity and poetry. The love of Phaon and the inviolate women of the Lesbian community are combined in poem XVII: 'The moon rose full, the women stood'. Sappho calls to her virginity, her 'only good', to come back, having been lost to Phaon. The inviolate state is 'that most blessèd, secret state/ That makes the tenderest maiden great', not the possession of a male's sexual attention. Sappho's loss of virginity effectively puts an end to her poetic gift:

> And when
> By maiden-arms to be enwound
>   Ashore the fisher flings,
> Oh, then my heart turns cold, and then
>   I drop my wings.

The connection between poetry and virginity is broached in *The New Minnesinger and Other Poems*, published by Katherine under the pseudonym Arran Leigh. The title poem discusses the craft of the woman-poet, 'she whose life doth lie/In virgin haunts of poesie.'[16] The virgin woman-poet, by virtue of her freedom from men, possesses the potentiality to be 'lifted to a free/and fellow-life with man' (p. 12). There appears to be a contradiction between 'free' and 'fellow-life'. With the stress placed on the 'free', there is a reverbation of the usage of 'enwound' in poem XX. Heterosexuality as the form of the relationship between men and women is a form of bondage. If this is replaced by the 'fellow-life' of equal comradeship, an idea much employed in this period and derived from Walt Whitman,[17] then the bondage, even in relationships between men and women is at an end. But whatever 'realm' a woman endeavours to enclose, she must 'ever keep/All things subservient to the good/Of pure free-growing womanhood' (p. 13). Virginity is not sterile in this formulation: it is simultaneously pure and productive. This version of femininity offers an ambiguous challenge to the terms of patriarchal culture. It exists apart from patriarchal dictates, but includes fellowship and equality with men. It embraces the productiveness of womanhood and an all-women community, and speaks of an equality of potency between men and women. It is the 'fellow-life' that is desired, and not men or heterosexuality. Poem LII goes so far as to produce life as a woman as superior to life as a man, through the figure of Tiresias.

> [Tiresias] as woman, know
> The unfamiliar, sovereign guise
> Of passion he had dared despise . . .
> He trembled at the quickening change,
> He trembled at his vision's range,
> His finer sense for bliss and dole,
> His receptivity of soul;
> But when love came, and, loving back,
> He learnt the pleasure men must lack,

> It seemed that he has broken free
> Almost from his mortality.[18]

Tiresias, in his youth, is said to have found two serpents, and when he struck them with a stick to separate them, he is said to have suddenly changed into a woman. Seven years later he was restored to manhood by a repeat of the incident with the snakes. When he was a woman, Jupiter and Juno consulted him on a dispute about which of the sexes received greater pleasure from marriage. Tiresias decided in Jupiter's favour – that women derived greater pleasure – and Juno punished Tiresias for this slight by blinding him. Michael Field turn this myth, that is more than a little disparaging about men's enthusiasm for marriage, into a positive valuing of women. Women are not only more sensitive, more feeling, the usual attributes of femininity, they are also more capable than men of experiencing pleasure. That pleasure is not to do with the greater size of women's psyches or souls. Love equals pleasure, and women feel more pleasure. If this is read in the light of the Gorgo poem, above, then that pleasure comes to take on distinctly physical aspects. The other interesting aspect of the Tiresias poem is that it holds both genders together at the same time. At the moment of transition from female to male, Tiresias has a masculine consciousness and a feminine memory, and is an emotional hermaphrodite. While the feminine is better, the moment of transition is one of fullness, with both genders working together. Tiresias is a representation of the absence of any clear split between male and female in Michael Field's utopian vision.

The construction of femininity in these poems is more complex than an unequivocal embrace of a non-sexual friendship. Michael Field represent Sappho as a wise, old(er) woman who remembers the rejections of youth and deplores the fickleness of younger women and their susceptibility to men. Her constancy to women, 'Maids, not to you my mind doth change' (*Long Ago*: XXXIII, p. 52), is contrasted with her reaction to the men whom she will 'defy, allure, estrange,/Prostrate, made bond or free'. To her maids she is a maternal or passionate lover, and to men she is manipulative and fickle. (The attitude to men is complicated by virtue of the poems being authored under the name of a man. The 'male' poet relates sexually to both men and women.) The volume concludes with poem LXVIX, 'O free me, for I take the leap', where Sappho flings herself from a cliff with a prayer to Apollo for a 'breast love-free'.

Michael Field's Sappho, therefore, is not the denizen of a lesbian or Lesbian idyll. Rather, she is the subject of a contradiction which emerges from those versions described above. On the one hand, Sappho the poet must be defended from accusations of immorality, while, on the other, Sappho the Lesbian must be salvaged from the Phaon myth. The Lesbian community of women is more than a society of friendship, but is also a site of poetic production and, moreover, the production of the Poet identity. Both are threatened by men and heterosexuality. The

'production' of poetry both images and guarantees the 'free' bonds of
the women makers. It is a lesbian writing which, familiarly, needs to
think itself as free from men, for the conditions of its own practice. It
defines itself as productive, rather than anti- or non-productive, not
simply to give itself the dignity that men's poetry has within the canon
and practice of poetry, but also to give voice to, and thus 'have', the
lesbian desires that are constructed by and construct the poetic product.
This is clearly not only an account of Sappho and Lesbos, but a grap-
pling with the nature and practice of the composite poet, Michael Field.
The poetry is the result of the joint productiveness of two women.

Sexuality is not, therefore, the only interpretative category in play in
Long Ago. The practice of Poetry is equally important, and it interweaves
with sexuality. In the preface to *Long Ago* there is an ambiguous appeal
to 'the one woman'. The volume is jointly authored, yet the voice of the
preface is in the first-person singular. This prefatorial voice advocates
worship of, and the apprehension of, an ideal of the Poet and the lover
in the poetry and person of Sappho. A direct connection is made
between Sappho's prayer and the prayer of this first-person voice:

> Devoutly as the fiery-bosomed Greek turned in her anguish to
> Aphrodite, praying her to accomplish her heart's desires, I have
> turned to the one woman who has dared to speak unfalteringly of
> the fearful mastery of love, and again and again the dumb prayer
> has risen from my heart –
> σὺ δαντα
> συμμαχος εσσο[19]

Here, the Greek is translated as 'you will be my ally'. The 'one woman' is
either Sappho, a lover, or a writing partner. This ambiguity of identity is
central to this volume of poetry. In *Long Ago* Michael Field are writing
with Sappho the Poet, and working with Sappho, Aphrodite, and the
partner in an imaginary alliance. The preface does not specify who that
mastery of love is directed to. But perhaps that is the point. In order to
speak 'unfalteringly' of woman's love for woman, it is necessary for
Michael Field to work in alliance with other women and other women's
formulations of such love. The construction in the preface is both
strategic and passionate, not a privatized emotion which continues detached from historical and social concerns. It is political, creating
changes in the presentation of love between women on the basis of the
available cultural models. Michael Field's appeal to 'the one woman' does
not rest upon a static image of monogamous romance, which while
apparently neutral and ahistorical is intimately connected with bourgeois values and patriarchal family structures, and which lesbianism has
the potential to sidestep or remake.

This passage begs a series of questions about desire and speech. The
dumb prayer rising, an as yet unaccomplished desire, a person who

could dare to speak are all potent, and about-to-be, differentiated from the existing 'mastery'. This yearns for something that is both utopian and physical, and the process of making one necessarily involves making the other. The metaphors of the invocation are all physical. Aphrodite's passion is not abstract, but fiery and residing in her in her breast. One lover turns to the other, the emotional and physical senses both contained in that reference to that action.

'The Fearful Mastery of Love'

If, in the late twentieth century, contemporary lesbians are determined to write our own dictionary of lesbian love and desire, there appears to be no such imperative behind the writings of Michael Field. Michael Field, rather than inventing a vocabulary with an unmistakable precision of meaning, deployed the language of classical scholarship, the language of love belonging to heterosexuality, the language of friendship (but never noticeably the language of blood relatives), and later the language of Catholicism. These differing languages represent a series of modulations both chronologically within their *oeuvre* and in the different forms of writing they practised. There is no single language which they employ to talk about each other and their relationship. Consequently, there is enough imprecision or ambiguity in the slippage around their words of love and desire for Faderman, misleadingly, to find sufficient material in their writings to call them romantic friends, when the terms 'romantic' and 'friend' are both so sloppy. It is, of course, equally misleading to call them lesbians. Although the term 'lesbian' is historically available, it is not a word they ever used of themselves to indicate a sexual relationship. They did, however, have other terms and metaphors.

In comparing themselves to Elizabeth Barrett Browning and Robert Browning, Michael Field assert *'we are closer married'*.[20] Marriage was an available metaphor or conceptualization for both women to apply to their relationship. Following Edith's death, Katherine invoked the words of the marriage service when making an approach to the literary periodical the *Athenæum* to 'write a brief appreciation of my dead Fellow-Poet, not separating what God had joined, yet dwelling for her friends' delight on her peculiar & most rare gifts'.[21] In the preface to *Works and Days* God is said to have joined Michael Field both as the Poet and as 'Poets and lovers evermore' (*Works and Days* p. xix). And, as a last example, to Havelock Ellis, on the subject of his attempts to discover who wrote which piece, they asserted 'As to our work, let no man think he can put asunder what God had joined.'[22] Faderman denies that there is any sexual meaning in these statements, insisting that since 'they were generally so completely without self-consciousness in their public declarations of mutual love',[23] the relationship must have been 'innocent'. It is difficult to understand how someone can make a declaration of any kind without being conscious of what they are doing. In addition to this, Faderman makes the error of deciding that their love for one another '*caused* them to convert to Catholicism' (p. 211; my emphasis), since this conversion was a way to guarantee being together eternally. Faderman's specious theory appears to be based wholly upon one paragraph in the published journals, written by Edith: 'It is Paradise between us. When we're together eternally, our spirits will be interpenetrated with our loves and our art under the benison of the Vision of God' (p. 324). Faderman derives the whole of their Catholic experience from this brief extract, which was written when Edith was dying. Moreover, Faderman ignores the evidence of the rest of the journals, which reveal their faith as being a good deal more than a mere instrumentalist insurance policy, and the history and pattern of Catholic conversion at that time, with many literary figures joining the Church and some, notably John Gray and Frederick Rolfe, becoming or attempting to become priests.

Michael Field's God is not a cosy, tea-table God, nor an Old Testament God of vengeance for the wicked and just deserts for the righteous. It is a construction of God as an authority that resists what men do – which is, dividing women in the name of femininity and the family. God provides a ground for utopian female artistic production. The language of the passage from the published journals raises both their love and their art, equally significant, to the knowledge and approval of God. The act of interpenetration is produced as the highest point of achievement for poet and lover. This is not a safe, lesbian-feminist, metaphor. The act of inter-penetration unites the two women not as Romantic Friends, but interprets the relationship as something that values it as an entering into the other's work and identity. Not surprisingly, Faderman does not comment upon it. It does not fit with the diffuse sensuality she ascribes to Romantic Friends.

Faderman bases the Romantic Friendship hypothesis on a specific construction of femininity. She presents it as the sole form of the relationship between loving women before the development of a female homosexual identity and pathology through political and scientific discourses, such as the work of the sexologists and the gay rights movements in Germany and France. Consequently, Faderman applies a modern version of relations between women to the late nineteenth century which precludes any consciousness of sexual interest. In doing so, she constructs all female friendships along the lines of the dominant culture. Faderman argues that, since sexual relationships between women were unacceptable to the dominant, and since women were constructed as the passionless gender and ignorant of sex, they could not possibly have had the knowledge, language, or experience of lesbian *desire*. Any Victorian woman, she maintains, would have been profoundly shocked by such an interpretation of their feelings, and therefore every woman's expression of love or passion must of necessity have been free from the taint of homosexual desire. Faderman does not even entertain the possibility that these women, knowing that the dominant culture condemned such feelings and relationships, could have developed their own strategies for talking about and explaining such expressions of sexuality. Instead she presumes that innocence is a superior form of loving compared to sexual experiences between women. She practises the condescension of history, and in doing so attempts to dodge the revelation of her own political agenda. Of course, Katherine and Edith did not have available to them the language, politics, and structures of contemporary lesbianism and feminism. But Faderman's insistence that they were too stupid to know any better rests upon a belief in linear progress from one age to the next. Contemporary lesbians, so the argument goes, are much wiser than their nineteenth-century sisters because they of course can see through the mechanisms used to oppress and limit women. By practising this evolutionary politics, Faderman manages to read over the top of all the strategies and devices that Michael Field, among many others, did deploy in order to create a cultural space for themselves. That these strategies did exist is beyond question, and they were various, from the appropriations of Greek culture to Carpenter's assertion that 'homogenic love', encompassing both male and female homosexuality, was a potentially superior social force to heterosexuality.[24]

Before going further, I want to make it clear that I am disquieted by the project of going into print criticizing another lesbian. This is an unsisterly thing to do, particularly given the open nature of this forum. Such debates ought not to be conducted in public and in a manner belonging to the practices of non-feminist, gentlemen's club scholarship. *Surpassing the Love of Men* is an invaluable catalogue of the works of hundreds of lesbians which have been suppressed or ignored. But opposition to the political agenda of the book's thesis and the new orthodoxy, which is finding such currency amongst lesbians, academic and non-academic, is in my view of paramount importance. This version of lesbianism appropriates to itself lesbian history and makes of it a reactionary sexual politics. In the introduction to *Surpassing the Love of Men* Faderman makes this claim:

> In lesbian-feminism I have found an analog to romantic friendship
> . . . I venture to guess that had the romantic friends of other eras
> lived today, many of them would have been lesbian-feminists.
> (p. 20)

My guess is that in 'Romantic Friendship' she found an analogue to radical lesbian-feminism. She displays yet another methodological error in her making of history into analogues, since this works to deny the material specificity of the past as well as the present. Both Romantic Friendship and lesbian-feminism are positions distinguished by the desexualized nature of relations between women. This denial of lesbian sexual practice is spelt out by Elizabeth Mavor in *The Ladies of Llangollen: A Study in Romantic Friendship*, a work which I believe owes a great deal to Faderman's study: 'Much that we would now associate solely with a sexual attachment was contained in romantic friendship: tenderness, loyalty, sensibility, shared beds, shared tastes, coquetry, even passion.'[25]

This reading of love declarations between women and accounts of women living together as wholly non-sexual is explained by Faderman as follows:

> Women in centuries other than ours often internalised the view of females as having little sexual passion . . . If they were sexually aroused, bearing no burden of proof as men do, they might deny it even to themselves if they wished. (p. 16)

Undoubtedly, women internalized the prescriptions of dominant ideology, but the leap from saying they took on board these prescriptions to the assumption that this internalization defined and limited all they believed and practised is quite breathtaking. In particular, it seems hardly credible that simply because women did not have penile erections they would not have recognized how sexual arousal felt and what it meant. Yet this is the outcome of the position adopted by Faderman and Mavor, which argues for a female nature utterly distinct from all things male and masculine. Both writers construct a time that is both more innocent and more separatist than our own. Lesbian separatists construct lesbianism and lesbians as superior, more creative, more sensitive, and more human. Romantic Friendship is an expression of lesbian separatism which takes the form of a relationship that is, in Mavor's words, 'more liberal and inclusive and better suited to the more diffuse feminine nature' (p. xvii) – not concentrated in an erect penis – and which, according to Faderman, 'had little connection with men who were so alienatingly and totally different' (p. 20). The prescriptions of lesbian-feminism extend even into what happens sexually between women. Two women together escape the oppression of phallic heterosexuality, but to arrive in a utopian region of non-sexual romance and intimacy they must never behave in a manner which in any way reflects that in which men behave towards women.

Paradoxically, the Romantic Friendship hypothesis is a celebration of many of the conventional attributes of femininity as it has been constructed by patriarchy, such as passivity, gentleness, domesticity, creativity, and supportiveness, and which condemns as irretrievably phallic other characteristics generally labelled masculine, including strength, capability, activity, success, independence, and lust. In claiming women-loving women as romantic friends, the hypothesis annihilates from history all those lesbians/lovers who gave histories to (or recognized themselves in the works of) sexologists such as Havelock Ellis,[26] or who, alternatively, formed part of lesbian subcultures based on sexual prefer-

ence and emotional commitment.[27] Faderman's model consigns lesbian
sexual activity to a male fantasy that routinely appears in pornographic
writing. She opposes the pornographic image of women's sexuality to
the 'true', non-sexual history of women's relationships which, it is
claimed, appears in their diaries and writings. Having lighted upon male
pornographic images of lesbian sex, Faderman concludes that if men
talk about women having sex through a particular discourse, then since
that discourse does not appear in women's writings, women did not have
sex together or relate sexually to each other.

I am not arguing that every close relationship between women was a
sexual one. The point is that the evidence should be looked at without
the limitations of lesbian-feminist presuppositions. The political imperative behind my argument is to avoid having lesbian and gay histories
misappropriated yet again, and this time from within the ranks of gay
writers. Faderman's work is a revisionist project whose critique is focused on 'non-routine acts of love rather than routine acts of oppression,
exploitation or violence'.[28] On the basis that these women lovers did not
behave like or pretend to be men, this position concludes that they are
'nice girls', not lesbians. As an alternative to this revisionism, I want to try
to begin an account of Michael Field's work and relationship that gives
them credit for awareness and strategic practice, and which has the
potentiality to include within its frame of reference class, race, and
power. This will reject the lesbian-feminist invention of a realm and an
age of harmonious femininity where all women are equal, provided they
do not indulge in politically-right-off sexual activity.

Fleshly Love and 'A Curve That Is Drawn So Fine'

In order to develop a framework in which to understand and talk about
love between women in Michael Field's work, I will now go on to look at
the references to desire between women, and examine the plurality of
ways in which they talked about their understanding of sexual and
emotional love between women.

Two instances of desire between women that are constructed as negative and unnatural appear in the journals. Travelling through Europe,
Edith falls ill in Dresden, and writes: 'My experiences with Nurse are
painful – she is under the possession of terrible fleshly love [which] she
does not conceive as such, and as such I will not receive it.'[29] The nurse is
presented as not recognizing her experience. Edith, however, does
conceive of this love as fleshly. It is certainly within Edith's conceptual
framework to apprehend one woman's feelings of physical desire for
another woman. This instance of fleshly sin does not belong to the
imagination of a pornographer. In this extract, the use of the words
'possession' and 'terrible' cannot be simply read as condemnatory, since
any unwelcome sexual attentions may appear to be a terrible possession

of the harasser. It is not clear, though, whether Edith would not accept fleshly love in any context, or whether it is this particular instance that is unwelcome.

The second example concerning fleshly love appears in the manuscript journal for 1908, referring to a painting they saw.

> A man named Legrand – a monstrous charlatan – who can by a clever trick give the infamies of the worldly Frenchwoman – especially in unconscious self-conscious exposure to her own sex . . . [as manuscript] female friends together. What is to be expressed is of Satan – and the means as ugly as the matter. The people round me say 'He must be a Genius' – I answer to myself A Demon-Spawned Charlatan.[30]

I have yet to trace this painting, but it obviously enraged Edith. She can read this picture as false and disgusting. The exposure is apparently to the female gaze, but actually for the male gaze. The prurience of that gaze is expressed through that 'unconscious self-consciousness', a wink at the audience, inviting the viewer in to enjoy the scene. This 'clever trick' is that of the pornographer. Two women apparently exist for their own pleasure, but they are actually on offer as double pleasure for the male viewer.[31] The unreality of the scene is evident to Edith. Her racism is evident in her ascribing of infamies to Frenchwomen (and German women too, as evidenced by her comments on the nurse). The point is, she recognizes Legrand's painting is a false image of how women behave to one another as 'female friends'. Edith repudiates the way in which patriarchal values frame and perceive relations between women. Legrand is a charlatan; his representation bears no relation to the truth. Yet this rejection is not the same thing as denying the existence of desire between women. However, what that truth is cannot easily be deduced from the writings.

Outside of the treatment of Sappho, which is a minefield of interpretative complexity, there is very little explicit analysis of the relationship between Katherine and Edith. Their primary concern is always with Michael Field the Poet, and it is the name itself I want to focus on now because it reveals to a large extent how they conceived of their practice as poets. That male-authored publications are usually better received and taken more seriously than female-authored works is a truism. Before the adoption of the joint persona they used the pseudonyms Arran and Isla Leigh, which brought them more favourable reviews than they ever had as Michael Field, and also the assumption that they were either a married couple or a brother and sister. Perhaps this misinterpretation is what led them to adopt the single pen-name. Although Katherine and Edith used metaphors of marriage to describe their love, it would be surprising if they had wanted to be publicly portrayed as a heterosexual couple. However, 'Michael Field' cannot be regarded as a true pseudonym, since it was widely known in a literary circle that included John Gray, George Meredith, and Oscar Wilde, as well as their friends Charles Ricketts and Charles Shannon, that they were two women. Much of their correspondence is addressed to them both under the heading of Michael Field and they often signed themselves with the joint name. The name contains a compelling contradiction: they both deploy the authority of male authorship and yet react against such camouflage. Michael Field is not a disguise. Nor is it a pretence at being a man.

None the less, they were appalled when they became known to their Catholic congregation as the women behind Michael Field. Edith confronted her confessor, Goscommon:

> I say I regret it is known; but that in the same way, I am glad he, as my Confessor, knows, for it will help him to understand some things I feel he has somewhat misunderstood, & also it is for a poet with his freedom of impulse to submit to the control & discipline of the Church.[32]

This anxiety for concealment is in marked contradiction to their previous willingness to be known. Wayne Koestenbaum offers the explanation that 'their aliases gave them a seclusion in which they could freely unfold their "natures set a little way apart"'.[33] Yet that desired seclusion became impossible when they submitted to the authority of the Church. Even though their attempts to develop a framework in which to talk about their love and desires in part depended upon a screen from the world, this effort did not rest wholly upon the use of a male pen-name. Rather, the development of the poetic persona Michael Field gave them another role in which to play out their understandings of their relationship. The persona is distinct from Katherine and Edith, and separate from their pet names Michael and Henry, which were in common currency among friends. Michael Field the Poet is always presented as the highest point of their work.

Complicated shifts took place when they converted to Catholicism. Entering the Roman Catholic Church evokes from Edith the two explicit references to sexuality I have found. In the 1907 volume of the journals she wrote, 'Since I have entered the Holy Catholic Church, I have never fallen into fleshly sin',[34] which presupposes that before she joined she had succumbed to such fleshly temptation. Here fleshly sin may be a reference to masturbation, but I am doubtful, given the second reference in 1908: 'When I came into this Church a year ago [I gave] a gift that was a vow of chastity.'[35] Not practising masturbation may constitute abstinence from fleshly sin, but chastity in this context seems to involve another person. This may be an indication that before conversion, there had been a sexual or erotic relationship between Katherine and Edith.

The physicality of the relationship is not so much implicit as embedded, especially in the late poems. An unpublished poem from the manuscript journals, 'My Love is like a lovely Shepherdess', is appended with a note from the writer of the poem, Katherine.

> Edith's peach & green embroidered gown came home this evening; – after seeing her in it I brake into the 1st part of the 1st verse of this song – then came down &, at my desk, in the evening light, wrote the rest of the verses. Friday July 19th.

The first part of the first verse reads

> My Love is like a lovely Shepherdess;
>   She has a dress
>   Of peach & green
> the prettiest was ever seen.[36]

After this, the poem goes into a pastoral idyll, where the poet adores the shepherdess through metaphors of spring, morning, and music. But the starting point for the pastoral is the appearance of the beloved. She is 'pretty' (6), 'virgin white' (15), with a 'tender face' (10). The specificity of the poem derives from an identifiable moment in their daily life, which is valued as the proper subject of poetry, although not for publication.

From *The Wattlefold*, a volume of previously unpublished poetry which was eventually published after their deaths in 1930, comes Katherine's poem 'Caput Tuum ut Carmelus'. It opens with these lines:

> I watch the arch of her head
> As she turns away from me.

And continues in the third stanza:

> Oh, what can Death have to do
> With a curve that is drawn so fine,
> With a curve that is drawn as true
> As the mountain's crescent line?[37]

This dwelling on the physical detail of the loved/desired object makes the physical presence the representation of the identity of that object. That fine curve stands in for both the fineness of the inner self and also for how the lover conceptualizes the relationship with the loved. That curve is a combination of art – it is drawn – and of nature – like a mountain, and this is indicative of one way in which the identity of the loved object as loved object is delineated through the poetry. While there are no explicit declarations of lesbian desire, there are these embedded constructions of identity expressed through relationship.

Edith, in one of her last entries before her death, wrote: 'We have had the bond of race, with the delicious adventure of the stranger nature, introduced by the beloved father.'[38] Since the word father is not capitalized, I hazard to guess that this is a reference to John Gray, a poet, a convert, a priest, Katherine's one-time confessor, and spiritual adviser to them both. He was also the long-time lover of the poet Marc-André Raffalovich.[39] The word 'race' here is intriguing, but again there is the notion of natures that are different. Although they had been in correspondence with Havelock Ellis,[40] there is no evidence in their work of any belief or interest in sexology, inversion, and the 'third sex'. That said, these remarks do seem to resonate with the notion of belonging to a 'breed apart'.

Their strategies for making sense of their love do not take the shape of pretending to be or believing themselves to be men, nor of understanding themselves to be romantic friends. In their treatment of their role as Michael Field and of their love for each other, Katherine and Edith construct a position of opposition against the misapprehensions and prejudices of the world. That opposition relies upon their alliance with one another, and with specific cultural formations that they recognize as expressive or reflective of that alliance. This is the impulse behind their declaration of 1893:

> My Love and I took hands and swore
> Against the world, to be
> Poets and lovers evermore. . . .
> Of judgement never to take heed,
> But to those fast-locked souls to speed,
> Who never from Apollo fled. . . .
> Continually
> With them to dwell,
> Indifferent to heaven and hell.[41]

The reference to Apollo marks the homoerotic nature of the relationship, and the indifference to heaven and hell seems to suggest they were refusing some large-scale social rules and norms. The roles of poet and lover are both integral to one another and essential to their rejection of the judgement of 'the world'. This is an implicitly political understanding of women as lovers, rather than a private and personal retreat from the world into Romantic Friendship.

There is no one strategy or organizing principle that they use to define themselves, a point which is demonstrated in the difference between the poem from 1893 and the prefatory poem from the 1875 volume *The New Minnesinger* by Arran Leigh (alias Katherine Bradley). 'To E.C.' refers to the 'mast'ring power' of the other woman's love, and the writer's need of that love which is 'forever voiceless' (p. vii). The 'lighter passions' will find a way 'into rhythm', and the voiceless need is premised upon the assertion that 'Thou hast fore-fashioned all I do and think' (p. vii). This difference marks the shift from a virtual silence about the love to the opening up of a framework in which to talk about that love.

Edith and Katherine's methods of explaining their love and desire are difficult to decipher because they are so unlike our own modes of explanation. But the fact that we have that trouble does not mean that they encountered the same problem. It is necessary to beware failing or refusing to recognize the complexity of the negotiations these women-loving women made. If we do, as Faderman has done, then all those negotiations made within a hostile dominant culture would lead to a particularly restricted view – a homogeneous and desexualized version. What I have attempted to do here is to begin the process of mapping out the complicated processes whereby the discourses of lesbianism might have been inscribed in the nineteenth century, and not to fall into a simplistic one-theory-fits-all position.

4 *Wilde*, Dorian Gray, *and gross indecency*

Joseph Bristow

I

'Those who find ugly meanings in beautiful places are corrupt without being charming. This is a fault', wrote Oscar Wilde in his series of provocative aphorisms prefacing *The Picture of Dorian Gray* (1891).[1] This chapter investigates how Wilde's only novel risked opening up a meta-phorical space in which male same-sex desire could be articulated as a potentially beautiful thing that the law rendered ugly by granting such desire a grotesque and incriminatory definition – namely, gross inde-cency. Taking its bearings from well-known aspects of Walter Pater's controversial aesthetics and their much-maligned interests in 'testing opinions and courting new impressions, never acquiescing in a facile orthodoxy',[2] the analysis that follows reads *Dorian Gray* as a dramatiza-tion of key preoccupations about the preservation of youth at the centre of late Victorian legislation on sexual relations. In these respects, the secret degeneration afflicting the hero's picture turns him into a hideous figure whose image bears witness – not to his innate immorality – but to the cultural representation of 'corruption'. Dorian Gray's tragically div-ided public beauty and private shame work as a double identity that places the fine values of art in opposition to the increasing power of the state – a state that was for the first time making condign judgments about what constituted a homosexual danger to the perceived moral well-being of the nation. The aesthetic and desiring energies invested in Dorian's equivocating 'picture' suggest a morality based on an ethics very different from that which in the statute books worded homosexuality in such punishingly negative terms. The novel, then, raises questions – rather than makes assertions – about how and why such an aesthetically ennobled image as Dorian's is, at one and the same time, 'gross' in its 'indecency'. In Dorian, Wilde was transgressing the dichotomy of public and private worlds in a manner very much of his era – as might be witnessed in a novel such as Robert Louis Stevenson's *Dr Jekyll and Mr Hyde* (1886). But Wilde was practically alone in going so publicly into print to develop, even advertise, available cultural models of homosexuality. His purpose was to expose the implicitly 'criminal' effects which led beautiful beings such as Dorian into the most fatal of crimes.

It has to be said, from the outset, that such an approach to *Dorian Gray* is in itself somewhat unorthodox. None the less, the reading presented here belongs to a gathering body of what may be labelled anti-homophobic or uncloseted criticism. Since the publication in 1985 of Eve Kosofsky Sedgwick's innovative theorization of the precarious divide between male homosocial and male homosexual desires, it has been possible to use a new vocabulary to address the homoerotic interests of Wilde's best-known works.[3] Sedgwick's pathbreaking study owes much to the work of lesbian and gay theorists, notably Gayle Rubin, whose rethinking of Claude Lévi-Strauss's anthropological inquiries into gift-exchange, taken together with René Girard's structural analysis of erotic triangulations in western narratives, forms the basis of an ambitious literary understanding of how male bonds are cemented by two prevalent and interdependent types of sexual loathing: homophobia and misogyny. Sedgwick examines the shifting boundaries of these formations of sexual hatred from the Renaissance (Shakespeare's sonnets) to the late nineteenth century (Henry James and Wilde). But given the meagre historical apparatus that Sedgwick sets in place to comprehend some three hundred years of increasingly prohibitive relations between men, it is, to say the least, difficult to see precisely how and why the late nineteenth century placed a strategic ban on male–male sexual contact. Similarly, Sedgwick supplies only a limited amount of information to indicate the structures of self-perception in which those subjects involved in homosexual practices were positioned. For a start – as Michel Foucault and Jeffrey Weeks remind us – the homosexual was only a 'homosexual' by the last decade of the nineteenth century.[4] Sedgwick, therefore, has offered literary historians a general – but none the less crucial – thesis into which a more particularized knowledge of homosexuality and homosociality may be inscribed.

Detailed work of this kind has already begun to emerge, and with important consequences for criticism of Wilde. One example of research probing the cultural models of homosexual desire available to late Victorians is Linda Dowling's outstanding essay on two related literary codes (the 'Dorian' and *poikilos*). These codes can be traced in the writings of Pater, John Ruskin, and Gerard Manley Hopkins (all Oxford men), indicating the degree of visibility potentially outrageous aspects of classical learning might in fact enjoy in a university ethos saturated with images of Ancient Greece. There is no need to rehearse Dowling's complex argument here but it is instructive to draw attention to her tentative conclusion about the ways in which 'Dorian' (namely, the hyper-Hellenic) and *poikilos* (meaning dappled, or 'pied', as in Hopkins's 'Pied Beauty') might be considered in potentially 'homosexual' contexts. Having illustrated Hopkins's disturbance with Walt Whitman's 'Calamus' poems – poems which attracted Hopkins as much as they repelled him – Dowling states:

> This is not at all to say that there is no such thing as a 'homosexual' code in later Victorian writing. But it is to suggest that whatever that code consists in (and even its outlines are not yet clear to us), it does not operate as a simple inversion of the dominant discourse. Instead, as Ruskin's persistent presence as a source and influence will remind us, the late Victorian 'homosexual' code . . . assumes a discontinuous and constantly shifting relationship to the discourse of the dominant group . . . What future studies of Victorian sexuality must strive to do, then, is to plot the varying adhesions and resistances that punctuate the relation between 'homosexual' and dominant discourses. Yet even to speak of 'the dominant discourse' is a perilous oversimplification. For what may appear from a point of view at the margin to be the fluent speech of power may seem from a point near the centre to be a subversive dialect of opposition. Hence, for example, the unstable institutional role of Greek studies at the ancient universities: J.A. Symonds found in Greek studies a haven, while opponents of 'Germanism' and university reform saw in them a hell, and it is precisely the continuing implication of 'homosexuality' in university politics that at times impels and at times impedes its emergence as a discourse.[5]

Dowling is indubitably correct to state that a homosexual coding is not necessarily an 'inversion' of a dominant discourse; it is more likely to be of the order of a Foucauldian 'reverse-discourse', whereby conventional terms are subverted from within. *Dorian Gray* is, to all appearances, an extension of the late nineteenth-century Gothic. And, indeed, that is how this novel has frequently (and not altogether misguidedly) been interpreted. But the Gothic – a variable term of classification in itself, with its strongly marked capacity for monstrous imaginings – provides a generic space in which many kinds of sexual otherness can take shape. Dorian Gray's Gothic spectre haunts the troubled conscience of the degenerating *fin de siècle*. And the novel adumbrates its hero's perverse desires by appropriating not only the conventions of the horror story but also a multiplicity of motifs from classical learning (Wilde, after all, was a first-rate scholar in the field).

Dowling's article does not touch on the work of Wilde. Yet, in an obvious sense, the implications for his links with Pater's homoerotic teachings are many, and the Oxonian connection with Pater forms a key component of Wilde criticism. The trouble is, moves have just as recently been made to dissociate Wilde from Pater's works. In fact, in what must amount to one of the most substantial items of Wilde scholarship to date – the edition of his Oxford Notebooks – astonishing pains are taken to unhitch Wilde from Pater's 'materialism'. That is, in this new account of

Wilde's Oxford education, he is no longer the Paterian spectator of life but one who is using criticism as a creative act to breathe energy – or soul – into art. In their exceptionally well-documented introduction to the Notebooks, Philip E. Smith and Michael S. Helfand return the whole of Wilde's art criticism (in which they include *Dorian Gray*) to his Oxford days: a brief period of intensive study when Hegel's writings on history made their greatest impact in Britain. (Oxford University was, of course, the main conduit for the transmission of Hegel in the nineteenth century.) Focusing on Wilde's many debts to Ruskin (namely, the spiritual influence of art), his response to Hegel (dialectical thinking), and the concomitant influences of theories of race health (taken from a variety of sources, but both Charles Darwin's *Descent of Man* (1871) and W.K. Clifford's theories of the 'tribal self' figure largely here), Smith and Helfand present an image of Wilde's intellectual development as one of progressive (but not unilinear) evolutionism, which is also proto-eugenic. Indeed, so constant and unwavering is this account of Wilde's dialectical thinking that no other influences can find their way into the apparently consistent logic of a body of 'art criticism' that has – to even a casual observer – a 'homosexual' content.

With such points (or prejudices) in mind, it is perfectly possible for these editors to claim that the transactions that occur between the protagonists in Wilde's essay on Shakespeare's sonnets ('The Portrait of Mr W.H.' (1889)) involve 'a transference of spirit', 'a dialectical process in which an unrealized aspect of the collective soul is brought to awareness by an outside agent: an individual, or some other form of artistic or cultural expression', and, finally, 'the psychology of transmission', with no reference to same-sex desire whatsoever.[6] Each of the actors in this essay on the forgery and/or authenticity of the love represented in the sonnets is shown to be an instrument of Wilde's complexly Hegelianized Ruskinism. That the essay on the sonnets forms part of a wider attempt on the part of homosexual writers to find a history for their prohibited pleasures does not enter their argument. (Roden Noel, Havelock Ellis, and John Addington Symonds, for example, were writing about Christopher Marlowe's and Thomas Otway's dramas to uncover the homosexual past.) *Dorian Gray*, which for Smith and Helfand marks the culmination of Wilde's 'art criticism', is similarly confined to an exclusively anti-Paterian allegory, displaying the necessity of dialectical thinking, the renunciation of the ego in favour of the transaction of spiritual influences – from art to life, and back again. The controversy that surrounded the publication of Wilde's novel, and led to the withdrawal of copies from bookshops, is mentioned nowhere at all. The homosexual allusions – especially those echoing many sections of Pater's *Studies in the History of the Renaissance* (1873) – are marginalized. Even Wilde's multiple uses of 'hedonism' – which, as John Stokes reminds us, was at this time one of several code-words for 'homosexuality' ('morbidity' would be another) – passes without notice.[7]

Yet the narrowing of the critical lens in this manner actually yields surprising results, picking up on features of Wilde's novel that earlier commentators have neglected. One significant aspect Smith and Helfand focus on is the emphatic reference to 'race' or 'race-instinct' that recurs in the narrative. The novel is populated with distinctly modern scientific allusions to a degenerate 'germ' (p. 112) that seems to consume Dorian's soul. Yet rather than view this violent instinct as a product of a society that outlaws certain desires, Smith and Helfand attribute the blame for Dorian's fate upon Pater's 'materialism', alias the hedonistic and 'wild struggle for existence' (p. 25) vouched for by Lord Henry Wotton – Dorian's mentor and corruptor. (Wotton, the arch-culprit, supposedly figures in Smith and Helfand's thesis as a Paterian demon.) All in all, the conclusion they draw is summed up in one sentence: 'Dorian's role in the story is to be an object lesson, to represent what hedonistic materialism might do to Western civilization.'[8] The novel has become an allegory of a contest between, on the one hand, Pater, and on the other, Ruskin mediated by Hegel.

Since Smith and Helfand's meticulous but highly selective account has more than an element of truth in it, the next advisable step would seem to be to act on Dowling's counsel and try to plot the 'varying adhesions and resistances' that lie between Wilde's homosexual textuality and the dominant, or acceptably authoritative, aesthetic debates to be found in *Dorian Gray*. The central metaphor on which the novel turns – that of a man and his portrait whose mortality and immortality swap roles – can be understood not solely in relation to Pater, Ruskin, and Hegel (or any of the other authorities cited by Smith and Helfand) but also with reference to the Criminal Law Amendment Act, and its final clause which outlawed acts of 'gross indecency'. Like Dorian's portrait, this law sought to preserve the face of British youth. To its critics (and victims), this law created the corruption it was designed to eradicate. In the context of *Dorian Gray*, it is important to remember that Henry Labouchère's amendment, which legislated against 'gross indecency', was commonly known as 'the blackmailer's charter'.

II

How Victorian Britain came to understand 'gross indecency' follows a rather circuitous path joining together hotly debated legislative issues concerning prostitution, consent, and birth control. Each part of this sexual history needs to be briefly mentioned in turn if we are to comprehend why so many 'ugly meanings' lurk in the shadows of Wilde's portrait of a wealthy, beautiful, and yet – for some reason – 'corrupt' young man.

In the 1890s, when the infamous 'Love that dare not speak its name' was alluded to in the Wilde trials, the idea of 'homosexuality' – as a specific type or person – was still restricted to medical textbooks. Before

that time, sexual intercourse between men was called sodomy or buggery, a crime punishable by death in England and Wales as late as 1836.
In the 1870s and 1880s, groups of men who engaged in (or were
suspected of) this form of sex were becoming more and more visible –
most notably in the figures of Ernest Boulton and Frederick William
Park, who were tried (unsuccessfully) in 1871 on the vague charge that
they, 'being men and dressed in female attire', intended to 'commit a
felony'. Found in the foyers of London theatres, these lavishly dressed
figures were thought by some to be prostitutes. Both of these female
impersonators were anally examined when under arrest. They crossed
identifications of gender for reasons that their prosecution could not
comprehend.[9] Later, in 1885, the law was used – almost, it would seem,
in the manner of an afterthought – to criminalize sexual contact between
men in the context of extensive legislation concentrating on female
prostitution (particularly the corruption of young working-class women
by well-off men): this was the Criminal Law Amendment Act. The
Labouchère amendment, outlawing 'gross indecency' between males
(even in private), is frequently cited as the crucial moment in characteriz-
ing, and establishing, the concept of the male homosexual in British
culture.

The Labouchère amendment largely arose in response to the numerous homosexual scandals of the early 1880s. Its aim, however, when
situated within the complete scope of the 1885 Act, was not so much to
prohibit same-sex relations between adult males but more to deter the
corruption of youth – both young men and young women. John
Marshall claims that 'if we examine the motives behind the anti-
homosexual amendment, we will see that the law was consistent with the
general drive against decadence and did not presuppose the existence of
a special type of person.'[10] The notion of 'gross indecency' was, in part,
an outgrowth from the concept of 'obscenity' – the 'filthy' and 'corrupt'
nature of which was written into the statute books in 1857 (the Obscene
Publications Act), and famously invoked against Annie Besant and
Charles Bradlaugh in their birth control campaign some twenty years
later. Again, the law sought to obscure sexuality – of any kind – from
public view. If seen, it would supposedly destroy the moral order, an
order maintained by hierarchies of class and gender, along with a
universal insistence on a division between private and public domains.
The intensified legal surveillance of sex – on the one hand, monitoring
women's interference with the passage of semen, and, on the other,
scrutinizing the penetration of the anus – obviously demonstrates how at
this time sexual desire was beginning to be perceived as a separate
formation from naturalized categories of gender.

The 1885 Act was significant – not least for *Dorian Gray* – because it
raised the age of consent for women from 13 to 16, creating entirely new
boundaries for heterosexual relations, and greatly extending, and

thereby making much more prominent, the definition of youth. By increasing the numbers of innocent young people, it follows that the law had expanded the realm of potential corruption too. Therefore, in terms of the passage of the 1885 Criminal Law Amendment Bill, the configuration of the notion of consent, aiming to represent natural and normal sexual relations, finally brought into relief a figure who threatened not only young women but also young men. The workings of this law meant that a new sexual type, 'gross' in his 'indecency', was defined against the altogether amplified proportions of those young people who had not reached the age of 'consent'. This man quickly came to possess a variety of names, competing versions of which are to be found in sexology, philosophy, and, of course, literature. He was both 'pederast' and 'invert', 'Uranian man' and the 'erotomaniac' (Wilde confessed in Reading Gaol that he had suffered from 'erotomania').[11]

As feminist historians have noted, the legislation of 1885, under which Wilde was tried a decade later, came in the wake of Josephine Butler's assault on the hypocritical 'double standard' that operated in the implementation of the Contagious Diseases Acts (1864, 1866, 1869). These Acts sought to control the transmission of venereal disease among members of the armed forces by confining infected prostitutes (or, most contentiously, women considered to be prostitutes) in lock hospitals. Butler protested that the Acts, by concentrating on the body of the diseased woman, failed to address the issue of male vice that created prostitution in the first place. For all her efforts to cast the blame on men over a period of twenty years, Butler and her allies could not shift the question of sexual abuse away from the woman's body – a body imaged as a site of disease which bred infection back into the family – on to the male's irresponsible behaviour. The trajectory of late nineteenth-century legislation on sex reveals that male lust was taken for granted as both natural and unchangeable. This was certainly the case until the advent of the Wilde trials, which altered, if not confounded, understandings of male sexuality.

By attending so much to the corruption of youth, the 1885 Act followed in the wake of those legal provisions covering contagious diseases by continuing the trend to deny women's sexuality, needs and wishes in the name of protecting women. Although feminists argued that the child prostitute was an innocent victim, their beliefs in fact forced the passing of a Bill that, once more, increased the power of the state to regulate the sexual lives of poor working-class women – which is precisely what Butler did not want. Purity associations soon joined her campaign, mixing reactionary politics with feminist aims in the name of 'national vigilance'. Together these different groupings helped to create the conditions whereby the law brought into view a formerly unimaginable type of man who would in later decades be known as the 'homosexual'. He, it is fair to suggest, had to bear the burden of moral contempt at a time when it was proving exceedingly hard to attribute the sinfulness of sex to the source of such a 'natural' form of corruption – the men who kept female prostitutes in business. Between the 1860s and the 1880s, the legal understanding of what comprised a sexual relation radically changed. A question about gender relations transformed into a heated discussion about sexual practices and the sanctity of the family unit. The main point that comes out of this brief historical sketch is made clear in Judith Walkowitz's observation: 'Shifting the cultural image to the innocent child victim encouraged new, more repressive, political initiatives over sex.'[12]

The Criminal Law Amendment Act, then, had many antecedents directing it towards the strict protection of the young. But law in the abstract, as Wilde knew, was the perpetrator of its own crimes. Youth, like the perpetual youth of Wilde's protagonist, can only be preserved when there exists, simultaneously, the most suppressed and misrepresented form of 'corruption' – the corruption of the law itself. Corruption is deemed in law to be something that must be hidden away – like the picture of Dorian Gray. A picture that cannot be put on show, and which materially degenerates under lock and key, may well be viewed, in Wilde's novel, as the product of a law that speaks out to silence what it, as law, has given voice to: homosexuality. In other words, the law produces the very category it most seeks to do away with. This instantaneous production and prohibition of a sexual type belongs to a pernicious and self-deceiving form of logical circularity. Dorian's career dramatizes the tragic consequences of this strategy, one that, Wilde suggests, can only be exposed by art – namely, his novel – and not the instrument of 'public morals', the law. In any case, *Dorian Gray* came into direct conflict with the law. Passages from this already infamous narrative contributed to the evidence that sentenced Wilde to Holloway Prison and, eventually, to Reading Gaol in 1895.

In court, Wilde remorselessly defended the purity of his art without identifying the sexuality that the law tried to (but could not) lay bare during the lengthy proceedings against the pugilistic Marquess of Queensberry. The record of the trials shows that Wilde's performance consisted of disastrous tactical evasions. The prosecution repeatedly attempted to locate in the novel 'perverted moral views', 'love . . . of a certain tendency', and the 'feeling of one man towards another'.[13] Asked to define what the 'Love that dare not speak its name' in Alfred Douglas's poem 'Two Loves' might signify, Wilde supplied an answer that construed the substance of the text purely within the lexicon of art:

> [I]n this century [it] is such a great affection of an elder for a younger man as there was between David and Jonathan, such as Plato made the very basis of his philosophy, and such as you find in the sonnets of Michaelangelo and Shakespeare . . . It is in this century much misunderstood, so much misunderstood that it may be described as the 'Love that dare not speak its name', and on account of it I am placed where I am now.

He went on to add: 'It is intellectual.'[14] Wilde protested that no work of art put forward views: 'Views belong to people who are not artists' – lawyers, for example. He rejected outright that 'flattering a young man, making love to him in fact, would be likely to corrupt him'.[15] But, as *Dorian Gray* implies, it is not flattery that makes young men into homosexuals. Instead, it is the law that persistently returns to the question creating the object it seeks to prohibit. The trials demonstrate that male homosexuality is thought to be an undoubted possibility (more natural than unnatural) when an older man 'influences' a male youth. The courtroom, of course, is not involved in a theoretical exercise to examine why an all too possible desire is, in another sense, undesirable. The legal desire to preserve youth is clearly agitated by the idea of an older man's interest in a young person of his own sex. If youth is to be kept innocent – for as long as possible – then it must, in one way or another, be desirable. To put it bluntly: preservation is here the public face of corruption. This is a paradox – a double standard – inherent in the actions of the law, and it is a contradiction that *Dorian Gray* turns into an alarmingly suggestive figuration for its time.

Even if 'homosexuality' was not named by Wilde's prosecutors – nor by Wilde in his novel – it had a new status and significance in the cultural consciousness, not only with regard to young people but also to questions of class. From the moment it was first published, *Dorian Gray* caused considerable concern in the press. In its original periodical form (in the American *Lippincott's Magazine*), it promptly received a hostile response from Charles Whibley in the Tory *Scots Observer*. (As a consequence, copies of *Lippincott's* were quickly withdrawn from sale by the largest retail outlet, W.H. Smith.) Whibley picked up on the homosexual content instantly: 'if he [Wilde] can write for none but outlawed noblemen and perverted telegraph-boys, the sooner he takes to tailoring (or some other decent trade) the better for his own reputation and public morals.'[16] These vituperative remarks refer to the Cleveland Street affair, which involved a number of wealthy men in a homosexual brothel off Tottenham Court Road where post office boys worked to supplement their incomes. In the Wilde trials, working-class young men were paraded in court to give evidence against him. *Dorian Gray*, the Wilde trials, and the Cleveland Street affair shared the same shocking elements: leading the young into vice; homosexual relations; and, in many respects most egregious of all, cross-class liaisons. What needs to be borne in mind here is that the corruption of youth is part of a larger formula – the upper-class contamination of working-class boys – each aspect of which makes the other look even more offensive to the Victorian bourgeois mind. (At the time when Dorian's crimes are considerably on the increase, he remarks: 'The middle classes air their moral prejudices over their gross dinner-tables, and whisper about what they call the profligacies of their betters in order to try and pretend that they are in smart society, and on intimate terms with the people they slander' (p. 118).) Whibley implies that the wealthy older men and the working-class youths share a sexual identity that threatens class relations and, more specifically, the middle-class ideology of self-help character- ized by the 'decent' tailor working for the good of 'public morals'. Tellingly, after the first day of the third trial, Wilde (outrageously) declared: 'The working classes are with me . . . to a boy.'[17]

Dorian Gray stands at the beginning of a self-consciously homosexual literary tradition opposing the social undesirability of cross-class sexual relationships and the decadent uncleanliness associated with them. As Weeks states, a good deal of homosexual fiction developed 'a pattern of what could be called "sexual colonialism", which saw working-class youth as a source of "trade"'.[18] For example, on one of Dorian's 'mysterious and prolonged absences' (p. 102) he is rumoured to have been 'brawling with sailors' (p. 112). Dorian's secret relations with 'foreign sailors' cross national and class barriers to disclose (but, importantly, not name) homosexuality. One transgression, therefore, implies another. The fact that Dorian mixes with these men suggests that he keeps their company for something other than 'brawling'. Wilde is strategically silent about Dorian's barely glimpsed life along the shadowy docks. Defining the nature of this life, of course, would certainly have risked prosecution. The 'homosexual' code had to be read through such obliquities.

Replying to Whibley, Wilde made three aphoristic statements that refused to name – to lend a positive term to – the offensively implied sexual interests of the novel: 'each man sees his own sin in *Dorian Gray*. What Dorian Gray's sins are no one knows. He who finds them has brought them.'[19] The 'sin' is produced, not discovered. It is a 'sin' only when it is named – and thus essentialized – as such. (It is important to remember that Wilde only took action against Queensberry when he was abusively categorized, in a celebrated misspelling, as a 'somdomite' by the Marquess.) As the preface to the novel declares: 'There is no such thing as a moral or an immoral book' (p. 17). Such a statement, refusing to comply with the conventional opposition of vice and virtue, may appear to be fired by a Romantic impulse to set apart aesthetics from politics (to transcend, in other words, material conditions). But, in fact, Wilde's novel illustrates the problematic links between art and the ethical decisions underpinning such a narrowly defined morality. It was Pater who recognized the complex moral structure of *Dorian Gray*: '[Dorian's] story is a vivid, though carefully considered, exposure of a soul, with a very plain moral pushed home, to the effect that vice and crime make people coarse and ugly.'[20] But what makes a vice vicious and a crime criminal to begin with? Virtuous public morals and the law, it seems. The 'moral' of this story, of course, cannot be spoken about in the same register as those 'public morals' that deem such writing 'indecent'. Instead, its desire-stricken 'picture' discloses how the aspirations of art have been woefully incriminated by the invidious prurience of bourgeois morality.

Seeing something of his own teachings within the novel, Pater remarked that 'Dorian himself, though certainly quite unsuccessful in Epicureanism, in life as a fine art, is . . . a beautiful creation.'[21] These words suggest that *Dorian Gray* is, to some extent, a rewriting of Pater's erudite fictional narrative of aesthetic development, *Marius the Epicurean* (1885), which follows a young Roman's maturation from paganism to a suspected conversion to Christianity. It was a rite of passage that appeared controversial because it presented Christian belief as an aesthetic attraction – a sensuous form of art – rather than a divinely imparted dogma. To Pater, Dorian is beautiful in so far as he is desirable as a youth who is perfect enough to be a work of art. It is in Wilde's aphorisms that a Paterian commitment to aesthetics – art for its own sake – may be seen to subvert proverbial moral wisdom. However, the aphorism is not modelled on Pater's elegant prose. Instead, it is here that an undoubtedly Hegelian turn of mind is at work. Aphorisms contain a dangerous knowledge for Dorian: they make other meanings, often lethal ones, available to him.

Dorian is surely seduced by aphorisms. He comes under the verbal spell of Lord Henry Wotton, the older man who provides Dorian with the pleasure-seeking philosophy that, to all appearances, is the cause of the young man's downfall. Wotton's enchanting aphorisms open up the shape and structure of Dorian's sexual exploits. They invert given values and make other meanings possible. This strategic 'inversion' is, as Jonathan Dollimore has pointed out, part of a politically oppositional reverse-discourse.[22] Many of these maxims explicitly parody proverbs unthinkingly dictated to the young. But the Wildean apothegm, as Dollimore implies, is more than simply parodic. Lord Henry's eloquence overturns commonly held assumptions to reveal the unethical bases of values all too readily deemed fit for young minds. For example, in one of his most characteristic overturnings of common sense, Lord Henry argues: 'It is only shallow people who do not judge by appearances. The true mystery of the world is the visible, not the invisible' (p. 32). This may well mean he is a Paterian materialist. But this aesthetics of the surface solicits other interpretations. It is the form as well as the highly critical content of these aphorisms that has a broader bearing on late Victorian culture.

Taking as her cue a remark made by Lord Henry about the virtues of a new and highly fashionable commodity, the cigarette – which forever promises, but never can fulfil, pleasure – Rachel Bowlby observes that Lord Henry's aphorisms absorb other aspects of the culture of consumerism undermining the authenticity of Dorian's portrait. Bowlby's analysis treats *Dorian Gray* within the context of the 'conspicuous consumption' that Thorstein Veblen remarked on in *The Theory of the Leisure*

Class (1899), and which permeates the upper-class society that prevails in Wilde's novel. Noting how bourgeois culture at this time witnessed the convergence of art and advertising – focused by a familiar example, Millais's commercial ideal of youth, 'Bubbles', used to promote Pears's soap – Bowlby indicates that Wilde's aphorisms are suffused in an atmosphere where the relations between art and commerce have been destabilized: 'the aphorism repeats the effects of pleasure of non-satisfaction attributed to its subject, securing a renewed quest for more satisfaction'.[23] Since they read like promotional slogans, these aphorisms mockingly place art criticism and advertising on more or less the same plane. It could also be said that since Wilde transposes his aphorisms from one text to another with such frequency in his whole canon of work, they float free from any pure source of authority. They mimic – only to criticize – the mass-produced phrases of the marketplace.

For Lord Henry, aesthetics concerns the elegance and persuasiveness of expression itself as much as anything else. He is endlessly enchanted by superficial qualities – by how an object looks and by the desires that object arouses, rather than by its deepest and most serious implications. The apparent assault on Pater may seem to hold good. However, throughout the novel, the point seems to be that whatever may be desired in the name of beauty cannot be seen for what it is. 'Bubbles' may advertise a bar of soap but Dorian Gray cannot promote sexual relations between men. To reiterate: the representation of homosexuality stands against, even if it draws on, the interests of consumer capital. Likewise, it displays the dangerous influence of Paterian hedonism in a world where the consequences of such a doctrine cannot freely exist. In a world where – to take the interwined issues at stake here – commerce, art, and sexuality have been radically reconfigured, it is still not possible to portray some of the desires shaped and encouraged by the increasingly rapid exchange of goods.

In *Dorian Gray*, pleasure remains in continual conflict with property, as well as proper behaviour. Dorian's first encounter with the painter Basil Hallward points this out. Dorian's beauty captivates Hallward so much that the painter falls in love with him: 'I knew that I had come face to face with some one whose mere personality was so fascinating that, if I allowed it to do so, it would absorb my whole nature, my whole soul, my very art itself' (p. 21). 'Personality' – a word repeatedly turned to by Wilde throughout the trials – both eludes and yet signals the object of homosexual attraction. Hallward captures Dorian's remarkable looks in paint to the extent that there is barely any distinction to be made between Dorian and his picture. The portrait marks the zenith of the painter's career. Lord Henry is impressed by the finished work. There follows a short but highly significant dialogue about who owns the picture – Dorian, Hallward, or its purchaser:

'Of course he [Dorian] likes it,' said Lord Henry. 'Who wouldn't like it? It is one of the greatest things in modern art. I will give you anything you like to ask for it. I must have it.'

'It is not my property, Harry.'

'Whose property is it?'

'Dorian's, of course,' answered the painter.

'He is a very lucky fellow.'

'How sad it is!' murmured Dorian Gray, with his eyes still fixed upon his own portrait. 'How sad it is! I shall grow old, and horrible, and dreadful. But this picture will always remain young. It will never be older than this particular day of June . . . If only it were the other way! If it were I who was to be always young, and the picture that was to grow old! For that – for that – I would give everything! Yes, there is nothing in the whole world I would not give! I would give my soul for that!'

'You would hardly care for such an arrangement, Basil,' cried Lord Henry, laughing. 'It would be rather hard lines on your work.'

'I should object very strongly,' said Hallward.

Dorian Gray turned and looked at him. 'I believe you would, Basil. You like your art better than your friends. I am no more to you than a green bronze figure. Hardly as much, I dare say . . . How long will you like me? Till I have my first wrinkle, I suppose. I know, now, that when one loses one's good looks, whatever they may be, one loses everything. Your picture has taught me that. Lord Henry Wotton is perfectly right. Youth is the only thing worth having. When I find that I am growing old, I shall kill myself.' (pp. 34–5)

Dorian's image provides the focus for the different, inquiring looks of all three men. Each is in competition with the other. In Dorian's picture, Lord Henry and Hallward see what they desire. This desire, however, can only exist as a representation, as art. The artwork itself has such a high price on it that the desire to possess it – and implicitly kill it – begins to intensify. In response to what appears to be an alienating commercial transaction (that is, putting the picture into the realm of property) Dorian fears he has lost control over his identity, since it seems that he is only desirable as a valuable artwork and nothing else. He strives to reappropriate his image – to become what he has been made to look like: an aesthetic object. But as soon as he enjoys the hedonistic lifestyle he has been led towards, the picture turns grotesque, and consequently has to be put into hiding. Thereafter Dorian can never be anything other than a picture, a falsifying image, to the world – of heterosexual norms, of conspicuous consumption, and of widening gaps between rich and poor – in which both his desire and his desirability are situated. Ed Cohen argues that this narrative displaces the erotic on to the aesthetic, making homosexuality problematically unrepresentable. That is, the picture has the function of an 'absent presence' which 'interrupts the novel's overt representational limits by introducing a visual, extraverbal component of male same-sex desire'.[24] Cohen means that homosexuality cannot be seen for whatever it may be. Only through an oblique reading of the painting can the homosexual 'moral' of Dorian's life be comprehended.

Having sat for his portrait, Dorian is able to see how he solicits the gaze of other men. But his position within this relay of looks is not the *raison d'être* for his sexual preference. The novel explores various structures and theories of deviant desire to witness the formation of Dorian's 'Greek' sensibility. Wilde's narrative moves from the same-sexual interests of narcissism implicit in the painting, to Lord Henry's misogyny, and finally to Dorian's outlandish experiments in cross-dressing (see pp. 107–9) to examine how homosexual desire might be articulated. He also introduces a proto-eugenic account of Dorian's hereditary sexual nature. Passing meditatively through the rooms of his family home, Dorian muses on the portraits of his scandalous ancestors gracing the walls:

> He felt that he had known them all, those strange terrible figures that had passed across the stage of the world and made sin so marvellous, and evil so full of subtlety. It seemed to him that in some mysterious way their lives had been his own. (p. 113)

Ancestry and heredity are controlling (because predestinarian) forces in Dorian's double life. But these, by turns, sensual, evil, and fantastic people from the past do not wholly account for the perverse vicissitudes of his desire. Slightly earlier, the narrator has pointed out that to Dorian 'man was a being with myriad lives and myriad sensations, a complex multiform creature that bore within itself strange legacies of thought and passion, and whose very flesh was tainted with the monstrous maladies of the dead' (p. 112). Such thoughts allow both heredity and many other causes, in all their multiformity, to give birth to the monstrosity that is Dorian's partially obscured sexual identity. This story explores different types of sexual daring and sexual loathing to suggest Dorian's dangerous homoeroticism.

First of all, misogyny figures as a defining feature of homosexuality. Dorian's initial crime involves the harsh rejection of a woman, the actress, Sybil Vane. (Her name puns on several things. She is, to begin with, a 'sybil' – a prophet – who is 'vain': both narcissistic and empty-headed. Moreover, as the narrative shows, she can only be loved 'in vain', a feature which extends to practically every one of the marginal women characters mentioned in the story.) This crime occurs early in the novel, by which time Dorian is almost wholly under the influence of Lord Henry. A working-class girl playing to a middle-class audience, Sybil is a hack actress who untiringly performs Shakespearean drama to pay the rent. She is exploited by her Jewish agent, Mr Isaacs, and Dorian's anti-Semitic jibes underline the depravity of her life. In his insatiable pursuit of transgressive desires, Dorian visits her downmarket theatre to watch her in a variety of comic roles. She plays parts involving cross-dressing, ones which in themselves disrupt conceptions of gender. Dorian muses: 'One evening she is Rosalind, and the next evening she is Imogen . . . I have watched her wandering through the forest of Arden, disguised as a pretty boy in hose and doublet and dainty cap' (p. 51). Neither boy nor girl in these costumes, Sybil exists in a world of factitious images that flout sex, class, and even the Bard. But the moment Sybil is disabused of the artificiality of the theatre – by discovering her 'real' love for Dorian – she can no longer succeed on the stage. Dorian instantly loses interest in her. She tells him: 'The painted scenes were my world. I knew nothing but shadows, and I thought them real. You came – oh, my beautiful love! – and you freed my soul from prison. You taught me what reality really is' (p. 74). Yet he finds her desirable only when she is associated with a despised Jew, a mother whose life thrives on sensation novels, and a theatre that vulgarizes Shakespeare.

Furthermore, it is later revealed that her brother, James, is a bastard. Sybil's love for the fairy-tale 'Prince Charming' – as Dorian is known in the dockland underworld of prostitution and social decay – clearly perturbs her brother. A cross-class love affair is sensed as a fatal attraction – and so it is. Towards the end of the novel, James Vane haunts the East End to avenge his sister's death. He will also die, if not at Dorian's hands, then by association with him. (Vane accidentally receives a fatal wound from a shooting party of which Dorian is a member.) Basil Hallward – whom Dorian murders for gaining access to the hidden painting – implores the by now lethal hero: 'Why is your friendship so fatal to young men?' (p. 117). Dorian's homosexuality symbolically spreads like an incurable, chancre-ridden disease. Elaine Showalter observes how his recriminatory picture appears to be pathologically eaten away by syphilis, noting the 'warped lips' and 'coarse bloated hands', the 'misshapen body and failing limbs' (p. 103): 'The sudden and uncontrollable frenzy in which "the mad passions of a hunted animal" (p. 122) seize Dorian . . . suggest the psychology of general paralysis.'[25] So sexuality can only maim, madden, and finally kill, annihilating both men and women, and all kinds of art. Bastardy; degeneracy; prostitution; homosexuality – all bear witness to the criminality of desire. Yet the more Dorian stares, nervously, at his portrait, the more it may seem that he is inevitably and wrongly caught up in a duplicitous world which legislates against his pleasures. And so his story goes from bad to worse.

After hearing of Sybil's death, Dorian expresses no guilt whatsoever. Lord Henry delivers the following detached account of her sad life: 'I am afraid that women appreciate cruelty, downright cruelty, more than anything else ... They love being dominated. I am sure you were splendid' (p. 86). This misogynistic tirade fully satisfies Dorian. Women are 'charmingly artificial, but they have no sense of art' (p. 85). When, much later, Dorian challenges another character, the Duchess, to define women, he is told, in one of Wilde's oft-repeated phrases, that they are 'Sphynxes without secrets' (p. 150) – without sexuality, the ultimate secret, it might be inferred. Even woman's 'mystery' or 'otherness' is rendered factitious. Artificial, not art; subservient, not dominant – women are the official objects of sexual interest, to be condemned in the process of being loved. In *Dorian Gray*, female sexuality is continually displayed as a theatrical spectacle. Lord Henry again: 'A woman will flirt with anybody in the world as long as other people are looking on' (p. 154). And, close to the start, Lord Henry claims that his own marriage enables him and his wife to live 'a life of deception' (p. 20). By exposing what he considers to be the shallow qualities of women, Lord Henry persuades Dorian to enter-tain other desires, other objects, ones kept out of view, outside the marriage market. Dorian 'felt the time had really come for making a choice. Or had his choice already been made? Yes, life had decided that for him – life, and his own infinite curiosity about life. Eternal youth, infinite passion, pleasures subtle and secret, wild joys and wilder sins' (p. 87). By now Dorian has turned away from women, whatever their class or reputation. Lord Henry opens up Dorian's mind: 'I represent to you all the sins you have never had courage to commit' (p. 70). These sins are serious, not shallow, and concern pleasure, not wedded union. Lord Henry has already pronounced that 'Men marry because they are tired; women, because they are curious; both are disappointed' (p. 48).

To become homosexual, Dorian has made a number of moves. He has, first of all, separated out property from art, locating desire as a force directed against convention (property relations) and towards the aesthetic beauty of other bodies, regardless of class or gender. Dorian, after all, says of his affair with Sybil: 'I did not treat it as a business transaction' (p. 68) – which is how officially respected sexual relations in marriage may be thought of. Second, his desire is driven towards those who manipulate roles and masks. Sybil, at the start, delights him because she is a common actress pretending to be something else – a boy, for instance. Lastly, Lord Henry denies that women possess the finest quali-ties of art. Misogyny here forms part of a struggling understanding of what motivates male homosexuality. Such cruel woman-hating attends the generally deleterious consequences that stem from the moral con-straints placed on all sexual desire. Dorian soon learns that only in the underworld, among unnameable sexual acts, can 'art' discover its erotic potential. This shadowy, private world is the best – because most improper – place for it. It is also where it is most imperilled.

That Dorian has turned to homosexuality emerges in the description of his friendship with Lord Henry. Their love

was really love – had nothing in it that was not noble and intellectual. It was not that mere physical admiration of beauty that is born
of the senses, and that dies when the senses tire. It was such love as
Michael Angelo had known, and Montaigne, and Winckelmann,
and Shakespeare himself. (p. 97)

Listing these famous artists, Wilde is exposing the 'grossly indecent'
subtext to be found in the successive chapters of Pater's *The Renaissance*,
the Conclusion to which was thought by some to endanger its young
male readers. There, Pater infamously encouraged 'the desire of beauty,
the love of art for its own sake'.[26] Pater's advocacy of such unrestrained
fervour for art disturbed his conservative contemporary, Sidney Colvin,
who remonstrated: 'by all means refine the pleasures of as many people
as possible; but do not tell everybody that refined pleasure is the one end
of life. By refined, they will understand the most refined they know, and
the most refined they know are gross.'[27] Gross indecency? The line
between what was considered to be refined and what was indecent was so
precarious that Pater seemingly was moved to withdraw the Conclusion
from subsequent editions. (There may, admittedly, be other reasons for
this retraction. The Conclusion reappeared in the fourth edition in
1893.) Colvin's comments indicate a prevalent attitude: if something is
beautiful it is probably immoral, especially if the working classes start
liking it.

Dorian wears a fine aristocratic face but possesses what may be
referred to as a working-class (debased, gross, indecent) body, as he
moves across and between different echelons of society. He is to be
found either in a 'delicately-scented chamber, or in the sordid little room
of the little ill-famed tavern near the Docks . . . under an assumed name,
and in disguise' (p. 103). He frequents places at the heart of the late
Victorian social conscience. In one episode, a politician states: 'The East
End is a very important problem' (p. 44). Set against this serious issue are
Lord Henry's flippant remarks: 'I don't desire to change anything in
England except the weather' (ibid.). This brief exchange belongs to the
after-dinner repartee of the upper classes where no one can accept the
vicious activities attributed to Dorian Gray – 'those who heard the most
evil things against him . . . could not believe anything to his dishonour
when they saw him' (p. 102). It is at points such as this that the full sweep
of Smith and Helfand's belief in the anti-Paterian representation of
Lord Henry comes into its own. Hedonism of Lord Henry's kind here
may reveal his complete contempt for improving social relations.

But, there again (to keep the Wildean dialectic in motion), Lord
Henry will not tarry with the witless pieties of political rhetoric. That
said, other writings by Wilde can be brought to bear on this piece of
dialogue; take this, for example, from 'The Soul of Man under
Socialism':

when scientific men are no longer called upon to go down to a depressing East End and distribute bad cocoa and worse blankets to starving people, they [the poor] will have delightful leisure in which to devise wonderful and marvellous things for their own joy and the joy of everyone else. (p. 1089)

Yet in a class-divided and gender-riven world where 'public morals' dictate standards of behaviour, there can only be the most formidable kinds of 'corruption', like that brought about by Labouchère's amendment. Late in the novel, Dorian threatens to expose the young scientist, Alan Campbell, for untold crimes if Campbell refuses to get rid of Hallward's murdered body. 'You have gone from corruption to corruption, and now you have culminated in crime' (p. 132), says the scientist. At this point, the picture begins to bleed. A site of beauty has become one of sin. Who or what is to blame? Pater or the law? Or even homosexual desire itself?

Let me offer a not entirely satisfactory answer to the 'multiform' possibilities opened up by the implicit 'moral' of this story. If Lord Henry embodies the worst of Pater's materialism – a self-seeking hedonism – it may follow that his evil influence on Dorian, introducing him to the yellow-wrapped book (J.-K. Huysman's *A Rebours* (1884), itself containing a homosexual incident), would seem to be an outright condemnation of Greek ethics. Dorian certainly leads his life to its fullest and most sensational ends, and the price he has to pay is his own mortality. Yet, in the course of his hedonistic indulgences, Dorian learns that what he takes pleasure in is not permitted in public; his delights are consigned to secrecy. His unspoken wish for sexual relations with men; his impossible liaisons with the lower-class Sybil and, later, the village girl, Hetty Merton – all of these things signal Dorian's displacement from conventional heterosexuality. His desires subsist on blackmail and the ruination of other people's lives. This fact alone, however, does not necessarily suggest that such desires should not be expressed or that hedonism itself is evil.

Dorian's fatal punishment, lying dead, a wrinkled husk of a man, having stabbed his monstrous bleeding picture (now the last will and testament of all his sins), anticipates Wilde's own in Reading Gaol. There, Wilde witnessed the appalling cruelty exercised towards children incarcerated for petty crimes. Two well-known pieces of correspondence on this theme describe the circumstances in which a friendly and caring warder lost his job because he had provided, out of his own pocket, sweet biscuits to a hungry child prisoner (see 'The Case of Warder Martin: Some Cruelties of Prison Life': pp. 958–69). The young person to be protected in these interlinked arenas – the courts and the prison – was, on the one hand, to be saved from the clutches of the homosexual, and on the other, to be imprisoned for minor thefts arising out of poverty. With this double standard in mind, it looks as if the law is its own criminal. But is it?

This chapter has attempted to argue that in *Dorian Gray* Wilde turns his hero into a figure whose life story implicitly interrogates the iniquitous effects of legislation on sex in the 1880s. Surely, in the light of all that has been said, child prostitutes required protection? They did – from the law, which persistently marked out women's bodies as sites of vice, instead of challenging the patriarchal governance of those bodies, and which, simultaneously, drove homosexual men into hiding. The Wilde trials, of course, shocked those who backed movements campaigning against the Contagious Diseases Acts. W.T. Stead's famous 'Maiden Tribute of Modern Babylon' published in the July and August 1885 issues of the *Pall Mall Gazette* is important here. This bestselling piece of investigative journalism into the 'white slave traffic' of young British girls to European brothels both landed Stead in prison and precipitated the passing of the Criminal Law Amendment Act. He wrote after judgment had been passed on Wilde:

> [T]he trial and the sentence bring into very clear relief the ridiculous disparity there is between punishment meted out to those who corrupt girls and those who corrupt boys. If Oscar Wilde, instead of indulging in dirty tricks of indecent familiarity with boys and men, had ruined the lives of half a dozen simpletons of girls, or had broken up the home of his friend's wife, no one could have laid a finger on him. The male is sacrosanct; the female is fair game.[28]

Stead would seem to be suggesting that the incrimination of homosexuals was serving as an excuse for the ongoing corruption of young women by men of Wilde's class. It is certainly the case that men involved in practices of 'gross indecency' in Britain have often received sentences that seem harsh by comparison with those delivered against men who have raped women. (But that is not to argue that the punishment for the one crime should or should not exceed the other. It is, instead, the fact that a juridically reviled male homosexuality grants a certain permission to the apparently 'understandable' impulses motivating heterosexual male rape.)

By the time of the Wilde trials, it was clear that the Labouchère amendment had diverted attention from the prime objectives of protecting girls to focus instead on the private world of male sexuality – a sexuality which, if at one time seen as natural in its lustfulness, was now particularly intriguing because of its (potential) wrong choice of object. In 1885 what was most familiar about men and sex (they were bestial) had become, ten years later, most strange (they were perverse). This turnabout in the legal comprehension of – or, indeed, puzzlement about – male sexuality can be connected, once more, to Wilde's principal textual strategy, the aphorism – that which playfully resembles received wisdom only to invert it, thereby exposing the mistaken complacency of its origins. At one point Sybil Vane, at her most wise, declares: 'Our proverbs want re-writing' (p. 62). For homosexual politics, *The Picture of Dorian Gray* marks the beginning of such a project: to rewrite and rethink how and why it is 'strange to live in a land where the worship of beauty and the passion of love are considered infamous'.[29]

5   Forster's self-erasure: Maurice and the scene of masculine love

John Fletcher

E.M. Forster's *Maurice* (1914/1971) should now be recognized as the one classic portrayal of 'masculine love' (the phrase is Maurice's own in chapter 45)[1] and the one explicitly homosexual *Bildungsroman* produced within the mainstream English literary tradition by a canonical author. Recent gay readings have begun to elaborate the terms of such a recognition in the face of the near universal chorus of hostile or disparaging criticism that the novel has met with.[2] After the homophobic antagonism of the straight-identified response at its worst (notably Cynthia Ozick, Jeffrey Meyers[3]), it is necessary to be wary of the opposite dangers of an anachronistic gay reading that finds in the novel only a reflection of its own preconceptions, as when Claude Summers claims that Forster embodies 'a modern gay liberation perspective' and hails *Maurice* as 'the first gay liberation masterpiece'.[4] The inappropriateness of such claims should be clear from Forster's Terminal Note, which makes evident his own pessimism and political resignation as late as 1960 on the particular question of law reform and the enactment of the recommendations of the Wolfenden Report (1957) for a partial decriminalizing of male homosexuality, let alone the more ambitious vision of social and sexual 'liberation' that has constituted the specificity of modern gay liberation politics.

Had *Maurice* been published at any point from 1914 until the late 1960s, it might have been an incalculable force for good, not only for its homosexual readers for whom it would have offered an affirmative vision of same-sex love from a culturally authoritative and prestigious source, but also as an ideological contestation of the dominant models of homosexuality, medical and theological, in the wider culture. Not just a liberal appeal *on behalf* of a minority for sympathy, but an imaginative act of homosexual self-definition, the novel might have opened up a public space for a homosexual discourse to challenge the dominant discourse *about* homosexuality. For all its problematic representation of lesbianism, the role played by Radclyffe Hall's *The Well of Loneliness* (1928) in nurturing lesbian identity and self-recognition during the dark decades of the mid-century might suggest something of the force and effects

64

Maurice's publication might have had. Even as late as the final revision and Terminal Note of 1960, when Forster's personal and social position was unassailable, its publication could have told considerably on public opinion, hastening the slow shift in attitudes and effecting the ideological conditions necessary for legislative and social change. Instead we have, with Forster safely dead, its belated appearance in 1971 as a marginalized Edwardian afterthought in a cultural moment now marked by the partial decriminalization of male homosexuality in 1967 and the emergence of the Gay Liberation movement from the Christopher Street uprising in 1969. One need only think of a film such as *Victim* (Dir. Basil Dearden, UK 1961), and the considerable personal courage of Dirk Bogarde in agreeing to put his career and status as a film actor on the line by appearing in it, to recognize in Forster's public silence the absence of anything remotely comparable to the perspectives and politics of modern gay liberation. *Maurice*'s closeted history, its fifty-seven years of non-publication, is the measure of that absence.

Paradoxically Forster's presentation of homosexual love is more celebratory and socially radical than Radclyffe Hall's self-lacerating and deeply conservative vision of lesbian *âmes damnées*, or the politics of liberal pity that inform *Victim*, both of which were more socially engaged and effective than the more radical but essentially timorous Forster. His personal quietism and self-protecting caution in relation to his novel are not, however, the result of the obviously homophobic or simply heterosexist ideologies that inform the work of many homosexual writers contemporary with him, such as Hall or Proust. The novel's final retreat to an unimagined and unimaginable 'greenwood', an impossible pastoral of homosexual outlawry, combines homosexual affirmation, a certain social radicalism and social disengagement in equal measures. None of this necessarily explains the novel's suppression and Forster's silence. There is, however, another constitutive element, more important than its apolitical pastoralism, that might go some way to explaining the puzzling, and for this gay reader, excruciating combination of celebration, loss and suppression that characterize the book and its history. This element one might call Forster's self-erasure, the gradual but systematic exclusion of the Forsterian intellectual from the novel's final vision of masculine love. It is with the significance of this exclusion that I shall be concerned in this chapter.

John Addington Symonds and 'Greek Love'

The most significant gay reading of *Maurice*, by Robert K. Martin,[5] shows Forster attempting in a diary entry of 1907 to constitute something like a homosexual tradition of writing. Forster's list includes both high cultural canonical authors from Marlowe and Shakespeare to Whitman, Samuel Butler, A.E. Housman and Fitzgerald, as well as the more popular writers of the schoolboy romance such as A.E.W. Clarke, H.N. Dickinson, Howard Sturgis, and Desmond Coke. In particular, Martin situates *Maurice* within the first attempts by homosexual male writers at the turn of the century to reflect theoretically on their sexuality. Of particular importance are the conceptions of male homosexuality elaborated by John Addington Symonds and Edward Carpenter. Martin discerns a 'double structure' in *Maurice* which consists of an opposition between two kinds of homosexuality, represented in the novel by Maurice's two lovers, the aristocratic Clive Durham and Clive's gamekeeper Alec Scudder, and the different kinds of love they offer Maurice. The novel's first half is devoted to the Maurice–Clive relation, Martin argues, and is 'dominated by Plato and, indirectly, John Addington Symonds and the apologists for 'Greek Love'; its second half is devoted to the Maurice–Alec relationship and 'dominated by Edward Carpenter and his translation of the ideas of Walt Whitman' (p. 36). The novel as homosexual *Bildungsroman* in Martin's view is constituted by Maurice's progress from 'the false vision of an idealised homosexuality' (p. 38) offered by Clive in the spirit of Plato and the Hellenists to the 'Dionysiac spirit evoked by Alec' (p. 42) in the tradition of Whitman and Carpenter. The novel's formal structure and its developmental trajectory are then a function of the divided genealogy of homosexual apologetics and self-reflection inherited by Forster from the late nineteenth century.

Martin's reading is a powerful one that enables us to glimpse something of the infra-structural logic of inclusion and exclusion that determines the novel's character system and its much criticized, but for Forster 'imperative', ending. It works, however, at the price of a certain over-polarizing of both the novel and its genealogy. In particular it seems historically incorrect to claim that 'in the first half of *Maurice* the attitudes of Symonds prevail: homosexuality is defined as a higher form of love and its spiritual superiority is preserved by its exclusion of physical consummation' (p. 39), while reserving the second half of the novel to Carpenter and 'physical love'. For while there are contrasts to be made between the closeted timidity of Symonds (which indeed has its parallels with Forster's life and non-publications) as against the public openness of Carpenter, Symonds as much as Carpenter is concerned to defend the physical expression of homosexual love, which explains both his concern with 'Greek love' and his commitment precisely to Whitman's work.

Symonds's conception of what he calls 'Greek love' in his privately published scholarly work, *A Problem in Greek Ethics* (1883),[6] is explicitly set up as a mediating term between opposites. He cites an older form of heroic friendship, exemplified by Homer's representation of Achilles and Patroclus in *The Iliad*, which is a non-sexual masculine love between warriors embodying martial ideals and values. This he distinguishes from the historically later practice of *paiderastia*, the love of a man and an adolescent youth, which he divides into the noble and the base varieties. What he calls 'Greek Love' is the mixed form of *paiderastia* which combines the manly ideals of heroic friendship with a cross-generational passion of an older man for a youth, but which 'exhibited a sensuality unknown to Homer' (p.17). It is ethically superior to the widespread sexual use of boys and men in classical Greece (who might be slaves, male prostitutes or aliens) by virtue of its status as a social institution that regulated relations between members of the citizen class. It transmitted and inculcated a set of virile ideals and behaviours, from the adult warrior/citizen to the youth destined to the same restricted membership of the Greek *polis*. It was a combined class/gender apprenticeship bound by libidinal ties. Despite the ambiguous and conflicting emphases in his source material, Symonds concludes: 'In these conditions the paiderastic passion may well have combined manly virtue with carnal appetite, adding such romantic sentiment as some stern men reserve within their hearts for women' (p. 29).[7]

Far from counterposing Plato to Whitman on the question of sublimatory renunciation as against sexual expression, Symonds is in fact Whitman's first major expositor and apologist in England. Symonds engaged in a twenty-year correspondence with Whitman, attempting to win from him an explicit recognition and acceptance of the sexual feeling between men implied and tacitly imagined in Whitman's poetic celebration of 'the love of comrades'. In his later text of 1890, *A Problem in Modern Ethics*,[8] Symonds sees Whitman's poetry as performing a function analogous to that performed by Socrates for Greek *paiderastia*, that is the rehabilitation and elevation of same-sex passions in a 'democratic chivalry' (p. 191). Whitman's final disingenuous repudiation of Symonds's suggestions about the sexual implications of his *Calamus* poems – 'morbid inferences – which are disavowed by me and seem damnable'[9] – indicates that no clear-cut polarization of Symonds against Carpenter, or of Plato against Whitman, on the question of the sexual expression of masculine love can be made to function as the novel's informing genealogy.

Edward Carpenter and the Primal Scene

It is, however, true that, as Martin argues, the novel is organized around a contrast between Maurice's two lovers Clive and Alec, and is the story of Maurice's movement from one to the other. The three male figures form the nucleus of the novel's character system, and the combination and substitution of terms their story plays out, is the working through of highly conflicted and overdetermined psychic and ideological material necessary for the novel's 'imperative' happy ending to be put in place. The binary opposition of false and true conceptions of homosexual love laid out by Martin simplifies the oppositions involved and the narrative's conflicting fantasies.

Forster's extraordinary account in the Terminal Note of 1960 of the novel's genesis gives us a glimpse of the fantasmatic dimensions involved. The novel arose out of a visit in 1913 to Edward Carpenter, at his home in Millthorpe in Derbyshire. Carpenter was an exponent of socialism and the Whitmanian doctrine of 'the love of comrades', and an avowed 'Uranian' openly living with his working-class lover, George Merrill. Forster approached Carpenter, he tells us, 'as one approaches a saviour':

> [H]e and his comrade George Merrill combined to make a profound impression on me and to touch a creative spring. George Merrill also touched my backside – gently and just above the buttocks. I believe he touched most people's. The sensation was unusual and I still remember it, as I remember the position of a long vanished tooth. It was as much psychological as physical. It seemed to go straight through the small of my back into my ideas, without involving my thoughts. If it really did this, it would have acted in strict accordance with Carpenter's yogified mysticism, and would prove that at that precise moment I had conceived.
>
> No other of my books has started off in this way. The general plan, the three characters, the happy ending for two of them, all rushed into my pen. And the whole thing went through without a hitch.[10]

This is the novel's primal scene, a moment of fantasmatic genesis in which Carpenter and his lover Merrill 'combined . . . to touch a creative spring' (p. 217). The heterosexual primal scene – of father, mother and infantile voyeur, classically described by Freud – is here replaced by a primal scene of masculine love in which by a strange displacement the male partners combine to touch and to inseminate the watching third. Merrill's touch on the backside transmits Carpenter's Whitmanian doctrine to Forster. The tableau of cross-class democratic harmony between upper middle-class intellectual and working man, in which the touch of the latter is 'in strict accordance with' what Forster mockingly calls 'Carpenter's yogified mysticism', condenses and displaces a number of elements that will be central to the novel. In particular there is the intellectual and manual division of labour, the form of a fundamental class relation, which is experienced as the emasculating split between the intellect and the body, the intellectual and his body, and especially the intellectual and the body of the man he desires, because it represents a virile being and capacity from which he feels alienated. The imaginary resolution of that division is signalled in Forster's peculiar paradox: 'it seemed to go straight through the small of my back into my ideas, without involving my thoughts' (p. 217). The motif of the thinking body that bypasses a debilitating intellectuality is characteristic of radical literary theories of the period – Forster's own 'flesh educating the spirit';

Edward Carpenter, Forster's Uranian ideal: an early gay masquerade of masculinity.

Yeats's 'unity of being'; T.S. Eliot's 'unified sensibility' that experiences an idea as immediately as the odour of a rose; D.H. Lawrence's 'sympathetic solar plexus' opposed to mental consciousness. Despite the short-circuiting of Forster's intellectuality, instead of drawing him into this spectacle of masculine combination and plenitude the scene produces in its observer, its touched recipient, a paradoxical sexual inversion – 'at that precise moment I had conceived'. Rather than an access of virility what Forster embodies is a displaced male femininity. Touched on the backside, he conceives.

The unusual ease and rapidity of Forster's literary conception and delivery suggest that 'the general plan, the three characters, the happy ending for two of them' that 'all rushed into my pen' and 'went through without a hitch' is a fantasmatic transcription or transference of the scene of male combination and conception in play between Carpenter, Merrill, and Forster that produced the novel. What is at stake is not a set of one-to-one equivalences between the male figures in each triad. The novel does not just transmit the Whitmanian 'love of comrades' exemplified in the combination of Carpenter and Merrill and finding its novelistic representation in the imperative happy ending that unites Maurice and Alec. This is Martin's account of the book, as the affirmation of a 'true' homosexuality – manly, democratic, sexual, socialist – sired by Walt Whitman out of Edward Carpenter. The fantasmatics of cultural transmission are stranger than that, and a detour through the psychoanalytic theory of primal scenes and primal fantasies will help us to see why.

In their classic essay, 'Fantasy and the Origins of Sexuality' (which reconstructs this crucial but under-theorized Freudian concept), Jean Laplanche and Jean-Bertrand Pontalis describe the fantasy of primal scenes as subjective myths of origins that 'claim to provide a representation of and a solution to the major enigmas that confront the child' (p. 19).[11] According to Freud, the infantile voyeur watching, sometimes actually but always in fantasy, the enigmatic scene of his own genesis represses its violent and traumatic import, only to work through its terms belatedly (*nachträglich*) in the moment of the Oedipal crisis. Here it confronts him with a set of symbolic options and positions, embodied in what is then recognized as a scene of heterosexual division and difference.[12] What was fantasized as a violent and enigmatic *arche* or origin is now assumed as a *telos*, a futurity that includes and positions the subject. Jean Laplanche's critical revision of the Freudian account in his recent theory of the enigmatic signifier argues that the power of the primal scene or its signifiers to insist – to produce a belated or deferred action far beyond the time and effects of their first inscription – is not to be understood as simply the result of the inclusive resolution of the original provoking enigma ('where do babies come from?', 'what is the difference between the sexes?'). It derives instead from all that resists or eludes the translation or resolution of the enigma. The enigmatic signifier,

The young Bob Buckingham, Forster's long-term (but married) companion –
dark, rugged, law-abiding.

argues Laplanche, is enigmatic for the other who transmits it as well as for its recipient. The continuing seductive and provoking power of the primal scene derives from what remains untranslated, enigmatic or repressed for the adult participants in that scene as well as for its childish witness.

If Forster went to Millthorpe to learn the mysteries of masculine love, he comes by his own account to function, if not as its antithesis, then as the depository of its difficulties. So his novelistic offspring condenses and encodes the oppositions that appear resolved or overcome in that scene, in particular the class opposition of gentleman and manual labourer combined in a body whose ideas are touched (touched up?) but not thought (like a Metaphysical poem read by T.S. Eliot). For in conceiving and bearing the novel, Forster becomes the site, at once intellectual and unmasculine, of what must resist or discomfort the mythic resolutions of manly love. The Lacanian child analyst, Maud Mannoni, has suggested that the child, caught up in the desire and discourse of the Other, functions as the symptom of its parents.[13] As a narrative of homosexual love, *Maurice* – the novelistic child of that scene of male genesis – has a poignancy that resides not just in the resolutions and pairings of its much decried happy ending, but in the exclusions and reversals that make it both possible and necessary – 'imperative'. In the poignancy of those exclusions and rejections – 'three characters, the happy ending for two of them' – we may read the effects of another story and the novel's 'other scene', a shadowy, early drama of loss and haunting repeated in Maurice's story of a coming to self-recognition and identity through a saving figure only to be rejected and abandoned by that figure.

In his 'Notes on the three men', Forster comments: 'Alec starts as an emanation from Milthorpe [*sic*], he is the touch on the backside' (p. 219). This is the one direct correlation between the novel and its scene of genesis, but even here the 'emanation' is considerably reworked and revised: 'he became less of a comrade and more of a person . . . the additions to the novel . . . are all due to him' (ibid.). Maurice and Clive, however, bear no simple correspondence to the other two figures in the novel's genesis, Carpenter and Forster, yet they are generated out of the field of tensions between them. They represent a novelistic translation of certain class and psychic patterns in which the theme of the intellectual apparently so harmonized in the relation between Carpenter and Merrill returns as a point of difficulty in which class, gender, and desire are all knotted together. In an essay written years later in 1944 on the centenary of Carpenter's birth (an essay which practises a characteristically Forsterian silence on the subject of Carpenter's homosexuality), Forster observed: 'at the end of his life when I came to meet him, he rather mistrusted me because, like himself, I had had the disadvantage of a university education'.[14] P.N. Furbank, Forster's biographer, tells us that

Forster had been rebuked by Carpenter for his excessive intellectuality: 'He made Forster ashamed of his fidgetiness and self-consciousness. To Forster's bright, intelligent remarks he would simply sometimes answer "Oh do sit quiet!" and Forster felt glad to sit quiet. He had never before felt such power in another man.'[15] From a similar professional upper middle-class and Cambridge background, Carpenter might be taken as a Uranian ego ideal for Forster through identification with whom access to the scene of masculine love might be given. For Carpenter, Forster clearly represented an earlier self, overly intellectual, self-conscious, unmanly. Both of them shared the structure of feeling characteristic of upper-class homosexuality in the period, a cross-class structure of desire in which what is at stake is a relation to the virility embodied in the working-class man. In his self-analysis written for Havelock Ellis and included as a case history in the latter's book *Sexual Inversion* (1897), Carpenter wrote:

> Now – at the age of 37 – my ideal of love is a powerful, strongly built man, of my own age or rather younger – preferably of the working class. Though having solid sense and character, he need not be specially intellectual. If endowed in the latter way, he must not be too glib or refined. Anything effeminate in a man, or anything of the cheap intellectual style, repels me very decisively.[16]

Clearly for Carpenter virility is potentially compromised by intellectuality with its risk of the glib, the refined, and the effeminate. 'Solid sense and character' are preferred as more appropriate to manliness. Forster also describes a similar structure of homosexual feeling in a memorandum of 1935 when he writes: 'I want to love a strong, young man of the lower classes and be loved by him and even hurt by him. That is my ticket . . .'[17]

Carpenter's own writings on homosexuality as 'the intermediate sex'[18] present a highly idealized account of the homosexual temperament as a synthesis of masculine and feminine attributes. Like Symonds his views were strongly influenced by the writings of the German homosexual apologist Karl Heinrich Ulrichs. Ulrichs's formulation of male homosexuality as a congenital, biologically determined condition involving 'a female soul in a male body' (*anima muliebris in corpore virili inclusa*),[19] clashes strongly with the Whitmanian celebration of manliness and 'the love of comrades'. The contradiction between Ulrichs and Whitman marks the writings of both Symonds and Carpenter (and is far more important than Martin's opposition of Whitman and Plato whom both Symonds and Carpenter see as compatible).

Carpenter wishes to see the 'healthy' Uranian male as supplementing his masculine constitution with certain 'feminine virtues' – tenderness, sensuality, intuition, emotionality, altruism, and self-sacrifice – involving the standard motif by which male femininity has been legitimized since the late eighteenth century – 'at bottom lies the artist-nature, with the artist's sensitivity and perception'.[20] It is precisely in these terms that Carpenter describes himself after describing his 'ideal of love': 'I am an artist by temperament and choice, fond of all beautiful things, especially the male human form; of active, slight, muscular build; and sympathetic, but somewhat indecisive character, though possessing self-control.'[21] The figure of the artist licenses the grafting of femininity on to a basically male nature and the prestige of a limited form of male androgyny.[22] The ideological danger in any crossing of genders is that the feminine will supplant or improperly dominate the masculine in the mixed type, that instead of an extension of the masculine beyond its traditional sphere a subversion of the masculine may result. This danger is signalled in the fear of effeminacy. The difficulty of drawing the line between the two – of preventing the passage of male femininity into the effeminate – is responsible for the defensive anxiety on this topic in Carpenter's writing. Carpenter produces two portraits of 'extreme specimens', of cross-gendering gone wrong: the effeminate male, unmuscular, hairless, high-pitched, mincing, chattering, sentimental, and skillful at the needle; and the masculine female, muscular, low-voiced, passionate, practical, untidy, and *outrée* in attire, wielding not the needle but the pistol and 'the fragrant weed'![23] The possibly emasculating dangers of femininity on the male are contained and countered by the cult of the male body, its constitution, deportment, and behaviour, as the privileged site of virility and its powers. Hence Carpenter's emphasis on his own active and muscular build despite his artistic nature, just as the 'normal' Uranian is accorded 'thoroughly masculine powers of mind and body', being 'often muscular and well-built' (p. 197).

Effeminacy and intellectuality then are conditions that displace the male body as the animating force of the personality, weakening its powers or inverting its nature, and so threatening its virility. The enigma or problem encoded in what I have called the primal scene of masculine love might be extrapolated as a question: can a male be homosexual, combine with another male, without a loss of virility? The implicit answer seems to be that the homosexual male can retain or augment his virility in relation to another male only if the disembodying effects of effeminacy and intellectuality can be kept at bay.

Intellectuality and its Discontents

It is out of the uneasy liaisons between manliness, homosexuality, and intellectuality that the Maurice–Clive relation is produced, and produced as a fantasy of their reconciliation. Edwardian 'Greek love' is here the form of the saving relation between normality and the intellectual, a redrafting of the Wilcox–Schlegel alliance in *Howards End* (1910). While sharing Forster's class and family background – public school, a home in the Surrey suburbs and Cambridge – Maurice is conceived as Forster's antithesis: 'I tried to create a character who was completely unlike myself or what I supposed myself to be: someone handsome, healthy, bodily attractive, mentally torpid, not a bad businessman and rather a snob' (p. 218). Forster's decision to make his homosexual protagonist a non-intellectual and an embodiment of Edwardian middle-class normality – 'Suburbia' – in everything but his sexuality, to make Maurice, *not* Clive, the novel's protagonist, may at first seem surprising. As a novelistic premise it avoids the more obvious pitfalls of a simply idealizing or apologetic narrative, a portrait of the artist as a young invert. Maurice's mental torpor, his ordinary uncritical immersion in the values of his family, class, and gender, the painful slowness of his struggle to self-awareness, serve to foreground his emergent homosexual difference, whether the enigmatic surplus of emotion in his boyish fits of tears or his discomfort with the normal expectations of him, precisely as a yeasting rather than a debilitating element. In Forster's words, it is 'an ingredient that puzzles him, wakes him up, torments him and finally saves him' (p. 218). Maurice's 'normality' also conveniently provides a virile body, uncompromised by effeminacy, as the site for a homosexual grafting and for his unsettling and disaffecting difference to work on. We may detect here another reworking of an earlier narrative as the Rickie of *The Longest Journey* (1907) leaves his crippled body to inhabit that of Gerald Dawes, the handsome and brutal athlete, his erstwhile tormentor at public school.

Clive is the concave to Maurice's convex. As the embodiment of Forster's Cambridge – 'the calm, the superiority of outlook, the clarity and the intelligence, the assured moral standards, the blondness and the delicacy that did not mean frailty, the blend of lawyer and squire' (p. 218) – he is the characterological formula that provides Maurice with the alternative by which Suburbia and Public School can be called into question and rejected. As a 'blend of lawyer and squire' Clive's intellectuality is situated by Forster in class terms. The historic association of the Law with the landed gentry has its first literary representation in English in Chaucer's General Prologue to *The Canterbury Tales* with the pairing of the Sergeant of the Law and the Franklin. In terms of Gramscian class analysis the profession of Law, like that of the Church, constituted the traditional intelligentsia, provided the organic intellectuals for the de-militarized, non-feudal capitalist gentry that emerged as the economically dominant class between the late fourteenth and the early seventeenth centuries.[24] Clive's studying at the Bar after Cambridge, and as a prelude to taking up his father's Parliamentary seat and 'representing the division' (p. 89), signals his acquiescence in a future determined by an historic pattern of class duties – in his mother's words, 'there was the game, there were his tenants, there were finally politics' (p. 89) – chief among which is the provision of an heir for Penge, the family estate.

The same configuration of a traditional intellectual formation based on the classics with a landed class position is invoked by Dr Barry in his patronizing placing of Maurice's own class origins on his being sent down from Cambridge:

> What do you want with a university degree? It was never intended for the suburban classes. You're not going to be either a parson or a barrister or a pedagogue. And you are not a county gentleman . . . Quite right to insult the Dean. The city's your place . . . I mean that the county gentleman would apologize by instinct if he found he had behaved like a cad. You've a different tradition. (p. 79)

Maurice feels the sting of Dr Barry's reproach for his refusal of his mother's request to apologize to the Dean and seek readmission to his college at Cambridge. He is a 'cad' for his attitude to the Dean and a 'disgrace to chivalry' for his rebuff of his mother. In Dr Barry's invocation of a code of gentlemanly behaviour and his association of it with a classical education and a county gentry class position – Maurice isn't an 'instinctive' gentleman but a member of the suburban middle classes destined for a stockbroker's job in the City of London – we can read the trace of one of the major ideological themes from the nineteenth century 'Condition of England' debate. In this, as in much else, Forster is the heir of Matthew Arnold. Arnold's writings diagnose a crisis of cultural leadership in mid-Victorian Britain, a power vacuum in which the dominant industrial bourgeoisie (Arnold's philistines) has not elaborated a code of values and behaviour that can command consent beyond what its narrow economic dominance can impose. He recommends the organization of a cultural apparatus – a state-sponsored compulsory education system on the French model – that would break from the narrow *laisser-faire* anti-state prejudices of the bourgeoisie and in which an education based on a vernacular national literature and history would be both heir and substitute for the previously hegemonic cultural formation of the landed classes (Arnold's Barbarians). Of those traditions neither a classical education nor an orthodox Anglican Christianity had the power to mould the formation of the new urban working class (Arnold's Populace) in their contention with the bourgeoisie for political representation and power.[25] Arnold's stark choice – Culture or Anarchy – signals a sense of social crisis that while decisive for the institutionalization of vernacular literary studies at different levels of the nineteenth-century national curriculum, nevertheless underrated the continuing prestige of the older traditions. The ability of the classical curriculum to insert itself into the massive extension of the public school system that incorporated precisely the suburban middle classes to which both Maurice and his creator, Forster, belonged, is registered with some irony in the anomaly of Maurice's Greek Oration on Prize Day at

Sunnington. The schoolboy Maurice addresses the Hague Peace Conference in defence of war: "'O andres Europenaici . . . Is not Ares the son of Zeus himself?" . . . . The Greek was vile: Maurice had got the prize for the Thought' (p. 28). This concession by the economically dominant class of certain areas of cultural and political leadership to the gentry and aristocracy is represented prototypically in Dickens's 'Condition of England' novel, *Hard Times* (1854). There, the elegant and languid Mr James Harthouse is brought north to meet the Coketown industrialists whose political representative in Westminster he is suited to be by virtue of his class background and education. Forster's own 'Condition of England' novel *Howards End* is his most Arnoldian and the Maurice–Clive relation is in part a homosexual reworking of the Wilcox–Schlegel alliance in which the Arnoldian intelligentsia (Margaret Schlegel) and the commercial bourgeoisie (Henry Wilcox) are reconciled on the mystified terrain of an essentially 'English' rural continuity, the old yeoman family farmhouse, Howards End, inherited through the maternal line and which significantly is neither a gentry estate nor a recently acquired bourgeois investment.

The very terms of the Maurice–Clive relation – the intellectual awakening of the mentally torpid bourgeois by the patrician intellectual – are highly overdetermined by a tradition of cultural diagnosis of which Forster is the heir and which constitutes a crucial matrix for the homosexual narrative he projects. Clive's intellectuality, his embodiment of alternative values and standards that judge Maurice's world, is not, however, a simple function of his gentry class origins or its traditional ideological representatives in the professions. For Clive represents a Cambridge – 'one corner of it' – that is associated with the free-thinking, homophile Apostles, minimally represented by the Wildean undergraduate Risley (Lytton Strachey) whose presence first provokes Maurice into venturing outside his narrow circle of old Sunningtonians and so meeting Clive. Raymond Williams analyses the Cambridge–Bloomsbury connection as a dissident and reforming professional fraction of a ruling class judged in its majority to be shortsighted, hypocritical, and philistine. It practised a social and intellectual critique that challenged the outlook of that class while acting as the agency of its liberalizing and modernizing adaptation to changing historical circumstances.[26] This combination of an often scathing rejection of received class values and outlooks, together with a continuing insertion into the class through influential and binding family connections and friendships, suggests one way of understanding Clive's successive embodiment and betrayal of Cambridge 'enlightenment' so central to the novel's homosexual drama.

Clive's intellectuality is also naturalized by the novel through a figuration of the male body – his 'neat little figure' (p. 40), 'the blondness and delicacy that did not mean frailty' (p. 218) – that suggests a certain femininity while excluding effeminacy. Such femininity serves as an

imaginary complement to the greater strength and robustness of
Maurice, with his 'well trained and serviceable body and a face that
contradicted it no longer. Virility had harmonised them and shaded
both with dark hair' (p. 103). Their bodily differences – blond and
delicate as against dark and hirsute – provide a tacitly sexual framework for the wary process of courtship that in chapter 7 is played out
during the Lent term between them in the theological disputes by
which Clive through a process of Socratic dialectic interrogates
Maurice's supposed religious faith. This he does by demonstrating to
Maurice that he neither understands nor actually believes in the doc-
trines of the Trinity and Redemption he is trying to defend. This
process of enlightenment is also a process of seduction as it is in *The
Symposium*, the Platonic text by reference to which Clive's first lover's
avowal so disastrously takes place. In this dialectic where Clive represents the enlightened intellect, Maurice represents the recalcitrant
and clumsy body:

> He wanted to show his friend that he had something besides brute
> strength. . . .
>   Maurice felt uncomfortable and looked at his own thick brown
> hands. Was the Trinity really a mystery to him? . . . he glanced at
> his mind. It appeared like his hands – serviceable, no doubt, and
> healthy and capable of development. But it lacked refinement. . . .
> It was thick and brown. (pp. 46, 48)

The body is also the seat of intuition and the feelings, which gives it, in
Forster's epistemology, an inarticulate wisdom that can outflank the
intellect even as it depends on it for self-recognition and expression.
Maurice's submission to Clive's forensic rigour, his surrender of his
unthinking religious orthodoxy, is also a sustained exercise in the intuitive and cautious seduction of his patrician educator: 'Outwardly in
retreat, he thought that his Faith was a pawn well lost; for in capturing it
Durham had exposed his heart' (p. 50). Maurice's ragging and affectionate manhandling of Clive – 'When Hall started teasing he was charmed
. . . and he liked being thrown about by a handsome and powerful boy'
(p. 69) – and Clive's responsive intellectual aggression against Maurice's
pieties – 'Durham couldn't do without him, and would be found at all
hours curled up in his room and spoiling to argue . . . Was there not
something else behind his new manner and furious iconoclasm? Maurice
thought there was' (p. 50) – together constitute the dialectic of Maurice's
inarticulate appeal, and Clive's answering will to articulate and name,
that will govern their relationship on the terms proposed by Clive. Clive
reads Maurice's unspoken appeal, we are told, in a peculiar expression
of his face, compounded of affection and impudence. Forster is here
concerned both with the growing intimacy between them and with the

difficulties, delays, and indirection entailed by the simultaneous taboo
on speech and absence of a language, a set of conventions that would
allow that taboo to be broken and which keeps their intimacy literally
'unspeakable':

> It occurred when they met suddenly or had been silent. It beck-
> oned to him across intellect, saying, 'This is all very well, you're
> clever, we know – but come!' It haunted him so that he watched for
> it while his brain and tongue were busy, and when it came he felt
> himself replying, 'I'll come – I didn't know'.
>   'You can't help yourself now. You must come.'
>   'I don't want to help myself.'
>   'Come then.' (p. 69)

Clive's 'coming' has first to constitute a set of terms to make up for the
absent language of recognition and avowal of homosexual love and to
defuse the destructive power of the taboos against it at work within both
of them. Chapter 7 concludes significantly with their first coded broach-
ing of the subject of 'Greek love' in response to the Dean's censorship of
the topic in a translation class – 'Omit: a reference to the unspeakable
vice of the Greeks' (p. 50) – and so with Clive's consequent advice to
Maurice to read the Platonic account in *The Symposium* over the Easter
vacation – 'He hadn't known it could be mentioned, and when Durham
did so in the middle of the sunlit court a breath of liberty touched him'
(p. 50).

Maurice's return in chapter 9 from the Easter vacation and his failed
courtship of Miss Olcott exhibits him in a painful transition between
suburbia and Cambridge, between the 'public-schoolishness' and 'insin-
cerity' induced by his family and the fragile and as yet unconsolidated
rapport with all that Clive quite literally embodies for him. The friends'
first meeting in the May term frames as a tableau Maurice's dependency
on Clive for his own sense of self:

> Maurice knew that he had lost touch. . . . Durham sat upon the
> floor beyond his reach. It was late afternoon. The sounds of the
> May term, the scents of the Cambridge year in flower, floated in
> through the window and said to Maurice, 'You are unworthy of us.'
> He knew that he was three parts dead, an alien, a yokel in Athens.
> He had no business here, nor with such a friend.
>   'I say, Durham –'
>   Durham came nearer. Maurice stretched out a hand and felt the
> head nestle against it. He forgot what he was going to say. The
> sounds and scents whispered, 'You are we, we are youth.' Very
> gently he stroked the hair and ran his fingers into it as if to caress
> the brain.
>   'I say, Durham, have you been all right?'

'Have you?'

'No.'

'You wrote you were.'

'I wasn't.'

The truth in his own voice made him tremble. 'A rotten vac and I never knew it,' and wondered how long he should know it. The mist would lower again, he felt sure, and with an unhappy sigh he pulled Durham's head against his knee, as though it were a talisman for clear living. It lay there and he had accomplished a new tenderness – stroking it steadily from temple to throat. Then, removing both hands he dropped them on either side of him and sat sighing. (p. 55)

This moment crystallizes vividly Clive's significance for Maurice. Clive's presence provokes him to an awareness of his regression to the values of suburban normality and its falsifying expectations. Disconnected from Clive and excluded from his world, 'a yokel in Athens', Maurice feels the very scents and sounds of Cambridge and the May term judging him: 'You are unworthy of us.' His desire for contact, to be again in touch, assumes poignantly literal form as he feels Clive's head, stroking his hair 'as if to caress the brain'. The inadequacy of speech is supplemented by a touch that reverses his exclusion: 'the scents and sounds whispered, "You are we, we are youth".' Desire is here the mode of connection between Maurice's aching inarticulacy and Clive's enlightenment, between the 'good, blundering' bourgeois and his educator, the Socratic intellectual. With the bizarre literalness of erotic feeling, Maurice's accession to 'a new tenderness' is expressed in his fondling of Clive's head 'as though it were a talisman for clear living'.

The terms of their exchange radiate out to other moments, in particular to the novel's ending. Despite Forster's governing conception – 'three characters, the happy ending for two of them' (p. 217) – the novel's final moment moves beyond the union of Maurice and Alec to return to Clive. The closing intensities of feeling centre on Clive's exclusion from the scene of masculine love concluded in the previous chapter in the boathouse at Penge with Alec's words: 'And now we shan't be parted no more and that's finished' (p. 210). The novel, however, isn't finished and it returns to the same elements we have seen at play between Maurice and Clive only to realign them in a different way. Maurice still represents the body and its claims – 'I'm flesh and blood, if you'll condescend to such low things . . .' – and Clive the intellect – 'I'm a frightful theorist, I know' (p. 212). Maurice's settling of accounts with his former lover and educator entail a championing of the right to sexual expression – 'I have shared with Alec . . . All I have. Which includes my body' – to be met with Clive's protest: 'But surely – the sole excuse for any relationship between men is that it remains purely Platonic' (p. 213). The intellectual defending 'platonic' values, the exclusion of the sexual body and its desires from male relations, is no longer the representative of enlightenment, the 'talisman for clear living', but the very voice of normality and its obfuscations: 'Even in his nausea Clive turned to a generalisation – it was part of the mental vagueness induced by his marriage' (ibid.). More than mental vagueness, Clive is the embodiment of emotional confusion and constriction – 'But his thin sour disapproval, his dogmatism, the stupidity of his heart, revolted Maurice, who could only have respected hatred' (ibid.). It is now Clive, 'relapsed into intellectualism', who represents the uneducated heart, an inauthenticity of the emotions and their attenuation. Newly articulate, Maurice gives a lengthy and trenchant judgement on the terminal stage of their relationship:

> You do care a little for me . . . but nothing to speak of, and you don't love me. I was yours once till death if you'd cared to keep me, but I'm someone else's now – I can't hang about whining for ever – and he's mine in a way that shocks you, but why don't you stop being shocked, and attend to your own happiness? (p. 214)

Maurice's challenge to Clive recalls the early terms of their relationship even as it reverses them:

> 'Who taught you to talk like this?' Clive gasped.
> 'You, if anyone.'
> 'I? It's appalling you should attribute such thoughts to me,' pursued Clive. Had he corrupted an inferior's intellect? He could not realise that he and Maurice were alike descended from the Clive of two years ago . . . (ibid.)

In his intellectual conceit, Clive is unable to recognize the values of his earlier self, especially the radicalism of the demand for emotional fulfilment now embodied in a Maurice who vanishes away in the darkness even as Clive talks of dinner jackets and appointments, leaving as a last trace 'a little pile of the petals of the evening primrose, which mourned from the ground like an expiring fire' (p. 215). The evening primroses first introduced to Maurice by Clive come to feature in Maurice's preliminary but unwitting exchanges with Alec on the night of their first lovemaking, as the mute sign of the unstated sexual currents between them, covering Maurice's hair with pollen and dubbed 'Bacchanalian' by old Mrs Durham. Now they mourn the expiring fire of Maurice's love for Clive. Clive's feeling for Maurice, however, has not expired, though he doesn't yet know this. The novel's penultimate paragraph evokes Clive's future memories of their first days together and the capacity of that lost, fugitive possibility of homosexual love to continue to haunt him:

To the end of his life Clive was not sure of the exact moment of departure, and with the approach of old age he grew uncertain whether the moment had yet occurred. The Blue Room would glimmer, ferns undulate. Out of some eternal Cambridge his friend began beckoning to him, clothed in the sun, and shaking out the scents and sounds of the May Term. (p. 215)

The power and poignancy of the writing here far exceeds the genuine narrative satisfactions but understated description of our last glimpse of Maurice and Alec in the boathouse. The return to Clive is essential because the novel's most powerful and unsatisfied yearnings turn on Clive, precisely because of his abandonment of Maurice and exclusion from the happy ending. However 'imperative' that happy ending – free of 'a lad dangling from a noose or . . . a suicide pact' (p. 218) – the novel's final chapter breaches its narrative closure. Given Clive's state of confusion as to the moment of Maurice's departure, and in time even the reality of the moment, the feelings evoked by the prose are in excess of anything simply attributable to Clive as a character. As a figure of loss and self-loss (not just of his lover but of the reality of his own experience) he is the locus and precondition for the novel's unsatisfied yearnings, for its profound identification with the state of loss. If the Blue Room and the ferns signal certain repudiated memories of intimacy at Penge – 'He hated queerness, Cambridge, the Blue Room, certain glades in the park . . .' (p. 152) – the evocation of Cambridge constitutes a complex of feelings that belong directly to neither character, but indicate a fantasy offered the reader and elaborated through and around the characters. The sights and sounds of Cambridge in the May term once excluded Maurice – 'You are unworthy of us' – but came to include him only through his connection with Clive – 'You are we, we are youth'. The potent combination of spring, youth and enlightenment (Cambridge) – we need to go to Tennyson's memories of Hallam at Cambridge for an equivalent[27] – now invest the figure of Maurice still making his appeal to Clive to 'come'. What can explain not only such a reversal but that still unassuaged appeal insisting at the novel's close in excess of its apparent happy ending?

Forster and the Lost Father

Forster . . . showed little desire to delve into his father's life or personality. When I once asked him 'What was your father like?', he answered with atypical tetchiness 'How should I know? He died before I was two.'[28]

Forster attempted an epilogue which gave the reader a glimpse of Maurice and Alec's future life as nomadic woodcutters in the greenwood then abandoned it – 'epilogues are for Tolstoy'. The present final chapter Forster asserted 'is the only possible end to the book' (p. 219). The lyrical remainder, after the happy ending, where in the ageing Clive's reveries the youthful Maurice for ever makes his appeal, points us back into the novel and an opacity at its heart.

If Maurice is the antithesis of both Clive within the narrative and his creator Forster framing it, then the surplus of yearning of which Clive is the textual representative without quite being the narrative motivation – like T.S. Eliot's Gertrude who arouses in Hamlet feelings which envelop and exceed her[29] – points towards an authorial identification. Like Forster at Millthorpe Clive is the intellectual excluded from the scene of masculine love. As a character he is the site of a number of reversals. From being the representative of Cambridge and its values which pass to the bourgeois Maurice, Clive becomes the embodiment of stupidity of heart, emotional tepidity, and expediency. From being the self-knowing platonizing homosexual he becomes the homophobic and uxorious heterosexual. With these reversals, Forster observes, 'Clive deteriorates, and so perhaps does my treatment of him. He has annoyed me . . . But it may be unfair on Clive who intends no evil . . .' (p. 219).

There is an opacity about the figure of Clive that is symptomatic of the text's occluded difficulties. We can partly approach it through Cyril Connolly's observation that of Maurice Hall the suburban hearty and Clive Durham the fastidious Apostle, 'it is Durham who would seem the true homosexual, Maurice the temporary one, like many an easy-going athlete who falls in with the homosexual mores of a university before going on to marry his best friend's sister'.[30] Putting aside Connolly's facile distinction between 'true' and 'temporary' homosexuals, one can recognize certain recurrent psychic and behavioural patterns associated with the terms in which Maurice and Clive are first established and which the novel disconcertingly reverses. Clive's conversion to heterosexuality is an anomaly at the heart of the book that remains inexplicable and unassimilable. Its arbitrariness is signalled in the rhetorical form of its presentation as a capricious, Hardyesque Fate, 'just a blind alteration of the life spirit, just an announcement, "You who loved men, will henceforth love women. Understand or not, it's the same to me".' Forster clothes his authorial fiat in various mystifying appeals to 'the body . . . deeper than the soul and its secrets inscrutable. . . . It was of the nature of death or birth' (p. 106). In response the reader can assemble various elements towards an explanation: Clive's influenza and his hysteria; his discovery of the pleasures of heterosexual flirtation; his family and class obligations; the corrosive nihilism that overwhelms the idealized sublimations of Greek love, 'the love Socrates bore Phaedo' (p. 91); the pilgrimage to Greece and Pallas Athene that discovers only 'dying light and a dead land' (p. 104); the blunt announcement to Maurice, 'against my will I have become normal. I cannot help it'; and the consequent despairing fatalism of the choric formula from Greek tragedy that echoes in the theatre of Dionysus, 'not to be born is best' (p. 104). All these point to a crisis in Clive's relation to Maurice, the failure of its idealizations, reserved for Wednesday nights and weekends within the bourgeois routines of their working lives at the Inns of Court or the City. What it doesn't substantiate, however, is the psychic consistency of Clive's sexual reorientation. The Merchant Ivory film of the novel (*Maurice*, UK 1987) is driven to supply the embarrassingly absent motivation for Clive's change by inventing an analogue for the Wilde trial in the sentencing and imprisonment of Risley for homosexuality. This suggests the familiar reality of social oppression and persecution as the explanation that is signally absent from Forster's text.

There are a number of different elements in Clive's normalization and the novel's expulsion and punishment of him. First of all one might hypothesize a certain satisfaction in the *escape* of the Forsterian intellectual into normality leaving the virile figure as the homosexual outsider, the representative of homosexual desire, not just its unattainable object but its lonely subject:

> His ideal of marriage was temperate and graceful, like all his ideals
> . . . they loved each other tenderly. Beautiful conventions received
> them – while beyond the barrier Maurice wandered, the wrong
> words on his lips and the wrong desires in his heart, and his arms
> full of air. (p. 144)

The return of this state of exclusion, loss and unsatisfied yearning in the figure of the ageing Clive in the final chapter, displaced and repeated from Maurice's experience of abandonment and rejection in Part 3, suggest – beyond the compensations and satisfactions brought by Alec's arrival through Maurice's window at Penge (itself a repetition of Maurice's arrival through Clive's window at Cambridge) – another scene. This is the scene of an emotional trauma that circulates and repeats *through* both characters without belonging to either, and which the possession of Alec cannot, for the novel if not for Maurice, lay to rest.

The novel's early chapters, while presenting Maurice as the representative 'mediocre member of a mediocre school' (p. 25), give him a distinctive psychic profile. Forster outlines two dreams that, we are told, 'will interpret him': the dream of George the garden boy and the dream of the friend. The latter is a frequent daydream – 'he saw scarcely a face, scarcely heard a voice say, "That is your friend" ' – from which 'he would emerge yearning with tenderness and longing to be kind to everyone, because his friend wished it, and to be good that his friend might become more fond of him' (p. 26). A recurrent point of reference throughout the narrative it bears especially closely, as the support of an idealizing function, on his love for Clive, while the fantasy of a mutually self-sacrificing pair of friends against the world is affirmed again with Alec. The dream of George is more elaborated, adversarial, and obscurely erotic. In it he attempts to collar (a blocking and embracing move) the naked garden boy as he runs down the field in a football game. The dream ends with the naked boy turning 'wrong' and a sense of brutal disappointment. It begins by relating the desired boy to an earlier and even more obscure figure:

> In the first dream he felt cross. He was playing football against a nondescript whose existence he resented. He made an effort and the nondescript turned into George, that garden boy. But he had to be careful or it would reappear. (p. 25)

The naked boy he desires but who eludes his embrace appears to be both a substitute for and a transformation of the resented nondescript who is the object of his anger and whom he seems intended to fend off or exclude. The dream clearly grows out of the moment of crisis recorded in the previous chapter. Here Maurice returns home from his last term at prep school to discover that George the garden boy is no longer employed by his mother. The news provokes an outburst of tears, 'a great mass of sorrow that had overwhelmed him by rising to the surface' (p. 22). The sorrow seems inexplicable except that its immediate context, in the conversation with his mother and the chapter as a whole, is a repeated emphasis on the figure of his dead father.

Significantly for all their physical, temperamental, and class differences, both Maurice and Clive share the same family situation as Clive acknowledges – 'you mentioned you had a mother and two sisters which is exactly my own allowance' (p. 44) – and critics have observed how a family situation marked by female predominance of mother and/or sisters, and a dead or absent father, is the 'allowance' of the male protagonists throughout Forster's fiction (as it was indeed Forster's own). In the novel's first two chapters the absence of the father is accompanied by a chorus of voices from both characters and the narrator, insisting on the figure of the father as the key to who Maurice is and the form his future is to take.

> He was a plump, pretty lad, not in any way remarkable. In this he resembled his father, who had passed in the procession twenty-five years before . . . (p. 16)

> 'Well, what did Mr Abrahams say? . . .
> 'Mr Abrahams told me to copy my father, sir.' (p. 17)

> 'Such a splendid report from Mr Abrahams . . . he says you remind him of your poor father . . .' (p. 21)

The Forsters, mother and androgynous son: all Little Lord Fauntleroy locks and possessive embraces.

'We are sending you to your father's old public school too –
Sunnington – in order that you might grow up like your dear
father in every way.'

A sob interrupted her . . . the little boy was in tears. (p. 22)

'He has quite a way with him already,' they told the cook. 'More
like his father.'

The Barrys . . . were of the same opinion . . . 'No one could be
deeply interested in the Halls . . . Like his father. What is the use of
such people?' (p. 23)

The unexplained 'great mass of sorrow' finds its context in the adult
insistence on the father and Maurice's repeated question, 'Where is
George?' The disappearance of the garden boy seems to rehearse the
death of the father and so provoke the rising of a sorrow that is already
in existence. This striking combination of paternal absence and insistence marks out a space where the child's night fears are shown to
flourish. It is an enigmatic, and in the Freudian sense, uncanny space of
mirrorings and doublings.

He had been such a man all the evening, that the old feeling came
over him as soon as his mother had kissed him good night. The
trouble was the looking-glass. He did not mind seeing his face in it,
nor casting a shadow on the ceiling, but he did mind seeing his
shadow on the ceiling reflected in the glass. He would arrange the
candle so as to avoid the combination, and then dare himself to put
it back and be gripped with fear. (p. 23)

As a formative moment this passage resonates with similar formative
moments in other *Bildungsroman*: Jane Eyre's moment of trauma in the
Red Room with its spectral self-reflection in the looking-glass and the
imagined return of the dead patriarch Mr Reed; Proust's little Marcel
yearning for his mother's goodnight kiss and watching with terror his
father's shadow ascending the staircase to his room. Frightened of
neither his direct reflection nor his shadow, Maurice's fear is located in
the doubling of a doubling, the moment of seeing 'his shadow on the
ceiling reflected in the glass'. His fear, like his tears, remains unexplained except that one might observe that in the moment of redoubling
the self-representation, both shadow and reflection, it is no longer
directly tethered to the self as its immediate effect. The shadow appears
to escape direct control, assuming an apparent autonomy in the spectral
world of the mirror. The phrase 'the land through the looking-glass'
appears later on as Clive's designation for the homosexuality he has
turned away from and which he appeals to Maurice to leave behind (pp.
152, 212). Maurice's fear of the shadow in the mirror is immediately
followed by fears of other shadows – 'sometimes blots like skulls fell over
the furniture. His heart beat violently, and he lay in terror with all his

household close at hand' (p. 23) – shadow-skulls that make the connection with death and have the power to terrify him in the very security of the family home. Faced with these terrors, the garden boy appears:

> As he opened his eyes to look whether the blots had grown smaller, he remembered George. Something stirred in the unfathomable depths of his heart. He whispered, 'George, George.' . . . He did not even know that when he yielded to this sorrow he overcame the spectral and fell asleep. (p. 24)

The thought of George has the power to comfort and Maurice's absorbing sorrow over his absence vanquishes the spectral world of shadows and skulls. This connection between George and the spectral, which he has the power to keep at bay, is represented in the dream where 'the nondescript whose existence he resented . . . turned into George. But he had to be careful as it would reappear' (p. 25). A number of elements, the double (feared or desired), the dead father and the question of homosexuality all converge on this enigmatic moment.

Psychoanalytic theory in its various forms has addressed the significance of such representations – the mirrored self, the dead father – in the formation of identity and sexuality. Freud's essay on 'The Uncanny' is particularly close to the concerns of this moment, with its account of the *heimlich* (the familiar, the domestic) invaded by the *unheimlich* (the uncanny, the unrecognizable double, the stranger), which is the return of what was once known and familiar.[31] Freud suggests that the double first appears in psychic life as a comforting representation (the narcissistically invested ego ideal) but later becomes the site for the formation of a new psychic agency, the paternal superego with its judgemental and threatening forms. Maurice's fears however seem not to have the classic lineaments of the Oedipal crisis, for the father in so far as he is represented by the nondescript and the skulls and shadows, is a spectral even deathly absence feared and resented, but also the object of that 'great mass of sorrow' that comes to attach itself to George the garden boy.

Maurice's 'land through the looking glass' constitutes a dream of obscure and shifting relations between the desired boy, the Ideal Friend and the mourned-for lost father, non-descript and resented. If Alec enters into the heritage of the naked garden boy, Clive moves from the position of the Ideal Friend to take over the burden of that shadowy paternal absence. Clive's rejection and abandonment of Maurice, having first awoken his desires and brought him to a first consciousness of them (the function of the Ideal Friend), has the emotional centrality to the novel that it does have because it gives a renewed occasion and form to that 'great mass of sorrow', repeating the experience of loss in which has been constituted the first image of desire. The identification of Clive with the father is clear from a curious passage in Chapter 30 where Forster explicitly evokes the ghost of the father as the embodiment of precisely the easy-going pattern of social and sexual conformity that

Edward Morgan Llewellyn Forster, Forster's father – prone, feline, intellectual.

Cyril Connolly has commented on and which Clive in his own way enacts:

> Mr Hall senior had neither fought nor thought. . . he had sup-
> ported society and moved without crisis from illicit to licit love.
> Now, looking across at his son he is touched with envy, the only
> pain that survives in the world of shades. For he sees the flesh
> educating the spirit, as his has never been educated, and develop-
> ing the sluggish heart and slack mind against their will. (p. 133)

Maurice, the embodiment of the homosexual body and its desires as
an educator of the spirit, is the object of a ghostly paternal envy, just as
he will be the object of a yearning nostalgia from a Clive who repeats the
father's conformity. Banished from the satisfactions of the narrative, the
novel's fugitive intensities of feeling – Maurice's childish sorrow and his
later anguished sense of abandonment, Clive's belated yearning, the
dead father's ghostly envy – locate in an uncanny limbo, the world of
shades, the land beyond the looking-glass, the text's unconscious point
of enunciation and fantasy. From this site of exclusion, a spectral authorial subject watches, nondescript and envious, as Maurice and Alec, the
Ideal Friend and the naked garden boy embrace together.

The apparent closure of that ending is sustained by a double absence.
Maurice is notable for the absence of a theory of inversion, of intermediacy
or cross-gendering such as we saw in Carpenter's writings and which
marks the writings of many of Forster's homosexual contemporaries as in
Proust and Radclyffe Hall. Also noticeable is its sexual inexplicitness or
reticence, the absence of the theme of sodomy so crucial to Forster's other
suppressed homosexual fictions which regularly turn on the act of
sodomy as the symbolic act of male inversion through which a range of
other differences – barbarian/Christian, missionary/native, officer/half-
caste, milkman/baronet – are played out.[32] One might read Forster's
confession of desire – 'to love a strong young man of the lower classes and
be loved by him and even hurt by him' – as a euphemistic expression of the
wish for such an act. Returning to the novel's primal scene, Forster at
Millthorpe visiting Carpenter the Uranian sage and Merrill his lover
(another proletarian George), we may read in its simultaneous construction of Forster as both a writing and a sexual subject – touched on the
backside, he conceives and delivers the novel – the very grounds of his
exclusion, feminized and inverted, from the scene of masculine love he
celebrates. In composing the novel's imperative happy ending as a vision
of sexual sameness, of virile doubling, Forster erases himself as a sexual
subject. The novel's concluding return to the figure of Clive suggests a
contradictory logic at work whereby the formation of the masculine
couple requires the exclusion of the unmanly intellectual with his disavowed paternal affiliation, only to repeat in displaced form the primordial experience of paternal loss and abandonment that the happy ending
was designed to assuage. Forster's attitude to his novel may be the result in
part of his own paradoxical absence from that 'happy ending'.

6 What is not said: a study in textual inversion

Diana Collecott

Silences shape all speech.
> Pierre Macherey, *A Theory of Literary Production*

SILENCE = DEATH
> ACT UP (AIDS Coalition To Unleash Power) slogan, USA

What are the words you do not yet have? What do you need to say?
> Audre Lorde, 'The Transformation of Silence into Language and Action', *Sister Outsider*

You will not find in what I say . . . any semblance of a woman whom you can love.
> Virginia Woolf, 'Reminiscences', Chapter 1, *Moments of Being*

Where does the body come in? What is the body?
> H.D., *Notes on Thought and Vision*

Turning In

Sexual Inversion is the second volume of Havelock Ellis's *Studies in the Psychology of Sex*, and the one which caused him most embarrassment. In the preface to the first American edition, he apologizes for publishing a study of the 'abnormal manifestations of the sexual instinct before discussing its normal manifestations', and presents this as compensatory behaviour for his own inclination to 'slur it over as an unpleasant subject'.[1] The same unease may be responsible for his stuttering insistence on the syllable *in* in his definition of *inversion* as 'the turning in of the sexual instinct towards people of the same sex' and his conclusion that this instinct is 'inborn'. Linguistic contortions such as these suggest that Ellis is teetering between the obligation to present homosexuality (of whatever kind) as unnatural and abnormal, and the awareness that this instinct 'to those persons who possess it appears natural and normal'. As a scientist he was conscious of the uncertainty principle that is active in different perceptions of the same phenomenon, and he passively incorporates this principle in his writing by citing authorities other than

91

himself – most notably 'several persons for whom I felt respect and admiration who were the congenital subjects of this abnormality'. How is the 'normal' reader to take such statements, and is a different interpretation permissible to the reader constructed as 'abnormal' according to Ellis's pathology? Where men are the norm, are all women abnormal? Or is the 'female invert' so doubly defined by her abnormality as to be excluded from discussion?

In this same preface, Ellis demurs to the 'normal' (heterosexual male) reader when he writes: 'If I had not been able to present new facts in what is perhaps a new light, I should not feel justified in approaching the subject of sexual inversion at all.' It is tempting to imitate this doctor's presumption of objectivity and to write here as an academic, concealing my other identities as a woman and a lesbian. Yet it is as a subject conscious of the discontinuities between these positions that I write. Should my text try to 'pass' as a 'straight' essay, or turn in on itself, using deliberate word-play to subvert the pre-Freudian norms of academic discourse? Should it display its embarrassing openings to other possibilities of interpretation, or of interpenetration between different systems of meaning? What degree of co-operation can it expect from the reader, in its eccentricity, double talk, interruptions, hesitations, scholarly presentations of 'new facts'? So much turns upon the reader, whose position is – what? He . . . She . . . 'The other who knows'.[2] And if not?

Lesbian Silence

Monique Wittig insists, in her Author's Note to *The Lesbian Body*, on the difference between homotextualities. Her book, she says,

> has lesbianism as its theme, that is, a theme which cannot even be described as a taboo, for it has no real existence in the history of literature. Male homosexual literature has a past, it has a present. The lesbians, for their part, are silent – just as all women are as women at all levels.[3]

Wittig's statement is as relevant now, in the late 1980s, as when it was written, in the early 1970s. During the intervening decade, many women in the academy have 'come out' as feminists, but few have come out as lesbians. Feminist critical attention to women's silences has itself been largely silent concerning the taboo on female homosexuality and its effects on literature. So long as gays pass as men and lesbians pass as feminists, heterosexism will be normative in education. This sustains a situation summed up by Adrienne Rich in 1975:

> Women's love for women has been represented almost entirely through silence and lies. . . .
>   Heterosexuality as an institution has also drowned in silence the erotic feelings between women. . . .[4]

The last sentence quoted here contains two words that are especially charged for lesbian writers and readers: 'silence' and 'erotic'. In the 1970s, (hetero)sexuality became a permissible subject for discourse, while (homo)sexuality was still subject to taboo. In the 1980s, a curious inversion of meaning has taken place, whereby (hetero)sexuality has been naturalized so that (homo)sexuality is marked as non-domestic and hence erotic. Yet, to reiterate Wittig, 'The lesbians, for their part, are silent': 'gay' means 'male' in most contexts, just as 'invert' means 'male' throughout most of Ellis's text. Even today, few speakers or writers on homosexuality bother to differentiate between those whom the culture constructs as men and those whom it constructs as women. The male body dominates current discussion in gay studies, while the female body is doubly deleted: is deleted as a maternal body, and as both subject and object of lesbian desire. This reduplicates the silence that Audre Lorde once broke with her cry: 'We have been raised to fear the *yes* within ourselves, our deepest cravings . . .'[5]

This situation leaves the lesbian conscious of herself as an absence from discourse, and the lesbian writer, teacher, or theorist in an historical position that does not synchronize with the relative recognition and the relative freedom of gay men to write, teach, and theorize. Wittig has suggested that 'The fascination for writing the never previously written and the fascination for the unattained body proceed from the same desire.'[6] While, under the shadow of AIDS, 'the unattained body' has become a figure of mourning for gay men, it remains a figure of absence for lesbians in most parts of the contemporary world. Let us not share the North American delusion that most lesbians are 'out', or that economic independence is not a *sine qua non* of homosexual expression. Virginia Woolf recognized these 'facts' in the 1920s. Although *A Room of One's Own* is now a canonical text for women's studies, few feminists are aware that in it Woolf identifies the task of articulating lesbian desire as one that involves rereading, as well as writing in previously unknown ways:

> And I began to read the book again, and read how Chloe watched Olivia put a jar on a shelf and say how it was time to go home to her children. That is a sight that has never been seen since the world began, I exclaimed. And I watched too, very curiously. For I wanted to see how Mary Carmichael set to work to catch those unrecorded gestures, those unsaid or half-said words, which form themselves, no more palpably than the shadows of moths on the ceiling, when women are alone, unlit by the capricious and coloured light of the other sex. She will need to hold her breath, I said, reading on, if she is to do it; for women are so suspicious of any interest that has not some obvious motive behind it, so terribly accustomed to concealment and suppression, that they are off at the flicker of an eye turned observingly in their direction. The only

> way for you to do it, I thought, addressing Mary Carmichael as if
> she were there, would be to talk of something else, looking steadily
> out of the window, and thus note, not with a pencil in a notebook,
> but in the shortest of shorthand, in words that are hardly syllabled
> yet, what happens when Olivia . . .[7]

Is this assumption of silence, this habit of 'concealment and suppression',
this necessary obliquity, outmoded in most lesbians' experience of both
living and writing? I suspect not, despite Adrienne Rich's confident
assertion that 'it is the lesbian in us who drives us to feel imaginatively,
render in language, grasp, the full connection between woman and
woman.'[8] Rich writes here as an out American lesbian with a surprisingly
unproblematic sense of the writer's task, and indeed of the nature of
language. Both of the effective verbs in this statement can be read in a
double sense. 'Drives' reads grammatically as a singular verb ('She *drives*
a car'); but it can also be read ungrammatically as a plural noun (as in the
'libidinal *drives*' of popular psychology). 'Grasp' means, literally, to have
direct physical contact with; figuratively, to comprehend or understand.
Whether conscious or unconscious on Rich's part, these double meanings override what other writers have felt to be a gap between experience and representation. There is even a deliberate implication that,
given 'full connection between woman and woman' – a connection that is
presumably physical as well as symbolic – signs and their meanings will
also achieve full connection.

For her part, and in her time and place, Virginia Woolf was convinced
that felt or perceived experience cannot be fully rendered in words, least
of all in patriarchal language. In her 'Reminiscences', Woolf addressed
her nephew Julian Bell in a passage that implicitly positions itself in
relation to the *Mausoleum Book* of her father and his grandfather, Leslie
Stephen:

> Written words of a person who is dead or still alive tend most
> unfortunately to drape themselves in smooth folds annulling all
> evidence of life. You will not find in what I say, or again in those
> sincere but conventional phrases in the life of your grandfather, or
> in the noble lamentations with which he fills the pages of his
> autobiography, any semblance of a woman whom you can love . . .[9]

Death marks Woolf's writing here, as it marks much writing by gay men
in our time. In 'Reminiscences' Woolf mourns a lost body: the body of
her mother. Her metaphor for written language turns the traditional
figure of speech as dress to clothe the bare body of meaning into a
shroud 'annulling all evidence of life.' By a similar inversion of meaning,
the contemporary poet James Merrill, in 'Investiture at Cecconi's (for
David Kalstone)', makes words perform in such a way that they represent the speaker's grieving dream for his friend.[10] Here the metaphor
modulates from tailor's fitting to mourning robe. Merrill seems to be

more confident than Woolf that language can convey, and not merely cover, lived experience. Yet Woolf wants 'written words' to stand for, or recover, what is lost; her passage continues:

> It has often occurred to me to regret that no one ever wrote down her sayings and vivid ways of speech, since she had the gift of turning words in a manner peculiar to her, rubbing her hands swiftly, or raising them in gesticulation as she spoke.

Woolf's own style turns here, from the 'conventional phrases' she associates with her father ('It has often occurred to me', etc.), to her mother's 'peculiar' manner of expression. As she recalls her mother's 'vivid ways of speech', her mother's actions become vivid too; articulation joins with 'gesticulation' and both manner and movement enter the writing: 'turning words . . . rubbing her hands . . . or raising them . . . as she spoke'. Thus written words are the means by which the mother's body is recovered, or at least represented, in the daughter's text. But the gestures of Julia Stephen also mark Virginia Woolf's recognition that words are only signs and that the body, though not 'annulled', is indeed lost.

Difference = Sameness

In the title essay of her volume, *In Search of Our Mothers' Gardens*, Alice Walker criticizes Virginia Woolf for omitting, from her discussion of women's freedom to write, any consideration of women bound to silence by slavery and racial as well as economic oppression.[11] In the face of such facts as the history of African-American women, are we justified in affirming what Adrienne Rich called 'the lesbian continuum', or should we focus on discontinuity, the absence of a universal lesbian identity? Ann Ferguson has suggested that, given differences of class and race, as well as historical differences, lesbians can be defined only by their opposition to the cultural norms of their time and place.[12]

Audre Lorde's memoir, *Zami: A New Spelling of My Name*, is a text vitally aware of its own oppositionality to the representative tradition of African-American autobiography. Moreover, its subject – the author's experience as a Black lesbian in New York in the 1950s and 1960s – defines itself through verbal and epistemological oppositions. Mapping the contradictions of her life as a student at Hunter College, and in Manhattan's lesbian bars, Lorde writes: 'Downtown in the gay bars I was a closet student and an invisible Black. Uptown at Hunter I was a closet dyke and a general intruder.'[13] This double life, with its different silences, is recalled in language that doubles back on itself in punning repetition:

> Lesbians were probably the only Black and white women in New York City in the fifties who were making any real attempt to communicate with each other; we learned *lessons* from each other,

the values of which were not *lessened* by what we did not learn. (my emphasis)[14]

Another passage recalling the gay-girls' bars of Greenwich Village is curiously reminiscent of Woolf's English fantasy of Chloe and Olivia:

Sometimes we'd pass Black women on Eighth Street – *the invisible but visible sisters* – or in the Bag or at Laurel's, and our glances might cross, but we never looked into each other's eyes. We acknowledged our kinship by passing in silence, looking the other way. Still, we were always on the lookout, Flee and I, for that tell-tale flick of the eye, that certain otherwise prohibited openness of expression, that definiteness of voice which would suggest, I think she's gay. *After all, doesn't it take one to know one?* (emphasis in original)[15]

Here African-American practices of double-talk come into play. The verb 'to pass' is a keyword, denoting mere passing in the street as well as the significant transition from Uptown (Black) to Downtown (White) Manhattan. For light-skinned 'blacks' who could *pass* as 'white', this was the traditional route to economic and social betterment: Nella Larsen's novella *Passing* counts the cost of such a transition across the colour line, for a woman who must deny kinship with her darker sister to sustain the fiction that she herself is white.[16] By contrast, Lorde's sisters 'acknowledged our kinship by passing in silence'. This inversion of usual social behaviour is introduced by a contradiction, 'the invisible but visible sisters', which compacts several levels of meaning. It reminds the reader that Black women are visible in the white community, while treated as invisible. So such sisters are women whose racial difference is marked by colour, while their sexual difference is unmarked, because perceived (both inside and outside the Black community) as more dangerous: so dangerous that the women cannot acknowledge it even to each other. Nevertheless, where Woolf writes of the 'half-said words' of women who are 'off at the flicker of an eye turned observingly in their direction', Lorde records a paradoxical 'openness of expression' and 'definiteness of voice' between women whose shared identity as lesbians was otherwise suppressed.

In a later polemical essay, Lorde recalls this chilling 'message . . . to Black women from Black men': 'if you want me, you'd better stay in your place which is away from one another, or I will call you "lesbian" and wipe you out'.[17] The fear of being 'wiped out' is taken into much lesbian writing and may account for many of its self-contradictions and obliquities. But when this fear is counterbalanced by lesbian desire, in works like *Zami* or the poetry of Gertrude Stein, it accounts for the erotics of these texts: their word-play, subversion of grammatical rules, resistance to literal reading or single-minded interpretation.

Black American speech has a rich range of practices known as *signifyin'*, which include opposite meanings for common words; hence, as fans of Michael Jackson know, 'bad' means 'good'.[18] The poet and polemicist June Jordan has defended Black English as distinctly different from White English, and equally valid for written use, including literary expression. She demonstrates this in her poem 'Getting Down to get Over (dedicated to my mother)' by signifyin' on idioms such as White Welfare jargon and Black Brother talk.[19] A poem like this requires diachronic as well as synchronic reading: it includes history, and obliges the reader to recognize that, historically, signifyin' has been a form of indirect or silent speech used by a people powerless within a particular cultural economy. Slaves, women, homosexuals, oppressed ethnic and religious groups, have always used forms of double-talk to elude punishment, censorship, or mere ridicule. Such talk can be interpreted only by another who is also 'other' – in Sedgwick's phrase 'the other who knows', for, in Lorde's inversion of the heterosexist sneer, 'doesn't it take one to know one?'

In the prose of *Zami*, Lorde is both more explicit about the political context of her writing, and more relaxed in her use of figures of speech, than Jordan is in her poem. However, a longer quotation from *Zami* will allow Lorde's text to speak with its own urgency:

> In the gay bars, I longed for other Black women without the need ever taking shape on my lips. For four hundred years in this country, Black women have been taught to view each other with deep suspicion. It was no different in the gay world.
>
> Most Black lesbians were closeted, correctly recognizing the Black community's lack of interest in our position, as well as the many more immediate threats to our survival as Black people in a racist society. It was hard enough to be Black, to be Black and female, to be Black, female and gay. To be Black, female, gay, and out of the closet . . . was considered by many Black lesbians to be suicidal.[20]

The alternative to individual suicide, as Lorde presents it, is a shared sense of difference. Her emphatic statement '*We were different*' is reiterated in a chant, preparing the reader for the writer's discovery of another Black woman whom she can love. 'We were different' is a complex statement, signifying two kinds of difference (between 'Black' and 'white' women, and between homosexual and heterosexual Black women); it also signifies sameness (between Black women, and between homosexual women), so that 'difference' is a sign of otherness that can be shared. Thus difference of colour may unite Black Women of different sexual orientation, while another difference unites lovers of the same sex. This paradoxical sense of sameness within alienation is enforced by Lorde's repeated use of two phrases, 'each other's' [*sic*] and 'our own' in the following passage:

> The Black gay-girls in the Village gay bars of the fifties knew each

other's names, but we seldom looked into each other's Black eyes, lest we see our own aloneness and our own blunted power mirrored in the pursuit of darkness.[21]

Her witty expression 'the pursuit of darkness' may well have Conrad's colonialist depiction of Africa in the corner of its eye. It plays on conventional notions of otherness: the general cultural association of blackness with evil, and the specific cultural association of lesbianism with witchcraft and proscribed desires. Recovering her longing for other Black women from the denigration of racists, anthropologists, and sexologists, Lorde celebrates difference as sameness, and renames herself as a lesbian whose African heritage validates female power and spirituality. Moreover, the passages that re-present, in 'written words', Zami's love-making with Black women consciously use incantatory rhythms and expressions associated with witchcraft. In one of these passages, the triple repetition of 'each other' provides the kind of override that Rich experienced in language charged with lesbian desire:

> *Our bodies met again, each surface touched with each other's flame, from the tips of our curled toes to our tongues, and locked into our own wild rhythms, we rode each other across the thundering space, dripped like light from the peak of each other's tongue.* (emphasis in original)[22]

In the climactic description of Zami's love for Afrekete, the trope of witchcraft is even more explicit. Introducing the 'crossroads' as a traditional sign of intersection between natural and supernatural powers, Lorde recalls the transition between Uptown and Downtown that was reversed when she met this Black female lover, and turns her words into a ritual of exorcism:

> *I remember the full moon like white pupils in the center of your wild irises.*
> . . .
> *Afrekete, Afrekete, ride me to the crossroads where we shall sleep, coated in the woman's power. The sound of our bodies meeting is the prayer of all strangers and sisters, that the discarded evils, abandoned at all crossroads, will not follow us upon our journey.* (emphasis in original)[23]

Coming Out

On the last weekend of October 1989, the Lesbian and Gay Studies Center at Yale University held its third annual conference, this time entitled 'Outside/Inside'. Over five hundred people attended – perhaps four times as many men as women. They included scholars from other American universities and gay activists from New York. On the first evening of the conference, most participants were watching Vito Russo's *The Celluloid Closet*, while a member of ACT UP was in the Yale Law School putting up posters for a presentation scheduled for the next day. A woman teacher at the Law School (who was not attending the conference) saw these genitally explicit posters and reported them to the Yale police as 'obscene'. The Yale police arrested the man responsible, and when members of the film audience protested at the arrest, they called in the New Haven police and eight more men were arrested. Bystanders, as well as those taken to the police station, were subjected to verbal and physical harrassment by the police. All those arrested were charged with breach of the peace and 'interfering' with a police officer in the course of his duty.

A statement issued by the Lesbian and Gay Studies Center concluded:

> The threat of violence we live with every day was realized in an instant in the middle of the street. Gay people assaulted and taken prisoner for bringing their sex to light and for voicing anger.

The President of Yale, called to account for the action of the University's own security corps, promised to hold an inquiry and blandly defended the rights of homosexuals to freedom of expression. A slip of the tongue – he referred to 'lays and gesbians' – hinted at his own difficulties with this concept. A week passed during which those arrested appeared in court in New Haven with full media coverage and were released on bail pending trial. Unidentified sympathizers with the police posted the Yale campus with the slogan, 'When gays act up, lock 'em up.'

On the Friday after the conference, a rally was held by the core of active lesbians and gays who remained on campus; no gay members of the university staff who had participated in the conference attended. Cameras and reporters from local and national TV networks were present. The rally was held in front of the President's office on Beinecke Plaza, right outside the library in which I was writing this chapter. I stopped writing to join in; we listened to speeches urging the President to 'come out' and make good the university's stated policy of non-discrimination. We applauded the students who insisted that the issue was our own bodies, our right to exist as gay or bisexual women and men. And we chanted slogans: 'Lesbian, lesbian, gay, gay/These words aren't so hard to say'; 'Hey, hey hey, ho, ho ho,/Homophobia's got to go'; 'No more violence/End the silence.' Most of us now wore badges showing a pink triangle on a black ground and the legend 'SILENCE = DEATH'.

A week later, there was a further court appearance in New Haven, and the charges against all nine of those arrested were dropped. The *Yale News* published a lengthy self-justification from the woman teacher who had complained about the posters, and the university released a transcript of her taped telephone conversation with the police which exposed the homophobia she denied. The President and his publicity officers held a press conference with one eye on the university's reputation for freedom of expression and inquiry, one on feminist protests against pornography and both on homophobic alumni on whom it depended for endowment. Dismissing the demand of the Lesbian and

Gay Studies Center that the police of both forces involved in the action be disciplined or fired, the President and the local Chief of Police agreed to some form of 'sensitivity training' for their men, and announced that the uniforms of the Yale police would in future be of a different colour to distinguish them from the New Haven police.

'Love Poem'

For literate women of my generation, either inside or outside the academy, who came alive to both lesbianism and feminism in the 1970s, two Americans were deeply influential: Audre Lorde and Adrienne Rich. In their essays and speeches, they made statements that were 'hardly syllabled yet' in our conscious minds, and formulated questions that we did not dare to utter. Such is Rich's statement about her earlier poetry: 'I hadn't found the courage yet to do without authorities, or even to use the pronoun "I" ';[24] or Lorde's challenge to other women-oriented women: 'What are the words you do not yet have? What do you need to say?'[25] In their different ways, they placed both feminism and lesbianism within a political arena and radicalized our understanding of the institutions of racism and heterosexism. Rich's book *On Lies, Secrets and Silence* inspired many of us to revise our own lives, and the lives and works of earlier women writers. Her own poetry – for instance, the sequence 'Twenty-one Love Poems' – created a context for the rereading of poets as diverse as Emily Dickinson and H.D. Lorde's exploration, in *Sister Outsider*, of the oppositions black/white, female/male, gay/straight was a polemical matrix for her own poetry.

Sister Outsider contains a conversation between Audre Lorde and Adrienne Rich which is also a record of Lorde's coming out as a 'Black lesbian poet'.[26] She connects this historic moment with the power of speech:

> Speaking up was a protective mechanism for myself – like publishing 'Love Poem' in *Ms* magazine in 1971 and bringing it in and putting it on the wall of the English Department.[27]

Notably, the poem appeared in a feminist magazine, but not in Lorde's next volume of poetry, *From a Land Where Other People Live* (1973). She tells Rich:

> My publisher called and literally said he didn't understand the words of 'Love Poem'. He said, 'Now what is this all about? Are you supposed to be a man?' And he was a poet! And I said, 'No, I'm loving a woman.'[28]

This example of 'speaking up' remains ambiguous: the speaker's 'I' can refer to either sex, unless uttered in a female voice. This is also the case with Lorde's 'Love Poem', which is explicit about the sex of the person loved but masks the sex of the lover under a neutral pronoun. It is this masking that the male publisher exploits, concealing his distaste for a woman loving a woman, under a cover of what? Subjective misunder-standing or covertly objective critique? The result is the same: censorship.

Is self-censorship already present in Lorde's decision, as a Black lesbian, to write in the anonymous tradition of white male lyricism? Love poems have, for centuries, been addressed from 'I' to 'you', with the sex of both partners unidentified. Masculist traditions of interpretation assume that the poet or speaking subject is male, and the beloved object is female, unless there is internal evidence to the contrary. Heterosexism must also account for the sex-changing of names in nineteenth-century translations of Sappho, and the suppression of Shakespeare's homoero-ticism. Yet it is these very conventions that have allowed homosexual writers to publish love poems with impunity. Few teachers discuss the gender of W.H. Auden's lover in 'Lay your sleeping head my love', or mention Amy Lowell's masculine impersonation in her love poems to Ada Russell. Contextual information of this kind has often been con-cealed by the writers themselves: Lowell's will instructed Russell to burn her love letters.[29] By contrast, Audre Lorde's autobiography *Zami: A New Spelling of My Name*, offers a context in which her 'Love Poem' must be understood – differently. Here is the full text of the poem:

Speak earth and bless me with what is richest
make sky flow honey out of my hips
rigid as mountains
spread over a valley
carved by the mouth of rain.

And I knew when I entered her I was
high wind in her forests hollow
fingers whispering sound
honey flowed
from the split cup
impaled on a lance of tongues
on the tips of her breasts on her navel
and my breath
howling into her entrances
through lungs of pain.

Greedy as herring-gulls
or a child
I swing out over the earth
over and over
again.[30]

When the lesbian context of this poem is not suppressed but assumed, details that might be misunderstood leap into meaning. The words 'I entered her', which must have disturbed Lorde's publisher, take their place in a pattern of spatial metaphors that maps the female body: '*sky . . . mountains . . . valley . . . forests . . .*'; '*hips . . . mouth . . . fingers . . . tongues . . . breasts . . . navel . . .*'.[31] The descriptions in the first stanza, which precede 'I entered her', must refer to the body of the woman speaking ('I'), and those which follow must refer to the body of the woman loved ('her'). The poem's meaning – and the reader's confusion – arise from the fact that these are, in a sense, the *same* body. Lorde's ecstatic last stanza reinforces this, reminding us in a mere simile ('Greedy . . . as a child') that this same body is the maternal body, the 'earth' from which we come and from which we are freed in love.

Text/Context/Intertext

The term 'lesbian context' has an extended meaning, beyond the biography of the writer. It brings into play writings by other lesbians, whether covert or overt, indeed any writing by women that gets its energy from erotic attraction between women. Hence Lorde's metaphors resonate unintentionally with those of Amy Lowell's poetic sequence 'Two Speak Together', as well as with the texts of poems by contemporaries such as Adrienne Rich and Olga Broumas. Moreover, when her 'Love Poem' is brought together with Monique Wittig's *The Lesbian Body*, the lesbian reader will recognize a shared eroticism that the heterosexual reader might categorize as violence. This body of material provides a common matrix for new lesbian writing, and for older writing by homosexual or bisexual women that has survived – often in isolation from its significant others. Indeed, the publication of contemporary lesbian poetry in the 1970s was part of a coming-out process for writings whose homotextuality was forgotten or unknown.

In 1982, when Audre Lorde's 'Love Poem' appeared in her first important selection, H.D.'s poem 'I Said' was printed for the first time, some twenty years after the poet's death.[32] It had been written in 1919 and inscribed 'To W.B.', that is, to Winifred Bryher, the young British writer who had fallen in love with H.D. the previous year. In 1919, aged twenty-five, Bryher was working on her first autobiographical novel, *Development*, and trying desperately to free herself from her parents in order to establish her own identity. In the same year, both H.D. and Bryher separately consulted Havelock Ellis about their sexuality. By the winter of 1919, when H.D.'s poem was written, Bryher had threatened suicide: a form of self-silencing still chosen by many homosexual men and women. 'I Said' is H.D.'s response to that threat – a threat specifically addressed to her as the beloved who must save W.B. from death in one form or another.[33]

As it is now presented to us, in the 1983 edition of H.D.'s *Collected Poems, 1912–1944*, 'I Said' is detached from this history. At the back of the book, an editorial note simply states that earlier typescripts are entitled 'To W.B.' In fact, these initials encode part of the history: they reflect the gender-free signature over which Hilda Doolittle chose to publish, and mark a stage in Winifred Ellerman's transition from her family name to her adoption by deed poll of the pen-name Bryher. In 1920, *Poetry* published a trio of love poems under the title 'Hellenics' by 'W. Bryher': this 'new spelling' of her name will have concealed the poems' Sapphic content from readers who missed an editorial note mentioning the visit to America of 'Miss Bryher and H.D. (Mrs. Richard Aldington)'.[34] Earlier that year, the two women had visited Greece together, accompanied as far as Athens by Havelock Ellis.[35]

Why do I trouble you, my reader, with such 'new facts'? Is it to remind us, as scholars and textual critics, of our own responsibilities for 'concealment and suppression'? Is it because the facts disturb me – like the phone call threatening suicide that tore me from the library where I wrote this? What are the critical implications of reinserting this poem in its lesbian contexts: the contexts of actual lives, then and now, and the literary contexts? In an attempt to respond to these questions, I want to postpone quotation from 'I Said', in order to consider further the problem of 'What is not said'.[36]

In his *A Theory of Literary Production*, Pierre Macherey argues that what is important in a literary work is 'what [it] cannot say'; he urges the reader to 'investigate the silence' behind the work, to ask ourselves:

> Can we make this silence speak? What is the unspoken saying? . . .
> To what extent can dissimulation be a way of speaking? Can something that has hidden itself be recalled to our presence?[37]

Macherey's theory was formulated for consideration of unconscious suppression. Does it have any application to the deliberate dissimulation of homosexual writers, and the condition of silence which the taboo on homosexual activity forces on their readers? Its usefulness, surely, is in drawing our attention to contradictions between what is said and what is not said in a given literary text. For Macherey, the signs of such contradictions will be, precisely, silence and dissimulation, and his method of interrogating these silences involves a shift to an ideological intertext where the 'unspoken' speaks.

We have already seen how Virginia Woolf, as imaginary reader of Mary Carmichael's as yet unwritten text, conspires with her to create a space for 'words that are hardly syllabled yet'. For Woolf, the markers of this joint enterprise between writer and reader will be a necessary obliquity: in writing of Chloe and Olivia, Carmichael will have to 'hold her breath', 'talk of something else' and use 'the shortest of shorthand'. For Michael Riffaterre, as for Woolf and Macherey, the reader has a crucial role in producing meaning. Riffaterre identifies the reader as 'the only one who makes the connections between text, interpretant and intertext', and he defines *intertext* as: 'any one of the various matrices that is active in the writing of a passage and vital to the reading of it'.[38] The word *matrix*, with its connotations of the maternal womb, is a resonant one for women readers, and especially those influenced by Julia Kristeva's claim that 'pregnancy still constitutes the ultimate limit of meaning'.[39] In the passage from *A Room of One's Own* cited above, Woolf substitutes for Kristeva's 'archaic . . . mother', an archetypal woman writer named Mary: it is she who is entrusted to record the love of Chloe for Olivia, which exists as yet only in Woolf's text. Some readers will identify the lost maternal body of Woolf's 'Reminiscences' as the intertextual matrix of all her writings, the matrix capable of almost endless extension.

The implications of this way of thinking are so extensive that I want to take them up in another essay on literary (re)production and lesbian collaboration. What matters here is how far the concept 'intertext' will stretch. If, as Catharine Stimpson has so nicely stated, 'Lesbianism partakes of the body', then the matrices of lesbian writing must embrace what have been described as 'the intertexts of relation and desire'.[40] An intertextual approach to lesbian texts thus requires us to acknowledge the silences within society's 'heterosexual presumption', and to acquire forbidden knowledge of writers' lives. It also requires a revision of reading practices, and especially the New Critical convention that a literary text contains within itself all the information necessary to its interpretation.

Where Macherey focuses on ideological contradictions between a text and its matrix, Riffaterre introduces the idea of the *ungrammatical*, arguing that 'any ungrammaticality within the poem is a sign of grammaticality elsewhere'. He goes on to say that this half-hidden relationship between the 'textually grammatical' and the 'intertextually ungrammatical' is so disturbing that 'the reader continually seeks relief by getting away from the dubious words, back to safe reality (or to a social consensus as to reality)'.[41] With texts like Audre Lorde's 'Love Poem' or H.D.'s 'I Said', such a retreat to safety is only done at the cost of reinforcing the social taboo on lesbian identity: the alternative, for readers and editors, is to encounter meaninglessness, as lesbians must in their daily existence. However, once such poems are identified as intertexts for each other, their contradictions and instances of ungrammaticality may, paradoxically, become meaningful.

'I Said'

H.D.'s poem 'I Said' has more fugitive intertexts than Lorde's poem: these include letters between Bryher, H.D. and their friends, including

Havelock Ellis, and unpublished prose and poetry found among Bryher's papers after her death.[42] In Bryher's fictional versions, the same episode is replayed in dialogues between two shifting characters: the lover's death-threat and the response of the beloved. In H.D.'s poetry, we find high rhetoric in place of naturalistic prose; this is the opening stanza of the four-part poem:

> I said:
> 'think how Hymettus pours divine honey,
> think how dawn vies
> in the shelter of Hymettus,
> with the clusters of field-violet,
> (rill on rill of violets!
> parted and crested fire!)
> think of Hymettus
> and the tufted spire of thyme,
> hyacinth, wild wind-flower,
> think of Hymettus
> beyond mist,' I said, 'and rain,'
> and you,
> "twere better, better being dead.'[43]

The repeated Greek name, (Mount) Hymettus, is a key to this stanza's patterns of assonance, and a means of displacing the drama from its actual context. When it is set aside, we find here elements that are also present in Lorde's 'Love Poem': *mountain . . . honey . . . rain*. These suggest a shared physical intertext, acknowledged only as landscape in H.D.'s poem. In 'Love Poem', metaphor is used to reveal rather than to conceal erotic experience; in 'I Said', breathless metonymies hint at what is not said. Thus, in a different lesbian poem, the same signs may mark what Macherey calls 'dissimulation as a way of speaking'.

To hear what the 'unspoken' is saying in this poem, we must attend to ruptures or interruptions; for instance, the abrupt parenthesis – (rill on rill of violets!/ parted and crested fire!)' – makes a rift in the text as if the mountain itself were breaking open like a volcano. H.D. was aware, from her reading of Pausanias' *Guide to Greece*, that Mount Hymettos is renowned for its flowers and honey-bees. She also thought it was an extinct volcano; an early holograph version of these lines reads: 'in the *crater* of Hymettus, rill on rill of violets – parted fire . . .' (my emphasis).[44] In the final version, the exclamation marks draw attention to the break in syntax, and we seem to be in the presence of metaphors for the female genitals rather than celebrations of an absent Greek landscape. 'Every peak is a crater. This is the law of volcanoes,' writes Adrienne Rich, 'making them eternally and visibly female.'[45] In later poetry, H.D. will syllable her sexuality in lines like these:

> I did not know how to differentiate

between volcanic desire
anemones like embers
and purple fire
of violets
like red heat
and the cold
silver
of her feet . . .[46]

Flower imagery has been used by both men and women to encode eroticism; it is essential to H.D.'s earlier poetry, and connects it with the tradition of homoerotic 'decadence' represented in England by A.C. Swinburne and Oscar Wilde: 'They talked of Greeks and flowers' is her veiled comment on these writers in the novel *Asphodel*, whose own title pays tribute to the Victorian classicism of W.S. Landor. Ros Carroll comments on H.D.'s use of the term 'Lesbian iris' in her essay on Sappho:

> The flower is both a metaphor for something which cannot be named, and a signifier for something that H.D. dare not name, not only because of social prohibition, but because it touches upon her own deepest fears, H.D. has absorbed the connections . . . between witchcraft, lesbianism and hysteria, all associated in some way with 'excessive sexual drive'.[47]

If H.D.'s fears about her own sexual desires and sexual ambivalence, reinforced by Ellis's pathological account of the female 'invert', act as unconscious censors on what is said, she is also skilful in consciously constructing a hermetic discourse that will contain meanings not stated in her text. In the lines from 'I Said' quoted above, two words of Greek origin stand out: *Hymettus* and *hyacinth*; they share a common first syllable, and 'hyacinth' can be read, like 'Hymettus', as a proper name. As a mere flower-name it is 'textually grammatical' with the poetic description of place; as the name of the beautiful young man with whom the god Apollo was in love, it directs the reader to a homosexual intertext that resonates in complex ways with the occasion of H.D.'s poem. In Greek legend, Hyacinth was killed, either accidentally or because of Zephyr's jealousy, by a wind-blown discus thrown by Apollo. In Farnell's *Cults of the Greek States*, which H.D. was reading along with Pausanias in 1919, Hyakinthos is identified as a vegetative divinity, like Kore or Adonis; his hero cult was celebrated each spring with flowers and mourning songs. This knowledge enlarges the meaning of the line "twere better, better being dead', by covertly introducing the idea of rebirth and the theme of heroic death.

Both ideas are present in the second stanza of the poem, where the speaker continues:

'But what grave heart,' I said,

'of beauty dies if you die:
at Marathon there bled
souls such as yours,
such souls as yours
stained those pale violets red,
her violets beyond Athens . . .'

The intertextual matrix of these lines includes the myths of both Hyacinth and Adonis, whose blood was shed as a result of passionate entanglements. The blood of Adonis sprang up as anemones, while Hyacinth's marked the wild iris with Greek letters spelling out his suffering: *ai ai*. In 1918, Bryher published her own translation of Bion's *Lament for Adonis*. Here is a heterosexual text offering florid versions of the same tropes that H.D. will use in 'I Said'. In Bion's poem, it is Aphrodite who mourns the young man lost to love: 'The Paphian weeps as Adonis bleeds and blood and tears change to flowers upon the earth. Roses are born out of the blood but the tears are windflowers.'[48]

'Windflowers' follow 'hyacinth' in H.D.'s poem, either through unconscious association with the wind-blown discus, or because Greek poets such as Sappho and Ibycus connect Eros with flowers and liken him to a sudden wind, that shakes the lover's limbs. H.D.'s 'purple hyacinth' ('Heliodora') is not the cultivated species, but the wild Greek iris. Lorde, too, may have the 'Lesbian iris' in mind, when she puns on the 'wild irises' of her lover's eyes. If so, she may also share with H.D. this image of Sappho's: '. . . as the shepherd men trample the hyacinth on the mountain with their feet, and on the ground the purple flower.' H.D. turned this fragment into a description of Sappho's poetic style that alludes to her actual writing: 'violets, purple woof of cloth, scarlet garments . . . the lurid, crushed and perished hyacinth, stains on cloth and flesh and parchment'.[49] Flowers were not only strewn on the graves of men and heroes; they were worn, according to Farnell, as signs of the earth mother, signifying birth as well as death. Their juices stain like ink or menstrual blood; their petals bruise like passionate flesh, 'lurid' in H.D.'s version of Sappho, as in the writings of Lorde and Wittig, as in the 'hyacinths like famished kisses' in the autobiographical prose of *Asphodel*.

Hyacinth and Adonis are both figures of eternal youth; indeed, Farnell tells us that the word *hyakinthos* 'in form and meaning corresponds to our word "young"'.[50] Dying, they re-enter the earth, like heroes killed in battle, and like their female counterpart, Kore, who returns with the flowers each spring to Demeter her mother. H.D.'s later poem, 'The Mysteries', celebrates the seasonal cycle of death and rebirth with imagery drawn from the rites of Adonis:

the grain
lifts its bright spear-head

to the sun again;
behold,
behold,
the dead
are no more dead . . .[51]

The word 'spear-head' is common to this poem and 'I Said', where it
refers to Athene's weapon, 'glittering' at the head of the Athenian army
and responsible for their victory at Marathon. Athene Nike is the
unnamed she of the line 'her violets beyond Athens', and the goddess
whom H.D. identifies elsewhere as 'my own especial sign or hiero-
glyph'.[52] In this way, Greek myth and legend are serving H.D. as what
Woolf called 'the shortest of shorthand': signs or hieroglyphs poised
between the text and its concealed intertexts.

Another such sign is the place-name Marathon. If *Hymettus* evokes the
Greek world in an ideal serenity, *Marathon* is a site of struggle: the
battleground where the Athenian spearsmen defended Greece against a
vaster army of invading Persians. Marathon is remembered in English as
the name of a foot-race that commemorated the endurance of the
solitary runner who carried the news of the victory to Athens, then died
of exhaustion. In H.D.'s poem the word connotes victorious resistance,
heroic death, and *brotherhood*. When she wrote the poem, the First World
War, in which she lost her dearest brother, was only just over. Even
when they hated modern warfare, women envied serving soldiers' close
bonds with their own sex, their youthful high-mindedness. War is idealized in H.D.'s references to Marathon so that the poet can praise W.B.
for her courage and self-sacrifice. Here her literary intertext is the *Persae*
of Aeschylus, himself said to have been wounded at the battle of
Marathon, and defeated by Simonides of Ceos in the poetry competition
to celebrate the victory. Poetry, too, may be a site of struggle.

The struggle of 'I Said' is between W.B.'s denial of her own courage
('"I am no Greek", you said') and H.D.'s insistence that there is heroism
in resistance to social pressures. In her reply to the suicidal younger
woman, the overt target is philistinism, but she covertly implies that
living as a lesbian involves an inversion of heterosexual values, a rereading of words and meanings. Under such conditions, 'lies' may be 'true':

. . . it seems to me Greek rather
to live as you lived,
outwardly telling lies,
inwardly without swerving or doubt –
'if I can not have beauty about me
and people of my own sort,
I will not live,
I will not compromise' –
and though I have heard many people

talk about life
and the indubitable comfort of being dead,
your words alone of them all
rang unutterably true,
you meant what you said.

This affirmation brings the second section of 'I Said' to a climax which is also the mid-point of the poem:

anyone to-day who can contemplate
the idea of death, abstract death,
(romantic though he be,
young without doubt, mad perhaps)
anyone to-day who can die for beauty,
(even though it be mere romance
or a youthful geste)
is and must be my brother.

The use of masculine pronouns here, not to speak of the expression 'my brother', is grammatical with the poem's celebration of masculine hero-ism, but confusing to the reader aware of its lesbian intertext, as the neutral pronouns 'I' and 'you' are not. Readers of H.D. will recall actual ungrammaticality in poems like 'Amaranth' of the same period, where names and pronouns have been changed from version to version, so that the outcome is an apparently heterosexual text, like some Latin trans-lations of Sappho. Is the sudden presence of masculine referents in 'I Said' due to confusion of gender-identity on the poet's part, or to deliberate dissimulation? If dissimulation, is it comparable to the fugitive fictional versions of this conversation in which Bryher presents herself alternately as a young woman ('Nancy') or a young man ('Ernest'), choosing in each case names with 'queer' or Wildean overtones?[53] H.D., at the rhetorical climax of her poem, seems to be endorsing Bryher's desire to be a man, while diverting Bryher's desire for herself into a fantasy of male fellowship. This form of double-talk is marked by further ruptures in the text, in the form of two parentheses, each of which contains the uneasy conditional 'though':

(romantic though he be
young without doubt, mad perhaps)

and

(even though it be mere romance
or a youthful geste)

In effect, these lines are less an endorsement of masculine heroism than a questioning of its premises; the brackets seem to mark spaces for the speaker's doubt, while the obscure word 'geste' is disturbing in this context. In one of the typescripts of the poem, which Bryher herself preserved, it is italicized and spelt *jeste*.[54] We seem to be in the presence of one of H.D.'s inspired bilingual puns. Her posthumous male editor has opted for the single meaning that is most coherent with the rest of the text: an anglicized version of French *geste*, that is an heroic poem, but one in the Romantic rather than the classical tradition. Yet H.D.'s original ambiguous spelling or misspelling catches many meanings in a knot, exemplifying Macherey's idea of the unconscious element in a literary work, and Riffaterre's notion of ungrammaticality. In English, a *jest* is something said or done for amusement, but it may also be an object of derision or a laughing-stock. In French, *geste* means gesture or movement, as well as act or deed; it can be an heroic act or a despicable deed. In either language, then, the word is a sign looking two ways, signifying approval or disapproval, acceptance or threat, joy or fear. Thus the word *jeste*, as H.D. spells it, marks the semantic insecurities of the lesbian context of 'I Said'. Hidden within it is the ambivalent position of homosexuals in a heterosexist society, and the doubly ambivalent position of homosexual women in a sexist society. This is no laughing matter, as suicides show, but a matter of life and death. Yet H.D.'s use of this odd word is playful, inviting the reader to read the text in several ways and to address the contradictions of her lover's position. By referring to 'mere romance or a youthful geste' she hints at W.B.'s immaturity, while also gesturing at the doomed heroic themes of the *chansons de geste*. The poem's title may seem to refer to one side of the dialogue, but a more complex statement is made by the entire text. The reader can attend to this only by listening to what is not said, and by being alert to what Riffaterre describes as 'the transformation of texts into larger wholes'.

'If I saw you would you kiss me?':
sapphism and the subversiveness of
Virginia Woolf's Orlando

Sherron E. Knopp

I

The 'longest and most charming love letter in literature', Nigel Nicolson
calls *Orlando*.[1] But the real-life relationship between Virginia Woolf and
Vita Sackville-West prompted more reserved comment from the two
men – Virginia's nephew, Quentin Bell, and Vita's son, Nigel Nicolson –
who first characterized it with authority. Bell tells us that Virginia in the
beginning 'felt shy, almost virginal, in Vita's company, and she was, I
suspect, aroused to a sense of danger'.[2] He concludes cautiously: 'There
may have been – on balance I think there probably was – some caressing,
some bedding together. But whatever may have occurred between them
of this nature, I doubt very much whether it was of a kind to excite
Virginia or to satisfy Vita.'[3] In *Portrait of a Marriage*, Nicolson confirms
Bell's account and hastens to add the weight of his own authoritative
judgement: 'Vita and Virginia did no damage to each other . . . The
physical element in their friendship was tentative and not very successful, lasting only a few months, a year perhaps. It is a travesty of their
relationship to call it an affair.'[4]

But it is also a travesty of their relationship to reduce it to petty niggling
over what they did or did not do in bed. In contrast to the hesitant,
ambivalent relationship nephew and son describe, the letters between
Virginia and Vita, published in 1978 and 1984 respectively, reveal an
attachment that lasted in its physical expression not just the 'few months, a
year perhaps' that Nicolson first speculated but at least two years beyond
that and probably more, and it continued in emotional intensity until
Virginia's death in March 1941. As co-editor of Virginia's letters, Nicolson
no longer minces words: 'It was the deepest relationship which Virginia
ever had outside her family'; 'they loved each other.'[5] Vita's co-editor,
Mitchell Leaska, concurs: 'Rarely can an enterprise of the heart have been
carried out so near the verge of archetypal feeling.'[6] Nevertheless, while
Nicolson still bridles at the erotic significance of the relationship – 'They
slept together perhaps a dozen times'; 'a strange and pleasurable experience, but unintoxicating, terminable'[7] – Leaska ignores it.

The novel that celebrates Virginia's love for Vita has generated its own share of critical ambivalence, although in this case Virginia, not her biographers, gives the cue for misconception in diary entries labelling *Orlando* 'an escapade', something written 'for a treat', 'too much of a joke perhaps'.[8] The nonchalance of the joke, however, is belied by the ardour of her absorption in the project. On 9 October 1927, she writes to Vita with excitement: 'But listen; suppose Orlando turns out to be Vita; and its all about you and the lusts of your flesh and the lure of your mind.' Four days later: 'I'm so engulfed in Orlando I can think of nothing else. . . . I make it up in bed at night, as I walk the streets, everywhere. I want to see you in the lamplight, in your emeralds. In fact, I have never more wanted to see you than I do now.'[9] By December the significance of the project – and her engagement in it – brooks no disguise:

> Should you say, if I rang you up to ask, that you were fond of me?
> If I saw you would you kiss me? If I were in bed would you –
> I'm rather excited about Orlando tonight: have been lying by the fire and making up the last chapter.[10]

Yet the extent to which Vita and Virginia did love each other – profoundly and, in every sense of the words, erotically and sexually (the frequency or infrequency with which they went to bed is irrelevant) – is something that continues to be resisted, denied, ignored, qualified out of significance, or simply unrecognized, even by the feminist revolution that has enshrined Virginia as its saint. There seems to be an unspoken agreement that whatever else one might call Virginia – asexual, bisexual, androgynous – she was not a 'sapphist'. Joanne Trautmann, for example, borrows the term 'homoemotionality' from Charlotte Wolff's ambivalent *Love between Women*[11] to describe Virginia's relationships with women, associating it on the one hand with a 'fierce sexlessness' and on the other with 'that bisexual state of mind called androgynous'.[12] The assumption seems to be that lesbian love is only or primarily sexual, that love involving the emotional intimacy of minds and hearts requires a different term. Yet no one categorizes heterosexual relationships on the basis of such dubious distinctions. In a recent collection of feminist essays, Jean Love acknowledges Virginia's 'venture into eroticism' but quotes Bell and Nicolson to support her opinion that it was nothing more than a brief experiment and then proceeds to read *Orlando* as a 'means of gaining perspective and detachment', 'a requiem mass' for a part of her life she was ready to leave behind.[13]

Critical discomfort with the novel mirrors biographical discomfort with the relationship. Those who dislike *Orlando* complain that it is too deeply rooted in Vita's life to have general appeal. Jean Love, for example, contends that its biographical elements lack the 'greater reach and power of transformation' of those in *To the Lighthouse*.[14] But since lovers are as significant as parents in most people's lives, one cannot help wondering if it is the sex of the lover rather than the novel itself that lacks broad appeal. At least one critic makes no secret of her attitude: 'I want to say from the outset that I am not interested in what Quentin Bell once called "the coarse physiological facts" of their physical affair.'[15] Others just discreetly look the other way. As J.J. Wilson notes, *Orlando* receives little or no mention in works in which one would expect it to be central.[16] Those who admire the book hasten to admit that it is only a minor interlude amid more serious acts of creation – as Vita was (so the biographical version runs) in Virginia's attachment to Leonard. Thus Leaska, who co-edited Vita's letters in 1984, judged *Orlando* 'brilliant but incongruous' in 1977 and omitted it from *The Novels of Virginia Woolf: From Beginning to End*.[17] The few critics who treat the novel sympathetically and at any length locate its claim to serious consideration elsewhere than in the sexual politics that are its *raison d'être* – in its genre as antinovel, for example (J.J. Wilson), or in its revisionary treatment of English history and literature (Howard Harper).[18] Thus, like the relationship that inspired it, the book is ignored, dismissed as an anomaly, or explained as something other than it is.

Nevertheless, *Orlando* was less of a joke than Viriginia usually let on and more than mere personal indulgence. To her own typically self-deprecating assessment ('not, I think "important" among my works'), she juxtaposed Leonard's with obvious self-vindication: 'L. takes Orlando more seriously than I had expected. Thinks it in some ways better than The Lighthouse; about more interesting things, & with more attachment to life, & larger. The truth is I expect I began it as a joke, & went on with it seriously.'[19] I want to argue, of course, that Leonard was right and that criticism has not even begun to suspect how right. The things we joke about, after all, are often those we care about too much to risk seriousness. But to see just how large and attached to life *Orlando* is, one must first get the relationship between Virginia and Vita right and then see it in context: what it meant to regard oneself as a lesbian (or, to use the term Virginia and Vita prefer, sapphist) and to engage in lesbian relationships in the 1920s and what it meant to *write* about one's perceptions and experiences.

II

Initially, of course, it was Vita who was the sapphist – a 'pronounced Sapphist, & may, thinks Ethel Sands, have an eye on me, old though I am', Virginia wrote in February 1923, two months after meeting Vita.[20] By January 1925 it is not clear whose eye is on whom when she boasts in a letter to Jacques Raverat about '*My* aristocrat . . . [who] is *violently* Sapphic, and contracted such a passion for a woman cousin, that they fled to the Tyrol. . . . To tell you a secret, I want to incite my lady to elope with me next.'[21] By December 1925, with Vita's departure to join Harold in Persia imminent, it is Virginia who is chafing with impatience: 'Well, it is partly that devil Vita. No letter. No visit. No invitation to Long Barn. She was up last week and never came. So many good reasons for this neglect occur to me that I'm ashamed to call this a cause for weeping. Only if I do not see her now, I shall not—ever: for the moment for intimacy will be gone next summer.'[22]

In contrast to Bell's vision of a timid, asexual Virginia pursued by a Vita 'very much in love' and motivated by 'a masculine impatience for some kind of physical satisfaction',[23] letters and diary entries suggest a Virginia eager for Vita's intimacy and fully aware of its probable sapphic consequences. For her part, Vita seems, both before and after the encounter at Long Barn, to have been acting exactly as she assured Harold she was in 1926: 'I am scared to death of arousing physical feelings in her, because of the madness. I don't know what effect it would have, you see: it is a fire with which I have no wish to play.'[24] Although neither alludes explicitly to what happened between them, Vita's terse diary entries for 17 December 1925 ('A peaceful evening') and 18 December ('Talked to her till 3 am. Not a peaceful evening')[25] sound very much like someone worried about fire. Virginia, in contrast, sounds like someone startled to have discovered in practice what she already knew in theory – 'These Sapphists *love* women; friendship is never untinged with amorosity' – and she expresses relief that her 'fears & refrainings' had proved to be 'sheer fudge'.[26] In her letter to Vita on 22 December – 'I woke trembling in the night. . . . Ah, but I like being with Vita'[27] – she sounds like someone happily abandoned to the flames. Looking back on the occasion a year later, Vita wishes in a letter 'that we could put the clock back. . . . I should like to startle you again, – even though I didn't know then that you were startled'.[28] Still another year later, she humorously congratulates herself for the aggression by which she made Virginia's acquaintance in the first place and thereby 'lay the train for the explosion which happened on the sofa in my room here when you behaved so disgracefully and acquired me forever'.[29] If Virginia did not actively solicit or initiate the lovemaking at Long Barn, Vita certainly had the impression that she wanted and expected it.

True, the physical side of this affair did not involve the kind of fiery passion that Vita so characteristically generated in others, that erupted in international elopements, destroyed marriages, and precipitated threats of murder or suicide. But if it was not a raging conflagration, it was none the less a real fire: 'Please come, and bathe me in serenity again. Yes, I was wholly and entirely happy. If you could have uncored me – you would have seen every nerve running fire – intense, but calm.'[30] Nor did it exempt Virginia from feeling the jealous emotions of any hurt lover when her 'calm fire' did not prevent Vita from pursuing other lovers – Mary Campbell especially, but one could name half a dozen others. Vita became interested in Mary Campbell in May 1927. In June she wrote Virginia a teasing letter:

> Do you know what I should do, if you were not a person to be rather strict with? I should steal my own motor out of the garage at 10 p.m. tomorrow night, be at Rodmell by 11.5 (yes, darling: I did a record on Friday, getting from Lewes to Long Barn in an hour and 7 minutes,) throw gravel at your window, then you'd come down and let me in; I'd stay with you till 5, and be home by half past six. But, you being you, I can't; more's the pity. Have you read my book? Challenge, I mean? Perhaps I sowed all my wild oats then. Yet I don't feel that the impulse has left me; no, by God; and for a different Virginia I'd fly to Sussex in the night. Only, with age, and soberness, and the increase of considerateness, I refrain. But the temptation is great.[31]

Vita's playful contrast between Virginia and Violet Trefusis, with whom Vita had 'eloped' in 1920 and about whom she had written *Challenge*, is more appropriate than either Vita or Virginia could realize at the time, but Virginia's response is equally significant: 'You see I was reading Challenge and I thought your letter was a challenge . . . whereupon I wired "come then". . . . You won't think from this that I mean I seriously expected you: it was all a kind of tipsy vision of driving along the downs with you in the dawn. I was very excited all day.'[32] For Virginia the stimulation of the mind provided pleasure as real and immediate as stimulation of the body.

But if she could not play the role of Violet herself, she did not want anyone else to have it either. By 4 July her usual affectionate banter changes to the undisguised sarcasm of jealousy:

> Yes you are an agile animal – no doubt about it, but as to your gambols being diverting, always, at Ebury Street [Vita's London address] for example, at 4 o'clock in the morning, I'm not so sure. Bad, wicked beast! To think of sporting with oysters – lethargic glucous lipped oysters, lewd lascivious oysters, stationary cold oysters, – to think of it, I say. Your oyster has been in tears on the telephone. . . . I'm a fair minded woman. You only be a careful dolphin in your gambolling, or you'll find Virginia's soft crevices lined with hooks.[33]

Still smarting with jealousy when she writes to Vita on 9 October to propose an *Orlando* about 'you and the lusts of your flesh and the lure of your mind', she adds in parentheses: 'heart you have none, who go gallivanting down the lanes with Campbell'. On 14 October, after telling Vita how she is 'engulfed' in making up *Orlando* and longing to see Vita 'in the lamplight, in your emeralds', she warns: 'If you've given yourself to Campbell, I'll have no more to do with you, and so it shall be written, plainly, for all the world to read in Orlando.' When a furious Roy Campbell discovered his wife's affair a month later and an upset Vita turned to Virginia for sympathy, Virginia's response – ' "I hate being bored" I said, of her Campbells & Valery Taylors; & this she thought meant I should be tired of her'[34] – made Vita cry. Vita wrote to Virginia the next morning: 'Darling forgive me my faults. I hate them in myself, and I know you are right. But they are silly surface things. My love for you is absolutely true, vivid and unalterable',[35] and Virginia answered the same night: 'You make me feel such a brute. . . . And I'm half, or 10th, part, jealous, when I see you with the Valeries and the Marys. . . . I'm happy to think you *do* care: for often I seem old, fretful, querulous, difficult (tho' charming) and begin to doubt.'[36]

Far from being a way to create distance in the relationship, *Orlando* was a way to heighten intimacy – not a substitute for physical lovemaking but an extension of it.

III

All this explains why *Orlando* meant so much to Virginia but not why it should mean so much to anyone else besides Vita. In addition to its private inspiration, however, *Orlando* is also a public proclamation – public enough for Virginia's 'suppose' ('suppose Orlando turns out to be Vita') to be weighted with a concern for consequences that would not let her proceed without Vita's permission: 'Suppose, I say, that Sibyl next October says "Theres Virginia gone and written a book about Vita" and Ozzie [Dickinson] chaws with his great chaps and Byard [of Heinemann] guffaws. Shall you mind? Say yes, or No.'[37] Queried by someone mentioned in the preface, in fact, Virginia was quick to apologize ('Ought I to have asked your permission?') and make excuses ('Why is Orlando difficult? It was a joke, I thought. Perhaps a bad one. I don't know. But I enjoyed writing it, and I should enjoy still more answering any questions about it, if put in person').[38] Nor did Vita underestimate what Virginia was asking: 'My God, Virginia, if ever I was thrilled and terrified it is at the prospect of being projected into the shape of Orlando. . . . You have my full permission.'[39]

Challenge provides an illuminating perspective on *Orlando*. Written in 1918 to 1919, in the middle of the affair with Violet, it was published in 1924 – but only in the United States. Although Vita transformed herself and Violet into 'Julian' and 'Eve' and moved the action to a Greek island, both families found the characters so identifiable they had the book withdrawn from publication in England.[40] Virginia had some of the facts wrong in January 1925 when she wrote to Raverat about her sapphic aristocrat's flight to the Tyrol, but the gist of the story had been public scandal. It is no wonder, then, that Vita was 'terrified' when Virginia conceived a book in which 'Sapphism [was] to be suggested', based on a personal involvement that was neither casual nor insignificant and focused on the life of a publicly known, easily identifiable 'pronounced Sapphist'. And it is no wonder Virginia took special care in her strategy: 'I am writing Orlando half in a mock style very clear & plain, so that people will understand every word. But the balance between truth and fantasy must be careful.'[41]

The risks involved come into even sharper focus when they are juxtaposed with another literary project about sapphism taking shape in 1927. Radclyffe ('John') Hall, an acquaintance of Vita's, was a dashing sapphic aristocrat herself and author of five successful novels. She was a member of the PEN club (Poets, Essayists, Editors, and Novelists), to which Vita also belonged (and into whose membership she had tried, unsuccessfully, to lure Virginia at the beginning of their friendship), and in 1927 her fourth novel, *Adam's Breed*, won the Prix Femina, which in 1928 went to Virginia for *To the Lighthouse*.[42] Lady Una Troubridge, who shared John's life until her death in 1943 only two years after Virginia's, records the genesis of *The Well of Loneliness* this way:

> It was after the success of *Adam's Breed* that John came to me one day with unusual gravity and asked for my decision in a serious matter: she had long wanted to write a book on sexual inversion, a novel that would be accessible to the general public who did not have access to technical treatises. At one time she had thought of making it a 'period' book, built around an actual personality of the early nineteenth century. But her instinct had told her that in any case she must postpone such a book until her name was made; until her unusual theme would get a hearing as being the work of an established writer.
>
> It was her absolute conviction that such a book could only be written by a sexual invert, who alone could be qualified by personal knowledge and experience to speak on behalf of a misunderstood and misjudged minority.
>
> It was with this conviction that she came to me, telling me that in her view the time was ripe, and that although the publication of such a book might mean the shipwreck of her whole career, she was fully prepared to make any sacrifice except – the sacrifice of my peace of mind.
>
> She pointed out that in view of our union and of all the years that we had shared a home, what affected her must also affect me and that I would be included in any condemnation. Therefore she placed the decision in my hands and would write or refrain as I should decide.[43]

Although Una's stiff solemnity is poles from Virginia's lively wit, the parallels between the two projects are striking. Like *Orlando*, *The Well* was to be a biography, a psychological 'case history'. Like *Orlando*, it jeopardized personal reputation, and explicit permission was sought and granted. As with *Orlando*, style and strategy were extremely important.

The stakes could not have been more effectively dramatized by what followed. *The Well of Loneliness* appeared in July 1928 – four months after *Orlando* had been completed, three months before it would be published. Almost immediately, it was blasted by the editor of the *Sunday Express* for its 'undiscussable' subject-matter and temporarily banned; in November, despite witnesses prepared to testify on its behalf, among them E.M. Forster, Desmond McCarthy, Julian Huxley, Vita Sackville-West, and Leonard and Virginia Woolf, it was declared obscene and banned permanently.[44]

Although Bloomsbury may have been 'as willing to discuss buggery as it was to discuss Boethius',[45] the general public, it turned out, fell somewhere between the *Sunday Express* editor – 'I would rather give a healthy boy or a healthy girl a phial of prussic acid than this novel'[46] – and Leonard Woolf's mother (as reported by Virginia in a letter to Vanessa):

> I am seventy six – but until I read this book I did not know that such things went on at all. I do not think they do. I have never heard of such things. When I was at school there was nothing like that. . . . But I think much of Miss Radclyffe Hall's book is very beautiful. There is the old horse – that is wonderful – when she has to shoot the old horse. . . . All that about the old horse and the old groom is very beautiful. But the rest of the book I did not care for.[47]

In fact, the literary merits of the book were irrelevant. What was on trial, as Vita and Virginia were both acutely aware, was sapphism. Vita wrote from Potsdam on 31 August 1928:

> I feel very violently about The Well of Loneliness. Not on account of what you call my proclivities; not because I think it is a good book; but really on principle. (I think of writing to Jix [Home Secretary William Joynson-Hicks] suggesting that he should suppress Shakespeare's Sonnets.) Because, you see, even if the W. of L. had been a good book – even if it had been a great book, a real masterpiece, – the result would have been the same. And that is intolerable.[48]

Virginia made the same point in a satiric letter to Quentin Bell on 1 November 1928:

> At this moment our thoughts centre upon Sapphism – we have to uphold the morality of that Well of all that's stagnant and lukewarm and neither one thing or the other; The Well of Loneliness. I'm off to a tea party to discuss our evidence. Leonard and Nessa say I mustn't go into the box, because I should cast a shadow over Bloomsbury. Forgetting where I was I should speak the truth. . . . Most of our friends are trying to evade the witness box; for reasons

you may guess. But they generally put it down to the weak heart of a father, or a cousin who is about to have twins.[49]

The publication of *Orlando* in the midst of this scandal gave Virginia her first public triumph. Leonard Woolf, noting that the book sold twice as many copies in six months as *To the Lighthouse* had in a year, calls it the turning point in her career,[50] and Bell matter-of-factly attributes its success to the sudden 'topicality' of 'the sexual theme'.[51]

IV

But what *is* the 'sexual theme'? *Orlando* is obviously not about the sapphic love of Vita and Virginia, even in a disguised way. The hero/heroine loves men and women over the course of 400 years, but no one of these is the subject. The central relationship is between Orlando and the Biographer, but although Virginia acknowledged the erotic pleasure it gave her to think and write about Vita, there is nothing overtly or even covertly erotic in the relationship between Orlando and the Biographer in the novel. If *Orlando* has any claim to be regarded as a lesbian novel, it is one of the best-kept secrets in literary history, having eluded even those who should be the first to know. Jeanette Foster sees *Orlando* merely as a positive portrait of bisexual experience in general, and even that only 'as it were in the abstract'.[52] In a chapter devoted to the 1920s, 'Radclyffe Hall's "Obscene" Best Seller', Dolores Klaich shrugs off the sexual high jinks of *Orlando* as, 'well, pure fantasy'.[53] Lillian Faderman mentions *Orlando* only as an example of works that 'hide their lesbian subject matter by whimsical devices'.[54]

Like Quentin Bell, Lillian Faderman neglects to identify *Orlando*'s 'lesbian subject matter'. But whimsy was only one part of Virginia's formula. The other part was truth – not just about Orlando's real identity but about sapphism itself, as a fact of life better confronted than repressed as undiscussable or exploited as pornography – the same truth Radclyffe Hall wanted to exemplify with her masculine/feminine heroine, Stephen Gordon, and the same truth Vanessa and Leonard feared Virginia would speak in the witness box and so 'cast a shadow over Bloomsbury'. One reason it has not been recognized perhaps is that recent critical enthusiasm for the concept of androgyny has isolated Woolf from more relevant discussions of masculine and feminine gender traits, namely the 'technical treatises' Radclyffe Hall mentions, by Carl von Westphal, Richard von Krafft-Ebing, and Havelock Ellis – the pioneering nineteenth-century 'sexologists', whose theories about gender and sexual identity supply common denominators for both the literary characters of Orlando and Stephen Gordon and the real-life self-images of Vita Sackville-West and Radcylffe Hall.[55]

Stephen Gordon, of course, exemplifies the classic paradigm. Her masculine tastes and accomplishments, her men's ties and cropped hair, her riding and fencing like a man, her intellectual literary career, her general ease with male activities and prerogatives, coupled with an aversion to female passivity and domesticity, all signal the sexual 'inversion' behind her radical usurpation of male sexual privilege. Although modern readers generally regard Stephen as an extreme stereotype, Hall did not miscalculate the extent to which other late nineteenth- and early twentieth-century lesbians, including the hero/heroine of *Orlando*, perceived themselves in ways similarly dictated by the 'scientific' theories of the day. Vita does not refer to the technical literature on sexual inversion as directly as does Hall, whose heroine literally discovers herself in the pages of Krafft-Ebing,[56] but the secret autobiographical account that she began in 1920, 'in an impersonal and scientific spirit', was intended to supply the kind of intimate information that 'a professional scientist could acquire only after years of study and indirect information, because I have the object of the study always to hand'.[57]

The psychological portrait she constructs confirms the classic characteristics of the 'invert' exemplified by Stephen Gordon. Her childhood is one, like Stephen's, in which she did 'dangerous things. . . . [K]ept my nerves under control, and made a great ideal of being hardy, and as like a boy as possible.'[58] She 'raised' an 'army' and 'commanded amongst the terrorized children of the neighborhood', had a 'khaki suit' but shed 'tears of rage . . . because I was not allowed to have it made with trousers'.[59] Then she gets to Violet and the first experiences of friendship: 'I feel I am doing this part very badly, very confusedly; it is very difficult to do, because I am afraid of taking too seriously what would, normally, have begun and ended as the kind of rather hysterical friendship one conceives in adolescence, but which had in it, I protest, far stronger elements than mere unwholesome hysteria'; 'I want to be frank. I have implied, I think, that men didn't attract me, that I didn't think of them in what is called "that way". Women did.'[60]

What Vita and Hall describe is not the dispassionate balance of masculine and feminine traits that constitutes an androgynous ideal, although androgyny may be involved in the pleasure both associate with male prerogatives, but the dominance of one set of traits over another to generate distinct kinds of erotic attraction. The focus on erotic engagement makes their concerns, in fact, more threatening than mere androgyny, as Vita implies in an 'apologia':

> I am not writing this for fun, but for several reasons which I will explain. (1) As I started by saying, because I want to tell the *entire* truth. (2) Because I know of no truthful record of such a connection – one that is written, I mean, with no desire to appeal to a vicious taste in any possible readers; and (3) because I hold the conviction that as centuries go on, and the sexes become more nearly merged on account of their increasing resemblances, I hold the conviction that such connections will to a very large extent cease

to be regarded as merely unnatural, and will be understood far better, at least in their *intellectual* if not in their physical aspect. . . . I believe that then the psychology of people like myself will be a matter of interest, and I believe it will be recognized that many more people of my type do exist than under the present-day system of hypocrisy is commonly admitted.[61]

Although she speculates that the increasingly androgynous development of the sexes will lead to greater intellectual acceptance of personalities like her own, she entertains no illusions that it will generate greater understanding of the erotic attraction involved.[62] Indeed, even as the 'sexologists' cleared the way for seeing conventional social, legal, and moral sanctions as wrong-headed and inappropriate, they contributed another obstacle when they labelled sexual 'inversion' a pathology.

Neither Vita nor Radclyffe Hall escaped such obstacles in their desire to present sapphic love accurately and honestly. At the end of *The Well*, Stephen imagines herself surrounded by thousands of 'marred reproachful faces' with 'the haunted, melancholy eyes of the invert', and her last words are an agonized prayer for the mere 'right to our exist-ence'. Vita is less melodramatic, but she associates her love for Rosamund and Violet with 'my perverted nature', a 'brutal and hard and savage' side of her that would 'drive over' Harold 'like an armoured chariot', in contrast to the 'seraphic and childlike' side capable of devo-tion through 'years of marriage'. Her awareness of this 'Dr Jekyll and Mr Hyde personality', moreover, she attributes to an 'intuitive psycholo-gist'.[63] The most she expects from a 'spirit of candour' and from 'the progress of the world' is not an end to disapprobation for 'such persona-lities' and 'the connections which result from them' but mere 'recog-nition, if only as an inevitable evil'.[64]

The remarkable achievement of *Orlando* – and Virginia's *public* gift to Vita – is the book's joyous celebration, in the very teeth of society and psychiatry, of just such a personality as Vita's and its attendant 'connections'.

V

In one sense, of course, the fantasy is a dodge. Stephen Gordon learning to fence 'like a man' from ex-Sergeant Smylie might be the tomboy next door – or in your own house. Orlando 'slicing at the head of a Moor which hung from the rafters' never lived next door to anybody except in a Renaissance romance. The passing of centuries and the changing of sexes might cause bafflement in *Orlando*, but moral outrage would seem excessive, even foolish. If one found Stephen Gordon's predilections disturbing, however, every realistic detail in the 500-page novel could help fuel a frenzy of moral outrage – as it did.

In another sense, though, *Orlando*'s fantasy is no dodge at all. Within the realistic parameters of *The Well of Loneliness* a woman who acts like a man can only see herself and be seen by others as a 'freak', 'flawed', 'maimed', 'abnormal', and (the cliché lurks just in the background) 'unnatural'. But Virginia's fantasy annihilates such categories to embrace a more profound truth about gender and sexual identity than Hall's realism can articulate:

> We may take advantage of this pause in the narrative to make certain statements. Orlando had become a woman – there is no denying it. But in every other respect, Orlando remained precisely as he had been. The change of sex, though it altered their future, did nothing whatever to alter their identity. Their faces remained, as their portraits prove, practically the same. His memory – but in future we must, for convention's sake, say 'her' for 'his' and 'she' for 'he' – her memory then, went back through all the events of her past life.[65]

Orlando is not a woman acting 'like' a man: Orlando *is* a man. *And* a woman. The situation admittedly puts a strain on conventional language and thinking, but there is nothing 'unnatural' about it. *Orlando* takes the 'dual personality' Vita described in her diary and transforms the 'brutal' side that loved Rosamund and Violet into the romantic passion of a Renaissance nobleman, while the 'seraphic', 'childlike' side capable of 'years of marriage' becomes the Victorian woman who marries Shelmerdine/Harold Nicolson with all due respect for nineteenth-century standards of female behaviour.

What society or psychiatry might make of the situation is its own problem. Virginia declared her thoughts about psychiatry in a letter to Molly McCarthy in 1924, when the Hogarth Press was publishing the complete works of 'Dr Freud':

> I glance at the proof and read how Mr A.B. threw a bottle of red ink on the sheets of his marriage bed to excuse his impotence to the housemaid, but threw it in the wrong place, which unhinged his wife's mind, – and to this day she pours claret on the dinner table. We could all go on like that for hours; and yet these Germans think it proves something – besides their own gull-like imbecility.[66]

With sly Chaucerian simple-mindedness, Orlando's Biographer makes an equal shambles of the social prejudice and scientific theory surrounding sexual 'inversion'. Noting that Orlando's experience caused her neither pain nor surprise, the Biographer sees no reason for anyone else to be disturbed either:

> Many people . . . holding that such a change of sex is against nature, have been at great pains to prove (1) that Orlando had always been a woman, (2) that Orlando is at this moment a man. Let biologists and psychologists determine. It is enough for us to state

the simple fact; Orlando was a man till the age of thirty; when he became a woman and has remained so ever since.[67]

Orlando's 'condition' is neither the congenital defect that Krafft-Ebing and others described nor the debilitating case of arrested development that Freud suggested, but a simple natural fact.[68]

Marriage, however, whether to a Shelmerdine or a Harold, would seem to indicate bisexuality rather than sapphism. Yet Vita distinguishes quite emphatically in her diary between the 'companionship' that was the main ingredient in her attachment to Harold and the 'passion' she felt for Violet's predecessor, Rosamund Grosvenor, even as she was becoming engaged: 'I wasn't in love with him then – there was Rosamund – but I did like him better than anyone, as a companion and playfellow, and for his brain and his delicious disposition'; 'It never struck me as wrong that I should be more or less engaged to Harold, and at the same time very much in love with Rosamund. The fact is that I regarded Harold far more as a playfellow than in any other light. Our relationship was so fresh, so intellectual, so unphysical, that I never thought of him in that aspect at all.'[69] Fortunately for Vita, Harold was as content with a predominantly 'unphysical' relationship as she was.

The scene in which Orlando meets Shelmerdine begins with a survey of late nineteenth-century pressures to marry, with the human race 'somehow stuck together, couple after couple'.[70] Oppressed by what she sees – 'It was strange – it was distasteful; indeed, there was something in this indissolubility of bodies which was repugnant to her sense of decency and sanitation'[71] – Orlando flees to the moor, breaks an ankle, and resolves to die as 'nature's bride', until she is discovered by a man on horseback:

> 'Madam', the man cried, leaping to the ground, 'you're hurt!'
> 'I'm dead, Sir!' she replied.
>
> A few minutes later, they became engaged.
> The morning after as they sat at breakfast, he told her his name.
> It was Marmaduke Bonthrop Shelmerdine, Esquire.[72]

The brisk style comically mirrors the matter-of-fact courtship Vita describes in her diary.[73] In the instantaneous sympathetic understanding that brings Orlando/Vita and Shelmerdine/Harold together (from which physical attraction is conspicuously absent), Virginia's fantasy again puts the issues of sexual identity in the spotlight: 'an awful suspicion rushed into both their minds simultaneously: "You're a woman, Shel!" she cried. "You're a man, Orlando!" he cried.'[74] In case anyone misses the point, it is repeated:

> 'Are you positive you aren't a man'? he would ask anxiously, and she would echo,
> 'Can it be possible you're not a woman?' and then they must put

it to the proof without more ado. For each was so surprised at the quickness of the other's sympathy, and it was to each such a revelation that a woman could be as tolerant and free-spoken as a man, and a man as strange and subtle as a woman, that they had to put the matter to the proof at once.

And so they would go on *talking* . . .[75]

Critics are quite right to call the relationship with Shelmerdine androgynous, but the primary implications of Orlando's character, as I argue, and the focus of the book have to do with a different kind of relationship.

Once she has become a woman, Orlando continues to don male clothing to seek out the company of her own sex. More important, Sasha, the Russian Princess, haunts the memory of Orlando the woman as powerfully and pervasively as she dominates the passions of Orlando the man. The fantasy that first validates Vita's masculine tendencies by giving her a Renaissance boyhood in which to fall in love with Sasha/ Violet insists with equal rigour on the reality and profundity of a *woman's* love for a woman:

And as all Orlando's loves had been women, now, through the culpable laggardry of the human frame to adapt itself to convention, though she herself was a woman, it was still a woman she loved; and if the consciousness of being of the same sex had any effect at all, it was to quicken and deepen those feelings which she had had as a man. For now a thousand hints and mysteries became plain to her that were then dark. Now, the obscurity, which divides the sexes and lets linger innumerable impurities in its gloom, was removed, and if there is anything in what the poet says about truth and beauty, this affection gained in beauty what it lost in falsity.[76]

Even minor female characters like the prostitutes Nell, Prue, Kitty, and Rose[77] have a serious dignity not bestowed on more prominent male characters. The anomaly of Orlando's marriage to Shelmerdine, in fact, occasions the clearest acknowledgement of theme in the novel:

She was married, true; but if one's husband was always sailing round Cape Horn, was it marriage? If one liked him, was it marriage? If one liked other people, was it marriage? And finally, if one still wished, more than anything in the whole world, to write poetry, was it marriage? She had her doubts.[78]

For she was extremely doubtful whether, if the spirit [of the age] had examined the contents of her mind carefully, it would not have found something highly contraband for which she would have had to pay the full fine. She had only escaped by the skin of her teeth. She had just managed, by some dextrous deference to the spirit of the age, by putting on a ring and finding a man on a moor, by loving nature and being no satirist, cynic, or psychologist – any one of which goods would have been discovered at once – to pass its examination successfully. And she heaved a deep sigh of relief, as, indeed, well she might.[79]

The examination Orlando passes 'by the skin of her teeth' could not be plainer, and *The Well of Loneliness* provided a timely illustration of the 'full fine' one could expect to pay for *not* passing.

VI

But the real triumph is Virginia's. 'You will never succumb to the charms of any of your sex – What an arid garden the world must be for you!' she wrote to Vanessa in 1927 while the ideas for *Orlando* were taking shape.[80] It makes sense that Orlando should follow *To The Lighthouse*, her most deliberately and consciously autobiographical novel, for it is part of the same impulse, so close to her and so potentially explosive that it required jesting – even to herself – to distance it. If it was easier to write, it was also rooted in a less problematic relationship than the one with her parents: the whole autumn in which the work went 'so quick I can't get it typed before lunch' is coloured by the pleasure it gave her.[81] There was urgency, too. 'Launched furtively but with all the more passion' in October,[82] *Orlando* seemed in retrospect, in December 1927, 'extraordinarily unwilled by me but potent in its own right . . . as if it showed everything aside to come into existence'.[83]

Nor is *Orlando* less 'experimental' than the novel that preceded it. If *To the Lighthouse* seemed to require 'a new name . . . to supplant "novel". A new ____ by Virginia Woolf. But what? Elegy?'[84] *Orlando*, she boasted, would 'revolutionise biography in a night'.[85] There is a clue to what she meant as early as November 1926, when she wondered whether the method of *To the Lighthouse* could now serve a different use – such as:

> some semi mystic very profound life of a woman, which shall all be told on one occasion; & time shall be utterly obliterated; future shall somehow blossom out of the past. One incident – say the fall of a flower – might contain it. My theory being that the actual event practically does not exist – nor time either.[86]

Orlando's Biographer 'untwine[s] and twist[s] again' – through four hundred years of family, cultural, social, and intellectual history – the 'odd, incongruous strands' of Vita's psyche,[87] so that ordinary time and actual events, the mainstays of conventional biography (witness critical efforts to pin down how many times Vita and Virginia went to bed, how many months, years, the 'affair' lasted),[88] have least to do with the more significant realities of personal identity Virginia was intent on capturing. Her success is attested by Harold in a letter from Berlin on 15 October

1928: 'It really *is* Vita – her puzzled concentration, her absent-minded tenderness. . . . She strides magnificent and clumsy through 350 years.'[89]

But Leonard's praise suggests more: 'in some ways better than The Lighthouse; about more interesting things, & with more attachment to life, & larger'. The single 'incident' that 'contains' Orlando's life in this revolutionary biography, so that the future really does 'somehow blossom out of the past' (although the 'actual event practically does not exist – nor time either'), is much more interesting than her original notion of 'the fall of a flower' and much larger than Vita herself. The 'event', of course, is Orlando's change of sex, which allows Virginia to place herself and her readers at the very core of Orlando's sapphic 'nature' – and to see that it is good. Also *funny*. As funny in its collisions with conventional thinking and acting as Rosalind's excursion into male privilege is in *As You Like It*, where the Forest of Arden, like Virginia's fantasy, obliterates the significance of ordinary time and actual events, where the boundaries of sexual identities are blurred beyond conventional sorting out, where a male actor playing a woman playing a man playing a woman tries on and casts off and tries on again all the stereotypical poses and conventional gestures of Petrarchan love, where the prejudices and injustices of a more strictly ordered world are temporarily held at bay, and where laughter is the route to wisdom and compassion. The humour of *Orlando*, like the humour of Shakespearean comedy, runs the gamut from slapstick to wit, but with one important difference. While Shakespeare's Orlando, like everyone else in the play, is eclipsed by Rosalind's complex passions and nimble wit, Virginia's Orlando and her Biographer exist in complementary balance with each other: Orlando all beauty, passion, action; her Biographer – now Keatsian, now Chaucerian, now Shakespearean – all voice and eloquence.

'If I saw you would you kiss me? If I were in bed would you – I'm rather excited about *Orlando* tonight: have been lying by the fire and making up the last chapter.' Virginia wrote *Orlando* as an act of love – identified Vita by name in the dedication – and, 'very clear & plain, so that people will understand every word', celebrated her sapphic nature with an insider's knowledge for 329 exuberant pages. 'That book is the cleanest thing I know', Harold wrote from Berlin, as he told Vita how the proprietor of a bar there had assaulted him with pornographic photographs and how he had gone off 'in a dudgeon and read a chapter of Orlando to cleanse [his] mind'.[90] Its impact on Vita, naturally, was stronger:

> My darling,
>   I am in no fit state to write to you. . . . I can only tell you that I am really shaken, which may seem to you useless and silly, but which is really a greater tribute than pages of calm appreciation, – and then after all it does touch me so personally, and I don't know what to

say about that either, only that I feel like one of those wax figures in a shop window, on which you have hung a robe stitched with jewels. It is like being alone in a dark room with a treasure chest full of rubies and nuggets and brocades. Darling, I don't know and scarcely even like to write, so overwhelmed am I, how you could have hung so splendid a garment on so poor a peg. Really this isn't false humility; *really* it isn't. I can't write about that part of it, though, much less ever tell you verbally.[91]

Vita had attempted, both in *Challenge* and in her diary, to write about sapphic love honestly and sympathetically, but *Challenge* had been suppressed despite her concealment of its erotic implications, and the diary remained secret. It is not surprising that she felt 'violently' about *The Well of Loneliness*, even though it was not a great or even very good book, even though in its pitch for tolerance it presented its heroine as an unfortunate and unwilling freak of nature. What Virginia gave Vita in the book that started as a joke and continued seriously until it shoved everything else out of the way is the first positive, and still unsurpassed, sapphic portrait in literature. Vita's response – light-years from Stephen's discovery of herself in the pages of Krafft-Ebing – goes right to the heart of the achievement: 'you have invented a new form of Narcissism, – I confess, – I am in love with Orlando – this is a complication I had not foreseen.'[92]

8 Sylvia Townsend Warner and the counterplot of lesbian fiction

Terry Castle

What is a lesbian fiction? According to what we might call the 'Queen Victoria Principle' of cultural analysis, no such entity, of course, should even exist. In 1885, after the passage of the Criminal Law Amendment Act outlawing homosexual acts in Great Britain, it was pointed out to Queen Victoria that the amendment only dealt with 'acts of gross indecency' between men; women, alas, were not covered. The queen responded – as if to a *non sequitur* – 'No woman would ever do that.' Desire between men was conceivable, indeed could be pictured vividly enough to require policing. Desire between women was not.[1] The love of woman for woman, along with whatever 'indecency' it might entail, simply could not be represented. According to this primal (il)logic, it would follow, therefore, that 'lesbian fiction' is also inconceivable: a non-concept, a nothingness, a gap in the meaning of things – anything but a story there to be read.

We pride ourselves nowadays on having made some intellectual advances on the Victorian position. We know that lesbian fiction, like lesbianism itself, exists; we may even be able to name a few celebrated (or reviled) lesbian novels – *The Well of Loneliness*, *Nightwood*, *Orlando*, *The Desert of the Heart*, *The Female Man*, and so on. And yet on what theoretical basis do we make such denominations? What characteristics inform our definition of 'lesbian fiction' itself? Is a 'lesbian novel' simply any narrative depicting sexual relations between women? If this were the case, then any number of works by male writers, including Diderot's *La Religieuse*, for example, or some of the other pornographic or semi-pornographic texts of male voyeurism, would fall under the rubric of lesbian fiction. Yet this does not feel exactly right. Would a lesbian novel be a novel, then, written by a lesbian? This can't be the case, or certain of Willa Cather's novels, say, or Marguerite Yourcenar's, would have to be classed as lesbian novels, when it is not clear that they really are. 'A novel written by a lesbian depicting sexual relations between women' might come closer, but relies too heavily on the opacities of biography and eros, and lacks a certain psychic and political specificity.

The concept of 'lesbian fiction', one has to conclude, remains some-

128

what undertheorized. It remains undertheorized, paradoxically, even in those places where one might expect to see it brought under the most intense scrutiny – in critical studies specifically dealing with the subject of homosexual desire in fiction. To date the most provocative and influential study on this theme has undoubtedly been Eve Kosofsky Sedgwick's *Between Men: English Literature and Male Homosocial Desire* (1985). This brilliant meditation on 'homosociality' in literature, which Sedgwick wrote, as she recounts in her introduction, out of a specifically 'antihomophobic and feminist' position, can justly be said to have galvanized the world of gay literary studies, at least as far as that world is presently constituted in the United States.[2]

And yet how is the question of lesbian fiction handled in this book? The answer, simply, is not at all. To be fair to Sedgwick, she is aware of the omission and candidly acknowledges it in her introduction. 'The absence of lesbianism from the book,' she writes, 'was an early and, I think, necessary decision, since my argument is structured around the distinctive relation of the male homosocial spectrum to the transmission of unequally distributed power relations.'[3] In other words, the very terms of Sedgwick's argument do not allow for any consideration of lesbian desire or its representation. But how can this be so?

Put in the most basic form, Sedgwick's thesis (which will already be familiar to many readers) is that English literature, at least since the late seventeenth century, has been structured by what she calls the 'erotic triangle' of male homosocial desire. Drawing on the work of René Girard, Claude Lévi-Strauss, and especially Gayle Rubin, whose classic feminist essay, 'The Traffic in Women', underpins much of the thinking here, Sedgwick argues that just as patriarchal culture has traditionally been organized around a ritualized 'traffic' in women – the legal, economic, religious, and sexual exchange of women between men (as in the cherished institutions of heterosexual love and marriage) – so the fictions produced within patriarchal culture have tended to mimic, or represent, the same triangular structure. English literature is 'homosocial', according to Sedgwick, to the extent that its hidden subject has always been male bonding – the bonding mediated 'between' two men through, around, or over, the body and soul of a woman. In fiction as in life, the 'normative man', she writes, uses a woman 'as a "conduit of a relationship" in which the true *partner* is a man' (p. 26).

In a series of bravura readings Sedgwick traces the persistence of the male–female–male 'homosocial paradigm' in English writing from Shakespeare and Wycherley through the novels of Sterne, Hogg, Thackeray, Eliot, and Dickens. What she discovers along the way is that homosociality also has its discontents. These arise, not unexpectedly, from the ambiguous relationship between homo*sociality* and homo*sexuality*. The system of male domination, according to Sedgwick, depends on the maintenance of highly charged attachments between men. 'It is crucial to every aspect of social structure within the exchange-of-women framework,' she writes, 'that heavily freighted bonds between men exist, as the backbone of social form or forms' (p. 86). At the same time, she points out, when these male–male attachments become *too* freighted – that is, explicitly sexual – the result is an ideological contradiction of potentially crippling magnitude. If a man can become 'like' a woman in the act of homosexual intercourse, what is to distinguish such a man from any woman? By doing away with the 'female middle term' and blurring the putative difference between 'male' and 'female', the overt eroticization of male bonds undermines the very conceptual distinction on which modern patriarchy is founded.

How then to separate 'functional' male bonds – those which bolster the structure of male domination – from those which weaken it? In Sedgwick's insinuating rereading of patriarchal cultural history, litera-ture itself has been a primary means of resolving, or of attempting to resolve, this potentially disruptive ideological problem. Its solution has been to emphasize, with an almost paranoiac insistence, the necessity of triangulation itself – of preserving the male–female–male 'erotic para-digm' precisely as a way of fending off the destabilizing threat of male homosexuality. The plots of classic English and American fiction, according to Sedgwick, are blatantly, often violently, homophobic: in Hogg's *Confessions of a Justified Sinner*, or Dickens's *Our Mutual Friend* – to take two of her more memorable examples – the homoerotic desire of man for man is shown to lead, as if by Gothic compulsion, to morbidity, persecution, mania, and murder. By activating what she calls the stan-dard plot mechanisms of 'homosexual panic', these novels, along with many others, reveal themselves as none too subtly disguised briefs on behalf of the mediated eros of male homosocial desire. The triangular male–female–male figure returns at the conclusion of each story – triumphantly reinstalled – as a sign both of normative (namely, hetero-sexual) male bonding and of a remobilization of patriarchal control.

The obsession with vindicating male homosociality at the expense of male homosexuality has not been confined, writes Sedgwick, to the works of the English literary tradition. Indeed, in the most ambitious formulation of her argument, she asserts that the entire European literary canon since the Renaissance might be considered a massively elaborated (and ultimately coercive) statement on male bonding. What makes a literary work 'canonical', in her view, is precisely in fact the degree of its absorption in the issue of male homosociality. She makes this provocative claim in a crucial passage – once again from the intro-duction – in which she explains the somewhat idiosyncratic assortment of texts to which individual chapters of *Between Men* are dedicated:

> The choices I have made of texts through which to embody the argument of the book are specifically *not* meant to begin to deli-neate a separate male-homosocial literary canon. In fact, it will be

essential to my argument to claim that the European canon as it exists is already such a canon, and most so when it is most hetero-sexual . . . I have simply chosen texts at pleasure from within or alongside the English canon that represented particularly interest-ing interpretive problems, or particularly symptomatic historical and ideological modes, for understanding the politics of male homosociality. (p. 17)

Literature canonizes the subject of male homosociality; in return, it would seem, the subject of male homosociality canonizes the work of literature.

Within such a totalizing scheme, with its insistent focus on relations 'between men', what place might there be for relations between women? Sedgwick is aware, or at least half-aware, that her theory in some way fails 'to do justice to women's own powers, bonds, and struggles' (p. 18). She freely acknowledges that her reluctance to distinguish between what she calls 'ideologizing' and 'de-ideologizing' narratives may have led her to present 'the "canonical" cultural discourse in an excessively protean and inescapable . . . form'. Yet at the same time she makes it clear that she can offer little in the way of comment on 'women's own cultural resources of resistance, adaptation, revision, and survival'. She is content to send out a somewhat perfunctory appeal to her readers for 'better analyses of the relations between female-homosocial and male-homosocial structures' (p. 18).

If the subject of female bonding sets up a kind of intellectual or emotional 'blockage' in Sedgwick's argument, the specialized form of female bonding represented by lesbianism seems to provoke in her, interestingly enough, even deeper resistance. In the one or two some-what strained paragraphs of *Between Men* that Sedgwick *does* devote to women's bonds, she more or less summarily dismisses 'lesbianism' as a useful category of analysis. In contrast to the spectacularly polarized arrangement she finds in the realm of male desire, she can see no real cultural or ideological distinction, in the case of women, between homo-sociality and homosexuality:

The diacritical opposition between the 'homosocial' and the 'homo-sexual' seems to be much less thorough and dichotomous for women, in our society, than for men. At this particular historical moment, an intelligible continuum of aims, emotions, and valu-ations links lesbianism with the other forms of women's attention to women: the bond of mother and daughter, for instance, the bond of sister and sister, women's friendship, 'networking', and the active struggles of feminism. The continuum is crisscrossed with deep discontinuities – with much homophobia, with conflicts of race and class – but its intelligibility seems now a matter of simple common sense. However agonistic the politics, however conflicted

the feelings, it seems at this moment to make an obvious kind of
sense to say that women in our society who love women, women
who teach, study, nurture, suckle, write about, march for, vote for,
give jobs to, or otherwise promote the interests of other women,
are pursuing congruent and closely related activities. (pp. 2–3)

Lesbians, defined here, with telling vagueness, only as 'women who love
women', are really no different, Sedgwick seems to imply, from 'women
promoting the interests of other women'. Their way of bonding is so
'congruent' with that of other women, it turns out, that one need no
longer call it homosexual. 'The adjective "homosocial" as applied to
women's bond', she concludes, *'need not be pointedly dichotomized as against
"homosexual"; it can intelligibly denominate the entire continuum'* (p. 3; my
emphasis). By a disarming sleight of phrase, an entire category of
women – lesbians – is lost to view.

In the face of these rhetorically tortured and – for Sedgwick – unchar-
acteristically sentimental passages, one's immediate impulse may be to
remark, somewhat uncharitably, that she has not 'gotten the point', so to
speak, of pointedly dichotomizing lesbian from straight existence. What
may appear 'intelligible' or 'simple common sense' to a non-lesbian critic
will hardly seem quite so simple to any female reader who has ever
attempted to walk down a city street holding hands with, let alone kissing
or embracing, another woman. The homosexual panic elicited by
women publicly signalling their sexual interest in one another continues,
alas, even 'at this particular historical moment', to be just as virulent as
that inspired by male homosexuality, if not more so.[4] To obscure the fact
that lesbians are women who have sex with each other – and that this is
not exactly the same, in the eyes of society, as voting for women or giving
them jobs – is, in essence, not to acknowledge the separate peril and
pleasure of lesbian existence.

Are we then simply to blame Sedgwick for succumbing, albeit belatedly, to the Queen Victoria Principle? I think not – for what I am calling,
perhaps too tendentiously, the 'blockage' in her theory, is intimately
related, paradoxically, to its strength. It is precisely because Sedgwick
has recognized so clearly the canonical power of *male–male* desire – and
has described so well its shaping role in the plots of eighteenth- and
nineteenth-century English and American literature – that she does not
'get the point' of *female–female* desire. For to do so would mean undoing,
if only imaginatively, the very structure she is elsewhere at such pains to
elaborate: the figure of the male homosocial triangle itself.

To theorize about female–female desire, I would like to suggest, is
precisely to envision the taking apart of this supposedly intractable
patriarchal structure. Female bonding, at least hypothetically, destabilizes the 'canonical' triangular arrangement of male desire, is an affront
to it, and ultimately – in the radical form of lesbian bonding – displaces it
entirely. Even Sedgwick's own geometrical model intimates as much. As

the figure below suggests, the male–female–male erotic triangle remains stable only as long as its single female term is unrelated to any other female term. Once two female terms are conjoined in space, however, an alternative structure comes into being, a female–male–female triangle, in which one of the male terms from the original triangle now occupies the 'in between' or subjugated position of the mediator (see Figure 1).

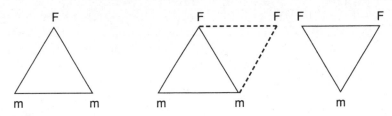

Figure 1

Within this new *female* homosocial structure, the possibility of male bonding is radically suppressed: for the male term is now isolated, just as the female term was in the male homosocial structure.

But one can go still further. In the original male–female–male configuration, we may recollect, the relationship between the dominant male terms was not static. Indeed, this was the inherent problem in the structure from the patriarchal perspective: that the two male terms might hook up directly, so to speak, replacing the heterosexual with an explicitly homosexual dyad. Yet exactly the same dynamism is characteristic of the female homosocial triangle. In the most radical transformation of female bonding – i.e. from homosocial to *lesbian* bonding – the two female terms indeed merge and the male term drops out. At this point, it is safe to say, not only is male bonding suppressed, it has become impossible – there being no male terms left to bond.

A pleasing elaboration of the Sedgwickian model, perhaps – but does it have any literary applications? If we restrict ourselves, as Sedgwick herself does, to the canon of eighteenth- and nineteenth-century English and American fiction, the answer would have to be no, or not really. Indeed, one might easily argue that just as the major works of realistic fiction from this period constitute a brief against male homosexuality (Sedgwick's point), so they also constitute, even more blatantly, a brief against female homosociality. Even in works in which female homosocial bonds are depicted, these bonds are inevitably shown giving way to the power of male homosocial triangulation. In Charlotte Brontë's *Shirley*, for example, a novel which explicitly thematizes the conflict between male and female bonding, the original female homosocial bond between Shirley Keeldar and Caroline Helstone (a bond triangulated through the character of the mill owner Robert Moore) is replaced at the end of the novel by not just one, but two interlocking male homosocial triangles, symbolized in the marriages of Robert with Caroline and of Robert's brother Louis with Shirley. True, *Shirley* represents an unusually tormented and ambivalent version of the male homosocial plot: but even Brontë, like other Victorian novelists, gives way in the end to the force of fictional and ideological convention.[5]

But what if we turn our attention to twentieth-century writing? Are there any contemporary novels that undo the seemingly compulsory plot of male homosocial desire? It will come as no surprise that I am about to invoke such a work, and that I propose to denominate it, without further ado, an exemplary 'lesbian fiction'. The work I have in mind is Sylvia Townsend Warner's 1936 *Summer Will Show*, an historical fiction set in rural Dorset and Paris during the revolution of 1848. What makes this novel paradigmatically 'lesbian', in my view, is not simply that it depicts a sexual relationship between two women, but that it so clearly, indeed almost schematically, figures this relationship as a breakup of the supposedly 'canonical' male–female–male erotic triangle. As I shall try to demonstrate in what follows, it is exactly this kind of subverted triangulation, or erotic 'counterplotting', that is in fact characteristic of lesbian novels in general.

Summer Will Show is not, I realize, a well-known piece of fiction – indeed quite the opposite. Even among Townsend Warner devotees it is still a relatively unfamiliar work, despite a Virago reprint in 1987. Warner's earlier novel *Lolly Willowes* (1926) remains generally better known; later works, such as the novel *The Corner That Held Them* (1948), the biography of T. H. White (1967), and the short story collection *The Kingdoms of Elfin* (1977) have attracted more critical attention.[6] What notice *Summer Will Show* has received has tended to be condescending in nature: because Townsend Warner wrote the novel during the period of her most passionate involvement with the British Communist Party and intended it in part as an allegory of the Spanish Civil War, it has often been dismissed as a 'Marxist novel' or leftist period piece. While not entirely an *un*read work of modern English fiction, *Summer Will Show* is at the very least an *under*read one.

Yet some of the resistance the work has met with must also have to do, one suspects, with its love story, which challenges so spectacularly the rigidly heterosexual conventions of classic English and American fiction. This story begins deceptively simply, in a seemingly recognizable literary landscape – that of nineteenth-century fiction itself. The tall, fair-haired heroine, Sophia Willoughby, is the only daughter of wealthy landed gentry in Dorset, the heiress of Blandamer House (in which she resides), and the wife of a feckless husband, Frederick, who, after marrying her for her money and fathering her two small children, has abandoned her and taken a mistress in Paris. At the start of the novel, Sophia is walking with her children, a boy and a girl, on a hot summer's day to the lime-kiln on the estate, in the hope that by subjecting them to a traditional remedy – lime-kiln fumes – she can cure them of the whooping cough they have both contracted.

Already in these opening pages, given over to Sophia's reveries on the way to the lime-kiln, we have a sense of her proud, powerful, yet troubled nature: like another Gwendolen Harleth or even a new Emma Bovary, she broods over her unhappy marriage and yearns ambiguously for 'something decisive', a new kind of fulfilment, some 'moment when she should exercise her authority' (p. 11).[7] While devoted to her children, she also feels constricted by them and infuriated at her husband for leaving them entirely to her care. As for Frederick himself, she harbours no lingering romantic illusions there, only 'icy disdain', mixed with a sense of sexual grievance. It is not so much that she is jealous – their marriage has been devoid of passion – but that she resents his freedom and his predictably chosen 'bohemian' mistress:

> For even to Dorset the name of Minna Lemuel had made its way. Had the husband of Mrs. Willoughby chosen no other end than to be scandalous, he could not have chosen better. A byword, half actress, half strumpet; a Jewess; a nonsensical creature bedizened with airs of prophecy, who trailed across Europe with a tag-rag of poets, revolutionaries, musicians and circus-riders snuffing at her heels, like an escaped bitch with a procession of mongrels after her; and ugly; and old, as old as Frederick or older – this was the woman whom Frederick had elected to fall in love with, joining in the tag-rag procession, and not even king in that outrageous court, not even able to dismiss the mongrels, and take the creature into keeping. (p. 31)

At the same time, however, Sophia feels an odd gratitude to the other woman: thanks to Minna, Sophia reminds herself, she is 'a mother, and a landowner; but fortunately, she need no longer be counted among the wives' (p. 20).

All this is to change as a result of the lime-kiln visit itself. With Sophia looking on, the lime-kiln keeper – a silent, frightening-looking man with sores on his arms – suspends each of the children over the kiln. Though terrified, they inhale the fumes and Sophia takes them home. In the next few weeks her attention is distracted by the arrival of her nephew Caspar, the illegitimate mulatto child of an uncle in the West Indies. At her uncle's request, she takes Caspar to Cornwall to place him in a boarding-school. Returning home, she finds her own children mortally ill: the lime-kiln keeper was in fact carrying smallpox and has infected both children. Sophia delays writing to her husband to inform him; yet Frederick comes anyway, having been recalled by a letter written by the doctor who is attending the children.

At once Sophia senses a subtle change in her husband, a mystifying new refinement, which she attributes – balefully, yet also with growing curiosity – to the influence of his unseen mistress. Listening to him repeat the words '*Ma fleur*' over his dying daughter's sickbed, it seems to Sophia as if a stranger were speaking through him: someone possessed of 'a deep sophistication in sorrow'. The intrusive cadence, she reminds herself angrily, must be copied from 'that Minna's Jewish contralto'. Yet afterwards, when both of the children are dead and Frederick has gone back to Paris, Sophia finds herself haunted by a memory of the voice – one that seems, 'according to her mood, an enigma, a nettle-sting, a caress' (p. 83).

With the death of Sophia's children, the crucial action of the novel commences. Distraught, grief-stricken, yet also peculiarly obsessed with her husband's other life, Sophia decides to seek him out in Paris, for the purpose (she tells herself) of forcing him to give her more children. Yet, as if driven by more mysterious urgings, she finds herself, on the very evening of her arrival, at the apartment on the Rue de la Carabine where Minna holds her salon. Entering the apartment unobserved, Sophia joins the crowd of guests (including Frederick himself) who are listening to their hostess tell a story.

The story, which is presented as an embedded narrative, is a hypnotic account of Minna's childhood in Eastern Europe – of the pogrom in which her parents were killed, of her own escape from the murderers, and of her eventual rescue by a vagrant musician. The experience of persecution has made her an artist, a story teller, a romantic visionary, and a political revolutionary. As Sophia listens, seemingly mesmerized by the Jewish woman's charismatic 'siren voice', she forgets entirely about Frederick and the putative reason why she has come. Suddenly the tale is interrupted: barricades are being put up outside in the streets; the first skirmishes of what will become the February Revolution are about to begin. Minna's listeners, mainly artists and intellectuals who support the revolt, depart, along with Frederick, who has not yet seen his wife. And Sophia, still as if under a spell, finds herself alone in the room with Minna.

She is utterly, heart-stoppingly, captivated. Not by Minna's beauty – for Frederick's mistress is a small, dark, and sallow woman, with 'a slowly flickering glance' and 'large supple hands' that seem to 'caress themselves together in the very gesture of her thought' (p. 127). Yet something in this very look, 'sombre and attentive', alive with tenderness and recognition, ineluctably draws Sophia to her. ('I cannot understand,' Sophia finds herself thinking, 'what Frederick could see in you. But *I* can see a great deal' (p. 154).) Minna in turn seems equally delighted with her lover's wife. Together they look out on the barricades: Frederick is below and now sees Sophia; he is piqued when she refuses his offer of a cab. Minna also ignores him, so he leaves. Minna then confides in Sophia her hopes for the success of the insurrection. Sophia, entranced yet also exhausted, falls asleep on Minna's sofa. When she awakens the next day her hostess is sitting beside her. Inspired by the strange 'ardour' of the Jewish woman's attention, the normally reticent Sophia suddenly finds herself overcome by an urge to recount the story of *her* own life. As if freed from an invisible bondage, she finds herself talking for hours. When Frederick returns that afternoon, he is momentarily 'felled' to discover his wife and mistress 'seated together on the pink sofa, knit into this fathomless intimacy, and turning from it to entertain him with an identical patient politeness'. For 'neither woman, absorbed in this extraordinary colloquy, had expressed by word or sign the slightest consciousness that there was anything unusual about it' (p. 157).

Nor, might it be said, does Townsend Warner. The attraction between Sophia and Minna is treated, if anything, as a perfectly natural elaboration of the wife–mistress situation. The two women, it is true, separate for several weeks, in part because Sophia is afraid of the depth – and complication – of her new attachment. While the political turmoil in the city grows, she stays with her wealthy, superannuated French aunt, Léocadie, who tries to reconcile her with Frederick. Yet she is drawn back into Minna's orbit soon enough, when she hears that Minna has given away almost all of her money to the striking workers and is destitute. Outraged with Frederick for 'casting off' his mistress (which is how Sophia describes the situation to herself), she determines to fulfil his 'obligations' herself. She returns to the now-shabby apartment on the Rue de la Carabine, and finding Minna weak with cold and hunger, decides to stay and care for her. As her absorption in the other woman grows – and is reciprocated – Sophia gradually feels her old identity, that of the heiress of Blandamer, slipping away. As if 'by some extraordinary enchantment', she is inexorably caught up in Minna's world and in the revolutionary activity in which Minna is involved.

Meanwhile Frederick, incensed by the alliance between his wife and his (now) ex-mistress, cuts off Sophia's allowance in order to force her to return to him. Yet his machinations serve only to intensify – indeed to eroticize – the intimacy between the two women. When Sophia tells her friend that Frederick has told the bank not to honour her signature 'as he is entitled to do being my husband', they suddenly comprehend their desire for what it is:

> 'You will stay? You must, if only to gall him.'
> 'I don't think that much of a reason.'
> 'But you will stay?'
> 'I will stay if you wish it.'
> It seemed to her that the words fell cold and glum as ice-pellets. Only beneath the crust of thought did her being assent as by right to that flush of pleasure, that triumphant cry.
> 'But of course', said Minna a few hours later, thoughtfully licking the last oyster shell, 'we must be practical.' (p. 274)

Townsend Warner, to be sure, renders the scene of their passionate coming together elliptically – with only a cry (and an oyster) to suggest the moment of consummation – yet the meaning is clear: Sophia has severed all ties with the past – with her husband, her class, and with sexual convention itself.

In the final section of the novel spring gives way to summer; the popular insurrection, dormant for several months, flares once again. Inspired by her new-found love for Minna, Sophia throws herself into political activity, becoming a courier for a group of communists who are collecting weapons in preparation for open civil war. Her last contact with her husband comes about when her nephew Caspar suddenly turns up in Paris, alienated and sullen, having run away from the school in Cornwall: Sophia is forced to ask Frederick for money to pay for the youth's schooling in Paris. Without her knowledge Frederick, who now cynically supports the government, instead buys Caspar a place in the Gardes Mobiles, the force opposing the now-imminent June rebellion.

Returning from one of her courier missions, Sophia finds that street fighting has begun in the neighbourhood around the Rue de la Carabine. Minna is already on the barricades. Together they join in the battle, loading and reloading the workers' rifles. The Gardes Mobiles launch an attack on the barricade and Sophia, to her surprise, recognizes Caspar in their midst. He plunges a bayonet into Minna, who falls, apparently mortally wounded. Sophia shoots Caspar in retaliation, but is herself captured and taken away with some other prisoners to be executed, only to be freed the next day because she is a woman. She searches frantically for Minna but cannot discover if she is alive or dead. The revolt has been put down and the workers' hopes seemingly destroyed. Returning to Minna's apartment, yet still harbouring a hope that her lover will return, Sophia opens one of the pamphlets that she had been delivering the previous day. It is Marx's *Communist Manifesto*. As she settles down to read – exhausted but also arrested by its powerful opening words – the novel comes ambiguously to an end.

I will return to this somewhat curious denouement in a moment: I would like to draw attention first to the more obviously revisionist aspects of Townsend Warner's narrative. For *Summer Will Show* – as I hope even my highly compressed account of its characters and incidents will have indicated – is a work obsessed with 'revising' on a number of counts. In the most literal sense the novel is a kind of revisionist fantasia: in recounting the story of her pseudo-Victorian heroine, Sophia Willoughby, Townsend Warner constantly pastiches – yet also rewrites – Victorian fiction itself. The opening scene at the lime-kiln, for example, both recalls and traduces the episode in *Great Expectations* in which Pip is dangled over a lime-kiln by the infamous Orlick: the 'great expectations' here belong, ironically, to the observer, Sophia herself. The early episodes involving the mulatto Caspar and the uncle in the West Indies likewise rework and subvert elements from *Wuthering Heights* and *Jane Eyre*. After Sophia's arrival in Paris, a curiously erotic scene in which Minna shows her her duelling pistols (pp. 154–6) is an almost direct parody of a similar moment in *Shirley*: Minna's guns are about to be given up to the striking workers of Paris; the guns that Caroline Helstone shows to Shirley Keeldar are their protection *against* the striking workers of Briarfield. Minna herself is a kind of revolutionary variant on a George Eliot heroine. Her Jewishness and political radicalism bring to mind characters and situations from *Daniel Deronda* and *Felix Holt*; her appearance – and passionate intelligence – may be modelled on Eliot's own. Yet she is far more deviant than any Eliot heroine is ever allowed to be. Tellingly, her very name appears to originate in the famous passage in *The Mill on the Floss* in which Maggie Tulliver declares her wish to 'avenge' all the unfortunate dark-haired heroines of English literature – 'Rebecca, and Flora MacIvor, and Minna, and all the rest of the dark unhappy ones.'[8] Maggie's Minna is the hapless heroine of Sir Walter Scott's *The Pirate*, abandoned by her lover on a frigid Scottish beach. By contrast, Townsend Warner's Minna – with her freedom from convention, her sexual charisma and survivor's instinct – is at once a satirical rewrite of the first Minna and a more resilient version of Maggie herself.

But it is not only English fiction that Townsend Warner is rewriting in *Summer Will Show*. In a somewhat tongue-in-cheek note composed in the 1960s, she revealed that in order to write the book she 're-read Berlioz's *Mémoires*, and with an effort put the French novelists out of my mind'.[9] Berlioz is certainly there, but so too are the French novelists. The scenes at Minna's Parisian salon have the flavour of Staël and Hugo, as well as of Stendhal and Balzac; Sophia's right-wing aunt Léocadie, along with her egregious confessor Père Hyacinthe, are straight out of *La Comédie humaine*. But it is Flaubert, obviously, and *his* novel of 1848, that Townsend Warner is most deeply conscious of displacing. Anyone who doubts the subterranean importance of *L'Education sentimentale* to *Summer Will Show* need only consider the name Frédéric – or Frederick – and the parodistic relationship that exists between Flaubert's anti-hero, Frédéric Moreau, and Townsend Warner's comic villain, Frederick Willoughby.[10]

To invoke Flaubert's masterpiece, however, is also to return – with a vengeance – to the Sedgwickian issue of erotic triangulation. For what is *L'Education sentimentale* if not a classic work, in Sedgwick's terms, of male homosocial bonding? Flaubert's Frédéric, we recall, acts out his emotional obsession with his friend Arnoux by falling in love first with Arnoux's wife, then with his mistress. Townsend Warner's Frederick, by contrast, not only has no male friend, his wife and his mistress fall in love with each other. In the very act of revising Flaubert – of substituting her own profoundly 'anti-canonical' fiction in place of his own – Townsend

Warner also revises the plot of male homosocial desire. Indeed, all of her revisionist gestures can, I think, be linked with this same imaginative impulse: the desire to plot *against* the seemingly indestructible hetero-sexual narrative of classic European fiction.

This work of counterplotting can best be figured, as I suggested at the outset, as a kind of dismantling or displacement of the male homosocial triangle itself. Granted, at the beginning of *Summer Will Show*, the hoary Sedgwickian structure still seems firmly in place: Sophia is more or less mired in the 'in between' position that patriarchal society demands of her. As the only heiress of Blandamer, 'the point advancing on the future, as it were, of that magnificent triangle in which Mr. and Mrs. Aspen of Blandamer House, Dorset, England, made up the other two apices' (p. 3), she has functioned, we are led to deduce, as the social mediator between her own father, who has been forced to give her up in marriage in order to perpetuate the Aspen family line, and Frederick, the son-in-law, who has enriched himself by allying himself with the Aspen patrimony.

Yet instabilities in this classic male–female–male triad soon become apparent. The deaths of Sophia's children are the first sign of a genera-lized weakening of male homosocial bonds; these deaths, we realize, are not just a transforming loss for Sophia, but for Frederick also, who loses, through them, his only remaining biological and symbolic connection to Sophia's dead father, his partner in the novel's original homosocial triangle. Significantly, perhaps, it is the son who is the first of the children to die: in a way that prefigures the symbolic action of the novel as a whole, the patrilineal triangle of father–mother–son here disap-pears, leaving only a female–male–female triangle, composed of Sophia, Frederick, and their daughter. Even at this early stage, one might argue, Townsend Warner represents the female-dominant triangle as 'stronger', or in some sense more durable, than the male-dominant one.

Yet other episodes in the first part of the novel suggest a disinte-gration of male homosocial structures. When Sophia delays writing to Frederick during the children's illness, her doctor, thinking the absence of her husband a scandal, writes to him without her knowledge. The letter is intercepted by the doctor's young wife, who brings it to Sophia and offers to destroy it. 'Why should all this be done behind your back?' exclaims the outraged Mrs Hervey, 'what right have they to interfere, to discuss and plot, and settle what they think best to be done? As if, whatever happened, you could not stand alone, and judge for yourself! As if you needed a man!' (p. 72). Admittedly, Sophia decides in the end to let the letter be sent, but the intimation here of an almost conspirator-ial bonding between the two women – against *both* of their husbands – directly foreshadows the more powerful bonding of Sophia with Minna. And as will be true later, a strong current of erotic feeling runs between the two women. 'She might be in love with me', Sophia thinks after Mrs

Hervey 'awkwardly' embraces her during one of their first meetings. Now, as she looks at the letter 'lying so calmly' on Mrs Hervey's lap, it suddenly seems only a pretext: 'some other motive, violent and unexperienced as the emotions of youth, trembled undeclared between them'. Later, they walk hand in hand in a thunderstorm, and Sophia briefly entertains a fancy of going on a European tour with Mrs Hervey – 'large-eyed and delighted and clutching a box of watercolour paints' – at her side (p. 78).

With the love affair between Sophia and Minna, one might say that the male homosocial triad reaches its point of maximum destabilization and collapses altogether. In its place appears a new configuration, the triad of *female* homosocial desire. For Frederick, obviously, is now forced into the position of the subject term, the one 'in between', the odd one out – the one, indeed, who can be patronized. Sophia and Minna do just this during their first supper together, following the memorable colloquy on the pink sofa. Sophia takes it upon herself to order the wine, a discreetly masculine gesture that inspires Minna to remark, 'How much I like being with English people! They manage everything so quietly and so well.' Sophia, catching her drift, instantly rejoins, 'And am I as good as Frederick?' 'You are much better', Minna replies. After a short meditation on Frederick's shortcomings, the two women subside into complacent amity. 'Poor Frederick!' says one. 'Poor Frederick!' says the other (pp. 161–2).

We might call this the comedy of female–female desire: as two women come together, the man who has brought them together seems oddly reduced, transformed into a figure of fun. Later he will drop out of sight altogether – which is another way of saying that in every lesbian relationship there is a man who has been sacrificed. Townsend Warner will call attention to this 'disappearing man' phenomenon at numerous points, sometimes in a powerfully literal way. When Sophia returns, for example, to the Rue de la Carabine to help the poverty-stricken Minna, only to find her lying chilled and unconscious on the floor, she immediately lies down to warm her, in 'a desperate calculated caress'. Yet this first, soon-to-be eroticized act of lying down with Minna also triggers a reverie – on the strangeness of the season that has brought them together, on the vast distance each has traversed to arrive at this moment, and on the man 'between them' who is of course not there:

> It was spring, she remembered. In another month the irises would be coming into flower. But now it was April, the cheat month, when the deadliest frosts might fall, when snow might cover the earth, lying hard and authentic on the English acres as it lay over the wastes of Lithuania. There, in one direction, was Blandamer, familiar as a bed; and there, in another was Lithuania, the unknown, where a Jewish child had watched the cranes fly over, and had stood beside the breaking river. And here, in Paris lay Sophia

Willoughby, lying on the floor in the draughty passage-way between bedroom and dressing-closet, her body pressed against the
body of her husband's mistress. (p. 251)

The intimacy, here and later, is precisely the intimacy enjoined by the
breakup of monolithic structures, indeed, by the breakup of triangulation itself. For what Sophia and Minna discover, even as they muse over
'poor Frederick', is that they need him no longer: in the draughty
passageway leading to a bedroom, the very shape of desire is 'pressed'
out of shape, becoming dyadic, impassioned, lesbian.[11]

What is particularly satisfying about Townsend Warner's plotting here
is that it illustrates so neatly – indeed so trigonometrically – what we
might take to be the underlying principle of lesbian narrative itself:
namely, that for female bonding to 'take', as it were, to metamorphose
into explicit sexual desire, male bonding must be suppressed. (Male
homo*social* bonding, that is; for lesbian characters in novels can, and do,
quite easily coexist with male homo*sexual* characters, as Djuna Barnes's
Nightwood, or even *Orlando* in its final pages, might suggest.)[12] Townsend
Warner's Frederick has no boyhood friend, no father, no father-in-law,
no son, no gang, *no novelist on his side* to help him re-triangulate his
relationship with his wife – or for that matter, with his mistress either.
To put it axiomatically: in the absence of male homosocial desire, lesbian
desire emerges.

Can such a principle help us to theorize in more general ways about
lesbian fiction? Obviously, I think it can. It allows us to identify first of all
two basic mimetic contexts in which in realistic writing plots of lesbian
desire are most likely to flourish: the world of schooling and adolescence
(the world of pre-marital relations) and the world of divorce, widow-
hood, and separation (the world of post-marital relations). In each of
these mimetic contexts male erotic triangulation is either conspicuously
absent or under assault. In the classically gynocentric setting of the girls'
school, for example, male characters are generally isolated or missing
altogether: hence the powerfully female homosocial/homosexual plots
of Colette's *Claudine à l'école*, Dorothy Strachey's *Olivia*, Christa Winsloe's
The Child Manuela (on which the film *Mädchen in Uniform* is based), Lillian
Hellman's *The Children's Hour*, Muriel Spark's *The Prime of Miss Jean
Brodie*, Catherine Stimpson's *Class Notes* or more recently, Jeanette
Winterson's *Oranges are Not the Only Fruit*, in which the juvenile heroine
woos her first love while attending a female Bible study group.

Yet the figure of male homosociality is even more pitilessly compromised in novels of post-marital experience. In the novel of adolescence, it is true, male homosocial desire often reasserts itself, belatedly,
at the end of the fiction: the central lesbian bond may be undermined or
broken up, usually by having one of the principals die (as in *The Child
Manuela* or *The Children's Hour*), get married (as in *Oranges are Not the
Only Fruit*) or reconcile herself in some other way with the erotic and

social world of men (as in *Claudine à l'école* or *The Prime of Miss Jean Brodie*). We might call this 'dysphoric' lesbian counterplotting. To the extent that it depicts female homosexual desire as a finite phenomenon – a temporary phase in a larger pattern of heterosexual *Bildung* – the lesbian novel of adolescence is almost always dysphoric in tendency.[13]

In post-marital lesbian fiction, however, male homosocial bonds are generally presented – from the outset – as debilitated to the point of unrecuperability. Typically in such novels, it is the very failure of the heroine's marriage or heterosexual love affair that functions as the pretext for her conversion to homosexual desire. This conversion is radical and irreversible: once she discovers (usually ecstatically) her passion for women, there is no going back. We might call this 'euphoric' lesbian counterplotting: it is an essentially comic, even utopian plot pattern. A new world is imagined in which male bonding has no place. Classic lesbian novels following the euphoric pattern include Jane Bowles's *Two Serious Ladies*, Jane Rule's *The Desert of the Heart*, and Claire Morgan's *The Price of Salt*, as well as numerous pulp romances of recent vintage, such as Anne Bannon's *Journey to a Woman* and Katharine V. Forrest's *An Emergence of Green*. In that it too begins with a failed marriage (that of Robin Vote and Felix Volkbein) even such a baroquely troubled work as *Nightwood*, paradoxically, might be considered euphoric in this respect: though its depiction of lesbian love is often malign, the novel takes for granted a world in which female erotic bonds predominate – so much so that the very possibility of male homosociality seems negated from the start.[14]

With its insouciant, sometimes coruscating satire on male bonding, *Summer Will Show* typifies the post-marital or conversion fiction: its energies are primarily comic and visionary. It is a novel of liberation. As Minna says to Sophia at one point: ' "You have run away. . . . You'll never go back now, you know. I've encouraged a quantity of people to run away, but I have never seen any one so decisively escaped as you" ' (p. 217). Yet is this the whole story? Given that the novel concludes with Minna herself apparently slain on the barricades, a victim of Caspar (who in turn is the pawn of Frederick), how complete, finally, is what I am calling, perhaps too exuberantly, its 'undoing' of the classic male homosocial plot?

That the ending of *Summer Will Show* poses a problem cannot be denied: Wendy Mulford, one of Townsend Warner's most astute critics, calls it an unconvincing 'botch' – though not, interestingly, for any purely narratological reason. For Mulford, Minna's bayoneting by Caspar is symptomatic of Townsend Warner's own emotional confusion in the 1930s over whether to devote herself to her writing or to revolutionary (specifically Marxist) political struggle. To the extent that Minna, the story-telling romantic, represents the potentially anarchical freedom of the artist, she has to be 'sacrificed', Mulford argues, in order to 'free the dedicated revolutionary' in Sophia, who functions here as a stand-in for the novelist herself. At the same time, Mulford conjectures, '[Townsend Warner's] unconscious was unable to consent to such a move' – hence the novel's descent into bathos and melodrama at this point.[15]

Yet Mulford already oversimplifies, I think, in assuming without question that Minna is dead. Granted, Minna seems to be dead (during the onslaught on the barricade Sophia sees Caspar's bayonet 'jerk' in Minna's breast) yet in a curious turnabout in the novel's final pages, Townsend Warner goes out of her way – seemingly gratuitously – to hint that she may in fact still be alive. Though unsuccessful, Sophia's attempts to locate Minna's body raise the possibility that her lover has survived: a witness to the scene on the barricades, Madame Guy, concedes that Minna was indeed alive when she was dragged away by soldiers; her daughter confirms it (pp. 397–8). Later visits to 'all the places where enquiries might be made' turn up nothing, but the man who accompanies Sophia reminds her that the officials in charge may be misleading her on purpose – the implication being that her friend may in fact be held prisoner somewhere (p. 399). The ambiguity is hardly resolved even at the last. When Sophia returns to Minna's apartment and takes up the *Communist Manifesto*, her peculiarly composed attitude seems as much one of waiting as of tragic desolation: far from being traumatized by seeing 'the wine that Minna had left for her' or Minna's slippers on the floor, she merely sits down to read, as though Minna were at any moment about to return. The utopian tract she peruses in turn hints symbolically at the thematics of return: if we take seriously the analogy that Townsend Warner has made throughout the novel between her heroine's political and sexual transformation, the inspiriting presence of the *Manifesto* here, with its promise of revolutionary hope resurrected, may also portend another kind of resurrection, that of Minna herself.

The novelist here seems to test how much implausibility we are willing to accept – for according to even the loosest standard of probability (such as might hold, say, in Victorian fiction) the possibility that Minna should survive her bayoneting by Caspar, an event which itself already strains credibility, must appear fanciful in the extreme. Yet it cannot be denied that Townsend Warner herself seems drawn back to the idea – almost, one feels, because it *is* incredible. Having offered us a plausible (or semi-plausible) ending, she now hints, seemingly capriciously, at a far more unlikely plot turn, as if perversely determined to revert to the most fantastical kind of closure imaginable.

Without attempting to diminish any of the ambiguity here, I think Warner's restaging of her conclusion – this apparent inability to let go of the possibility of euphoric resolution however improbable such a resolution must seem – can tell us something useful, once again, about lesbian fiction. By its very nature lesbian fiction has – and can only have – a profoundly attenuated relationship with what we think of, stereotypically, as narrative verisimilitude, plausibility, or 'truth to life'. Precisely because it is motivated by a yearning for that which is, in a cultural sense, implausible – the subversion of male homosocial desire – lesbian fiction characteristically exhibits, even as it masquerades as 'realistic' in surface detail, a strongly fantastical, allegorical, or utopian tendency. The more insistently it gravitates toward euphoric resolution, moreover, the more implausible – in every way – it may seem.

The problem with Townsend Warner's novel – if in fact it is a problem – is not so much that it forfeits plausibility at the end but that it forfeits it from the start. There is nothing remotely believable about Sophia Willoughby's transformation from 'heiress of Blandamer' into lover of her husband's mistress and communist revolutionary, if by 'believability' we mean conformity with the established mimetic conventions of canonical English and American fiction. The novelist herself seems aware of this, and without ever entirely abandoning the framing pretence of historicity (the references to real people and events, the 'Berliozian' local colour), often hints at the artificial, 'as if' or hypothetical nature of the world her characters inhabit. Metaphorically speaking, everything in the novel has a slightly suspect, theatrical, even phantasmagorical air. Revolutionary Paris resembles a stage set: the rebels near Minna's house are arrayed like 'comic opera bandits' (p. 177); a bloody skirmish in the streets is a 'clinching raree-show' (p. 171). Trying to convince her to return to her husband, Sophia's aunt Léocadie becomes a 'ballerina', with Frederick 'the suave athletic partner, respectfully leading her round by one leg as she quivered on the tip-toe of the other' (p. 203). Elsewhere Frederick is a 'tenor' plotting with the 'basso' Père Hyacinthe (p. 192). The captivating Minna, in turn, is a 'gifted tragedy actress' (p. 217), a 'play-acting Shylock' (p. 212), or someone 'in a charade' (p. 268). Sometimes Minna leaves the human realm altogether, metamorphosing into something from fairy-tale or myth – a 'Medusa', a 'herb-wife', a 'siren', a 'sorceress' – or a creature out of beast fable or Grandville cartoon. She is a 'macaw', Sophia thinks, a 'parrot,' 'some purple-plumaged bird of prey, her hooked nose impending', or perhaps the 'sleekest' of cats (p. 326). Her passion for Minna, Sophia concludes, is like the poet's – 'of a birth as rare/As 'tis of object strange and high . . . begotten by despair/Upon impossibility' (p. 289).

These built-in intimations of artifice and romance, of delight and high fakery, present on almost every page of *Summer Will Show*, work against the superficial historicism of the narrative, pushing it inexorably towards the fantastic. Of course a hankering after the fantastic is present elsewhere in Townsend Warner's writing: *Lolly Willowes*, we recall, begins as a seemingly straightforward tale about a spinster in an ordinary English village, but swerves abruptly into the marvellous when the spinster joins a coven of witches led by the Devil. Indeed the development of Townsend Warner's writing career as a whole suggests a progressive shifting away from realism toward the explicitly anti-mimetic modes of allegory and fable: in her last published stories, collected in *The Kingdoms of Elfin*, she dispensed with human subjects entirely, choosing to comme-morate instead the delicate passions of a race of elves.

Yet the fantastical element in *Summer Will Show*, is not, I think, simply a matter of authorial idiosyncracy. Other lesbian novels display the same oscillation between realistic and fabulous modes. One need only think again of *Orlando* or *Nightwood*, or indeed of Joanna Russ's *The Female Man*, Elizabeth Jolley's *Miss Peabody's Inheritance*, Lois Gould's *The Sea Change*, Sarah Schulman's *After Delores*, Margaret Erhart's *Unusual Company*, Michelle Cliff's *No Telephone to Heaven*, or any of Jeanette Winterson's recent novels, to see how symptomatically lesbian fiction resists any simple recuperation as 'realistic'. Even as it gestures back at a supposedly familiar world of human experience, it almost invariably stylizes and estranges it – by presenting it parodistically, euphuistically or in some other rhetorically heightened, distorted, fragmented, or hallucinatory way. In the most extreme manifestations of this tendency the pretence of mimesis collapses completely. In Monique Wittig's *Les Guérillères* or Sally Gearheart's *The Wanderground*, for example, two explicitly utopian lesbian novels, the fictional world itself is fantastically transfigured, becoming a kind of sublime Amazonian dream space: the marvellous inversion, in short, of that real world – 'between men' – the rest of us inhabit.[16]

What then *is* a lesbian fiction? Taking Sylvia Townsend Warner's *Summer Will Show* as our paradigm, we can now begin to answer the question with which we started. Such a fiction will be, both in the ordinary and in a more elaborate sense, non-canonical. Like Townsend Warner's novel itself, the typical lesbian fiction is likely to be an under-read, even unknown, text – and certainly an under-appreciated one. It is likely to stand in a satirical, inverted, or parodic relationship to more famous novels of the past – which is to say that it will exhibit an ambition to displace the so-called canonical works which have preceded it. In the case of *Summer Will Show*, Townsend Warner's numerous literary paro-dies – of Flaubert, Eliot, Brontë, Dickens and the rest – suggest a wish to displace, in particular, the supreme texts of nineteenth-century realism, as if to infiltrate her own fiction among them as a kind of subversive, inflammatory, pseudo-canonical substitute.

But most importantly, by plotting against what Eve Sedgwick has called the 'plot of male homosociality', the archetypal lesbian fiction decanonizes, so to speak, the canonical structure of desire itself. In so far as it documents a world in which men are 'between women' rather than vice versa, it is an insult to the conventional geometries of fictional eros. It dismantles the real, as it were, in a search for the not-yet-real, something unpredicted and unpredictable. It is an assault on the banal: a re-triangulating of triangles. As a consequence it often looks odd, fantastical, implausible, 'not there' – utopian in aspiration if not design. It is, in a word, imaginative. This is why, perhaps, like lesbian desire itself, it is still difficult for us to acknowledge – even when (Queen Victoria notwithstanding) it is so palpably, so plainly, there.

9 The African and the pagan in gay Black literature

David Bergman

Eldridge Cleaver's attack on James Baldwin in *Soul on Ice* (1968) was, according to Baldwin's biographer W.J. Weatherby, extremely 'important to Baldwin's developments' and 'helped to shape [Baldwin's] racial attitudes in middle age'. It came 'like a slap in the face bringing Baldwin to attention, making him reexamine his own situation'.[1] At a distance of more than twenty years, Cleaver's 'Notes on a Native Son' (1968) still seems a remarkable, forceful, but, in its way, perverse response to Baldwin, and one that functions to highlight the problem gay Black authors face in writing gay Black literature. Cleaver discredits Baldwin as a Black writer, not because he ignores Black issues, but because he is homosexual. In this chapter I want to explore the logic of Cleaver's attack, which for all its homophobic irrationality, does come out of a remarkable awareness of the encoding of homosexuality in African-American literary practice. This exploration will take us back to the works of the Harlem Renaissance, and particularly the work of Alain Locke and Countee Cullen who borrowed the white homosexual discourse about Ancient Greece in order to invoke an African classical past.

Cleaver begins his essay on Baldwin respectfully enough. 'After reading a couple of James Baldwin's books,' he remembers like a latter-day Keats dipping into Chapman's Homer, 'that continuous delight one feels upon discovering a fascinating, brilliant talent on the scene, a talent capable of penetrating so profoundly into one's own little world that one knows oneself to have been unalterably changed and *liberated*.'[2] In a gesture of both humility and subservience, he imagines the pleasure of sitting 'on a pillow beneath the womb of Baldwin's typewriter and catch[ing] each newborn page as it entered this world of ours'.[3] But such obstetric fantasies do not last long, and the sex change that this scenario signals soon becomes 'the racial death-wish' of 'many Negro homosexuals', who 'unable to have a baby by a white man . . . the little half-white offspring of their dreams . . . redouble their efforts and intake of the white man's sperm'.[4] Cleaver's sympathy and appreciation are hampered and finally erased by Baldwin's 'decisive quirk . . . which corresponds to his relationship to Black people and to masculinity'.[5] In short,

148

Cleaver rejects Baldwin as homosexual, because as homosexual, Baldwin must be anti-Black.

Although remarkably simple, Cleaver's sexual politics are central to his work. He argues that slavery has made the Black man into 'a black eunuch' who has 'completely submitted to the white man.'[6] Thus, all Black people, both male and female, must help Black men retrieve their masculinity. In 'To All Black Women, From All Black Men', the concluding essay in *Soul on Ice*, Cleaver sees the Black male crossing 'the naked abyss of negated masculinity', afraid to look Black women in the face because he might 'find reflected there a merciless Indictment of [his] impotence and a compelling challenge to redeem [his] conquered manhood.'[7] He then bids the Queen-Mother-Daughter of Africa, the Black Bride of His Passion: 'Let me drink from the river of your love at its source, let the lines of force of your love seize my soul by its core and heal the wound of my Castration, let my convex exile end its haunted Odyssey in your concave essence which receives that it may give.'[8]

In such a Freudian-charged atmosphere, it is no wonder that gay men threaten Cleaver. Uncertain of his own masculinity, he lashes out at what he fears he himself might be. Cleaver's paranoiac anxieties are particularly excited by Baldwin's critique of racial anger, Cleaver's principal tool for rebuilding the edifice of Black masculinity. When Baldwin comments that in Richard Wright's books 'violence sits enthroned where sex should be', Cleaver accuses Baldwin of engaging in a 'despicable underground guerrilla war, waged on paper, against black masculinity',[9] and he defends Wright's characters on the grounds that although 'shackled with a form of impotence, [they] were strongly heterosexual'.[10]

Cleaver was not the only critic who had difficulty appreciating Baldwin's work because of his depiction of homosexuality. The white critic Robert A. Bone also argued that Baldwin's homosexual viewpoint invalidated his art:

> Few will concede a sense of reality, at least in the sexual realm, to one who regards heterosexual love as 'a kind of superior callisthenics.' To most, homosexuality will seem rather an invasion than an affirmation of human truth. Ostensibly the novel summons us to reality. Actually it substitutes for the illusions of white supremacy those of homosexual love.[11]

I am uncertain what Bone really means in this crucial passage besides the fact that he thinks that writers who depict explicitly homosexual characters as good people are placing themselves beyond the pale of heterosexual sympathy, appreciation, and understanding. But I am not at all sure how such a depiction is 'an invasion . . . of human truth'. Does Bone mean homosexuals do not exist? Do not feel love? Are utterly deluded? The word *invasion*, suggesting some penetration of defence, makes me think that Bone fears some 'rearguard' action on the 'body' of truth. Nor can I explain how 'homosexual love' is a substitute for 'white supremacy'. But I do not want to leave the impression that Bone is the extremist and Cleaver the moderate. Toward the end of his essay, Cleaver pronounces: 'Homosexuality is a sickness, just as are baby-rape or wanting to become the head of General Motors.'[12] What is clear is that in the feverish atmosphere of the 1960s, Baldwin's depiction of homosexuals disturbed both white and Black readers, and excited rather extreme examples of homophobia.

But in calling Baldwin's works homosexual, I am distorting them. Baldwin is careful to make all his characters bisexual – David and Giovanni; Rufus, Vivaldo, and Eric; Leo and Christopher; Crunch, Arthur, and Jimmy are never depicted as 'faggots', by which Baldwin means exclusively and effeminately homosexual. Even as in the case of *Just Above My Head* (1979) in which Arthur Montana is never shown in any sexual relations with a woman, we are assured in the beginning that although 'Arthur slept with a lot of people – mostly men', it was 'not always' men, and although 'he was a whole lot of things, he was nobody's faggot'.[13] In fact, despite Bone's and Cleaver's assertion that Baldwin elevated homosexuality, gay Black men such as Samuel Delany found his portraits far from affirming.[14]

Even as late as 1984, Baldwin spoke of his discomfort with the term 'gay'. Asked if he felt 'like a stranger in gay America', Baldwin answered:

> 'Well, first of all I feel like a stranger in America from almost every conceivable angle except, oddly enough, as a black person. The word "gay" has always rubbed me the wrong way. . . . I simply feel it's a world that has very little to do with me, with where I did my growing up. I was never at home in it.'[15]

Moreover, he steers readers away from specifically gay interpretations of his work. He told Richard Goldstein, '*Giovanni* is not really about homosexuality. It's about what happens to you if you're afraid to love anybody. Which is much more interesting than the question of homosexuality.'[16] Although I understand and sympathize with Baldwin's desire to 'universalize' the themes of his novels, I also feel that he is making them blander than they are. For *Giovanni's Room* (1956) is not about just any obstacle to love, but quite specifically about internalized homophobia. To make it otherwise risks turning the novel into 'a little morality play in modern dress, in which the characters tend to be allegorical' – which is what Leslie Fiedler said of it in one of the novel's original reviews.[17] Two of *Giovanni's Room*'s strengths are the realism and the historical precision of its sentiments and attitudes, for the novella makes sense only in a culture in which homosexual relations are relegated exclusively to the *demi-monde*. As Claude J. Summers accurately states, 'It reflects in its ambiguities the homophobic tenor of the Eisenhower years even as it challenges those assumptions.'[18]

I cannot say to what extent Baldwin's resistance to calling himself gay or reading his works within a gay context is a personal belief or the result of homophobia in both the Black and white communities. But after Cleaver's attack, Baldwin emphasized racial much more than sexual issues. To Goldstein, he remarked, 'The sexual question comes after the color question. It is simply one more aspect of the danger in which all black people live.'[19] When sexual issues arise – as in the dialogue with Nikki Giovanni – Baldwin defends the male heterosexist position against Giovanni's Black feminist criticism. Baldwin, however, admits that the homosexual theme in his writing threatened his career in ways the Black theme did not. It lost him his first publisher, Alfred A. Knopf,[20] and by his own admission, 'a certain audience . . . I wasn't supposed to alienate'.[21]

Baldwin does admit to a certain amount of fag-baiting among Blacks, but contends it is less than among whites. Asked if people ever called him 'faggot' in Harlem, he answered:

Of course. But there's a difference in the way it's used. It's got less venom, at least in my experience. I don't know anyone who has ever denied his brother or his sister because they were gay. . . . a black person has got quite a lot to get through the day without getting entangled in all the American fantasies.[22]

Yet other accounts, even in his own fiction, suggest that gay Black men are seriously oppressed by the Black community. In an interview, Blackberri, a gay singer, remembers 'the magic summer' of his teenage years in Baltimore when he fell in love with the boy 'up the street'. 'We sat on the steps and talked all night long. He'd have his head in my lap, and we'd sit there until the sun came up.' But when people saw them holding hands, 'all hell broke loose. Lots of verbal attacks, people throwing rocks at us, being chased and stuff.'[23] The late Joseph Beam reflects in his essay 'Brother to Brother' that the 'fiery anger' that blazes as a result of racism 'is stoked additionally with the fuels of contempt and despisal shown me by my community because I am gay. *I cannot go home as who I am.*'[24] So violent is the Black reaction to homosexuality that even Cleaver deplores it as a scapegoating mechanism 'not unrelated . . . to the ritualistic lynchings and castrations inflicted on Southern blacks by Southern whites'.[25] Yet he admits that this 'classic, if cruel . . . practice by Negro youths of going "punk-hunting" . . . seeking out homosexuals on the prowl, rolling them, beating them up' is not limited to the South but is 'a ubiquitous phenomenon in the Black ghettos of America'.[26]

Max C. Smith argues that homosexual African-Americans have developed two basic strategies to cope with the homophobia in the Black community: by becoming, in his words, either 'Black Gays' or 'Gay Blacks'.[27] 'Gay Blacks are people who usually live outside the closet in predominantly white gay communities.' Smith estimates they make up only 10 per cent of all Black homosexuals. The vast majority are Black Gays who, according to Smith, 'are so strongly into our African-American identity that we would rather die than be honest enough with our homosexuality to deal with it openly'.[28] Homosexual African-Americans, according to Smith, must choose between identifying themselves as gay or Black; they cannot be both. As A. Billy S. Jones, whose own father was gay and advised his son 'to be tough, to be discreet, to marry, and to have children',[29] laments:

> The means by which we cope with our Blackness in mainstream America does not give us the means for coping with gayness. Just because Black Americans have a history of being discriminated against, of being victims of institutionalized racism, does not automatically free us from other forms of prejudice nor give us an understanding of the oppressions and injustices waged against others – even other Black gays.

In fact, Jones finds that 'A strong sense of Black nationalism or separatism, which often does not embrace homosexuality, will give some of my children's peers enough reason to make their lives miserable.'[30]

Throughout his career Baldwin insisted that homosexuality is a private matter and best kept away from public view. Although Baldwin took this position before Cleaver's attack, he held more tightly to it afterwards, even though this privatizing of sexual relations runs counter to his analysis of social power relations, which insists that institutions both reflect and reinforce people's unconscious psychological problems. Since for Baldwin 'the sexual question and the racial question have always been entwined', it makes no sense to declare the former a private matter and the latter a public one.[31] Yet in 1954 he wrote that André Gide's 'homosexuality . . . was his own affair which he should have kept hidden from us',[32] and thirty years later he averred: 'It seems to me simply a man is a man, a woman is a woman, and who [*sic*] they go to bed with is nobody's business but theirs . . . . that one's sexual preference is a private matter.'[33] In his last book *The Evidence of Things Not Seen* (1985), a jumbled account of the Atlanta child-murder cases, he repeats the speculation that Wayne Williams's motive for the murders – and Baldwin is uncertain of Williams's guilt – was to get back at his father, Homer Williams, who, frustrated over losing his job as a teacher, 'sodomized the son'.[34] Nevertheless Baldwin castigates the Defence for not finding 'a way to have prevented the question of homosexuality from being raised at all', since none of 'the crimes for which Wayne Williams had been arrested . . . were classed as sexual crimes'.[35] Yet even Baldwin admits that 'a great deal' of the non-sexual classification of those crimes 'depends on what one makes of the word, *sexual*', since the bodies of the boys were found naked.[36] Baldwin addresses the homosexual question of the murders only briefly, and when he does, his contradictory stances show his discomfort.

Yet another measure of Baldwin's discomfort with the subject is that in all his voluminous non-fiction writing, only one short piece centres on homosexuality, his 1954 review of Gide's *Madeleine* (1952), which although written with most of the articles that were published in *Notes of a Native Son* (1955), was not reprinted until *Nobody Knows My Name* (1960). Baldwin addresses sex between men almost exclusively in his novels, and in his one essay hardly articulates the belief that Cleaver accuses him of asserting, 'that there is something intrinsically superior in homosexuality'.[37]

To the contrary, in 'The Male Prison' (1954) Baldwin writes: 'The two things which contribute most heavily to my dislike of Gide were his Protestantism and his homosexuality', two of the attributes Baldwin held in common with him.[38] What Baldwin found objectionable was not Protestantism and his homosexuality separately, but the way they interacted in Gide's sensibility, since the battle between his sex and his religion limited Gide's capacity to be, 'in the best sense of that kaleidoscopic word – a man'.[39] In Baldwin's view, Gide's Protestantism forced him to separate erotic love, which in Gide's case was homosexual, from spiritual love, which for Gide took the form of a heterosexual love for Madeleine. But because Madeleine was his wife, Gide always felt guilty for failing to perform sexually while retaining her as a spiritual object. Yet because he preserved Madeleine as a spiritual ideal, Gide could minimize his homosexual guilt. As a result, Baldwin finds that Gide's 'Heaven and Hell suffer from a certain lack of urgency'.[40]

Baldwin's real objection is not that Protestantism and homosexuality are opposed, but that for Gide they so cunningly work together to exaggerate the gynophobia and asceticism of Protestantism. Because Gide can so easily retain Madeleine as a non-sexual, spiritual object, he never has to perform the difficult task of loving someone both physically and spiritually. Yet by making Madeleine his *wife* and thus retaining the possibility of heterosexuality – and here Baldwin exhibits his much-admired subtlety and complexity – Gide keeps open 'a kind of door of hope, of possibility, the possibility of entering communion with another sex'.[41] Baldwin praises Gide in so far as Gide entertains the possibility of heterosexuality and resists the puritanism of his Protestantism, but he criticizes Gide for relenting too easily to the narcissism of homosexuality and the self-righteousness of Protestant self-sacrifice.

Baldwin ends his review with a paean to heterosexuality: only heterosexuality can prevent Protestantism from falling into its latent homosexual asceticism, gnosticism, and narcissism; in short, only heterosexuality can keep Protestantism from dividing the spiritual from the sexual: 'When men can no longer love women', Baldwin writes, 'they also cease to love or respect or trust each other, which makes their isolation complete. Nothing is more dangerous than this isolation, for men will commit any crime whatever rather than endure it.'[42]

Although he does not mention bisexuality, one can see why it becomes so important to Baldwin: a homosexuality derived from a fear of the other sex, or a heterosexuality derived from a contempt of one's own, are merely different forms of racism. Consequently, Baldwin sees Gide's prison as 'not very different from the prison inhabited by, say, the heroes of Mickey Spillane'.[43] Both the homosexual and the ultra-macho heterosexual are ruled by the need to control and contain their fears and contempt. Without such clear controls, when they find themselves 'in a region where there is no definition of any kind, neither of color, nor of male and female', they feel as Vivaldo does in *Another Country* (1962), 'only the leap and the rending and the terror and the surrender'.[44] Cleaver views Baldwin's critique of the reaction formation of machismo as an attack on Black manhood and as an assertion of gay superiority. But the target of Baldwin's attack is the rigid exclusivity of either sexual orientation, which he maintains is an 'artificial division' and 'a Western sickness' that limits 'the capacity for experience'.[45]

Baldwin's attitude to Protestantism is extremely complicated, and as his article on Gide makes clear, it is inextricably tied to his attitudes toward sexuality. In so far as Protestantism is puritanical and polarizes concepts into simple dualism – good from bad, spiritual from physical, heterosexual from homosexual, man from woman – it is destructive. But in so far as Protestantism breaks down these categorical barriers and teaches the need for love, understanding, and empathy, it is a source of enormous good. A world without religion disintegrates into the tyranny of narcissism, but a theocratic society soon becomes hypocritical, brutal, and self-righteous.

The conflicts between religion and sexuality are central to Baldwin's early short story, 'The Outing', collected in *Going to Meet the Man* (1965). 'The Outing' (1957) tells of the Mount of Olives Pentecostal Assembly's boat trip to Bear Mountain one Fourth of July. On board the little steamer, Father James gives a sermon whose effect is so intense that the congregation

> might have mounted with wings like eagles far past the sordid persistence of the flesh, the depthless iniquity of the heart, the doom of hours and days and weeks; to be received by the Bridegroom where he waited on high in glory.[46]

Baldwin's strategy in 'The Outing' is to honour the high rhetoric and rich poetry of Pentecostal homiletics while exposing its hostility to the worldly and bodily. For Baldwin, the outing is a strangely ironic journey into the heart of darkness, since for the Assembly there is little difference between the Congo and the Hudson:

> On the open deck sinners stood and watched, beyond them the fiery sun and the deep river, the black-brown-green, unchanging cliffs. The sun, which covered earth and water now, would one day

refuse to shine, the river would cease its rushing and its numberless dead would rise; the cliffs would shiver, crack, fall and where they had been would then be nothing but the unleashed wrath of God.[47]

For Father James, the Bridegroom's love is indistinguishable from His 'unleashed wrath', and the beauty of the Hudson Valley is soon reduced to the wasteland of Armageddon.

Nowhere is the Pentecostal theology more destructive, in Baldwin's view, than in its attitude towards children. On the one hand, people are obliged to follow the divine injunction to be fruitful and multiply. Yet, on the other, siring children mires one further into 'the sordid persistence of the flesh'. Father James's love for his sons – particularly his eldest, Johnnie – is eaten away by bitterness since they represent his weakness before the 'depthless iniquity of the heart'. Baldwin's work from first to last is imbued with the deepest devotion to the family; no love can do more good than parental love, but parental hatred is the most destructive hatred of all. In his dialogue with Nikki Giovanni, Baldwin sees that the biggest threat to Blacks is that 'in gaining the world', they may lose 'the ability to love their own children'.[48] But Baldwin's concern for the binding and healing love of parents (and conversely with the almost unclosable, festering wounds of parental hate) has its sources in his own life in which he was the object of his father's violent paranoia, a paranoia whose magnitude required institutionalization. In 'The Outing' as well as in another story in *Going to Meet the Man*, 'The Rockpile' (1965), Baldwin exposes a father's hypocrisy in calling his brutal discipline of a son an act of love.

If the apocalyptic vision of Pentecostalism is inhospitable to nature and harmful to parental love, it is utterly destructive toward homosexual love, no matter how innocent or redemptive. 'The Outing' narrates that crucial moment when the childlike love of one boy for another is transformed into the adult awareness of the sinfulness of same-sex affection. In transforming love into sin, the puritanism of Pentecostalism warps the developing erotic and emotional life of the very children it claims to love and care for. Baldwin's resistance to the puritanical pressures of Pentecostalism may be gauged by the names he gives the boys – Johnnie and David – names that resonate with biblical significance, alluding to both the beloved apostle and the king whose love for Jonathan 'surpassed the love of women'.

Baldwin, who was a preacher in his early teens, recalls the guilt and anguish that he felt about his developing homosexual feelings. 'It hit me with great force while I was in the pulpit', he told Richard Goldstein. 'I must have been fourteen. I was still a virgin. I had no idea what you were supposed to do about it . . . Terrors of the flesh. After all, we're supposed to mortify the flesh, a doctrine which has led to untold horrors. This is a very biblical culture; people believe the wages of sin is death.'[49] In 'The Outing', the children must act 'as though their youth, barely begun, were already put away'. The elders find in the way the children moved, 'no matter how careful their movements . . . a pagan lusting beneath the blood-washed robes'. The adults 'considering [the children] with a baleful kind of love, struggled to bring their souls to safety in order . . . to steal a march on the flesh, while the flesh still slept'.[50] In *Just Above My Head* this twisted view of sexuality leads the father to commit incest with his preacher daughter as a way of consummating a love that has no other outlet. 'The Outing' ends with David embracing Johnnie, 'but now where there had been peace there was only panic and where there had been safety, danger, like a flower, opened'.[51] A religion that hates the flesh and abhors nature is exactly the sort of religion which will sow these particular *fleurs de mal*, and Baldwin abhors Father James as Blake abhorred the grey beadles for 'binding with briars our joy and desire' and transforming the Garden of Love into a graveyard.

Many gay Black writers have echoed Baldwin's difficulties with the Black church. James S. Tinney, who ministers to the nation's first Pentecostal church for Black gays, recalls how in other Pentecostal churches he attended 'the "holiness or hell" judgment was continually applied to homosexuals'.[52] When Tinney informed his wife that he was gay,

> she immediately called the pastor and his wife and other close confidants to pray for me. . . . Thus I was once a subject of an attempted exorcism. That in itself was extremely painful to my own sense of worth and well-being.[53]

The hypocrisy of Pentecostalists to homosexuality pains Tinney still more. For while it is probably untrue that 70 per cent of the Pentecostal congregation is gay – an estimate Tinney has heard – nevertheless, Tinney insists that 'if our churches were to instantly get rid of the homosexuals in them, they would cease to remain "Pentecostalist." For the gospel choirs and musicians (the mainstay and pivot of our "liturgy") would certainly disappear.'[54] Tinney paints a portrait of an uneasy truce between the strictures of dogma and the demands of reality.

> Despite the anti-sexual theme which characterizes much of Pentecostal preaching, a certain practical tolerance . . . exudes itself. The conscious way in which the presence of homosexuality was recognized (whether approved or not) contributed to a feeling that it was really no worse than women wearing open-toe shoes or saints missing a mid-week prayer meeting. In such an atmosphere the mind easily reaches its own conclusions: either the church doesn't take seriously its own preachments or else homosexuality is as culturally and temporally conditioned as the strictures against wearing red.[55]

But Black Pentecostal churches are not alone in assuming this hypocritical attitude toward homosexuality. Leonard Patterson, who served as an associate minister at the world-famous Ebenezer Baptist Church in Atlanta encountered the same experience. He was told, 'in effect, that as long as I played the political game and went with a person [unlike his white lover] who was more easily passed off as a "cousin", I would be able to go far in the ministry'.[56] When Patterson refused to drop his white lover, he was 'attacked verbally from the pulpit, forbidden to enter the study for prayer with the other associate ministers, and had seeds of animosity planted against [him] in the minds of certain members'.[57] The poisonous combination of Protestantism and homosexuality seems not to be limited to Gide's notebooks, but to extend to Black churches as well.

I make this analysis fully aware of the danger Amitai Avi-Ram warns white readers against falling into, namely, imposing the European Christian opposition of 'soul and body or between the sacred and sexual' on Afro-American religious beliefs, or conversely, 'oversexualizing the Afro-American [concept of] "soul" ' in order to distinguish it more easily from the dualisms of Euro-American theology.[58] The very real problem that Avi-Ram locates is one I hope to avoid. But it seems to me that Baldwin in 'The Outing' and Tinney and Patterson in their essays argue that Black churches often themselves lose track of the continuum between body and soul when challenged by homosexuals who refuse to hide their homosexuality, and that Black preachers lapse into such dualism when faced with the boundless gradations of sexual orientation. Black churches have trouble simultaneously honouring the continuum of sexual responses and remaining true to the African-American religious beliefs that posit a continuum of body and soul. And the difficulty of maintaining this continuum of theological and sexual category is reflected in Eldridge Cleaver's response to Baldwin. By calling on 'Queen-Mother-Daughter of Africa, Sister of My Soul, Black Bride of My Passion, My Eternal Love' to heal his sexual and spiritual wounds, he exemplifies in secular terms the continuity between body and soul that is the hallmark of Afro-American theology, yet in his response to Baldwin he lapses into a strict dualism of sexual identity.

The reason these questions about dualisms versus continuums, European Christianity versus Afro-American theology, play themselves out so directly in Pentecostalism is that, according to Tinney,

> Historians of religion are pretty well agreed that there are more surviving Africanisms (the drums, the dance, the state of possession, the emphasis on spirits, the ecstatic speech known as tongues, the healing magic, the use of inanimate objects which are blessed and transmit blessing) in Pentecostalism than in any other religion in the diaspora.

Thus Pentecostalism is a way not merely of being united with God, but of finding 'continuity with the Africanity in my heritage'.[59] Indeed, as

Tinney explains, one of the more difficult problems faced is how African a Black Christian church can be before it descends into paganism.[60]

Yet if one's 'Africanity' and Christianity may not entirely blend, for Tinney homosexuality and Africanity are continuous. Max C. Smith insists against the weight of Black popular belief that 'within some Black African societies homosexuality isn't legally and culturally condemned. The American Blacks' bias against gays is due to our forced socialization into Dixie Christian culture during slavery'.[61] Thus gay Black Christians wish to bring together their sexuality and their African heritage, and see the puritanical nature of Black Baptist and Pentecostal churches as falsely driving a wedge between Black gays and their African heritage.

Eldridge Cleaver keeps his attack on Baldwin from becoming merely a homophobic exercise by situating Baldwin's homosexuality in relation to Africa. Cleaver argues that homosexuality blocks Baldwin's – and, by extension, all Black homosexuals' – identification with his African origins. The way this argument emerges in Cleaver typifies the kind of breathtaking paradoxes of his thought. According to Cleaver, Norman Mailer is a better example of Black manhood than James Baldwin: while Mailer, 'the white boy, with knowledge of white Negroes [was] travelling toward a confrontation with the Black, with Africa', Baldwin, 'the black boy, with a white mind, was on his way to Europe'.[62] The gay Black men, like their counterparts in the Black bourgeoisie – and Cleaver sees the two as identical – have 'completely rejected their African heritage, consider the loss irrevocable, and refuse to look again in that direction'.[63] For Cleaver the 'only way out' of Baldwin's supposed problem of racial and sexual self-hatred 'is psychologically to embrace Africa, the land of his fathers, which [Baldwin] utterly refuses to do'.[64] Thus Cleaver locates Baldwin's alleged homosexually warped vision of Black culture not in *Giovanni's Room*, which he never mentions, nor in *Another Country*, but in Baldwin's essay 'Princes and Powers' (1957), an account of the 1956 Conference of Black Writers and Artists, in which sexuality never appears, but where, according to Cleaver, Baldwin shows 'revulsion . . . [for] Negritude and the African Personality'.[65] Cleaver's equation of Black homosexuality and anti-African sentiments may at first seem odd and strained, but it derives from a long and fascinating line and is perhaps Cleaver's most subtle and telling move in this strangely truculent essay.

This is not the place, nor am I the person, to argue whether homosexuality or other forms of sexual relations exist between men in sub-Saharan Africa. The issue is not, by any means, a literary or academic one. This very question has stymied AIDS researchers exploring routes of HIV transmission in Africa. Nevertheless, Gill Shepherd, an anthropologist, has extensively studied male and female homosexuality among the Swahili Muslims of Mombasa, a group of mixed blood Arab-Africans, and reports that 'Lesbians and homosexuals are open about their behaviour' and that there are 'well-established rules for fitting them into everyday life'.[66] She also reports that 'The Swahili for a male homosexual is *shoga*, a word also used between women to mean "friend." '[67] I mention this because the street sense in the Black community is that homosexuality is a habit picked up from whites, a remnant of slavery. So we have that voluble factotum of the rap music world, Professor Griff, lecturing the press:

> You have to understand something. In knowing and understand-
> ing Black history, African history, there's not a word in any African
> language which describes homosexual. You [journalists] would like
> to make them part of the Black community, but that's something
> brand-new to Black people. If you want to take me up on that, then
> you find me, in the original languages of Africa, a word for
> homosexual, lesbian or prostitute. There are no such words. They
> didn't exist.[68]

My point is not that Griff is a reliable expert, but rather he speaks with such authority because he states what is the received notions of his audience.

Even sophisticated Black academics have difficulty maintaining the slippery hold on African mythology and anthropology when it comes to sexuality. The formidable Henry Louis Gates, Jr, for example, inter-rupts his discussion of Esu, the Yoruba god of interpretation, to state: 'Despite the fact that I have referred to him in the masculine, Esu is also genderless, or of dual gender . . . Each time I have used the masculine pronoun . . . I could have just as properly used the feminine.'[69] Then Gates lapses back into the masculinist and heterosexist language he has used up to this point. Somehow the polymorphous perversity of Esu is lost in translation, and the continuum of African thought reduced to the binarism of western ideology. Even for the best-intentioned Black scho-lars, sexuality in Africa remains problematic.

The problem of the gay Black's relationship to Africa begins in the work of Alain Locke – the Howard University professor, Rhodes Scholar, and Harvard Ph.D. – who was intellectually and sexually in-volved with various members of the Harlem Renaissance. His seemingly successful campaign to seduce the wary Hughes makes for interesting reading in Arnold Rampersad's biography of the poet.[70] Locke is fre-quently, and in many ways correctly, viewed as one of the more forceful and articulate intellectuals to argue for African-Americans to study their origins in Africa, and 'the most direct catalyst' of the Harlem Renaissance, which gave voice to the Negritude movement.[71] Neverthe-less, as James B. Barnes has pointed out, 'Locke was often as ambiguous and enigmatic in his terms of definition as was the theme he was endeavouring to define.'[72] Locke's interest in Africa and the ambiguity and enigmatic quality of his language about Africa are at least partly motivated by a desire to create a cultural context for Black homosexuality, a subject that at the time could only be dealt with indirectly.

Locke's strategy is no different really from the strategy of upper-class gay Englishmen at the turn of the century, for whom, as David Halperin argues, the 'the Greeks provided an ideological weapon against the condemnatory reflexes of . . . Christian conscience, offering [them] in its place, "a new guide for life".'[73] Group after group, as I have discussed in my book *Gaiety Transfigured*, tries to find cultural permission for homosexual behaviour through recourse to some earlier – usually more primitive – state before Christian morality.[74] Melville and Stoddard's journey toward the Polynesian derives from this impulse, as do many of Cavafy's lyrics and Lowes Dickinson's writings on the Greek way of life. Similarly gay Black men sought the same legitimation of desire in an African past and cultural matrix. And like 'the self-censorship which', according to Halperin, 'Lowes Dickinson evidently exercised', Alain Locke found it advisable to couch his sexual politics in ambiguous and enigmatic terms.[75]

The key to Locke's rhetoric may be found in the letters he wrote to Hughes in his campaign of seduction, a correspondence of which Rampersad gives a lively account. Early on, Locke tells Hughes of his identification with Germany, since

> Germans had a gift for friendship, 'which cult I confess is my only religion and has been ever since my early infatuation with Greek ideals of life.' 'You see,' he went on, 'I was caught up early in the coils of classicism.'[76]

In later letters, the two discovered they were 'pagan to the core'.[77] Rampersad believes this coding was so obvious that even the youthful Hughes was only 'pretending not to understand', coyly refusing to take the hint.[78] In fact the polarities that Locke sets up between ancient and contemporary, classic and modern, Greek and American, pagan and Christian were the standard codes of the Uranian writers and such fellow-travellers as A.E. Housman, Countee Cullen's ideal.

Those enigmatic and ambiguous terms in Locke's criticism merely turn Greece into Africa. 'What the Negro artist of to-day has most to gain from the arts of the forefathers,' Locke wrote, 'is perhaps not cultural inspiration or technical innovation, but the lesson of a classical background, the lesson of discipline, of style, of technical control pushed to the limits of technical mastery.'[79] He concludes with this peroration:

> If African art is capable of producing the ferment in modern art that it has, surely this is not too much to expect of its influence upon the culturally awakened Negro artist of the present generation. So that if even the present vogue of African art should pass, and the bronzes of Benin and the fine sculptures of Gabon and Baoule, and the superb designs of the Bushongo should again

become mere items of exotic curiosity, for the Negro artist they ought still to have the import and influence of classics in whatever art expression is consciously and representatively racial.[80]

What makes African art classical is that it embodies 'rigid, controlled, disciplined, abstract, heavily conventionalized' elements similar to the classical Greek plastic expression, and its moral tone – 'disciplined, sophisticated, laconic and fatalistic' – bears a striking resemblance to the Hellenic temperament.[81] Indeed, Locke makes a quite explicit comparison between Greek classicism and African classicism, a comparison which asserts that at present the African variety may be more useful:

> This artistic discovery of African art [by European modernists] came at a time when there was a marked decadence and sterility in certain forms of European plastic art expressions, due to generations of the inbreeding of style and idiom. Out of the exhaustion of imitating Greek classicism and the desperate exploitation in graphic art of all the technical possibilities of color . . . form and decorative design became emphasized. . . . And suddenly with this new problem and interest, African representations of form . . . appeared cunningly sophisticated and masterful.[82]

We should not ignore Locke's inbreeding metaphor because it provides a vital insight into his larger cultural politics. For Locke, African classicism enters as a *deus ex machina* to solve the incestuous problems of Greek classicism and European aesthetic inbreeding, and places the African-American at an advantage over the European in the coming years. To be sure, the Black has suffered from the importation of European values (and Nordic blood), and the art of the Blacks in America is a pale imitation of European artistic expression. However, that infusion of European influence has kept the African-American artist from suffering the degenerative inbreeding that has affected his European colleagues, and now Black American artists stand to benefit, as no European could, from the rediscovery of their classical African roots.

One benefit, according to Locke, is that Black Americans are in a better situation to throw off the shackles of western oppression and participate in the austere, disciplined, and highly sophisticated paganism of African classicism.

> The universality of the Spirituals looms more and more as they stand the test of time. They have outlived the particular generation and the peculiar conditions which produced them; they have survived in turn the contempt of the slave owners, the conventionalization of formal religion, the repression of Puritanism, the corruption of sentimental balladry, and the neglect and disdain of second-generation respectability. They have escaped the lapsing

conditions and the fragile vehicle of folk art, and come firmly into the context of formal music. Only classics survive such things.[83]

Locke's elegant periods emphasize both the process of the Spirituals' transmission and their transformation into classics. The pagan sources of the Spiritual, its origins in African life, have survived 'the conventionalization of formal religion' as well as 'the repression of Puritanism'. The Protestant message of Black Spirituals, like the Christian interpolations in *Beowulf*, are merely recent excrescences on the classically stylized surfaces of the pagan originals, crude fig leaves across the heroic torso. Indeed, Locke divides the Spiritual into four groups – ritualistic prayer songs, evangelical 'shouts', folk ballads, and work songs – only to deny these division into secular and religious. 'It is not a question of religious content or allusion – for the great majority of the Negro songs have this – but a more delicate question of caliber or feeling and type of folk use.'[84] In merging secular and Spiritual concerns, these classic works of art elude the conventions of puritanism and formal European religions while suggesting a deeper and more flexible religious feeling.

Yet Locke avoids the next logical rhetorical step: to see this classical African heritage as immediately connected to the American Black. Some aspects of the African heritage have survived, according to Locke, like the rhythms of the Spirituals, or their frightening rapid shifts of emotion. But Locke insists that the thread connecting American Blacks to Africa is virtually severed:

> Music and poetry, and to a certain extent the dance, have been the predominant arts of the American Negro. This is an emphasis quite different from that of the African cultures, where the plastic and craft arts predominate. . . . Except then in his remarkable carry-over of the rhythmic gift, there is little evidence of any direct connection of the American Negro with his ancestral arts. . . . The characteristic African art expressions are rigid, controlled, disciplined, abstract, heavily conventionalized; those of the Aframerican, – free – exuberant, emotional, sentimental and human. Only by the misrepresentation of the African spirit, can one claim any emotional kinship between them. . . . The emotional temper of the American Negro is exactly opposite. What we have thought primitive in the American Negro – his naïveté, his sentimentalism, his exuberance and his improvising spontaneity are then neither characteristically African nor to be explained as an ancestral heritage. They are the result of his peculiar experience in America and the emotional upheaval of its trials and ordeals.[85]

I have quoted Locke at some length because he echoes the position of many gay white intellectuals at the turn of the century and anticipates the problematic cultural issues Baldwin faced forty years later. Like Symonds and Dickinson, Locke feels he lives in a sentimental, puritanical, undisciplined society that needs both the chastening and the broadening of classicism, which in turn would give room and support to homosexual feelings. But like Baldwin, Locke finds himself both attracted to and distanced from the African. While the African has a grandeur missing in American Black culture, it lacks the definitive agony that the 'peculiar experience in America' forces on Blacks. Baldwin, in particular, also doubts whether contemporary Africa really is less homophobic, more accepting than African-American society.

Homosexual desire, Black Protestantism, and African classicism played themselves out in particularly stark and subtle ways in the work of Countee Cullen, friend of both Langston Hughes and Alain Locke, and boyhood teacher of Jimmy Baldwin. Cullen's poem 'Heritage' (1923) introduces Locke's essay on 'The Legacy of the Ancestral Arts' (1925), and forms – since Locke was the editor of the anthology – a gloss on Locke's position.

The poem begins with the school essay question: 'What is Africa to me?', but soon eroticizes the question: is it 'Strong bronze men and regal black/Women from whose loins I sprang/When the birds of Eden sang?'[86] Within the first sentence, Cullen brings together images of Africa, homoeroticism, and allusion to the Judaeo-Christian concept of the fall. In the second stanza Cullen gestures to push Africa back into the geography books, but it cannot be so easily repressed. Like the snake, Africa reveals itself to him, and the opening question, 'What is Africa?', becomes by the end of stanza two the more suggestive – and forbidden – question, 'What's your nakedness to me?'[87]

Cullen links Africa and erotic fantasies by one of the oldest conventions of lyric poetry – the sleepless night:

> So I lie, who always hear
> Though I cram against my ear
> Both my thumbs, and keep them there,
> Great drums beating through the air. . . .
> So I lie, and find no peace
> Night or day, no slight release
> From the unremittent beat
> Made by cruel padded feet,
> Walking through my body's street.
> Up and down they go, and back
> Treading out a jungle track.
> So I lie, who never quite
> Safely sleep from rain at night
> While its primal measures drip
> Through my body, crying, 'Strip!
> Doff this new exuberance,
> Come and dance the Lover's Dance.'[88]

These neatly turned tetrameter lines echo with more than the jungle drums. One can hear some of T.S. Eliot's Prufrock (1917) and perhaps a bit of Wallace Stevens's 'Sunday Morning' (1915) in the celebratory dance, but most of all Cullen has 'caught the tread of dancing feet' that Oscar Wilde hears in 'The Harlot's House' (1885). The pent-up sexual energy is not just the call of Africa, nor is its luridness justified by a heterosexual object. Homosexual implications freight the next short stanza, which returns 'Heritage' to its Christian mooring:

> My conversion came high-priced.
> I belong to Jesus Christ,
> Preacher of humility:
> Heathen gods are naught to me –
> Quaint, outlandish heathen gods
> Black men fashion out of rods,
> Clay and brittle bits of stone,
> In a likeness like their own.[89]

Clearly heathen gods, far from being naught to Cullen, are very precious, especially if they look like the 'strong bronze men' who haunt his imagination. The price for Christ is renouncing those rods fashioned by the men into gods, these phallic deities, and Cullen seems highly reluctant to pay it. The poem ends with the prayer, 'Lord, forgive me if my need/Sometimes shapes a human creed.'[90] Christianity of the puritanical sort practised by Black churches does not allow Cullen the human need for humans. Its strict separation of spirit and matter does not satisfy Cullen's more pagan (and homosexual) requirements. Africa becomes both the despised Sodom and the long-sought Eden of the homoerotic against which Cullen stuffs his ears and for which his heart sings. In such ways Africa is far more problematical for the gay than for the heterosexual Black American writer.

If Cullen and Locke feel themselves cut off as Christians and Americans from an ancestral identification with Africa, Langston Hughes feels alienated by race. Hughes's autobiography, *The Big Sea* (1940), begins with his journey to Africa when as a young man he hired on as a seaman aboard the S.S. *Malone*. During the crossing, Hughes waited 'anxiously to see Africa . . . My Africa! Motherland of the Negro peoples!'[91] Putting in at Dakar, Hughes is disturbed that Africa looks nothing like what he expected, a discomfort which is partly sexual, since 'at first you couldn't tell if the Mohammedans were men or women'.[92] But as the ship sails southwards he comes to recognize 'The great Africa of my dreams'. Yet now his pain is greater, for as Hughes writes, 'there was one thing that hurt me a lot when I talked with the people. The Africans looked at me and would not believe I was a Negro.'[93] Hughes's identification with an African ancestry is blocked not by his desire, but by Africans themselves who recognize in Hughes the admixture of many racial features – English, Jewish, and Cherokee. For Hughes, the American Black can no longer claim an African motherland.

Although genes more than sex block Hughes's identification with an African heritage, Rampersad makes clear that the trip was a source of sexual anxiety for Hughes. During this trip Hughes first had sex with another man, 'a swift exchange initiated by an aggressive crewman', according to Rampersad, who adds in case there was doubt, 'with Hughes as the "male" partner'.[94] Later, according to Rampersad, 'to Langston's great disgust, one of the firemen openly brought young black boys to the ship and sodomized them for a shilling or so. Hughes longed for the ship to leave.'[95] Hughes was not disgusted by the prostitution – accounts of which he gives quite casually, even mentioning his own occasional visits – but apparently by the openness of the sodomy. Or was it the low wages? What is clear is that Hughes found Africa off-putting, and that sex had some role in his alienation.

I hardly need mention that both these homosexual incidents are dropped from Hughes's account of the voyage in *The Big Sea*. Indeed, homosexuality, or rather transvestism, appears explicitly only once in *The Big Sea*, in a chapter ironically titled 'Spectacles in Color'. Hughes describes attending the annual Hamilton Club Lodge Ball, a drag affair in which 'prizes are given to the most gorgeously gowned of the whites and Negroes'. As if to distance himself Hughes writes,

> the pathetic touch about the show is given by the presence there of many former 'queens' of the ball, prize winners of years gone by, for this dance has been going on a long time, and it is very famous among the male masqueraders of the eastern seaboard.[96]

This chapter is one of the clearest examples of Hughes's technique of indirectly and silently commenting on a subject by placing accounts in juxtaposition. In *The Big Sea*, the Hamilton Club Lodge Ball segues into Countee Cullen's lavish wedding to Yolande Du Bois, W.E.B. Du Bois's only child, as if the 'male masqueraders' from one drag ball had merely waltzed over to another. Given the indirect way Hughes is forced to make his points about homosexuality, the sexual ambiguity of the 'Mohammedans' begins to loom larger as a sign, as do other odd remarks. Hughes recalls docking at Horta where 'Some of the boys made straight for women, some for the wine shops. It depended on your temperament which you sought first. . . . I bought a big bottle of cognac.'[97] What should we make of this sign of 'temperament', or in this portrait of Ramon, Hughes's cabin mate: 'he said he didn't care much for women. He preferred silk stockings'?[98] For a writer like Hughes who plays on an innocent ambiguity for his most sophisticated effects, Africa is a background at once too ambiguous and too clear for comfort. For both Cullen and Locke, Africa was the problematic site of a classical, homosexual past.

When Cleaver attacked Baldwin, claiming his homosexuality was an obstacle to his identification with Africa, Cleaver's analysis hits rather strongly, not only at problems in Baldwin's own position, but at problems in other Black writers and intellectuals who were gay or whose sexual orientation – like Hughes's – was ambiguous. Even after Cleaver's attack, at a time when Baldwin in his public statements attempted to side with the machismo of much Black popular sentiment, Baldwin was still unable to see Africa in its own terms and without the aid of a specifically Black American lens. His difficulties are quite evident in *Perspectives: Angles on African Art* (1987), one of the last projects he worked on. Susan Vogel, a curator at the Center for African Art, selected a number of works, then asked ten individuals to choose the ones they liked best and write comments about their choices. The commentators, whom Vogel calls 'cocurators', are an eclectic group, including David Rockefeller, William Rubin, Ekpo Eyo, and Romare Bearden. Baldwin's first choice is a wood statue from Madagascar in which a woman is kneeling on a man's lap, her head above his, her breast at hair level, so that the man must reach up to touch it. Baldwin identifies it as 'a mother and child' although the man has an enormous erection that rests against the woman's hand which in turn rests beside her vagina. Baldwin's statement that the statue 'speaks of a kind of union which is unimaginable in the West',[99] although implying a kind of intuitive sympathy, seems not only to beg the question but to suggest his unwillingness to acknowledge what is before him. When he turns to a Luba stool he sees Samson, and illuminates the work with references to Auden.[100] In two women holding hands on top of a Luba staff, Baldwin recognizes 'the women who live in Harlem'.[101] A Djenne figural scene reminds Baldwin 'of a song we used to sing in church called Peace in the Valley'.[102] In his final selection, a Cameroon stool causes Baldwin to meditate that 'the Western idea of childhood, or children, is not at all the same idea of childhood that produced me. . . . white people think that childhood is a rehearsal for success. . . . But black people raise their children as a rehearsal for danger.'[103] Again Africa is seen as merely an extension of Harlem, although I doubt that even in Harlem 'children' have the thigh-long penis granted to one of the figures carved on the stool. Despite Baldwin's repeated claims to have intuited the African spirit, one is continually reminded by how obsessively he projects American images – even negatively – on to African art, so that the footstool is distinguished as 'not like Mt. Rushmore'.[104]

As I mentioned earlier, Cleaver locates Baldwin's deepest difficulties with African identity in 'Princes and Powers', an essay which does not deal with homosexuality explicitly. Yet I think Cleaver recognizes the very subtle ways issues of gender are encoded, transformed, and deflected by Black homosexual writers, especially in the repressive atmosphere of the mid-1950s. Cleaver's reading of 'Princes and Powers' as a homosexual text provides his most daring insights into the cultural politics of gender.

In a startling coincidence, Baldwin addresses the same issue of Black classicism that is so central to Locke, 'classic here taken to mean', by Baldwin, 'an enduring revelation and statement of a specific, peculiar, cultural sensibility'.[105] Like Locke, Baldwin doubts that African and Black American art can meaningfully be connected. To argue, as Leopold Senghor does, that Wright's *Black Boy* (1945) is 'involved with African tensions and symbols' is so to dilute the notion of a classical heritage that it no longer contains any substance.[106] Moreover, as Baldwin points out, 'In so handsomely presenting Wright with his African heritage, Senghor rather seemed to be taking away his identity.'[107] A classicism so pervasive, so genetic, able to operate even when all other cultural, social, and systemic reinforcement is missing is nothing more than instinct, and one cannot claim that instinct conveys moral virtue. Like post-hypnotic suggestion, acts generated by an unconscious heritage cannot claim to be the work of the person who performed them. The writer merely becomes the instrument of a cultural force beyond his control; Baldwin rejects such a role for the artist and for the citizen. 'A culture', he insists, is not 'something given to a people, but, on the contrary and by definition, something that they make themselves'.[108] Baldwin draws from the concept of individual volition two key beliefs: first, colonial attempts to Europeanize Africans cannot succeed unless Africans help make such a culture; and second, culture can never be something passively finished since it exists only as it is made. Baldwin stands Eliot on his ear: the only tradition that counts is one of individual talent.

Baldwin rather self-consciously locates his cardinal virtues of individuality and volition within the Protestant ethic. His essay on André Gide indicates how problematic a move that is for him, and in 'Princes and Powers' Baldwin is quite aware of the dangers since, as he writes of the French, Christian apologetics has produced 'a legal means of administering injustice'.[109] Yet, whatever the sins of the Europeans have been, 'one of the results of 1455 [when the church had determined to rule all infidels] had, at length, been Calvin and Luther, who shook the authority of the Church in insisting on the authority of the individual consciousness'.[110] In claiming that European culture was bad because it oppressed the individual wills of Africans, Africans were relying on the very cultural principle of moral persuasion they were rejecting. Christian culture, for Baldwin, provided the terms of its own critique and thus the means of its own correction, while relying on some intuited native African classicism that was transhistorical, transgeographic, even transracial created an authority with no internal mechanism for correction. Baldwin approves of George Lamming when he quotes Djuna Barnes (and the sexual-political significance of the source should not be ignored): 'Too great a sense of identity makes a man feel he can do no wrong. And too little does the same thing.'[111] If Cleaver argued that Baldwin could not be an African because he was gay, Baldwin answers, at least in 'Princes and Powers', that he cannot be much of an African because he is too much of a Protestant.

Baldwin makes clear the tensions between the Protestant culture of American Blacks and the pagan culture of Africans in yet another disagreement with Senghor. Although Baldwin was willing to concede that 'The culture which had produced Senghor seemed, on the face of it, to have a greater coherence as regarded assumptions, traditions, customs, and beliefs than did the western culture', nevertheless 'Senghor's culture . . . did not need the lonely activity of the singular intelligence on which the cultural life – the moral life – of the West depends.' Indeed, the coherence of African culture – and the authority of that coherence – produces, according to Baldwin, 'necessarily, a much lower level of tolerance for the maverick, the dissenter, the man who steals the fire'.[112] Baldwin sees one choice: either a coherent culture of tribal conformity in which leaders control all values, or a more fragmentary culture of the west in which tolerance is required for the moral and creative acts of individuals. From a country where Blacks are a minority and where the hierarchy oppresses homosexuals, Baldwin not surprisingly sides with the culture of tolerance for individual differences. As he did in the Gide essay, Baldwin finds in 'Princes and Powers' that Protestantism is capable of producing – even if it has not always produced – not just the puritanical seeds of sexual oppression, but moral openness towards and tolerance of sexual minorities because of its self-correcting mechanisms. African culture is potentially more homophobic, more racist, more intolerant than a Christian culture. Cleaver sees Baldwin's homosexuality at work in his advocacy of the liberal humanism of Protestantism, and by rejecting what he sees as a homosexual desire for 'tolerance', Cleaver refuses to credit the other dimensions of Baldwin's position.

But it seems to me that even within the context of 'Princes and Powers', Baldwin is unwilling to settle for the either/or of Protestantism or Africa, homosexual tolerance or pan-African uniformity. '[Black Africans] were all now, whether they liked it or not,' Baldwin insists, 'related to Europe, stained by European visions and standards, and their relationship to themselves, and to each other, and to their past had changed.'[113] Blacks – African or American – could not turn back the clock to a time before the European invasion of their culture. In Aimé Césaire, Baldwin found a figure who seemed to bring together both the Protestant tolerance of difference and the African authority of origin. According to Baldwin, Césaire 'had penetrated into the heart of the great wilderness which was Europe and stolen the sacred fire. And this, which was the promise of their freedom, was also the assurance of his power.'[114]

Baldwin posits in this passage the figure of a Black Prometheus, and the gay dimensions of such a figure should be obvious to us now, carrying with it both the Greek way of life and a tolerance of the oppressed (including, the sexually oppressed). It joins, as Locke did, both a Greek and African classicism – austere, disciplined, but open to difference and variety. It gives voice to the rebel, the maverick, the oddball without placing the iconoclast outside the culture it seeks to alter and whose errors it tries to correct. Baldwin, it is true, cannot sustain or even explore such a figure either in his essays or in his novels. The Black Prometheus – whose fires erotic and intellectual are never extinguished – is but the passing rhetorical gesture in an essay filled with rhetorical gestures. But it positions Baldwin within a line he nowhere acknowledges – a line of both gay *and* African-American writers – a line which Cleaver's essay seems to have driven him off, a line which those after him have found difficult to trace and extend.

10   Who was afraid of Joe Orton?

Alan Sinfield

Oscar Wilde: [Secrecy] seems to be the one thing that can make modern life mysterious or marvellous to us. The commonest thing is delightful if one only hides it.[1]

Joe Orton: The whole trouble with Western Society today is the lack of anything worth concealing.[2]

Joe Orton went to study at the Royal Academy for Dramatic Art in 1951, in the heyday of Terence Rattigan, Whitehall farces, religious verse-drama and Agatha Christie. The Wolfenden Report on homosexuality was still six years away, and the film *Victim* ten. Theatre was often 'queer', but it was always discreet. In the late 1950s, Orton showed no interest in the socially and politically aware plays of Osborne, Delaney, and Wesker, though they accompanied and contributed to a great increase in public discussion of homosexuality – by 1958 the Lord Chamberlain, the Crown official whose task it was to censor stage plays, was obliged to allow serious treatment of the topic. Orton and his lover Kenneth Halliwell were conducting a more distinctive and anarchic cultural critique by redesigning the covers of library books.[3]

However, in 1963, with the mysterious menace of Pinter's plays in the ascendancy, Orton wrote *Entertaining Mr Sloane*. In 1966 *Loot* was successfully produced – London was swinging and 'permissive' and Orton was asked to write a film script for the Beatles. He died in 1967, the year when male homosexual acts were made legal (provided there were only two people, in private, aged over 21, and not in the armed services, the merchant navy, the prisons, Northern Ireland or Scotland). In 1968 stage censorship ended, and explicit gay plays – *Spitting Image, Fortune and Men's Eyes, Total Eclipse* – were produced in London. Plays in the London theatre in 1969 besides Orton's *What the Butler Saw* included *Boys in the Band, Oh, Calcutta!* and *Hair*; it was the year when the unprecedented resistance of gays to police harassment at the Stonewall Inn in New York's Christopher Street led to the formation of the Gay Liberation Front. So Orton's involvement in theatre spans the crucial period when the scope for homosexuals, both in

170

British society and in the theatre, was sharply contested. This was the period when Gay Liberation became conceivable.

This chapter explores how Orton's plays effected quite specific negotiations of these changing opportunities for theatre and male homosexuals (in this chapter I discuss men in Britain; the histories of lesbians generally and of men in other countries, though partly similar, are distinct). Orton exploited and contributed to the process through which homosexuality gradually became publicly speakable, and, as theatre audiences split and reformed, he was a focus of ideological conflict. Yet, I will argue, the terms of that conflict finally trapped Orton and limited his audience and his sexual politics, particularly in the play critics have most praised, *What the Butler Saw.* I invoke another gay play as a possible model of a gay cultural politics.

Silence and the Closet

Typically, from Ibsen to Christie and Rattigan, naturalistic plays disclose a danger to the social order. Often it takes the form of a socially unacceptable character – an outlaw-intruder who threatens the security of the characters and, by inference, the audience. Usually the problem is satisfactorily contained at the final curtain, though dissident authors might suggest that the disruptive intruder or misfit manifests in some ways a superior ethic or wisdom.[4] Pinter's plays reorganized this pattern. In them the sense of mysterious, ominous presence is often embodied in an intruder, though now its focus is not social propriety but an unstable compound of metaphysical vacuity and sexual challenge. Its ultimate residence may be the psyche of the threatened character. Notoriously, the danger hovers also in silences in the dialogue, pregnant now not with class disapproval but with a loosely 'existential' anxiety about emptiness and disintegration.

The outlaw-intruder pattern had obvious resonances for male homosexuals, especially of the middle and upper classes. They felt obliged to 'pass' as heterosexual, and thus themselves effected the intrusion of an 'undesirable' element into good society. They might fear the irruption of knowledge about homosexuality and hence their own exposure; further, they might themselves introduce the threatening lower-class person to whom they might be attracted (this was a common pattern and constituted the dominant concept of the homosexual liaison).[5] J.R Ackerley remarked, almost in passing, how he and his friends were 'outcasts and criminals in the sight of the impertinent English laws'; Peter Wildeblood said in 1955 that he 'would be the first homosexual to tell what it felt like to be an exile in one's own country'.[6] Homosexuality hovered upon the edge of public visibility, defining normality against a deviation so horrific that its occurrence could scarcely be admitted.

Pinter's version of the outlaw-intruder was apposite to homosexuality at this time: both were imagined as mysterious and violent, lying in wait in the silences, explicitly nowhere but, by so much, potentially everywhere. Homosexuality might manifest itself as an over-emphatic and hence potentially violent inflection in a relationship. It might even be lurking, scarcely recognized, in the psyches of 'normal' people. Most of Pinter's early plays have a homosexual inflection. There are intense male relationships in *The Birthday Party* (Goldberg and McCann; 1958), *The Dwarfs* (1960), *The Caretaker* (1960) and *The Dumb Waiter* (1960). In *The Birthday Party* Stanley resists Lulu's advances and is 'mothered' by Meg; in *The Homecoming* (1965) Lenny boasts of violent relations with women but is easily disconcerted by Ruth. It is not that these plays are 'really', 'underneath', about homosexuals; to say that would be to override the ambiguity which at the time was crucial. During those decades of discretion we should not imagine homosexuality as *there*, fully formed like a statue shrouded under a sheet until ready for exhibition. The closet (as discreet homosexuality was named when it came under scrutiny in the 1960s) did not obscure homosexuality – it created it. Freud makes a similar point when he disputes that one should expect to find 'the essence of dreams in their latent content': the important thing is the dream-*work* which produces such images.[7] Similarly, oblique homosexual representation should be studied for the *process* that constitutes it so, and for the social reasons that demand such a process.

As censorship gradually relaxed, Pinter wrote *The Collection* (1961). There is tension in the (evidently) homosexual relationship of Harry and Bill and in the marriage of Stella and James because, it emerges, there is a question whether sexual congress has occurred between Stella and Bill. Homosexuality is to be inferred from the usual stereotypical cues – the 'artistic' ménage of Harry and Bill, the fact that Bill is a dress designer, and the domineering attitude of the wealthier and older Harry. Martin Esslin deduces that Bill may have wanted to sleep with Stella because he 'may have been made into a homosexual by an older man who offered him social advancement, a good job, life in a middle-class milieu'.[8] We never find out what 'actually happened', of course. The need to infer the sexuality of Harry and Bill produces an additional layer of obscurity. Customary discreet indirection about homosexuality feeds neatly into Pinter's blend of mystery and menace.

While the Chamberlain's power persisted, Pinteresque mystery was a convenient mode for handling homosexuality on the stage. In *The Trigon*, by James Broom Lynne (produced at the Arts theatre in 1963), Arthur and Basil are presented through manifest homosexual hints – as the play opens, Arthur is wearing Boy Scout uniform and playing a record of 'Dance of the Sugar-Plum Fairy'. Their intentions towards their friend Mabel are evidently half-hearted (compare Stanley and Lulu in *The Birthday Party*) – it is said that if they both addressed her 'She wouldn't know which way to turn.'[9] But there is no indication of sexual feeling, as such, between the two men. The intruder, Charles, is also mysterious – though compatible with the stereotypical notion that homosexuals gain satisfaction from breaking up other people's relationships. He expels Basil and Arthur from their flat, but it is suggested that they will be better for the self-knowledge he has produced: 'It's no good either of us thinking of Mabel. Or any other woman for that matter. We'll make plans for each other. No third party' (p. 152).

This conclusion ought to mean that Arthur and Basil come to terms with their sexual relationship, but that cannot be shown. Inexplicitness makes *The Trigon* unactable outside its time. Of course Basil and Arthur are discreet about homosexuality (if wearing Boy Scout uniform and playing 'The Sugar-Plum Fairy' is discreet). And they may delude themselves about the chances of making it with Mabel. But there is no dramatic reason for them to be discreet when they are alone together. The reason is extra-dramatic: they are being overheard by the audience, and this makes their privacy public and subject to censorship. To the reviewer of *Theatre World* (July 1964) the characters were 'inexplicably bound together emotionally'. The mystery in this play has nothing to do with the absurdist project usually attributed to Pinter, it is simply the limits of what James Broom Lynne was allowed to say.

Entertaining Homosexuality

Entertaining Mr Sloane followed *The Trigon* into the Arts theatre in 1964 and was published in the same volume of *Penguin Modern Plays*. The whole manner was in the air, provoked by the demands of speaking the unspeakable in the conditions of that moment. However, Orton's use of 'Pinteresque' indirect dialogue and the mysteriously powerful intruder is cunning and distinctive. He incorporates them into the action, making them required by the concerns of the characters. We understand the middle-aged Eddie to be homosexual because it is the only way of making sense of his toleration of Sloane, his interest in Sloane's physique and sex life, and his horror of heterosexuality. Eddie is indirect in his approach to Sloane because he assumes he must be cautious. Sloane evidently reads this indirection: he suggests that Eddie is 'sensitive'. But Eddie denies it, insisting, 'I seen birds all shapes and sizes and I'm most certainly not . . . um . . . sensitive' (p. 204). Sloane carefully plays Eddie along because, as Orton explained, Sloane knows the score but 'isn't going to give in until he has to'.[10]

In *Sloane* obscurity and indirection make sense *within* the action as the inhibitions of discretion. The play makes apparent the operations of the closet; it comments on the discretion of the censor and polite society, as well as being subject to it. Orton also makes sense of 'Pinteresque menace'. The attractive youth, Sloane, has killed a man who wanted to photograph him, and this danger is not merely arbitrary, metaphysical, or paranoid, but part of that experienced all the time by homosexuals. In *Serious Charge* by Philip King (1955) and *The Children's Hour* by Lillian Hellman (1934; produced at club theatres in 1950 and 1956) an attractive, dishonest, and violent young person tries to ruin a plausibly homosexual adult by accusing him/her of homosexuality (the accusations are false, but suspicion is allowed to remain, humouring conventional notions about artistic, bachelor vicars and intense, unmarried lady schoolteachers). In actual life, often, homosexuals are subject to violent assault and murder. By the end of the play Sloane has killed two men, and Kath and Eddie are rash to assume that he won't kill again.

The changed use of obliquity and innuendo in Orton's plays was possible partly because, by the mid-1960s, understanding was no longer the special secret of a few. A perverse benefit from the witch-hunt against homosexual men in the early 1950s was enhanced visibility and a great increase in public discussion – provoked also by the Kinsey Report (1948). In the United States, where persecution was even more vigorous, John D'Emilio observes that 'attacks on gay men and women hastened the articulation of a homosexual identity and spread the knowledge that they existed in large numbers'.[11] Commentators have often observed that in the 1950s homosexuality came to be considered less an evil or a sin, and more a medical or psychological condition. That is true, but also, increasingly, it was discussed as *a problem*. A Church of England pamphlet was called *The Problem of Homosexuality* (1954). This was the era of the problem (juvenile delinquency, unmarried mothers, the colour bar, latch-key children . . .); and it involved an expectation that the state would encourage public discussion and then pass laws to improve matters. The Wolfenden Committee on homosexual offences (and prostitution) was set up in 1954 after a minister for home affairs declared: 'Quite clearly, this is a problem which calls for very careful consideration on the part of those responsible for the welfare of the nation.' By the end of the decade Gordon Westwood believed that his 1952 objective, of bringing 'the problem of homosexuality . . . out into the open where it can be discussed and reconsidered', had been achieved.[12] Homosexuality was no longer unspoken. When *The Killing of Sister George* by Frank Marcus was playing at Wimbledon in 1967, Orton prophesied: 'I don't suppose they'll understand what the play is about.' 'Don't you believe it,' Halliwell replied. 'They'll know very well what it's about.' Orton acknowledges: 'He was right. It became clear, from the opening scenes, that they understood and weren't amused.'[13]

They could have found out from BBC radio comedy. In 1960 Peter Burton experienced the homosexual slang 'Polari' as 'our own camp secret language with which we could confound and confuse the *naffs* (straights)'.[14] But from 1964 Polari expressions such as 'bona' (attractive), 'varda' (look at), 'omee' (man) and 'polonee' (woman) featured regularly in the dialogue of two very camp men in the Light Programme comedy series *Round the Horne*, with Orton's friend Kenneth Williams as

Julian (Jules) and Hugh Paddick as Sandy. Here is a typical instance from March 1967, with the couple as journalists:

> PADDICK. Can we have five minutes of your time?
> HORNE. It depends what you want to do with them.
> WILLIAMS. Well, our editor said, Why don't you troll off to Mr Horne's lattie . . .
> HORNE. Flat or home – translator's note.
> WILLIAMS. And have a palare with him . . .[15]

For regular listeners, as well as for gays, the 'translation' would be unnecessary. Its offer was part of the joke, signifying that the private was in the process of becoming public. In 1967–8 the laws on homosexuality and stage censorship were changed. By 1969 Lou Reed was a cult hero, and by 1972 Alice Cooper and David Bowie took gender-bending into the pop charts. Unevenly, in diverse institutions, homosexuality was becoming less secret.

He Do the Police

In the heyday of Noël Coward, audiences divided according to whether they would pick up hints of homosexuality. From the mid-1960s the split was hardly over decoding competence, but around a contest as to what could be said in public. Homosexual nuances in Coward's plays either were not heard, or they were rendered tolerable by the acknowledgement (in their indirection) that such matters should not be allowed into public discourse. As homosexuality became more audible, it became the subject of explicit contest.

Some people were certainly upset. When *Sloane* was considered for television the company's legal officer thought it disgusting: 'Perfectly horrible and filthy. I don't know why we want to consider such a play.'[16] She had understood what it was about. Outside London, *Loot* provoked walk-outs – 'Bournemouth Old Ladies Shocked', reported *The Times*.[17] But the shockable audience understood that homosexuality (and other such causes) were at issue. Furthermore, it was confronted by another audience, associated typically with the Royal Court theatre, that wanted to see progressive plays. In the subsidized sector of theatre especially, the left-liberal intelligentsia was winning space for its kinds of representation – to the extent that a 'taboo' subject like homosexuality was hardly challenging to the people likely to attend a production known to feature it. This audience had come to indulge what was being called 'permissiveness', and felt confirmed in their progressive stance. In 1966 Frank Parkin found between 75 and 94 per cent (depending on social class) of CND supporters agreeing that laws against homosexual acts by consenting adults should be repealed.[18] While *Sloane* was running, establishment West End producers complained fiercely about 'dirty plays' – particularly at the subsidized Royal Shakespeare Company. Their objections were used to advertise *Sloane* – so far from being a disadvantage, the scandal was played up.[19] Compare what happened when Wilde was arrested: *An Ideal Husband* and *The Importance of Being Earnest* had been attracting large audiences, but Wilde's name was taken off the hoardings and the plays soon closed.[20]

However, *Entertaining Mr Sloane* does contain a challenge for a progressive audience (this was my experience). It resides not in the homosexuality, but in the lack of interpersonal feeling which, in the character of Sloane, produces psychopathic violence. This disappoints a left-liberal pleasure in Sloane's initially relaxed attitude to homosexuality, and frustrates a wish to see diverse kinds of sexuality justified by the affective quality of the relationship. Further, progressive plays generally presented the young person as a victim of the grown-ups (for instance, *A Taste of Honey* by Shelagh Delaney, *Five Finger Exercise* by Peter Shaffer, *Roots* and *Chips with Everything* by Arnold Wesker). In part Sloane is such a victim – at the end Kath and Eddie are able to force him into their 'family.'[21] But he is also the unsocialized hooligan whom conservatives were invoking as grounds for clamping down on all youthful self-expression. He is set up in some ways as the attractive character among the four, but kicking old men to death is carrying intergenerational conflict a bit too far.

Loot was better attuned to the liberal-progressive audience (I went with a group of fellow students – it was someone's birthday). The play is on the side of the boys, Hal and Dennis, and attacks officialdom and traditional moral attitudes. Some of the dialogue is in a discreet manner, but deployed so as to challenge hypocrisy and bogus formality ('And even the sex you were born into isn't safe from your marauding').[22] Above all, *Loot* excited the youthful left-liberal intelligentsia by its treatment of the police and the law. During the relative social harmony of the 1950s, unusually, the image of the friendly 'bobby' was relatively unchallenged (though homosexuals always had reason to distrust it). But repressive attitudes to political demonstrations from around 1960, and then to drugs, gradually shifted left-liberal opinion. In 1965, while Orton was writing *Loot*, the case of Detective Sergeant Harold Challenor came to prominence. He had arrested, beaten, and planted a brick and an iron bar on people demonstrating against the Greek monarchy (because it sponsored the right-wing government in Greece). Orton, says Kenneth Williams, became 'obsessed with Challenor', and as the play was reworked the part of Inspector Truscott was developed.[23]

It is not usually stressed that Orton's critique of police malpractice goes far beyond anything previously seen in the theatre, or indeed other media.

> TRUSCOTT. (*shouting, knocking* HAL *to the floor*). Under any other political system I'd have you on the floor in tears!
> HAL. (*crying*). You've got me on the floor in tears.

*   *   *

TRUSCOTT. And you complain you were beaten?
DENNIS. Yes.
TRUSCOTT. Did you tell anyone?
DENNIS. Yes.
TRUSCOTT. Who?
DENNIS. The officer in charge.
TRUSCOTT. What did he say?
DENNIS. Nothing.
TRUSCOTT. Why not?
DENNIS. He was out of breath with kicking.[24]

To have such things said in public, I recall, was as exciting as the relaxed attitudes to homosexuality attributed to Hal and Dennis. In the closing moments McLeavy tells Truscott 'You're mad!' The response recalled the Challenor case: 'Nonsense, I had a check-up only yesterday' (p. 274). Orton even worked into the text Challenor's actual words, reported in court: 'You're fucking nicked, my old beauty.'[25] Hilariously, the Lord Chamberlain would not allow 'fucking'. With the repressive state apparatus starkly displayed, he was still chasing after naughty words.

Introducing *Loot*, Simon Trussler said it outrages 'every expectation of a *morally* appropriate outcome'. However, in an article Trussler remarked the difference between '*kinds* of audiences': one kind 'may understand *Loot* because they share its moral assumptions', the other will prefer Whitehall farces and 'either ignore *Loot* or hate it'.[26] For left-liberals its critique was exhilarating. McLeavy's fate does not trouble us much, for he has foolishly worshipped the authority that victimizes him. The ending of *Loot* is triumphant because it displays most completely, in Truscott's behaviour, the corruption of established power and authority. (The effect is similar in the last moments of at least two other early 1960s new-wave plays, Wesker's *Chips with Everything* and Giles Cooper's *Everything in the Garden*.) Further, the final lines propose that Hal, Dennis, and Fay should all live together. This arrangement offers to resolve unconventionally but pleasantly a tension among the three most likeable characters. In fact it is exactly the happy ending of Noël Coward's *Design for Living* (1932). But times have changed and in *Loot* the idea can no longer be welcomed innocently – 'People would talk. We must keep up appearances' (p. 275). In so far as this does not repudiate the *ménage à trois* as such, it is pleasing to left-liberals and, in so far as it exposes the hypocrisy of 'people' once more, it is a final blow against convention.

After difficulties in the provinces, *Loot* was a hit in London. Its success could be partly because traditionally minded people enjoyed feeling indignant – Hal says of his father, 'His generation takes a delight in being outraged.'[27] But mainly it was because younger people were excited by it.

The Moment of Orton

The 1960s intensified both libertarian and reactionary attitudes and their conflict was staged in the theatre. These were the circumstances that permitted Orton's notoriety. Earlier, he would not have been tolerated; later he would not be so significant (though he would be the subject of determined recuperation). We might call it the moment of Orton. The plays' prominence depended on the social atmosphere of the 1950s – which produced and talked anxiously about, but did not enact, Wolfenden. They were written to scandalize the Aunt Ednas (and remember, this 'middlebrow' follower of theatre was invented by Rattigan). But the condition of their presentation and success was the fact that discretion and the audience that assumed it were already under pressure. By making visible the structure of the closet, the plays helped to make its dismantling possible. The 1960s liberalization that helped make Orton a celebrity, therefore, also set a limit to his moment.

Orton (like most people) had difficulty seeing himself as part of a trend. He enjoyed watching audiences upset by *Loot*, and believed his 'authentic voice' was 'vulgar and offensive in the extreme to middle-class susceptibilities'.[28] He scarcely realized that they were already on the run and that there was enthusiastic support for the critique he was mounting. This is partly because he had few links with the student culture of the subsidized theatre audience and distrusted its earnestness. He had studied at the Royal Academy of Dramatic Art in the early 1950s, well before the student radicalism of the CND generation, and his attitudes to homosexuality and theatre tended to assume the milieu of Coward or Rattigan. (Osborne partly shared Orton's background, and this helps to explain his poor fit with the progressive movement he initiated. He edged back to the discreet, upper-class theatrical world of Rattigan in *Hotel in Amsterdam* (1968) and *West of Suez* (1971).) Orton wanted commercial managements to present his plays. He thought Kenneth Tynan wouldn't dare include 'Until She Screams', the sketch he submitted for *Oh, Calcutta!* in 1967; but this piece had basically been written in 1960. As Simon Shepherd remarks, Orton 'had a rather inflated idea of his own shockingness: they did dare do his sketch. Orton's underestimate of the sexual "liberation" of others is a mark not just of his vanity but of his isolation.'[29]

The confusions of the moment of Orton were manifested institutionally. So vigorous was the left-liberal theatre audience that it encroached on the West End, partly through the efforts of progressive impresarios to make a distinctive space for themselves. Michael Codron and Donald Albery were looking for 'disturbing' plays, and hence keen to produce *Sloane*; Codron thought it 'might turn out to have the most exciting commercial possibilities since *The Caretaker*'.[30] By the mid-1960s the boundary between West End and subsidized theatre was blurred, and Orton was unclear about where he belonged. His *Ruffian on the Stair* and

The Erpingham Camp were presented by the Royal Court (in 1967), and when *Loot* wasn't going well Orton doubted whether it was right for commercial theatre and thought of putting it into the Royal Court or the National.[31]

More damagingly, Orton's commercial success kept him among the older type of discreet theatre homosexual, who identified with a privileged, leisure-class outlook in which conservative attitudes to homosexuality and theatre went together and constituted an inevitable and largely desirable state of affairs.[32] They believed – rightly – that more openness would spoil their kind of accommodation to homosexuality (even as it spoiled the Orton moment). In his diaries Orton shows virtually no interest in other gay plays, or in the new 'fringe' companies, or in moves to abolish stage censorship, or even in the legalization of male homosexuality. Rattigan commented: 'Orton thought it very funny that I, of all people, should have thought his play so good.'[33] Actually, they were not so far apart, for Orton's satire depended on Rattigan's world.

Who Saw the Butler?

What the Butler Saw includes powerful satire against the oppressive constructions of medicine and psychiatry, and creates continuous gender confusion, with cross-dressing and 'inappropriate' sexual advances. But it was not too disturbing for Orton's discreet friends. They were very enthusiastic about it[34] and encouraged him to have it produced by Binkie Beaumont and Tennents, with Ralph Richardson, at the Haymarket – in other words, in the heart of traditional West End theatre. Evidently Orton thought he was setting a trap: he wanted a conventionally 'lovely' set so that 'When the curtain goes up one should feel that we're right back in the old theatre of reassurance.'[35] But Orton doesn't consider why Beaumont should want to do the play; it is he, Orton, who was trapped. Commentators agree that the text was played without flair – it wasn't the censor (by then defunct) who would not allow Churchill's 'missing part' to be produced on stage, but Richardson, the Beaumont star.[36] The production pleased neither of the divergent audiences who were striving to claim theatre for their point of view.

Nevertheless, *What the Butler Saw* has been praised by the best commentators on Orton. Albert Hunt suggests that it 'would, presumably, have been revised and tightened had he lived', but still admires the way it destroys 'the sexual stability on which the mechanics of bedroom farce depend'.[37] Hunt adduces the description by Dr Prentice of his wife:

> My wife is a nymphomaniac. Consequently, like the Holy Grail, she's ardently sought after by young men. I married her for her money and, upon discovering her to be penniless, I attempted to throttle her. She escaped my murderous fury and I've had to live with her malice ever since.[38]

It had been complained that if Mrs Prentice is indeed so liberal about sex then the principal motive of the action becomes absurd – namely her husband trying to keep from her his attempt to seduce his secretary. This is the point, says Hunt: the logic of farce collapses.[39] But that logic requires the assumptions of a 1950s farce audience. By 1969 very many people no longer believed that it is important to conceal adultery, that Christian imagery is sacrosanct, even that female sexual desire is shocking and/or funny. Brian Rix, sponsor of the Whitehall farces, had remarked in 1966: 'with the more tolerant climate there now is, we could put on a farce about adultery and our audience wouldn't bat an eyelid.' And he attributed 'the more liberal attitude' partly to Royal Court plays. Orton was not unaware of the issue. In the same article he is quoted as complaining: 'A lot of farces today are still based on the preconceptions of a century ago, particularly the preoccupations about sex. But we must now accept that, for instance, people *do* have sexual relations outside marriage.'[40] Things were moving faster than he realized. Back in 1962, Giles Cooper's *Everything in the Garden* was powerful when it showed conventional middle-class people finding themselves involved in prostitution and murder and getting used to the idea. In 1969, for many people, the concern in *Butler* with adultery and nakedness was merely quaint – and the speech about Mrs Prentice's 'nymphomania' sounded like it was straining to shock (and nothing is done with Prentice's 'murderous fury'). Progressive audiences would be disappointed at the failure to develop the homosexual theme after the initial interview between Prentice and Nick.

Simon Shepherd observes that instead of a return to order at the end of *What the Butler Saw*, incestuous desire is revealed. He believes the audience, 'like any comedy audience . . . *sees* itself to be like the characters in expecting an ending to disorder; but discovers that ending to be alien and uncomfortable. Thus trapped the audience is driven wild. The first performances succeeded: people stormed out or barracked the players.'[41] But suppose one did not find incest between consenting adults so very terrible? To be sure, the play upset some of Richardson's older admirers in the preliminary week in Brighton (I saw it there). And it was booed and jeered on the opening night in London, though this was not a naïve response but an organized campaign by the group of gallery first-nighters, followers of traditional theatre, that had already disrupted Colin Spencer's *Spitting Image* a few months previously.[42] But – my title question – who was afraid of Joe Orton? Was it important to taunt those people in 1969, especially at the price of framing *Butler* in terms they would react against? The play's title, which refers to ancient seaside machines showing 'sexy' pictures of women's knickers and suspenders for a penny, was of course meant to be ironic, but it holds Orton bound to the framework of attitudes that he wants to oppose. Furthermore, he could affront the Aunt Ednas only by failing to engage with other audiences. A different kind of farce, plucking at the susceptibilities of a sophisticated liberal audience, was just ahead in the work of Alan Ayckbourn and Michael Frayn. And plays on explicit gay themes – *The Killing of Sister George, When Did You Last See My Mother?, Staircase, Spitting Image, Fortune and Men's Eyes, The Madness of Lady Bright, Total Eclipse* – had been produced in London (most of these began in 'alternative' venues; all but the last two transferred to the West End).

Jonathan Dollimore has also praised *Butler*: he calls it 'black camp', and remarks the irony, parody, and pastiche, held together by 'a stylistic *blankness*'. He argues that the play insinuates 'the arbitrariness and narrowness of gender roles, and that they are socially ascribed rather than naturally given'.[43] The play is thus in the mode of Wilde who, Dollimore shows, validates the artificial, the non-natural, the insincere. Wilde thus subverts the demand for depth – for authenticity, sincerity, and the natural; and these are 'dominant categories of subjectivity which keep desire in subjection'.[44] So we may see that sexual relations are not essentially thus or thus, but are based on manners, convention, custom, ideology, power. This is indeed what *Butler* does some of the time. It 'becomes a kind of orgy of cross-dressing, gender confusion and hierarchical inversion', and the dialogue calls into question the 'natural' – in circumstances where the speaker is in fact mistaken, because of cross-dressing, about the 'naturalness' of the very example he is using.[45] But even so, much of the comedy depends on believing that such attitudes are outrageous, and that, whatever their clothes, Nick is really a boy and Geraldine really a girl. I am inclined to see Orton's refusal of depth as indicating weakness rather than strength. This is not the assured position, perhaps the arrogance, of Wilde; it is looking over its shoulder to see how Aunt Edna is responding.

There is an alternative strategy to Wilde's cultivation of artificiality, as Dollimore shows. It appropriates parts of the dominant discourse, asserting the naturalness of gay relations and seeking to use sincerity and authenticity against their usual implication. This strategy was cultivated by Radclyffe Hall and André Gide. Of course, it may be no more than a pathetic plea to be allowed to share the power of the oppressor. But, alternatively, it may seize the ideology of depth and authenticate the unorthodox. And hence it may contribute to the development of what Foucault calls 'a reverse discourse', whereby 'homosexuality begins to speak on its own behalf, to forge its own identity and culture, *often in the self-same categories by which it has been produced and marginalised*, and eventually challenges the very power structures responsible for its "creation".'[46]

This latter was in fact the main strategy of the 1960s homosexual law reform capaign[47] and, shortly after Orton's death, of Gay Liberation – to produce and believe in positive representations of homosexuality ('gay is good'; the validation of surface over depth was slightly later, stimulated by such diverse concepts as the pink economy, poststructuralism, and high-energy disco-dancing). Orton was out of step with that reforming tendency; he refused nature, depth, and sincerity at least partly because, although he felt an intuitive opposition to the prevailing sexual ideology, he had difficulty conceiving a positive view of the homosexual.[48] He was stuck, in other words, in the Orton moment.

To be sure, Orton shows an untroubled practice of homosexuality in some characters – Sloane, Hal, and Dennis, perhaps Nick. But none of them is apparently *a homosexual*. The instance of that is the older, closeted Eddie in *Sloane*, and his devious exercise of power makes him unattractive. This is reminiscent of Coward who, I have argued elsewhere, validates deviant sexuality when it is part of a general bohemianism but makes his specifically homosexual characters unappealing.[49] Orton was very concerned that there should be nothing 'queer or camp or odd' about Hal and Dennis – 'They must be perfectly ordinary boys who happen to be fucking each other. Nothing could be more natural.' He also objected to Eddie appearing camp.[50] This seems radical; it is against stereotypes and appropriates nature. On the other hand, 'we're all bisexual really' is the commonest evasion. Hal and Dennis are said to be indifferent to the gender of their partners ('You scatter your seed along the pavements without regard to age or sex').[51] That was an unusual and disconcerting thought; it takes the implications of cross-dressing and superficiality quite literally; it could be utopian. But it also keeps a distance from very many actual homosexuals; it was not how Orton lived, or others that he knew. At this time male homosexuals were struggling to be gay, not to be indifferent to sexual orientation. Of course, we all think we want to get away from stereotypes. However, these are not arbitrary external impositions, but are implicated in the whole construction of sexuality in the modern world; they figure, positively and negatively, in gay self-understanding. You challenge them not by jumping clear but by engaging with them.

'Spitting Image'

It may be that Dollimore's two strategies can be combined – so that the strategy of superficiality deconstructs normative assumptions about patriarchy, heterosexuality and the family, and then the strategy of sincerity asserts the claims of unorthodox sexuality. I would suggest that Caryl Churchill's *Cloud Nine* (1979) does this. So does *Spitting Image* by Colin Spencer. This was produced in 1968, when the abolition of the Lord Chamberlain's censorship function made it suddenly possible to present plays that would make sense to and for a gay audience. To be sure, homosexuals had frequented discreet plays, even regarding theatre as a specially homosexual medium, but that discretion enshrined heterosexist assumptions. *Spitting Image* is written to make best sense to a

gay audience eager for its own theatre. It opened at the Hampstead
Theatre Club, a suitable location for a progressive audience, and proved
strong enough to gain a brief West End transfer to the Duke of York's.
There, *The Times* reported, it received 'loud boos from the gallery and
sustained applause from the stalls': it upset the old-fashioned moralists
and energized gays and radicals.[52]

To general astonishment and fear, one partner in a male homosexual
couple, Gary and Tom, conceives and bears a child (who calls them
Daddy One and Daddy Two). Familiar structures are shifted on to this
strange situation.

> DOCTOR. Yes, yes, any other symptoms, Mr Dart?
> TOM. Oh, just the normal ones, you know.
> DOCTOR. Normal?
> TOM. I mean, well, morning sickness in the first two months and
> then . . .[53]

Normality disintegrates in such a bizarre application. The relation of
mother and infant is one of the strongest sites for the ideology of
sincerity, nature, and depth, but its images scatter. 'It's so difficult to
adjust to . . . one gets so used to the idea of mother, like you know, on
those TV commercials' (p. 33). The play misses no opportunity to get the
language of patriarchy, family, and heterosexuality to entangle itself.
When a girl friend tries to kiss him Gary retreats: 'It's wrong. I'm a
mother . . . I can't go around kissing girls' (p. 37). The authorities want
to get hold of the parent and child, and decide that their tactic should be
to 'break up the family unit' (p. 35): they use the term 'family' even as
they plot against Gary and Tom because they are not a family.

But also, as they struggle against hostile officials and stereotypes, the
gay couple appropriate the genuine and human. A psychiatrist asks:
'and would you say that you are the active partner of this relationship?'
Tom replies: 'Eh? No, not really. I mean, it comes and goes. Sometimes
one thing, sometimes another' (p. 28). I recall people in the audience
applauding at this repudiation – in public – of one of the heterosexual
myths that aspire to organize gay sexuality. Gary and Tom are not
sentimentalized – most of the time they are bickering because of the
strain of the situation ('Doctor Spock says that parents often find it
difficult to adjust' (p. 33)). John Russell Taylor found them 'an entirely
believable married couple, living and growing together and apart. Few
heterosexual plays have done this so well.'[54]

Of course, gay men were to repudiate the manoeuvre that 'tolerates'
us so long as we appear to approximate to supposed heterosexual norms
(though in 1968 this was a provocative claim). However, *Spitting Image*
never allows the heterosexist values that it is appropriating to settle
down. It both subverts the ideology of depth *and* claims it for gays. It
would be difficult to say which is happening when Gary, disappointed at
Tom's lesser commitment, makes an emotive speech about parenthood:

> You're all surface aren't you mate? All you think about is the kind
> of place we live in, your pay packet, the films, plays, dinner-parties
> we used to go to. That was all your whole bloody life. Haven't you
> ever stopped for one minute and thought that we've created a new
> human being, a tiny creature who looks for us for love, guidance
> and security, who trusts both of us absolutely? (p. 36)

It is an appeal to depth, embedded in a situation where it must be
absurd. Spencer said he wanted to present both the reality of a love
relationship and the responsibility of having a child, and a farcical attack
on bureaucracy: 'The whole play's style had to change gear constantly.'[55]

The civil service and government assume that such offspring must be
studied, hidden, and prevented:

> The confusion would be unimaginable, it would distort the whole
> legal system. Think of the manpower lost in the professions and
> industries if these damned pansies are always prancing off becom-
> ing mothers. . . . Homosexuals of all races, colours and creeds
> would suddenly be given the hope of creating offspring. And what
> is more likely than that the offspring themselves will have the same
> sexual abnormalities. The whole world would be overrun – ugh!
> (pp. 33–4)

This homophobic utterance deconstructs itself by invoking the potential
of what was soon to be called gay power. Indeed, it transpires, in the
play, that many such children are being conceived. Daddy One responds
by organizing a national movement (though Daddy Two is initially
apathetic). The tactics are specifically reminiscent of the Suffragettes but
also, in a stroke of inspiration, they anticipate the mass solidarity of Gay
Liberation.

> But don't you see? Before we were alone, utterly alone, a freakish
> development. Now we are stronger . . . At first we're bound to be a
> deprived minority. The Government will be trying to hush the
> whole thing up. Well I'm not going to let it. . . . (p. 40)

Spitting Image is organized around a biological impossibility – that is
the repudiation of the conventional ideology of depth. But the ending is
gloriously triumphant. Gary and Tom's offspring is not only unusually
strong, intelligent, and humane (he worries dreadfully about the
Vietnam War), he is also able to infiltrate Downing Street at night and
affect the Prime Minister's mind by auto-suggestion. As a result the law
is changed, producing 'happy homosexuals' (p. 45). Daddy Two conceives. Nor is the effect limited to gays: Tom's mother is converted ('Well
if the papers say it's all right, I suppose it is', p. 45), and the Prime
Minister repudiates militarism. Gay Liberation correlates with peace and
love generally; indeed, the genuine freeing of a major oppressed group,
if it occurred, would perhaps amount to that.

Of course, the triumphant ending is even more of a fantasy than the rest – 'Funny how people's attitudes have changed' (p. 45). But fantasies are important: they mark the boundaries of the plausible, and may help us to see that plausibility is a powerful social construction – dominated, of course, by patriarchy, heterosexuality, and the family. Nancy K. Miller has noted the way women writers are frequently accused of falling prey to implausibilities in their fiction. They are said to manifest sensibility, sensitivity, extravagances – 'code words for feminine in our culture' – at the expense of verisimilitude. But such 'improbable' plots may be read as comments on the prevailing stories of women's lives – they manifest 'the extravagant wish for a *story* that would turn out differently'.[56] That is, the wish of women for power over their lives cannot be expressed plausibly within dominant discourses, only as fantasy. The improbability in *Spitting Image* is utopian, but it also alludes to that fact, and to the scale of social change that would have to occur for gays to become acceptably empowered.

Colin Spencer's play has continuing resonances for gay culture. The obvious analogue for its main situation now is the oppression of lesbian mothers, whose children are taken from them in the way that is attempted in *Spitting Image*. And the government decision to place the gay parents compulsorily in an 'enclosed colony', telling them they have 'a rare disease' (p. 39), is all too like modes of control that have been proposed for people with AIDS.

Gay men have found support in the notion that homosexuals have been creators of Art (well, it's got to be better than disc jockeys and royalty). To be sure, we can and should uncover the underlying gay significance in such work. But that very act tends to reinforce a notion that gay creativity must be covert. Decoding the work of closeted homosexual artists ought to produce a recognition of oppression, rather than a cause for celebration. Theatre has long been a site of homosexual culture, but it had always to be glimpsed through ostensibly heterosexual texts and institutions. *Spitting Image* represents a new break, because although in a public mode and a public venue, it is written not for the Aunt Ednas, but for gays. It appropriates theatre for an explicit gay culture, anticipating the Gay Sweatshop company. Other audiences are invited, but they will have the perhaps disconcerting experience – which gays have all the time – of sitting in on someone else's culture. *Spitting Image* signals the possibility of a non-closeted gay subculture.

It is through involvement in a subculture that one discovers an identity in relation to others and perhaps a basis for political commitment. A subculture creates a distinctive circle of reality, partly alternative to the dominant. There you can feel that Black is beautiful, gay is good. Such a sense of shared identity and purpose is necessary for self-preservation. However, subcultures may also return to trouble the dominant. They are formed partly by and partly in reaction to it – they redeploy its cherished values, downgrading, inverting or reapplying them, and thereby demonstrate their incoherence. Their outlaw status may exert a fascination for the dominant, focusing fantasies of freedom, vitality, even squalor. So they form points from which its repressions may become apparent, its silences audible.

11 Constructing a lesbian poetic for survival: Broumas, Rukeyser, H.D., Rich, Lorde

Liz Yorke

Growing up during the 1950s and 1960s in a conventional working-class family, I did not have any words to enable me to know about women-loving women – the much-censored word *lesbian* had virtually disappeared from the world around me, and certainly did not enter into my consciousness. In poetry, lesbian voices have also been subjected to extensive public or personal censorship. Indeed, this artificial silencing underlies the feminist critic's difficulty in locating lesbian voices within this genre. In her introduction to *Lesbian Poetry: An Anthology* (1981), Elly Bulkin suggested that 'it was easy, a few years ago, to think that lesbian poetry didn't exist'.[1] It *did*, of course, but it was neglected, 'lost', altered by others – or represented in coded forms by the poets themselves. Bulkin points to the 'impossibility of identifying [lesbian poets] unless they were represented by poems about subjects connected directly and explicitly to lesbian oppression and/or sexuality'.

Historically speaking, it is hardly news to say that lesbians have been excluded from the cultural symbolic order. They have found themselves situated at the margins of acceptability and have been virtually eradicated from many public discourses – including male-dominated poetry. Lesbian voices have literally been silenced, lesbian experience and identity have been erased and, for centuries, lesbians have been systematically dispossessed of their heritage. Yet as poets, writers, and academics, we are not bound to accept such silencing, invisibility, and erasure. In our work we must be attentive to the silences to identify, theorize, and explore what Diana Collecott has called the 'gap between experience and representation' – that is, the gap between lesbian lives and those dominant discourses which problematically avoid, distort, suppress, or condemn the actualities of lesbian existence.[2] The necessity is to challenge and oppose such dominance as a matter of urgency, for our *survival* within cultural forms depends on it.

When a lesbian begins to write her own story in her own words, she also begins to redefine herself and her community – in her own terms – within public discourses. Her disruptive words, traditionally barred from the consciousness of conventional poetic practice, blatantly exceed the limits of what is linguistically permissible within patriarchal representation. The task of this chapter is to examine how lesbian poets have negotiated the difficult gap between silence and speech in their attempts to construct within the symbolic a language adequate to lesbian experience. The lesbian writer has long been 'conscious of herself as an absence from discourse' and, in the face of censure, has traditionally adopted strategies of concealment involving a 'necessary obliquity'.[3] Above all, the struggle to articulate a poetic for survival has meant a struggle with fear, with internalized homophobia, and, of course, with the otherness and difference of being lesbian.

As Adrienne Rich has commented, 'women writers are now beginning to dare to enter that particular chamber of the "unspeakable" and to breathe word of what we are finding there'.[4] In so doing, the lesbian writer may well bring to language the distress, anger, and fear of *being the other*. She may also, much more disturbingly, celebrate and claim the *joy* of lesbian existence within language. In refusing to collaborate with the mechanisms of silencing, the lesbian writer articulates the suppressed alternatives to the conventional male/female heterosexual relation. In that the lesbian can and does challenge patriarchal definitions of herself, she defiantly identifies herself *for* herself: she makes herself, her sexuality, and her body visible – in spite of repressive discursive practices. Here, Olga Broumas's lines lovingly transform the terms of lesbian sexuality: the woman's patriarchally named 'cunt' is considered to be 'miraculous' and 'a seething of holiness'. Symbolized as a 'small cathedral', her body's interior becomes a 'light-filled temple' in which worshippers light many candles to mark their profound respect. In addressing her lover, Broumas suggests that

A woman-made language would
have as many synonyms for pink/light-filled/holy as
the Eskimo does
for snow . . .

      You too, my darling, are
folded, clean
round a light-filled temple, complete
with miraculous icon, shedding
her perfect tears[5]

Clearly, Broumas has defiantly brought to this poem a lesbian interpretation of her lover's body to affirm the ecstatic sensuality of lesbian sexual love. Lesbian poets, however tyrannically they have been marginalized within discourse, have often devised strategies of writing that can be set against definitions assailing them from homophobic culture. In this chapter, I explore how poems by Olga Broumas, Muriel Rukeyser, H.D. (Hilda Doolittle), Adrienne Rich, and Audre Lorde re-present lesbian libidinal difference, sexual identity, and cultural identity – in their *own* terms.

The task for the lesbian poet is, I should say at the outset, not one of searching for the repressed 'authentic' lesbian voice. Rather, it involves identifying and powerfully articulating the repressed representations, practices, and languages which construct lesbians as intelligible and sexually complex beings able to make a critical challenge to the regulatory practices of patriarchal discursive systems. For lesbian writers this involves deconstructing the heterosexual matrix which stabilizes phallogocentrism. For example, the transcendent 'I' of lyric poetry presents itself as a free subjectivity and at the same time denies/conceals its heterosexual masculinist bias. The western lyric tradition has long presented itself through a universal 'I' voice. Collecott has spoken of this 'anonymous tradition of white male lyricism' in which love poems have been addressed 'from "I" to "you"', with the sex of both partners unidentified'.[6] Such apparently gender-neutral language acts as a mask which allows the presumption of heterosexuality to go uncontested: 'masculist traditions of interpretation assume that the poet or speaking subject is male, and the beloved object is female, unless there is internal evidence to the contrary'. While, as Collecott suggests, these conventions have allowed homosexual writers to publish 'with impunity', they have also functioned to perpetuate the exclusivity of heterosexual norms in all their inequity. Lesbian writing needs to contest these sites of gender-neutral language, and this means resignifying differences and desires in gender-specific language to re-produce the lesbian sexual body in both its variation *and* its specificity.

Historically, lesbian poets have too often been driven to hide behind the mask of gender neutrality. As Adrienne Rich comments: 'Along with persecution, we have met with utter, suffocating silence and denial: the attempt to wipe us out of history and culture altogether. This silence is part of the totality of silence about women's lives.'[7]

For lesbians living within a hostile patriarchy, survival has depended on secrecy, on deviousness and the deliberate exclusion of specific aspects of our private sexual and emotional lives. Bulkin points to the impossibility of identifying lesbian contributions to culture as such, and the 'potential for erroneous (or, at best, incomplete) reading' of lesbian work.[8] For a poet to celebrate a lesbian relationship directly and openly, she has to have reached an acceptance, intellectually and emotionally, of lesbian sexual difference. Here is Muriel Rukeyser writing in 1973:

> Yes, our eyes saw each other's eyes
> Yes, our mouths saw each other's mouth
> Yes, our breasts saw each other's breasts
> Yes, our bodies entire saw each other
> Yes, it was beginning in each
> Yes, it threw waves across our lives

Yes, the pulses were becoming very strong
Yes, the beating became very delicate
Yes, the calling   the arousal
Yes, the arriving   the coming
Yes, it was there for both entire
Yes, we were looking at each other[9]

What is the sexual difference to be celebrated here? The 'difference' lies
in the sameness of the different women's bodies, the reciprocity of their
desires for each other, the delicacy of their lovemaking. It can be seen in
the concern of the speaker as she notes whether each moment of
recognition and further arousal has been reached by the other –
through each noticing and responding to the other's 'look'. The body
that 'looks' is the same sex as the body that is looked at, and the women's
sexual rhythms and responses have the same form. These particular
lovers take care that both partners are orgasmically satisfied – 'Yes, it was
there for both entire'. Rukeyser's use of chiasmus as a structuring figure
for lesbian desire is intriguing: the contrasting parallel phrases 'the
calling', 'the coming', 'the arousal', 'the arriving' may be considered as a
kind of spatial metaphor. The Greek root of the term chiasmus is *chiasma*
– a cross-shaped mark. Here, the figure takes the shape of an intertwin-
ing cross – which conveys a strong sense of the powerfully tender and
erotic bond between women who have said 'Yes' to each other's desiring
sexual bodies.[10]

Coming to recognize and use the complexity of difference as a resource for poetry in the struggle against persecution of lesbians and gay
men requires the poet to abandon reticence, secrecy, and self-hatred:

Among our secrecies, not to despise our Jews
(that is, ourselves) or our darkness, our blacks,

     . . . never to despise
the homosexual who goes building another
with touch   with touch   (not to despise any touch)
each like himself, like herself each
You are this.[11]

Again, through the use of similes, the poet explores the sameness-in-
difference – the difference-in-sameness – of homosexuality. Same-sex
love between men is clearly different from that between women and yet
it is also 'like'. In this complex word-play, the word 'like' becomes very
mobile, moving between genders and putting in parallel the key marks
of sexual difference. The poem both acknowledges differences *and*
collapses prominent distinctions of class, race, and sexuality. Blacks,
Jews, and homosexuals become 'ourselves' indistinguishable from 'them'
– no longer the other in their difference from us, we become them, they
become us – 'You are this'. Damaging projections on to the other are to

be reintegrated into the field of identity. Unconsciously acquired intern-
alizations are, likewise, to be examined and held up to question.
Constructing a poetic for survival thus requires the poet courageously to
explore the unacknowledged fears, the 'darkness', 'the secrecy' within –
and so requires her to refuse to accept the disparagements and discriminations discursively produced by an anti-Semitic, racist and sexist
hetero-patriarchy.

But before 1973, creating a lesbian voice was far from easy for
Rukeyser. Bulkin describes having 'read through Rukeyser's work without thinking of her possible lesbianism until *after* I had heard that she
had agreed to participate in the lesbian poetry reading at the 1978
Modern Language Association convention'. Rukeyser did not make the
convention and died in 1980. But Bulkin was compelled to reassess her
approach to Rukeyser's work: 'sending me back to her work, the discovery allowed me to understand for the first time that the opening
poems in *The Speed of Darkness* [1968] celebrate coming out'.[12] Rukeyser's
oblique and ambiguous representation in 'What Do I Give You?' (one of
the opening poems of that 1968 collection) gives us little indication that
she is a lesbian writer whose lesbianism may not be spoken of and whose
memories could not enter into the language of her poetry:

> What do I give you?   This memory
> I cannot give you.   Force of a memory
> I cannot give you: it rings my nerves among.
> None of these songs
> Are made in their images.
> Seeds of all memory
> Given me give I you
> My own self.   Voice of my days.
> Blessing;   the seed and pain,
> Green of the praise of growth.
> The sacred body of thirst.[13]

Following Bulkin's example by reading retrospectively, we can see that
Rukeyser speaks – if only indirectly and in gender-neutral language – of
the effects of repressive censorship on the lesbian poet. To produce and
develop a lesbian reading practice is vitally necessary if we are to recognize and understand the poetics of lesbian survival. As Collecott
suggests, this requires 'a revision of reading practices, and especially the
New Critical convention that a literary text contains within itself all the
information necessary to its interpretation'.[14]

It is clear that, under conditions of censorship, Rukeyser may not
draw on her own reminiscences. She may not make poetry out of the
substance of her own life's experiences, out of her own emotional
complexities, her own cultural attachments: 'None of these songs/Are
made in their images.' The poet is driven instead to use symbolic 'seeds'

to encode her memories, to give voice to 'my days', to give 'you' (the reader? who else? her lover?) 'My own self.' She does not speak openly of her pains and blessings, nor of her relationship to imposed or internal-ized silencing. All is veiled by the movement into symbolic/mythic refer-ence. Without contextual knowledge of Rukeyser's own life and of her lesbianism, it would be easy to miss the point of this poem.

The poem that opens *The Speed of Darkness*, and which is placed immediately preceding the above poem, is 'The Poem as Mask, *Orpheus*'. This equally cryptic poem is hardly speaking out about its lesbianism. Yet, given the knowledge that Rukeyser is a lesbian poet, it may be read as a manifesto, as a coded declaration of the necessity for lesbian poets to break through the façade mythopoesis provides and identify themselves for themselves within discourse.[15] Rukeyser clearly indicates her wish to 'sing her own music' and her passionate desire to position herself as no longer utterly fragmented but rather as a 'rescued' subjectivity able to reach towards a sense of her uncompromised integrity as a lesbian:

> When I wrote of the women in their dances and wildness, it
> was a mask,
> on their mountain, gold-hunting, singing, in orgy,
> it was a mask; when I wrote of the god,
> fragmented, exiled from himself, his life, the love gone down
> with song,
> it was myself, split open, unable to speak, in exile from myself.
>
> There is no mountain, there is no god, there is memory
> of my torn life, myself split open in sleep, the rescued child
> beside me among the doctors, and a word
> of rescue from the great eyes.
>
> No more masks! No more mythologies!
>
> Now, for the first time, the god lifts his hand,
> The fragments join in me with their own music.[16]

The poet states that her writing had previously been masked. Jacob Korg suggests that the use of the poetic mask was developed substan-tially by Ezra Pound who tried to 'convey character or states of mind through style in poems written through fictional or historical characters'. Pound viewed these poems 'as steps in a search for his own identity which he carried on by first creating and then casting off "complete masks of the self in each poem"'.[17] Here, masked or personified as Orpheus, the poet is 'in exile' from herself; she is 'unable to speak', 'split open', fragmented. The male god Orpheus, who had functioned as a masculine projection, functions as a persona to conceal the voice of the *poet*. Rukeyser's use of the personal reflexive pronoun 'me', repeated three times, emphasizes her desire to disclose the subject behind this mask – the silenced, torn-apart identity of the lesbian poet. She begins a reconstructive process of re-membering and reminiscence, attempting a symbolic reintegration of the 'fragments' of her disintegrated self. Reviewing her 'torn life', the 'child' is rescued, and so the poet's own voice may be heard. Rukeyser seems to be rejecting her earlier poetic strategies. Now 'there is no mountain, there is no god', and she very evidently desires to sing her 'own music'. In the wry reversal of the concluding lines, when 'the god lifts his hand', we may well ask – is he waving farewell? is he releasing her? Or is he beckoning her to speak her own words, sing her own song? It is tempting to think that in retaining the figure of Orpheus, Rukeyser is signalling her continuing allegiance to the use of Greek mythology as an alternative cultural resource having especial resonances within homosexual writing. But, in fact, very few of her later poems actually do so. When Rukeyser does refer to Greek myth again her usage is ironic. Henceforth, when she speaks, she speaks as herself.

Yet the Greek poet Sappho is an inspirational and very special precursor for a great many lesbian poets. Lesbian and bisexual poets have, despite their ambivalent reactions to Sappho's possible suicide, frequently mythicized the resonances of their lives in poetry that draws its symbolic imagery from sapphic sources. Modern and contemporary poets have built on her surviving fragments to invent a classical inheritance where none truly exists. As Susan Gubar has remarked, since so many of the original Greek texts were destroyed 'the modern woman poet could write "for" or "as" Sappho and thereby invent a classical inheritance of her own' – through what Gubar calls a 'fantastic collaboration'. Women poets could, therefore, reach for that 'long-lost ecstatic lyricism that inscribes female desire as the ancient source of song'.[18] Rachel Blau Du Plessis follows Gubar when she claims that

> to need Sappho as a literary woman is to participate in an erotic-textual chain of longing that occurs for several reasons, not the least that Sappho has been left in fragments, and hence can be fleshed out, re-animated by being rewritten.[19]

Du Plessis argues further that modernist poet H.D. 'inspired herself repeatedly by engagement with Greek materials, imitated and reproduced them to produce herself as a writer'.[20] This classicizing impulse allows the writer to assume both 'real and imagined' personae and revise them in texts that emerge 'aslant to reigning conventions'. These strategies may also be used both to project *and* to veil the self. As Du Plessis points out:

> despite the unstinting Greek contexts and references, it is possible to see (as Norman Holmes Pearson has suggested) the whole set of lyrics only coincidentally Greek: the landscapes are American,

the emotions are personal, the 'Greek' then becomes a conventional but protected projection of private feelings into public meanings.[21]

H.D. chose to locate her poetic within the ancient world of Sappho and frequently invoked the gods and goddesses, the religious ceremonial and symbology familiar to us from pagan classical texts. The appropriation of ancient myth has particular value to a twentieth-century woman writer engaged in the task of reconstructive re-vision. She may use it to support and sustain an alternative cultural perspective; to resymbolize a scene, plot, or narrative; to project and re-enact within a transformed setting her personal story; or she may dramatize some moment that has been important to her in her personal life.

H.D. frequently and deliberately echoed Sappho's lyricism, her extreme simplicity of style, her intense sensuality and her fine emotional delicacy. Sappho's sparse, short lines, her clarity of image, her personal dramatic narratives – all were vital parts of H.D's speaking 'for' or 'as' Sappho, as she displaced and mythicized her experience into poetry. 'From citron bower', an extract from 'Hymen (1921)', can be read as a semi-ironic 'temple service' of lament which enacts ceremoniously the coming of (heterosexual) love to the bride at the Temple of Hera. 'Hymen' is directly related to Sappho through its form, its imagery, its trajectory of desire, and its symbolic reference:

> From citron-bower be her bed,
> Cut from branch of tree a-flower,
> Fashioned for her maidenhead.
>
> From Lydian apples, sweet of hue,
> Cut the width of board and lathe.
> Carve the feet from myrtle-wood.
>
> Let the palings of her bed
> Be quince and box-wood overlaid
> With the scented bark of yew.
>
> That all the wood in blossoming,
> May calm her heart and cool her blood
> For losing of her maidenhood.[22]

This poem echoes the sense of grief in Sappho's 'Fragment 34'. The song is a lament for a maidenhead, its imagery 'Lydian' – soft, slow, luxurious, feminine. The Cretan quince-apple, sacred to Aphrodite, speaks tellingly of erotic connection; it is also the sacred apple of the tree of life and death in Hera's garden. The sensual appeal of fragrant wood and fragrant blossom is ambivalently linked to death; the yew is emblematic of grief in Greek mythology; and the myrtle signifies life in death. The bed may blossom to 'calm her heart and cool her blood', but as we read the poem, the carved wood becomes ever more overlaid, box-like, coffin-like, closed in – as these symbolic references resonate. Sung by a chorus of boys, the final section tells how the desire of the woman becomes more and more eclipsed, 'mute and dumb', before the 'fiery need' of the male 'plunderer'.[23] Ultimately, we are told, 'Where love is king' there is little need to 'dance and sing'. The consummation of heterosexual love renders her speechless – it is not quite a moment to be celebrated:

> Where love is come
> (Ah, love is come indeed!)
> Our limbs are numb
> Before his fiery need;
> With all their glad
> Rapture of speech unsaid,
> Before his fiery lips
> Our lips are mute and dumb.[24]

A deathly failure of light, colour, and sound signals the end of the service. 'Blinded the torches fail' and *'flicker out'*; the music *'dies away'* and is *'finally cut short'*; *'the purple curtain hangs black and heavy'*; the figures *'pass out like shadows'*; and the service concludes in gloomy darkness and in silence. The over-romanticized *'flame, an exaggerated symbol'* of heterosexual love was hardly a figure to be welcomed. Thus it appears that H.D. has encoded the patterns of the heterosexual marriage on the surface but the sorrow and mourning of a lesbian *funeral* underlie the writing. In this liturgy of lament, as in Sappho's poetry, the direction of emotional attention is towards the woman. The feeling underlying this service is the profound sense of loss experienced by the 'concealed' lesbian poet who represents, complexly, her passionate concern and caring for the plundered, wan-faced bride: muteness, numbness, and grief appear to overwhelm her as the one she loves (herself or another) is 'taken' into heterosexual alliance.

H.D. surely has played hide and seek with the mask and the myth to find a way of creatively rehearsing situations and experiences drawn from her life. In working within and against a modernist aesthetic, H.D. makes use of the unsatisfactory heterosexual codes that so distort lesbian realities – in order to produce a lesbian encoding of her alternative story. In constructing a performative drama as a way to enact her grief, the poet also contests the socially instituted meaning of the heterosexual encounter. She subverts its power to transfix and fascinate, and thereby works to deconstruct its coercive ideological force. Ultimately the poet creates a subversive matrix in which the normative terms given within heterosexual discourses are rendered absurd and ridiculous. The intelligibility of lesbian desire, attachment, and loss does not reside in 'joy decreed' or in the *'flamboyant bird, half emerged in the sunset'* – such images, ones emanating from the powerful discourses of heterosexual love, are rendered either as seductive or as ridiculous.[25] Rather, it lies with the 'flute and trumpet wail', the *'black and heavy'* signifiers of (concealed) lesbian loss and grieving.

Lesbian loss and grief become literally unmentionable where compulsory heterosexuality rules discourse. The loss or death of a lover, or separation, or an unsatisfiable yearning for an unavailable woman become unrepresentable, unintelligible to a world in which their existence is denied. Lesbian sadness or grief; the unsatisfied longing for tenderness, for an intimacy lost or never found – the confused strands that constitute the breadth of lesbian experience – all need to be made coherent and distinctly lesbian. Fully articulated themes of lesbian grief, separation, and loss dominate Rich's much later poem, 'Splittings (1974)'. At the same time, however, the poem is a celebration of the freedom to 'choose to love   this time   for once/with all my intelligence'. A spoken-of loss can be given a matrix of intelligibility, the limits of loss may be ascertained, the pain assuaged.

> I am not with her   I have been waking off and on
> all night to that pain   not simply absence but
> the presence of the past   destructive
> to living here and now   Yet if I could instruct
> myself, if we could learn to learn from pain
> even as it grasps us   if the mind, the mind that lives
> in this body could refuse   to let itself be crushed
> in that grasp   it would loosen[26]

Like H.D., Rich seeks to come to terms with an experience of separation from her lover. In the poem, this profound sense of grief is linked to the infant's experience of the estranging separation from and the ultimate splitting from the mother. The poet speaks of her anguish on hearing the inward echo that repeats the 'cry' of 'primordial loneliness', *'the pain of division'* that is comparable to the mother–daughter relationship. The poet's words proceed hesitantly, change direction, turn back on themselves, and assume multiple tones, positions, and voices. There is no certainty, except that self-division is fundamental to existence: the voice(s) speak(s) out of that pain, become(s) it:

> *We are older now*
> *we have met before   these are my hands before your eyes*
> *my figure blotting out   all that is not mine*
> *I am the pain of division   creator of divisions*
> *it is I who blot your lover from you*
> *and not the time-zones nor the miles*
> *It is not separation calls me forth   but I*
> *who am separation   And remember*
> *I have no existence   apart from you*

The destructive 'dark breath' of separation and loss is viewed here as a pain that is leftover; it is 'not simply absence but/the presence of the past'. Some way must be found to counter or cope with this destructive reminiscence, so as 'not to suffer uselessly   yet still to feel'. The poet dramatizes this lesbian's acknowledgement of her present pain, recognizing its propensity to carry with it 'configurations of the past'. She seeks to limit her anguish to the particularity of the present relationship, the separation of the lovers. Yet, at the same time, paradoxically, the poet fantasizes a unity of relation. Just as the baby may 'memorize the body of the mother/and create her in absence', so too does the poet experiment with images that recreate a sense of the lover's presence. In a contradictory movement which involves a degree of disavowal, almost a self-conscious denial of her lover's absence, the poet seeks to contain and limit the pain of separation, division, and difference. In this willed fantasy, she invokes the very physical presence – the 'mind and body' – of her lover:

> I will not be divided   from her or from myself
> by myths of separation
> while her mind and body in Manhattan are more with me
> than the smell of eucalyptus coolly burning   on these hills

The woman speaker is in San Francisco, her lover 'in Manhattan'. Yet the lover is 'more with me', more present to her body's senses than 'the smell of eucalyptus'. This sensuous affirmation plays with traditional heterosexual ideologies of romantic love: the illusion that oneness and completion is possible through the agency of the lover. A phantasmatic relation of body to body underpins this imaginary unity of relation. The metonymy of the (mother's) body – what Jane Gallop has emphasized as 'the register of [the mother's] touching, nearness, presence, immediacy, contact' – is reiterated many times in Rich's poem.[27] Throughout, there is a tantalizing sense of closeness to *and* distance from the body of the mother/ lover. Desire plays across the contiguities of feminine *jouissance* and sparks the pleasure of *contact* enjoyed in this fantasied relation, as well as the poignancy of the loss of that connection to the mother's body:

> Does the infant memorize the body of the mother
> and create her in absence?   or simply cry
> primordial loneliness?   does the bed of the stream
> once diverted   mourning   remember wetness?

I have noted elsewhere the fascinating parallels between the work of Adrienne Rich and Luce Irigaray.[28] In the following passage, Irigaray points to the political strategy necessary for women to survive despite the ravishments of hetero-patriarchal discourses:

> Let's not be ravished by their language again: let's not embody
> mourning. We must learn how to speak to each other so that we can

embrace across distances. Surely, when I touch myself, I remember
you. But so much is said, and said of us, that separates us.

This restorative fantasy of contiguity – of imaginary contact represented
in the poem – is not comparable to the heterosexual fantasy which
symbolizes woman as the 'stand-in' for the lost object. In the final section,
the woman states:

> I refuse these givens   the splitting
> between love and action   I am choosing
> not to suffer uselessly   and not to use her
> I choose to love   this time   for once
> with all my intelligence

In ultimately repudiating the 'givens' – the imposed choices, the useless
sufferings – of conventional heterosexual discourse, the poet refuses
either to take refuge from the world in the lover, to give up power for
love 'as women have done', or to hide from power in her love, 'like a
man'. Instead, the poet accepts the responsibility of a choice *outside* the
violating consistencies of gender polarity. Insistently, Rich eschews the
'refuge' of the dualistic world of complementary heterosexual roles,
neither abnegating nor hiding from her own power as a woman to
choose for herself what she wants. In this poem, written in 1974 and
included in her 'coming-out' collection *The Dream of a Common Language*,
Rich is able to explore the specificity of lesbian relationship and her
experience of loss overtly without recourse to the veil of ancient myth or
the devious mask of obliquity.

I want to turn now to the Black lesbian poet Audre Lorde, whose
profoundly political writing is, as Gail Lewis remarks, dedicated 'to an
acceptance, understanding and use of difference in the struggle to
change the world'.[29] Her personal quest for survival – not separate from
her politics – compels her to speak out about her own heart-rending
campaign against invasive cancer of the breast. Reading of Lorde's
struggle not to die, I want to celebrate her life of resistance – and her
life-giving words which will continue to survive, to do battle against the
aggressor – '*those of us who live our battles in the flesh must know ourselves as
our strongest weapon in the most gallant struggle of our lives*'.[30] Lorde spells
out the particular aggressions she faces as a Black lesbian: 'battling
racism and battling heterosexism and battling apartheid share the same
urgency inside me as battling cancer'.[31] And for all of these struggles,
Lorde says:

> I require the nourishment of art and spirituality in my life, and
> they lend strength and insight to all the endeavours that give
> substance to my living. It is the bread of art and the water of my
> spiritual life that remind me always to reach for what is highest
> within my capacities and in my demands of myself and others. Not
> for what is perfect but for what is the best possible.[32]

Throughout her work, the spiritual life is inseparable from both personal and political struggle for survival. And cancer, racism, heterosexism, and apartheid are intimately related to the forms of her spirituality as it becomes symbolized in her writing. The retrieval and reconstruction of the suppressed voices of marginalized spiritual traditions remains particularly important in the context of Lorde's poetry. Drawing on the rich resources of Black African folk-tales, Lorde is able to create sites which contest the racist and heterosexist constructs of not only white western patriarchy, but also of white western feminism. The poet utilizes these alternative mythologies for inspiration in the struggle to construct a poetic of survival that will not transmit the old colonial message untransformed. Her recourse to a fictive matrilineal world does not in my view constitute a regressive nostalgic return to origins. It is, rather, an attempt to fabricate a poetic matrix which is committed to dramatizing and resymbolizing sexual ambiguity, creating a confusion of gender categories, and offering a celebration of racial and sexual differences as both defiant and productive. This is a celebration similar to that which we have found in Rich's work. But Lorde takes this project further, in that she also offers a feminist challenge to patriarchal Christianity, the dominant form of faith her community has inherited from the colonizing white missionaries.[33]

In her poem 'Dahomey', Audre Lorde reaches back to the Black African culture of Abomey, specifically to the Dahomeyan Amazons, those 'highly prized, well-trained, and ferocious women warriors who guarded, and fought under the direction of, the Panther Kings of Dahomey.'[34] Yoruban spirituality informs this complex reworking of the ancient myths of Nigerian communities:

> It was in Abomey that I felt
> the full blood of my fathers' wars
> and where I found my mother
> Seboulisa
> standing with outstretched palms hip high
> one breast eaten away by worms of sorrow
> magic stones resting upon her fingers
> dry as a cough.

Rejection of white western feminism's pacifist emphasis leads Lorde to acknowledge and feel 'the full blood of my fathers' wars'. Lorde does not condemn violence as such, but sees its use as valid in the war against racism and apartheid. Where white feminism has a long history of opposing the violence of war, Lorde accepts its necessity. It is valuable to compare how white lesbian feminist Adrienne Rich condemns those men who commit war in this short extract from 'The Phenomenology of Anger (1972)', a poem which relates to the Vietnam War:

> This morning you left the bed

we still share
and went out to spread impotence
upon the world

I hate you.
I hate the mask you wear, your eyes
assuming a depth
they do not possess . . .[35]

These lines are not about hating men simply for being men, but about hating the mask of indifference and the acts of violence perpetrated by men under conditions of war. In 'Dahomey', Lorde refuses to make that condemnation and thus takes up a very different position from Rich. However, in identifying with and supporting to the full the urgent projects which lead Black 'fathers' into war, she is not uncritical. Lorde's poem does not sing the praises of masculist heroism; she ambiguously recognizes both the horror of the blood as well as the situation of the anguished Seboulisa, 'one breast eaten away by worms of sorrow'.

Seboulisa, the goddess of Abomey is, in the Dahomeyan pantheon, 'the Mother of us all'.[36] She is also a local representation of Mawulisa. Mary K. DeShazer sees Lorde as 'paying homage' to Seboulisa: 'Lorde celebrates Seboulisa as a mother of both sorrow and magic, a sorceress who will help her daughter find a language from which to speak.'[37] This link between the mother and the daughter has great importance in Lorde's work overall yet, as we shall see, it is not exclusive.

Lorde comments that 'Mawu is regarded as the Creator of the Universe, and Lisa is either called her first son, or her twin brother'.[38] She is thus a composite being combining a powerful mother and subordinate son or brother – a mythic figure in which the boundaries between male and female are blurred and in which gender categories collapse. In this poem, links of kinship and family are important, as are the relationships between women. Yet Seboulisa, 'the Mother of us all', is not 'pure' woman or even biological woman: she is to be understood as a sexually ambiguous figure possessing mixed gender attributes.

As this composite figure of Seboulisa suggests, Lorde does not limit her poetic to a reductive matriarchalism, or any other exclusionary politics – she will not accede to any politics which fails to negotiate difference: 'difference must be not merely tolerated, but seen as a fund of necessary polarities between which our creativity can spark like a dialectic'.[39]

So, in refusing to condemn either male or female violence, Lorde also refuses to ally herself with Rich's pacifist position. Instead, she situates herself alongside the male, like the African Amazon, ready to do battle as a woman who is 'not enjoined from the shedding of blood'.[40] She accepts the necessity for the 'brother' and 'nephew' to stitch 'tales of blood'. Are these tales of the past? Or are they ones to be stitched in readiness for future encounters with the white racist oppressor? Again, Lorde's poetry constitutes a radical challenge to the gender asymmetries characteristic of the white western patriarchy, which would limit female participation in the culturally constructed forms of militarized power, its defences and hostilities. Lorde fuses an ancient mythic world with what could be a contemporary world of brass workers and cloth: the mundane world of work is not separate from the spiritual world in Lorde's poetic. There is, however, underlying this poem, a clear-sighted realist recognition of the world of necessity for Black peoples: the need for both male and female to be ready to counter actual, often physically enforced, subjugation; and also the need to empower Black men to respect themselves.

An aside here to mention Lorde's relationship to her own son – and her own necessity to find ways to empower him to respect himself – is perhaps relevant. In caring for Jonathan after he had been bullied, Lorde recounts how she had to check herself from hissing at her son in anger and frustration at his tears – ' "the next time you come in here crying . . ." and I suddenly caught myself in horror'. She had recognized how she, as his mother, was playing her part in perpetuating the 'age-old distortions about what strength and bravery really are'. She adds: 'Jonathan didn't have to fight if he didn't want to, but somehow he did have to feel better about not fighting.' [41] Empowerment, self-respect for boys and men growing up in a patriarchal world – Black or white – is not easily found or earned. As caring mother to her son, Lorde finds herself having to acknowledge her own impotent fury – her own pain at watching her son suffer the violence of the street corner – and it is a struggle for her to find ways to empower him, to help him achieve a measure of self-respect.

Despite Lorde's support of the necessity for violent, bloody, militant action, for typically masculine modes of confrontational politics, she does not fully approve of unmuted phallic power. In 'Dahomey', Eshu, the male god of language who 'transmits and interprets', is mocked by the women. His 'iron quiver/standing erect and flamingly familiar' is silenced, rendered 'mute as a porcupine in a forest of lead'. His potential for penetrative violence, his phallic weaponry – the 'iron quiver', the 'forest of lead' – is tamed. Eshu is often teased and, according to Lorde's notes, he is even often 'danced by a woman with an attached phallus'. [42] This figure stands erect, displays a 'huge erect phallus', is potent, virile – and, importantly, is also female. This humorous, probably intentional ambivalence towards masculinity – or the masculine female – is left unresolved within the poem. Indeed, the prankster, as an 'unpredictable' and 'mischievous' figure of parody, becomes a site or location where gender confusion proliferates so that the attributes of what the white western world has considered masculine and feminine become comically denaturalized. Here differences no longer carry a fixed meaning. Gender is rendered complex and its intelligibility questioned. The discourses that organize sexuality on the basis of anatomical distinctions are flouted – here biology is not destiny – and so laughter rules.

In contrast, Lorde attributes to the woman a position of serious responsibility towards the men. The 'woman with braided hair' has the awesome power to spell and prophesy over Shango, 'one of Yemanja's best-known and strongest sons', the god of 'lightning and thunder, war and politics'.[43] Women in this culture have spiritual and political power and are prepared to use violence, but, in this instance, it is only the violence of the tongue, of metaphor: 'I speak/whatever language is needed/to sharpen the knives of my tongue' ('Dahomey'). The poet's voice dynamically represents its power in the image of the drums whose 'speech' is honoured throughout old Africa. Her dignity, symbolized in the composure and poise of the woman's quiet integrity, is to be respected: 'whether or not/you are against me/I will braid my hair/even/in the seasons of rain.'

Desire for the mother, and for cultural unity, focuses this poem: the woman speaker searches for and finds her mother. Seboulisa, as personal mother and as mythic mother, is filled with sorrow. The mutilation of her breast may, in this context, be seen as signifying the agony inflicted by the white aggressor on generations of Black cultures. ('Racism. Cancer. In both cases, to win the aggressor must conquer, but the resisters need only survive'.[44] As I write, Lorde's current life fuses with the myth of Seboulisa, as she courageously continues to resist not only racism, but also cancer: a foremother herself.) The absent breast has not been purposely removed in order to hold the Amazonian bow in battle, but has been 'eaten away by worms of sorrow'. Seboulisa's 'outstretched palms hip high' suggest her mute appeal to end her suffering, the suffering of the Black mother responsible for her peoples. She is ready with her magic stones, her poetry. She continues to carry out her responsibilities towards her people in working her word-magic for the future.

As Lorde's poetry all too clearly reveals, a vital necessity for Afra-American women, alienated from their ancient matrilineal cultural roots by the ideological supremacy of white European forms of thought, is the retrieval of the hidden knowledges of non-European cultures. The persistence of racist and colonialist oppression requires a strategy of resistance. In Lorde's terms, such a strategy emerges out of the desires for/of the 'Black mother, the poet' whispering her subversive charter for the future:

> The Black mother within each of us – the poet – whispers in our dreams: I feel, therefore I can be free. Poetry coins the language to express and charter this revolutionary demand, the implementation of that freedom.[45]

The movement here from dreams, feelings, and desires towards survival and change, from ideas into action through the naming of her strong demand for 'freedom' – including the implementation of that demand – shows the Black mother/poet's urgent call for vast social change. As poet she will find words – her sister's or her mother's, her foresister's or her foremother's – to set against the white patriarchal words that colonize her.

In *Zami*, Lorde represents her own mother Linda as a fierce disciplinarian who knew how to 'frighten children into behaving in public', a 'very powerful woman' who fired her daughter's imagination with stories of her home in Carriacou (a small island off the coast of Grenada).[46] 'When I visited Grenada I saw the root of my mother's powers walking through the streets. I thought, this is the country of my foremothers, my forebearing mothers, those Black island women who defined themselves by what they did.' In this biomythography, the dream of Carriacou becomes closely bound up with desire for the mother – the desire for roots, for a homeland of fruits, trees, and flowers, for a land peopled by her Black mother's foremothers and other women.

The word *foremother*, according to Joanne Braxton, means a female ancestor, 'one who has preceded and who has gone on, but by definition, foremother can also mean one who has gone in front, someone who has been a leader, someone who has stood at the foreground of cultural experience'.[47] The term includes all those women who have taken a leading role in contemporary politics or cultural life, those who have worked for the maintenance of Black relationships, and Black connection. Chinosole speaks of the related concept of the matrilineal diaspora as referring to the capacity of Black foremothers

> to survive and aspire, to be contrary and self-affirming across continents and generations. It names the strength and beauty we pass on as friends and lovers from foremothers to mothers and daughters allowing us to survive radical cultural changes and be empowered through differences.[48]

Lorde's project of resignifying difference and contesting 'mythical norms' defined as 'white, thin, male, young, heterosexual, christian, and financially secure' is crucially empowered through the figures of 'Foremothers'.[49] The poem 'Call', which concludes her most recent book of poetry *Our Dead Behind Us* (1986), in particular constitutes a sophisticated and strongly developed challenge to the power over minds of the figure of the white western male God. 'Call' is a prayer/poem addressed to Black African divinities 'whose names and faces have been lost in time'.[50] The poet calls upon the Black matriarchal warrior figure Aido Hwedo, holy ghost mother, symbolized in the poem as the Rainbow Serpent. The Black woman's faith in the 'most ancient Goddesses' of Black Africa is strongly affirmed:

I have not forgotten your worship
nor my sisters
nor the sons of my daughters
my children watch for your print
in their labors
and they say Aido Hwedo is coming.
I am a Black woman   turning
mouthing your name as a password
through seductions   self-slaughter
and I believe in the holy ghost
mother
in your flames beyond our vision

Oya, Seboulisa, Mawu, Afrekete – goddesses from the ancient African capital of Dahomey – are set alongside historical and human heroines. 'Thandi Modise   winged girl of Soweto', Rosa Parks and Fannie Lou Hamer, Assata Shakur and Yaa Asantewa, her own mother and Winnie Mandela are all invoked as images that affirm the Black woman as a warrior figure – shouting, ready and prepared to do battle against the white oppressor. The women sing and speak the Word (or the teaching) of the Black African ancestral inheritance. White male western deities have no place in this ancestral value and belief system. In contesting the power of the colonizing white patriarchal God, Lorde reconstructs a strong alternative system of faith that is centred in the Black woman, and which she asserts in very powerful and polemical forms.

None the less, the pain of exploring the relation between her self and her mother has been, for Lorde, intense. 'Story Books On a Kitchen Table' speaks of a Black mother who cannot accept her daughter's identification as lesbian. This poem records the mother's anguish at her daughter not 'becoming' a heterosexual adult. That said, anger does not prevent them both from grieving deeply about their differences and consequent separation from each other. In the poem, the lesbian daughter in her sexual difference has become her mother's 'nightmare':

Out of her womb of pain my mother spat me
into her ill-fitting harness of despair
into her deceits
where anger re-conceived me
piercing my eyes like arrows
pointed by her nightmare
of who I was not
becoming.[51]

One of her own mother's 'deceits' is recounted in *Zami* – when her little daughter was spat on, an apparently commonplace event in New York in the 1930s. Her mother is described ambivalently by the poet as fussing about 'low-class people who had no better sense nor manners than to spit into the wind no matter where they went, impressing upon me that this humiliation was totally random'.[52] Lorde seems to be both grateful for and made uncomfortable by her mother's way of coping. As she explains, her mother's 'deceits' are grounded in her positive desire to protect her daughter from the humiliations of racism. When Lorde speaks of her mother's 'pain' and 'despair', however, we become aware that the two women are very different politically. Her mother still bears the scars from the traumas inflicted by the pernicious racism of white supremacist culture and dare not confront her oppressor. That the heterosexual mother cannot accept her lesbian daughter's sexuality also creates a difficult situation for both of them, but especially for the daughter who cannot and will not fulfil her mother's expectations of her. But it is because her Black mother 'left in her place/iron maidens to protect me' that Lorde, the lesbian daughter, will survive. Coming to the painfully clear-sighted recognition that no 'white witches' will offer 'any kind enchantment/for the vanished mother/of a Black girl', the Black girl-child is under no illusions about what is possible in reality.

Despite her mother's 'going away' from her and her subsequent sense of loss, Lorde reclaims her powerful mother, seeing her as a 'Black dyke': 'to this day I believe that there have always been Black dykes around – in the sense of powerful and woman-oriented women – who would rather have died than use that name for themselves. And that includes my momma'.[53] A large part of *Zami* is devoted to an account of her relationships with women, as mothers, friends and as lovers: with her schoolgirl friend Genny (who commits suicide); with Ginger (her voluptuous first lover); with the unresponsive Bea; and then, in Mexico, with the mature and sophisticated alcoholic, Eudora. And there are further loves – Muriel and Afrekete. *Zami* explores the gay scene of the McCarthyite 1950s – as a role-playing world in which butch/femme conventions operated. Lorde felt unable to enter fully into adopting the 'mean' and 'tough' masculine image of the virile butch mode, nor could she identify with the 'cute' and 'passive' exaggeratedly feminine femme: 'I was given a wide berth. Non-conventional people can be dangerous, even in the gay community.'[54] Lorde here speaks of her own marginality as a Black woman within that already marginal gay-girl world:

> Most Black lesbians were closeted, correctly recognizing the Black community's lack of interest in our position, as well as the many more immediate threats to our survival as Black people in a racist society. It was hard enough to be Black, to be Black and female, to be Black, female and gay. To be Black, female, gay, and out of the

closet in a white environment, even to the extent of dancing in the Bagatelle, was considered by many Black lesbians to be simply suicidal.

In such a world, survival was not always possible: 'Many of us wound up dead or demented, and many of us were distorted by the many fronts we had to fight upon. But when we survived, we grew up strong.'[55] Living as a Black lesbian in a racist society involves living with constant fear. In her poem 'A Litany for Survival' Lorde reveals how Black women learn to be afraid 'with our mother's milk':

And when the sun rises we are afraid
it might not remain
when the sun sets we are afraid
it might not rise in the morning
when our stomachs are full we are afraid
of indigestion
when our stomachs are empty we are afraid
we may never eat again
when we are loved we are afraid
love will vanish
when we are alone we are afraid
love will never return
and when we speak we are afraid
our words will not be heard
nor welcomed
but when we are silent
we are still afraid

So it is better to speak
remembering
we were never meant to survive.[56]

Black lesbians, compelled to stand outside of the definitions of what will pass and who is acceptable, seem to have a choice. This choice is between self-destruction – that is, either becoming something that will make it possible to be taken inside the system, being assimilated, becoming an insider – and finding alternative structures outside the system that will allow, justify, and acknowledge their existence. Survival in Lorde's terms, when so many do not survive, is learning how to move beyond fear, beyond despair – through love. In the words of the quotation on the frontispiece of *Zami*: '*In the recognition of loving lies an answer to despair.*' Black women dare not refuse to be conscious of what they are living through or feeling at any time. As Lorde affirms, the close scrutiny of that 'dark place' within is the route to survival: 'as we learn to use the products of that scrutiny for power within our living, those fears which rule our lives and form our silences begin to lose their control over us'.[57]

As we have seen, Lorde positions herself as a Black lesbian warrior – an identity constructed in strong resistance to the conventional structures of a white hetero-patriarchy. In claiming and affirming Black lesbian sexual difference, she has argued that Black lesbian survival depends on recognizing and exploring difference – 'as a springboard for creative change within our lives'. Her template for survival is learning to talk across differences between woman and woman, Black and Black, Black and white, lesbian, gay and heterosexual: 'we have no patterns for relating across our human differences as equals. As a result those differences have been misnamed and misused in the service of separation and confusion.'[58] Unacknowledged fear of the 'strangeness' of lesbian otherness, which lies at the root of that confusion, may remain guiltily ignored and unspoken, giving rise to the distortions and hostility of homophobia.

Internalized homophobia comes under close examination in Lorde's poem 'Letter for Jan'. In this 'letter' the poet reaches out to a silent and afraid woman, desiring her to move beyond her fear and loathing of what she imagines as a rapacious lesbian sexuality, to a point where she can experience lesbian sexual difference as non-threatening, even as 'full of loving':

> No I don't think you were chicken not to speak
> I think you
> afraid I was mama as laser
> seeking to eat out or change your substance[59]

Fears of homophobic intensity link themselves, perhaps predictably, to the terrifying intrapsychic image of 'mama as laser', the devouring, avenging, guilt-producing, punitive mother. Does homophobia derive from this disavowed figure, angry, hated, condemned and ultimately projected on to the strong, independent, sexually free lesbian? In the poem, we encounter a 'Mawulisa bent on destruction by threat/who might cover you'. The fear to be acknowledged is that of being overwhelmed, seduced, and then drowning in the kind of exotic hothouse eroticism that could wipe out her voice, her identity, her own 'praise song'. In her essay, 'Uses of the Erotic: The Erotic as Power', Lorde argues that the erotic as a source of power has been corrupted and distorted: 'we have been taught to suspect this resource, vilified, abused, and devalued within western society'.[60] Suspicion, contempt, and distrust of female erotic power fuel homophobic fears: lesbian sexuality in the first section of 'Letter for Jan' becomes seen as rampant and overbearing in its forms, comparable to the sexualized aggressions of macho-heterosexuality:

> that would seduce you open
> turning erotic and delightful as you
> went under for the third time

> your own poetry and sweetness
> masked and drying out
> upon your lips

The fear is neither about the lesbian as she is nor lesbianism as it is commonly lived, but instead concerns 'me as I might have been' – a too casual 'quick chic', a too powerful 'god mother', or someone who is ready 'to reject you back into your doubt/smothering you into acceptance/ with my own black song'. This is an intrapsychic 'nightmare' figure bearing anger, ready to reject, able to 'swallow you into confusion', 'buy you up', 'burn you up'. Entering into that terror and that loathing is to enter into the fear of difference and otherness. Lorde identifies the therapeutic task as working with the distortion and 'darkness', the 'mis-naming' that produced that particular silence – as well as exploring the moment of closure that so devastatingly prevented 'Jan' from speaking. The intrapsychic and sociopolitical work to be done is 'to extract these distortions from our living at the same time as we recognise, reclaim, and define those differences upon which they are imposed'.[61] The danger-ous fantasy of the rapacious lesbian must be recognized for what it is: a disparaging homophobic stereotype which covers over, drowns, and so wipes out the specificities of lesbian identity –

> When all the time
> I would have loved you
> speaking
> being a woman full of loving
> turned on
> and little bit raunchy
> and heavy
> with my own black song.

Lorde's insistence on exploring difference, and re-presenting lesbian sexual desire and lesbian eroticism in her own terms is a crucial political strategy:

> The future of our earth may depend upon the ability of all women to identify and develop new definitions of power and new patterns of relating across difference. The old definitions have not served us, nor the earth that supports us. The old patterns, no matter how cleverly rearranged to imitate progress, still condemn us to cosme-tically altered repetitions of the same old exchanges, the same old guilt, hatred, recrimination, lamentation, and suspicion.[62]

Blatantly exceeding the limits of what is discursively permitted within patriarchal discourses, Lorde's disturbing poem brings to awareness the suppressed negative in the homophobic response to lesbian difference.

All the poets I have looked at here, Broumas, Rukeyser, H.D., Rich and, of course, Lorde – in their different ways – subvert, contest, or displace conventional heterosexist poetic discourses. Through these poets' different strategies, lesbian libidinal differences, sexualities and cultural identities have disruptively entered language and history. Each poet develops a lesbian strategy of survival appropriate to the particular dangers she faces within her own location and historical situation. In all instances, their pain, celebration, and courage are a testimony to their determination to survive despite marginalization and homophobic ostracism. Indeed, constructing a poetic of survival demands just such a courageous strategy in which same-sex desire is represented in all its specificity and diversity – through a matrix that is textually, ontologically, and culturally intelligible.

12 Reading awry: Joan Nestle and the recontextualization of heterosexuality

Clare Whatling

I

Feminist communities have never lacked for writings on or discussions about sex and sexuality. The 1970s and early 1980s in particular saw a veritable explosion of such studies, dealing with everything from the case for political lesbianism to the myth of the vaginal orgasm. Suddenly it seemed as though everything was open to discussion, and so in time a politicized lesbian-feminism began to be seen as a necessary precondition for an effective feminist revolution. As a new freedom began to characterize the movement on one level, however, it became apparent that on a more profound level certain issues were being left out, were indeed being subject to a gradual but determined erasure. Within the lesbian-feminist community a list of unmentionables grew up. Penetration, the use of artificial sex aids (dildoes), the eroticization of dominance and submission (which was how lesbian butch/femme was now characterized), intergenerational sex – indeed anything smacking of power difference or potential inequality was decisively expurgated from the feminist revolutionary canon. Good lesbian-feminists no longer did these things. Such practices were, it was said, the products of a lesbianism vitiated and contained by heterosexuality.

This situation continued with little comment up to the end of the 1970s. As the 1980s commenced, however, dissenting voices began to be heard, voices that announced themselves betrayed by a movement which had initially proposed to reflect their needs. These voices challenged the prevailing lesbian-feminist view. They proclaimed that not only had the practices recently outlawed by the lesbian-feminist movement been taking place under cover of silence and fear for years, but that there was nothing intrinsic to these practices that should be theorized as fundamentally antithetical to feminism. For a long time these voices spoke from the wilderness. Only during the last few years has the controversial work of lesbian-feminists such as Joan Nestle, Dorothy Allison, Gayle Rubin, and Pat Califia reached a wider audience. Their views have hardly gone uncontended. To the increasingly popular feminist anti-pornography movements in America and Britain, the contemporary lesbian affirmation of pornography, consensual power exchanges and other sexualities alternative to those laid down by 1970s lesbian-feminism is seen merely as a resurgence of a libertarianism saturated in patriarchal ideology. Califia, Nestle and the others are feared as pollutants to the rest of the movement, corrupting its standards of sexual and political purity. The common response to this fear has been a stringent policing of desire by some feminists, who have vilified their more controversial sisters as not only traitors to the feminist cause, but also, most spectacularly, as 'heterosexual lesbians'. The resulting schism has provoked a polarization of debate within the feminist movement that has to date been highly damaging.

At the centre of the current controversy over lesbian sex lie certain practices, and, most importantly for my concerns in this chapter, certain texts. I shall be considering one of these texts in detail, Joan Nestle's collection of short stories and essays, *A Restricted Country* (1987), to argue for a more affirmative way of understanding ideas about sexual power and sexual pleasure that until only recently received a very bad press within the movement. What lies particularly at stake in the controversy over these texts are certain questions of reading. The claim that expressions of radical lesbian sexuality are corrupted by patriarchal values that have infiltrated revolutionary lesbian culture, reabsorbing its potential subversiveness into the master discourse, implies that the literary representation in this instance partakes of the oppressor's language rather than forging ahead with a new language of its own, a language ideally untainted by previous and reactionary forms. As I hope to demonstrate here, such an understanding of literary representation is inadequate. To address the questions of representation that concern me I will need to look, albeit briefly, at the situation of lesbian-feminism in the 1970s.

Lesbian-feminist politics of the 1970s and the orthodoxies they established were, in part, a reaction to the entrenched naturalization of gender divisions operating within western patriarchal society where women under patriarchy submit to men who assume social, economic, and sexual dominance. An increasing number of feminists felt it more logical to turn their desires away from men (where women's emotional dependence and apparent sexual submissiveness might be seen to be in contradiction with their political independence), and towards the women with whom they shared emotional empathy and political energy. Since women were of the same sex and therefore equal, so the argument went, there would be a reduction of role stratification in sexual and social relations, thereby ushering in the new order all the more swiftly. Elizabeth Wilson explains the thinking underpinning this kind of lesbian politics:

> Lesbianism no longer, therefore, involves the adoption of roles; on the contrary it comes to be seen as the escape route from the socially constructed gender roles imposed on all women (and men) in our society.[1]

Out of this escape route the notion of 'political' lesbianism was born where women believed they could train themselves to relate exclusively, politically, emotionally and even sexually to 'their own kind'. That a sexual politics of this type rests on a particularly idealistic view of individual volition is now recognized by many feminists.[2] It is a utopian argument which dreams of a free space, a sanctuary where a lesbian culture might exist independently, uncontaminated by external – namely heterosexual – influences. Like all utopias it has been subject to contention. One dilemma in particular struck feminists even in the 1970s: if sexual roles were to be deemed politically inadmissible, what was to be done about the apparent acquiescence in role-play and the presumed eroticization of dominance and submission within the already existing culture of butch/femme lesbians? Dating from the 1920s, inhabiting throughout this time a multitude of complex but highly influential forms, lesbian butch/femme had played a central role in emerging urban lesbian cultures. Yet how could butch/femme be engaged with except as an unfortunate hangover from the pre-feminist days of strict role designations and sexual difference – a heterosexual manifestation to which, it was argued, butch/femme lesbians contributed a sad imitation? Obviously, by the calculations of 1970s feminists, it could not. Butch/femme style had therefore to be consigned to the old heterosexual order and thrown out with the old-style heterosexual gender constraints. That the wholesale rejection of butch/femme involved a calculated process of intolerable exclusion is made clear by Joan Nestle: 'As a way of ignoring what butch–femme meant and means, feminism is often viewed as the validating starting point of healthy lesbian culture.'[3]

Role-play, the taking on of heavily gendered characteristics of extreme femininity or of visible masculinity, has been the most troubling issue here, since to the revolutionary lesbian-feminist of the 1970s role-play is an evasion of one's 'true self', an authentic core of being that necessarily transcends role conditioning. Such an essentialist understanding of the self is always at the centre of this particular brand of 1970s feminism. Thus a passage from Sidney Abbott and Barbara Love's *Sappho Was A Right-on Woman*, a popular lesbian-feminist tract of its time, can claim:

> Gay role-playing is another way out of confronting oneself. If a lesbian plays a male or female role in a relationship, she is living out roles written by the society. Whatever role is played, butch or femme, the lesbian will eventually find it hard to be herself, to know who she is.[4]

Role-play marks a betrayal of 'the self' because it is merely an imitation (and by implication, a somewhat tawdry one too), of its heterosexual 'original'. It represents, strangely enough, the security of 'the norm', that is, of a heterosexual role-playing society which older, more traditional lesbians cannot do without, even to the point of 'pretending' to be men themselves. And so Abbott and Love can say of butch/femme:

> There is a strong possibility that heavy butch and femme role-playing serves the function of burying guilt. If only men can marry women, then a woman who lives existentially as a man will not consciously feel guilty for loving another woman. In her own reality she will be seeing someone of the opposite sex as will the femme.[5]

Questionable psychologizing apart, this passage presents many difficulties, notably the invocation of the term 'pretence' (that infinitely adaptable notion as our current state legislation on homosexuality in Britain clearly demonstrates).[6] That Abbott and Love's assumption must finally ground itself on an understanding of masculinity as a 'real' to which the butch lesbian then acts out a 'pretence' is only one of the issues that goes unanalysed in the strictures laid down in *Sappho Was a Right-on Woman*.

The problem I have with Abbott and Love's political position is a conceptual one. Their lesbian-feminism wants to start anew, to forge a utopia in which an autonomous lesbian culture might flourish. The new world demands new values. Theoretically this can be characterized as the 'spring into free space'[7] celebrated by Mary Daly, who believes that by a conscious effort women can transcend their individual oppression. An artistic analogue might be the deployment of 'natural' imagery of fruit and flowers as emblems of the female genitalia, a pastime made popular by the 'rediscovery' of artists such as Georgia O'Keeffe in the 1970s. That there is nothing natural about such a use of nature or 'the natural', since everything is already part of a received meaning and thus tainted by association, is more obvious to us in the light of poststructuralist thought.[8] In this sense terms can be adopted and transformed, subverted and parodied, but they cannot be *naturally* derived. This is then the main distinction between 1970s lesbian-feminism and the works of Joan Nestle that I wish to discuss. Nestle's writings have a quite different engagement with the existing culture: one not of refusal, but of appropriation and subversion.

Joan Nestle is one of the women to defend and theorize the butch/femme commitment against the charges that it refigures the oppressive structures and inequalities of the heterosexual marriage relation. Here she describes her position as she perceived it, and as she felt herself perceived, within post-war American society:

> In the late 1950s I walked the streets looking so butch that straight teenagers called me a bulldyke; however, when I went to the *Sea*

Colony, a working-class Lesbian bar in Greenwich village . . . I was a femme, a woman who loved and wanted to nurture the butch strength in other women.[9]

The butch/femme stance does not necessarily imply a direct visual copying of heterosexuality. Nestle's statement rather demonstrates the exorbitant trust our culture puts in the specular. It also illustrates how appearance can deceive. In fact Nestle argues that it is not the similarity with heterosexuality in this instance which offends; what provokes is not the imitation but the clear statement of sexual independence:

My understanding of why we angered straight spectators so is not that they saw us modeling ourselves after them, but just the opposite: we were a symbol of women's erotic autonomy, a sexual accomplishment that did not include them. The physical attacks were a direct attempt to break into this self-sufficient erotic partnership.[10]

In the McCarthyite 1950s only men could be safely represented as the bearers of sexuality. That one of a woman's few means of announcing her sexual autonomy over the normative image of 'woman' as passive, yielding, receiving, might be to take on masculine garb attests to the reception of this fact. It also suggests its recuperation, hence the complexity of the butch style:

None of the butch women I was with, and this included a passing woman, ever presented themselves to me as men; they did announce themselves as tabooed women who were willing to identify their passion for other women by wearing clothes that symbolized the taking of responsibility. Part of this responsibility was sexual expertise.[11]

The 'passing' woman is the woman who in straight society could pass for a man, and who would frequently hold down a job claiming to be one. Within the bar culture she would of course be recognized as someone quite different, namely a *woman* who 'passes'. To condemn such a woman as 'acting like a man' shows only too obviously the inadequacy of the erotic categories at large in our society.

A similar account must be made of the butch's apparent opposite, the femme who, though traditionally the more undertheorized of the two, has been equally misapprehended and habitually treated either as a victim or a sexual dupe. As Nestle points out:

Many Lesbians dismiss me as a victim, a woman who could do nothing else because she didn't know any better . . . but I wasn't a piece of fluff and neither were the other fems I knew. We knew what we wanted and that was no mean feat for young women of the 1950s, a time when the need for conformity, marriage and babies was being trumpeted at us by the government's policy makers.[12]

Since she inhabited the conventional regalia of the heterosexually identified woman the femme could often pass for heterosexual, until, that is,
she was seen out alongside her butch lover. That the femme, because she
'looked like a woman', was not recognized for the sexual heretic she
surely is, once again suggests the fatally limited perspective of the
heterosexual contract.

In 'The Fem Question', her article designed to correct some of the
more searing misapprehensions of the femme identity, Nestle recognizes the double-bind of construction and reaction that the butch/
femme statement inhabits in being defined within, though not by, the
heterosexual paradigm:

> Colonization and the battle against it always poses a contradiction
> between appearances and deeper survivals. There is a need to
> reflect the colonizer's image back at him yet at the same time to
> keep alive what is a deep part of one's culture, even if it can be
> misunderstood by the oppressor, who omnipotently thinks he
> knows what he is seeing. Butch–femme carries all this cultural
> warfare with it. It appears to incorporate elements of the hetero-
> sexual culture in power; it is disowned by some who want to make a
> statement against the pervasiveness of this power, yet it is a valid
> style, matured in years of struggle and harboring some of our
> bravest women. The colonizer's power enforces not only a daily
> cultural devaluing but also sets up a memory trap, forcing us to
> devalue what was resistance in the past in a desperate battle to be
> different from what they say we are.[13]

The irony of the sexual-political structures Nestle describes is that a
certain kind of lesbian-feminism, in reading butch/femme out of context, plays into the very hands of the oppressor in defining butch/femme
by his terms. Butch/femme therefore, is paradoxically read as (straight!)
mimesis, directly imitating the heterosexual relation with little alteration
of its terms, where it needs to be understood instead as a kind of
Irigarayan mimesis,[14] existing independently and even ironically in
relation to those forms within which it is, however, still defined.

For this reason it is imperative to be aware of the codes which operate
within a given community to recognize its resistances. The importance of
comprehending such codes can be seen when we look to the sexual
languages that inhabit the lesbian bars. What to the uninitiated ear
seems to be clichéd or even oppressive, in fact manifests a complex
network of desire, solicitation, and importantly, trust. Nestle writes:

> Women who were new to the life and entered bars have reported
> they were asked: 'Well, what are you – butch or femme?' Many fled
> rather than answer the question. The real questions behind the
> discourse were, 'Are you sexual?' and 'Are you safe?' When one

moved beyond the opening gambits a whole range of sexuality was possible.[15]

Nestle is determined to stress that there is more scope for movement than a mimetic reading of butch/femme will allow:

> Butch and femme covered a wide variety of sexual responses. We joked about being a butchy femme or a femmy butch or feeling kiki (going both ways). We joked about a reversal of expectations: 'Get a butch home and she turns over on her back.'[16]

While this may be true of Joan Nestle's understanding of the lesbian culture of the Sea Colony, the bar she frequented throughout the 1960s, it seems that the reality may have been more complex. Where information is limited there is a danger of universalizing that little bit we do know about the bar cultures, although as a privileged informant Nestle is always concerned to contextualize her own experience.[17] Davis and Kennedy's recent study of New York lesbian bar culture from the 1940s to the 1960s suggests the differences that existed between bars in different periods and at various locations.[18] Their analysis shows that attitudes towards role ambivalence in general hardened in the bars of the 1950s and they suggest that this corresponds to a polarization of role definitions within heterosexual culture at this time. Butch/femme therefore might merely be seen as a new and necessary form of resistance, since it served to announce lesbians' public visibility precisely in the way that most challenged the dominant culture's investment in dress as the chief signifier of (hetero)sexual difference. As gender differentiation eased off in the 1960s, according to Davis and Kennedy, so too did the bar cultures' policing of their own style statements. This argument implies then an occasional relation (though never an absolute correlation) between lesbian and heterosexual mores that deserves further exploration by a committed lesbian anthropology or sociology. Yet the study finally demonstrates the debatability of these issues where there is such diversity of opinion between lesbians who experienced the communities at first hand.

Undoubtedly the issue of role stratification within the lesbian community inhabits a complexity that we can only begin to suggest here. For example, it is probably the case that some lesbians did and do see themselves as being born into particular roles or sexual stances. In believing this they paradoxically invoke the notion of the natural that in other contexts has been used against them in so far as heterosexuality is habitually invoked as the natural, and lesbianism is seen as the perversion of this. That there are on the other hand ambiguities to sexual statements that on first sight appear rigid is likely, given the complexities of the gender definitions and positions I have described. Unfortunately, butch/femme has remained so undertheorized within a feminist movement concerned solely with its exclusion that the subjective interpretations of such role-play remain largely unexplored within a public context. This situation leaves us with more questions than we yet have answers for. Still, why should we consider the 'passing woman' of the bars to be more essentialist in her identification with that which is conventionally described as the masculine, than the lesbian-feminist who recognizes the convention but believes it inhibits her 'true self'? Might it be that the former woman has a larger investment in forging her identity, an altogether greater imperative to construct herself more completely in the face of violent social hostility to her sexual stance?

In her essay 'Butch-femme Relationships: Sexual Courage in the 1950s', Nestle makes a remark which, though fitting in context, has interesting reverberations for our understanding of butch/femme. She says, 'We were two women not masqueraders.'[19] One of the things that is striking in Nestle's portrayal of butch/femme relations, however, is the significance and significations attributable to dress and it would surely not be unreasonable to assume from her writings that some element of masquerade is in play within the butch/femme relation, although this is not to term it a mere imitating of the heterosexual. For butch/femme is a style, an identification, specifically and visually stated in dress.[20] Nestle would not deny this view. Speaking of the femme stance she observes: 'Oh, we had our styles – our outfits, our perfumes, our performances.'[21] The danger she anticipates is that these styles will once again be misconstrued. Yet the notion of masquerade, while always ambiguous, need not be pejorative. How masquerade is interpreted is necessarily a matter of context, a context which can radically transform the statements being made. Consider for a moment the notion of masquerade as theorized by Joan Riviere:

> Womanliness therefore could be assumed and worn as a mask, both to hide the possession of masculinity and to avert the reprisals expected if [the woman] was found to possess it – much as a thief will turn out his pockets and ask to be searched to prove that he has not stolen the goods.[22]

It is possible to argue that the butch/femme style takes Riviere's premises to fascinating new extremes. Note how, for example, Riviere's account of womanliness as masquerade finds its apotheosis in the femme, smart embodiment of feminine accoutrements. In contrast to Riviere's paradigm, however, the femme's appropriation of the feminine as dress and as style is not intended to disguise her power in pursuit of a man, but to attract the butch and to signify to her that she is willing to transgress traditional feminine boundaries.

The butch on the other hand refuses femininity and takes on the dress of the male, not to become the unsexed creature Riviere believes her to be,[23] but to announce her sexual identity to the world. What the butch/femme style shows is that women can adopt or refuse 'femininity', something that goes beyond even Riviere's examination of masquerade, and a fact that in turn testifies to femininity's adaptability and 'unnaturalness'.[24] To sum up, the butch/femme stance of the 1950s, instead of figuring a rigid imitation of heterosexual roles, in fact plays with visual assumptions about gender and sexuality, taking the limited erotic categories available to lesbians at the time and transforming them into something very different and highly subversive, far beyond the recognition of the culture of their time. This is, I believe, why Nestle can say, 'When we broke gender lines in the 1950s, we fell off the biologically charted maps.'[25]

As Judith Butler observes in *Gender Trouble, Feminism and the Subversion of Identity*, we are all familiar with the ways in which appearance misleads and can be used to question that which we otherwise hold to be 'natural' or 'real' or 'innate'. This is illustrated in drag, for example. Talking about Divine, the star of John Waters's film *Female Trouble*, Butler observes:

> Her/his performance destabilizes the very distinctions between the natural and the artificial, depth and surface, inner and outer through which discourse about genders almost always operates. Is drag the imitation of gender, or does it dramatize the signifying gestures through which gender itself is established? Does being female constitute a 'natural fact' or a cultural performance, or is 'naturalness' constituted through discursively constrained performative acts that produce the body through and within the categories of sex?[26]

Butler is arguing that this kind of gender/sexual play presents us with the opportunity to reconstruct gender identities into new, multiple, and innovative forms, identities which have traditionally been framed only in terms of a heterosexual paradigm. Butch/femme, through the manifold possibilities of their expression, may thus give the lie rather than the proof to heterosexuality's presumptive norm. To cite Butler again:

> The 'presence' of so-called heterosexual conventions within homosexual contexts as well as the proliferation of specifically gay discourses of sexual difference, as in the case of 'butch' and 'femme' as historical identities of sexual style, cannot be explained as chimerical representations of originally heterosexual identities. And neither can they be understood as the pernicious insistence of heterosexist constructs within gay sexuality and identity. The repetition of heterosexual constructs within sexual cultures both gay and straight may well be the inevitable site of the denaturalization and mobilization of gender categories.[27]

This mobility of gender and sexual definitions, she goes on to observe, 'brings into relief the utterly constructed status of the so-called heterosexual original. Thus, gay is to straight *not* as copy is to original, but, rather as copy is to copy.'[28] Butch/femme adopts this heterosexual iconography, presumed to be natural, and questions it, investing it with new meaning by a radical displacement of its forms. Perhaps, the more convincing the impersonation, the more radically it destabilizes the distinction between the natural and the artificial. Nestle: 'In some sense, Lesbians have always opposed the patriarchy: in the past, perhaps most when we looked like men.'[29]

II

So far this chapter has considered the refusal by the 1970s feminist movement of certain forms of lesbian eroticism. It has then attempted to demonstrate how this refusal is predicated on a misperception of these forms. Its argument is that such forms present not a mere rehearsal of heterosexual conventions but a radical restating of heterosexuality's naturalized terms. In this section I intend to explore this contention further by looking at some of the erotic fiction of Joan Nestle in order to show how it is informed by a similar polemic.

Classified as 'erotica'[30] the stories in *A Restricted Country*, perhaps in being interspersed with more theoretical works, have a greater air of respectability than the writings and graphics that have their only outlet in the still miniscule lesbian porn industry. In some ways of course one can actually see the publication of 'erotica' by a feminist publishing house as more transgressive of feminist sanctions on political correctness since, being available in a broad range of radical and feminist book-shops, these stories challenge an audience that the more specifically designated pornography would not normally reach. Nestle's use of the term pornographer as a self-description is ambivalent. Where she will label her writing erotica in the book, she will elsewhere describe it as pornography, 'Whatever's the upsetting term',[31] as she remarks in an interview. This is an interesting comment since it suggests not merely a desire to shock, but also an intention to shift the register of what is considered acceptable and so to displace norms.[32] Whether this inten-tion is evinced in her work or not is open to debate. Here I can only present a brief analysis of her variously named 'erotica' and 'pornogra-phy' and address a few of the points for which Nestle has been most castigated.

The first difficulty that arises in addressing Nestle's work is one of classification. Are these writings fiction (a problematic enough term in itself), designed to thrill or arouse? Are they autobiography, narrative testaments to the erotic imagination that Nestle elsewhere claims she wants to evoke? Can they be read as social documents, a journey into lives and bodies for so long silent about their sexuality? Are they fantasy? Can they be all of these, and if so, is their polemic radical or reactionary? A work that raises all these questions is Nestle's early autobiographical piece 'Esther's Story', a political celebration of butch/femme and an example of erotic writing that was attacked as being pornographic by the copywriter who refused to print it. Situated within a contemporary lesbian politics split by definitions of what does or does not constitute pornography, 'Esther's Story' inhabits an extremely complex and debatable position as a product of contending readings.

I have already described the difficulty of conceptualizing the complexity of the 'passing woman'. 'Esther's Story' marks a brief encounter with such a woman. Nestle's portrayal suggests the inadequacy of existing categories for an understanding of the 'passing' woman's commitment to her identity. To the heterosexual world, Esther is a man, at best a specular trick. For Nestle by contrast, she is a challenging woman desired for her strength:

> I looked at her, at the woman in a neat white shirt and grey pants and wondered how her passengers could be so deceived. It was our womanness that rode with us in the car, that filled the night with tense possibilities.[33]

Discrepancies and contradictions blend and our own assumptions crumble. 'Tough', as well as 'passing', Esther appears to Nestle in the bar, and to the reader if she chooses to look, in a much more complex manifestation than our expectations allow for. Captured, though only for a moment, in the paradox of her identity, 'a small slim woman who dressed butch',[34] Esther is neither less butch, nor less 'womanly' for this. Nestle's description encourages us to readdress our expectations and assumptions about the 'passing woman' without, however, compromising Esther's commitment to her chosen identity. For in Nestle's framework terms usually deemed incompatible find their juxtaposition. 'Tough', 'trembling', 'tender', 'demanding', 'caring', all these epithets find a place within the butch/femme encounter, not as opposites, binaries implying the superiority of one, but as shared equals.

In publishing this story, Nestle was, among other things, accused of engaging in 'unequal patriarchal power sex',[35] presumably meaning butch/femme. That there are power differences between the two women cannot be denied. Still, there is an equality of differences here, implied throughout by Nestle. The engagement is, she admits, a mutual testing: 'I was testing my boundaries, and I think she was too.'[36] Nestle is candid about its terms:

> We both had power in our hands. She could turn from me and leave me with my wetness, my need – a vulnerability and a burden. I could close up, turn away from her caring and her expertise.[37]

Still, Nestle does admit that for her this encounter involves more risk than usual:

> Usually I was in control . . . From the first with Esther, I knew it

would be different. I was twenty and she was forty-five. I was out only two years, and she had already lived lifetimes as a freak. Her sexuality was a world of developed caring and she had paid a dear price for daring to be as clearly defined as she was.[38]

This is testimony to Esther's sexual expertise, a characteristic commonly accredited to the butch. The butch's role as the dominant instigator of sex is of course the aspect of the butch/femme encounter which has most continually been misunderstood by our age, which stresses a different kind of mutuality. Yet as Davis and Kennedy's study of New York lesbian bar culture suggests, the dynamics of the butch/femme relation in this instance cannot be read in heterosexual terms since their focus of pleasure is entirely other. For in the butch/femme encounter of this kind, the butch receives pleasure not through her own release, but from the pleasure she gives to the femme. According to Davis and Kennedy:

In a [heterosexual] culture that viewed women as sexually passive, butches developed a position as sexual aggressor . . . However, the active or 'masculine' partner was associated with the giving of sexual pleasure, a service usually assumed to be 'feminine.' Conversely, the fem, although the more passive partner, demanded and received sexual pleasure and in this sense might be considered the more self-concerned . . . partner.[39]

The terms commonly associated with the conventional heterosexual encounter are thus reversed rather than repeated.

This passage from 'Esther's Story' is also an acknowledgement of the other woman's strengths and courage and the way in which these affect the encounter. For the encounter is not only about sex, but a sexuality that makes recognizable statements far outside the bedroom, since there are not only significant age differences between the two women but differences of culture and life experience too. Esther is a Puerto Rican passing woman who has spent half her life in Ponce where she was married and bore sons. She brings cultural and experiential differences to the encounter which are complicated by Nestle's own history as a Jewish working-class lesbian growing up under the shadows of poverty, homophobia, and anti-Semitism. Complicated but not evaded, since the differences between the women are those that we surely would not wish to negate since they present above all the richness and variety of women whose experiences can be shared, but whose distinctiveness is stated even within the jubilant paradox that 'two women could dare each other so'.[40] The otherness of this encounter is therefore part of its courage and joyfulness, in that each woman can acknowledge the differences in the other without feeling them to be a threat.

That Nestle is not alone in her celebration of difference within same-sex relations is illustrated by Jane Gallop's 'Annie Leclerc: Writing a Letter with Vermeer'. In her analysis of Leclerc's 'A Love Letter', Gallop sees Leclerc as emphasizing difference rather than similarity between women who choose to share their lives. Gallop notes:

> For her, love is the celebration of difference, the encounter with difference, which risks sounding heterosexist, but she will not accept the notion that homosexuality is the pleasure of sameness. She wants to affirm difference in homosexuality, however much a contradiction in terms.[41]

Leclerc employs Vermeer's portrait, *Lady Writing a Letter with her Maid* in her attempt to describe the excitement she obtains from the contemplation of erotic differences between women. Identifying with the bourgeois lady, says Gallop, Leclerc none the less feels desire for the maid, and admits:

> I love the woman servant . . . oh no, not out of pity, not because I would take up the noble mantle of redressers of wrongs . . . but because I want to touch her, to take her hands, to bury my head in her chest, to smother her cheeks and neck with kisses.[42]

It is in the contemplation of the difference between herself and the maid that Leclerc locates her desire. That such desire brings with it immense problems does not go unacknowledged by Gallop. As she observes, not only does it have identifications with a phallic tradition that operates around a desire for those with less power or privilege, but it could also be seen as romanticizing this tradition. None the less, Gallop concludes that Leclerc's desire for the maid is finally more affirming than oppressive because it is at least clear about its own terms, a fact about which the desire that hides itself beneath the 'mantle of redressers of wrongs' plainly is not. Gallop continues, 'in its very explicitness in Leclerc's text [this desire] allows us to see more clearly what is usually suppressed, repressed, or sublimated in our relation to the other woman'.[43] Like Gayatri Spivak's notion of the 'simultaneous other focus . . . not merely who am I? But who is the other woman?'[44] that Gallop invokes, this state of self-awareness is never easy and rarely simple. In its determination to recognize difference and its refusal to trust in facile universalisms, such self-awareness is, however, absolutely necessary if exclusions are to be renounced.

More contentious in some ways than the works we have been considering up to now, since it is not obviously identified as 'in the past', is Nestle's 'The Gift of Taking', which in its title alone suggests some of the more insistent paradoxes of the deployment of power in sex. Here Nestle asks us to readdress our attitudes and assumptions about the place of power in eroticism, both to acknowledge its fact, and to recognize that its deployment need not be coercive. For, in the very particular context Nestle describes, submission can also mean strength: 'My submission in this room with this woman is my source of strength of wisdom.'[45] We can only understand this submission in terms of the specific encounter Nestle describes, where submission does not imply weakness or entrapment, and where power can be as gentle as it is demanding, with 'hands that are strong enough to leave their mark without losing their tenderness'.[46] Nestle's description constitutes not only a recognition of the fact of power, but an exploration of its reflection and its reversal. Thus, powerful in the outside world, the fictional Joan can alternate here, both in exploring her dependence on this woman and in her willingness to have her for this moment at least, and so take the lead. In the room she exchanges a known position for something different. In attempting to describe this kind of exchange elsewhere, Nestle remarks that it 'isn't based on my submissiveness to another woman's strength, it's based, I would say, on strengths of difference'.[47] Here then is a mutuality of a different sort from that sanctioned by the cultural feminists. *Their* idealized merging of 'kindred spirits' can now be seen more in terms of extinction by rather than absorption in the other. What Nestle insists upon above all is the right to change, to alter one's position, and to explore many roles, desires, and needs at any given time. This she finds in 'Margaret', the woman who can be two different women at once:

> When she is on her back, her body's fullness begs for touch. When she is above me, her muscled back, her wide shoulders, her powerful forearms present a different kind of woman, but always the softness of her breasts precedes her.[48]

Such an exploration of power differences may manifest itself in a testing of one's partner, a playful teasing and daring that is respectful while being candid about its power dynamics. So Nestle can mount her butch lover, dare her, play with her, and taunt her, asking, 'What kind of wimpy-assed butch are you?'[49]

Nestle's 'A Change of Life' expresses this sense of movement and change in a more extreme way. 'After forty femmes turn butch',[50] observes Nestle, a doctrine she then embraces in the encounter that succeeds. 'Let me be butch for you; I have been a femme for so long',[51] she says. This is, however, a change of life which still expresses and plays around the old form: 'I know I am trying to feel like something other than the woman I usually am.'[52] Nestle suggests a flexibility of self which allows for the coterminous existence and play of identities and desires. She also claims the right to be open about these, to give expression to their formally outlawed, still maligned existence. Thus she writes of the dildo that she can finally admit to enjoying: 'No need to hide the word anymore. No need to hide my desires.'[53]

III

I hope to have demonstrated in my analysis of butch/femme that to describe its focus as 'heterosexual' is not only simplistic, but ignores the complex workings and delicate balances of power in forms that are honest in their acknowledgement of power differences and the pleasures they can yield. I do not of course mean to imply that sex is therefore more innocent when staged within butch/femme, that butch/ femme's honesty about the positive exchange of power in sex puts it beyond critique. To argue this would be to escape one Foucauldian paradigm only to fall into another,[54] for just as sex is never free from power, so it is never innocent of power's implications. In fact its claims must be continually problematized.

In her essay, 'Identity Politics and Sexual Freedom', Jana Sawicki refers to sexuality as a 'pluralism in which nothing goes'.[55] In arguing this she refers to a comment made by Foucault in an interview shortly before his death; he observes: 'My point is not that everything is bad; but that everything is dangerous.'[56] In other words, he is saying that everything needs to be put under continuous critique where nothing is presumed to be the norm. Foucault's words should be warning enough against the libertarian impulse we see at times in the work of sex-positive lesbian writers, an impulse from which Nestle is not immune. To make sex the focus of individual liberation, as Nestle sometimes does, and to see sex's freedom of expression as constituting the very essence of the self, is to make claims which are themselves not above suspicion. Raising such objections is not to go towards the opposite extreme, however, to maintain that there is nothing affirmative in the way that Nestle is prepared to recognize what her opponents refuse – and that is the fact of the existence of power dynamics in even the most loving and mutual of encounters. For what Nestle's work does is to *reinform* our understanding of the relation between power and sex. The presence in Nestle's writing of that which we as feminists have been taught to think of as the linguistic paraphernalia of the patriarchy (the occurrence of terms like 'penetration', 'tear', 'thrust', 'forces', and so on) is part of this strategy. For what their use here tells us is that there is nothing intrinsically bad about these words (which does not mean they cannot be critiqued). They become in fact the property of those who deploy them and can be wrested from the oppressor if necessary.[57] Consider the femme's appropriation of the sartorial conventions of femininity where the clothes are not oppressive in themselves but rather for what they signify at a given time, that is, as being required wear under patriarchy. Change the context, and the meaning changes too. This could also be argued of Nestle's play on the conventions of heterosexual courtship (here I am thinking of the arrival of the drink and the flowers from Esther, or Joan's gift of the négligé to her young femme lover in 'A Change of Place'). Cynics might remark that these attentions merely acquiesce in the 'already oppressive' conventions of romance *per se*. I am, none the less, tempted to read them otherwise since, in their gentle and knowing play on these conventions (Esther's amused smile speaks volumes), they elicit the assurance that lesbianism has as much right to the glamour of these forms as any other relation. The gender play that informs these moments enacts a reversal of our expectations and cannot be accused of merely imitating heterosexual forms. Rather, a redefinition of conventional forms is set up in images such as that of 'penetration *by this woman's hand*'.[58]

Nestle's erotica does not, of course, remain unproblematic in its constructions, and it is certainly not beyond committing some extravagances in the heat of the moment. The concluding passage to 'A Change of Life' is only one instance .of a certain libertarianism at work in her writing. 'But now I do not want my own movement to change the world,' she says, 'I want hers – her hips to call forth the new order.'[59] Such effusions might be a warning not to take 'the sheets' too literally out on to 'the streets'! On some occasions there seems to be in her fiction an almost too insistent stress on variety where difference becomes imperative to, rather than a facet of, performance. We see this emphasis most particularly in her story 'The Three', where it seems that every traditional feminist injunction is determinedly and self-consciously transgressed. As Elizabeth Wilson wryly puts it: 'At times I did feel timid and unadventurous when comparing my own experience with [Nestle's] heroic tales of untrammelled lust.'[60] The very multiplicity of positions explored and taboos broken can indeed prove exhausting, and it could be said that in certain instances Nestle's work performs not so much a play on heterosexual convention as an acquiescence in its sexual fix.[61] Such a state would characterize the moments of essentialism we sometimes glimpse in her work.[62] Essentialisms, undeniably, whenever they do occur, always need to be critiqued. Nestle's occasional unwillingness to problematize her own investment in the sexual ideologies of the dominant group (there is no reference in her book for example to the increasing commodification of the lesbian sex industry, nor to its increasing relation to big capital) is also worrying when we compare it with her otherwise committed investigation of the political and social lines of complicity between different interests and ideologies.

The relation of lesbian sex writing and graphics to pornography is a fascinating one, and worth exploring. It is a relation which I have not specifically considered here, as my concern has been to explore the relation between lesbian eroticism and its appropriation of a more mainstream heterosexuality. Despite this bias, my study has been informed by an understanding of pornography as a product of certain social formations. What is considered at any time to constitute pornography is thereby understood to be less a matter of content than of the context in which the material is read. It is in this spirit that I have attempted to describe the appropriative strategies of a writer like Joan Nestle. That Nestle's writings could be likewise appropriated for use within a male heterosexual context is without doubt an ongoing concern. Writers have little control over the reception of their work once published. Recent feminist experience has shown that even the most politically well-intentioned material is hardly invulnerable to adverse appropriation.[63] In the end we may only profess the conviction that, like the Sheba Collective on the publication of their own *Serious Pleasure* anthology (1989), 'At a certain point our confidence must override our fears.'[64]

In *Serious Pleasure* sex and politics have a tenuous but ongoing relation which reflects as intently on the writings of a lesbian-feminist like Joan Nestle as it does on Sheba's own productions. In trying to find the mean between political correctness and personal desire *Serious Pleasure* is sometimes crude, more often subtle in its explorations, offering no hard and fast answers, but providing a continued questioning of its own parameters. It is this self-questioning, this unwillingness to lay down injunctions or to inhibit careful exploration, that I find so affirming in the work of Joan Nestle. Earlier, the question of the politics of Nestle's writings was raised. There is, of course, no sense in which the works described in *A Restricted Country* can be innately radical or any more likely in themselves to usher in a new age of sexual liberation and tolerance. Any such claims when made for these writings must be undermined. In conclusion, however, I would argue that these writings do take on a political function in relation to the feminist movement, since in existing and being the subjects of contention they reopen a debate which has previously been refused. In this respect, they make public as well as private statements. Their *politicization* by the feminist movement alongside their continual sexual and gender reversals, their deconstruction of naturalized heterosexual forms, make them very political texts indeed. And it is for both these reasons that I read these texts less in terms of the danger of a co-option of lesbian eroticism by heterosexuality, than in the potential for the co-option of heterosexual forms by a knowing and playful lesbian sexual politics.

Afterword

In her preface to *A Restricted Country* Nestle tells of the multiple identities which have come to inform her life. These include her lesbian self, her feminist self, her socialist self and her own sense of what it means to be a Jew. Each of these identities has played its part in the thinking behind my approach to this essay, an essay which, while it has no pretensions to a sociological study, does I hope manifest an awareness of the politics and dangers of exclusion. What I have to admit here, however, is my partial failure in this ideal. I refer to my failure to *name* Nestle's sense of her own Jewishness, a sense of Jewishness which I believe now is central not only to her politics, but to the tone, the inflection, the voice that comes through so clearly and magnificently in her writings. I acknowledge this failure now, and thank Lianna Borghi for shocking me into an awareness of my own blind spot in this instance.

Further reading

This booklist is limited to a selection of monographs and collections in the overlapping fields of lesbian and gay criticism of literature in English. Many of the titles listed below have much more specialized bibliographies.

Bennett, Paula, *Emily Dickinson*, Key Women Writers (Hemel Hempstead: Harvester-Wheatsheaf, 1990).

Bergman, David, *Gaiety Transfigured: Gay Self-Representation in American Literature* (Madison: University of Wisconsin Press, 1991).

Boone, Joseph A. and Cadden, Michael (eds), *Engendering Men: The Question of Male Feminist Criticism* (New York: Routledge, 1990).

Butters, Ronald M., Clum, John M., and Moon, Michael (eds), *Displacing Homophobia* (Durham, NC: Duke University Press, 1990).

Dellamora, Richard, *Masculine Desire: The Sexual Politics of Victorian Aestheticism* (Chapel Hill: University of North Carolina Press, 1990).

Dollimore, Jonathan, *Sexual Dissidence: Augustine to Wilde, Freud to Foucault* (Oxford: Oxford University Press, 1991).

Faderman, Lillian, *Surpassing the Love of Men: Romantic Friendship and Love between Women from the Renaissance to the Present* (New York: Morrow, 1981; London: The Women's Press, 1985).

Foster, Jeanette, *Sex Variant Women in Literature* ([1956] Baltimore: Diana Press, 1975).

Fuss, Diana (ed.), *Inside/Out: Lesbian Theories, Gay Theories* (New York: Routledge, 1991).

Hobby, Elaine and White, Chris (eds), *What Lesbians Do in Books* (London: The Women's Press, 1991).

Jay, Karla and Glasgow, Joanne (eds), *Lesbian Texts and Contexts: Radical Revisions* (New York: New York University Press, 1990).

Koestenbaum, Wayne, *Double Talk: The Erotics of Male Literary Collaboration* (New York: Routledge, 1989).

Lilly, Mark (ed.), *Lesbian and Gay Writing* (London: Macmillan, 1990).

Moon, Michael, *Disseminating Whitman* (Cambridge, MA: Harvard University Press, 1991).

Mulford, Wendy, *This Narrow Place – Sylvia Townsend Warner and Valentine Ackland: Life, Letters and Politics, 1930–1951* (London: Pandora, 1988).

O'Rourke, Rebecca, *Reflecting on 'The Well of Loneliness'* (London: Routledge, 1990).

Palmer, Paulina, *Contemporary Women's Fiction: Narrative Practice and Feminist Theory* (Hemel Hempstead: Harvester-Wheatsheaf, 1989).

Rule, Jane, *Lesbian Images* (London: Peter Davies, 1976).

Sedgwick, Eve Kosofsky, *Between Men: English Literature and Male Homosocial Desire* (New York: Columbia University Press, 1985).

Sedgwick, Eve Kosofsky, *Epistemology of the Closet* (Berkeley: University of California Press, 1990; Hemel Hempstead: Harvester-Wheatsheaf, 1991).

Sinfield, Alan, *Literature, Politics and Culture in Post-War Britain* (Berkeley: University of California Press, 1989; Oxford: Basil Blackwell, 1989).

Summers, Claude J., *Gay Fictions: Wilde to Stonewall: Studies in a Male Homosexual Tradition* (New York: Continuum, 1990).

Woods, Gregory, *Articulate Flesh: Male Homo-Eroticism and Modern Poetry* (New Haven, CT: Yale University Press, 1987).

Yingling, Thomas, *Hart Crane and the Homosexual Text: New Thresholds, New Anatomies* (Chicago: University of Chicago Press, 1990).

Yorke, Liz, *Impertinent Voices: Subversive Strategies in Contemporary Women's Poetry* (London: Routledge, 1991).

Zimmerman, Bonnie, *The Safe Sea of Women: Lesbian Fiction 1969–1988* (Boston: Beacon, 1990; London: Onlywomen Press, 1991).

Notes

1 Introduction

1 See, for example, Chris Baldick, *The Social Mission of English Criticism 1848–1932* (Oxford: Oxford University Press, 1983), pp. 45–6.
2 Michel Foucault, *The History of Sexuality: An Introduction*, trans. Robert Hurley (Harmondsworth: Penguin Books, 1981), p. 43.
3 Eve Kosofsky Sedgwick, *Epistemology of the Closet* (Berkeley: University of California Press; Hemel Hempstead: Harvester-Wheatsheaf, 1991), pp. 15–16.
4 David Van Leer, 'The Beast of the Closet: Homosociality and the Pathology of Manhood', *Critical Inquiry*, 15:3 (1989), pp. 587–605.
5 Janet Todd, *Feminist Literary Criticism: A Defence* (Cambridge: Polity Press, 1988), p. 118.
6 'Male feminism' makes its appearance in two important collections: Alice Jardine and Paul Smith (eds), *Men in Feminism* (New York: Methuen, 1987), and Joseph A. Boone and Michael Cadden (eds), *Engendering Men: The Question of Male Feminist Criticism* (New York: Routledge, 1990).
7 Mandy Merck, 'Difference and its Discontents', *Screen* 28:1 (1987), p. 2.

2 The cultural politics of perversion: Augustine, Shakespeare, Freud, Foucault

1 The issues and arguments outlined in this chapter are explored more fully in Jonathan Dollimore, *Sexual Dissidence: Augustine to Wilde, Freud to Foucault* (Oxford: Oxford University Press, 1991).
2 All quotations from Freud's writings are taken from the Pelican Freud Library. Volume and page numbers are included in the text.
3 Kenneth Lewes, *The Psychoanalytical Theory of Male Homosexuality* (London: Quartet, 1989). Those analysts Lewes cites include Edmund Bergler ('the most important analytic theorist of homosexuality in the 1950s', p. 15), who wrote: 'I have no bias against homosexuality . . . [but] homosexuals are essentially disagreeable people . . . displaying a mixture of superciliousness, false aggression, and whimpering . . . subservient when confronted with a stronger person, merciless when in power, unscrupulous about trampling on a weaker person' (cited by Lewes, p. 15).
4 Michel Foucault, *The History of Sexuality*, vol. 1, *An Introduction* (New York: Vintage, 1978). See especially part 2, ch. 2.
5 Foucault, 'Introduction' to George Canguilhem, *The Normal and the Pathological* (New York: Zone Books, 1989), p. 22.
6 Francis Bacon, 'Advertisement Touching an Holy Warre', in *Works*, ed. J. Spedding and R.L. Ellis (1857–61; Stuttgart: Fromann, 1961–3), vol. 7, pp. 33–4.

7 Robert Burton, *The Anatomy of Melancholy*, ed. Holbrook Jackson (London: Dent, 1932), first partition, p. 136.

8 Leo Bersani, *The Freudian Body: Psychoanalysis and Art* (New York: Columbia University Press, 1986).

9 Augustine, *City of God*, trans. Henry Bettenson (Harmondsworth: Penguin Books, 1972). All page references to this edition are given in the text.

10 David Hume, *Dialogues Concerning Natural Religion*, part X, in Steven M. Cahn (ed.), *Classics of Western Philosophy* (Indianapolis: Hackett, 1977), p. 741; Lactantius, 'The Wrath of God' in *Lactantius: The Minor Works* (Washington, DC: Catholic University of America Press, 1965), pp. 92–3. I am grateful to Tony Nuttall for these references.

11 Charles Journet, *The Meaning of Evil*, trans. Michael Barry (London: Geoffrey Chapman, 1963), pp. 43, 46, 66.

12 Jacques Maritain, *St Thomas and the Problem of Evil* (Milwaukee: Marquette University Press, 1942), p. 2.

13 John Hick, *Evil and the God of Love* (Glasgow: Collins, 1968), p. 68.

14 ibid., p. 264.

15 Quotations from *Othello* are taken from the Signet Classic Shakespeare edition, ed. Alvin Kiernan (New York: New American Library 1963).

16 Cited in Simon Shepherd, *Marlowe and the Politics of Elizabethan Theatre* (Brighton: Harvester Press, 1986), p. 142.

17 Alvin Kiernan, 'Introduction' to *Othello*, Signet Classic Shakespeare, pp. xv–xviii.

18 Richard Marienstras, *New Perspectives on the Shakespearean World*, trans. Janet Lloyd (Cambridge: Cambridge University Press, 1985), chs 5 and 6.

19 *Homily against Disobedience and Wilful Rebellion* (1571), in *Certain Sermons or Homilies: Appointed to be Read in Churches* (London: Society for the Promotion of Christian Knowledge, 1890), p. 615. Further references are included in the text.

20 On the demonic representation of Black people in Elizabethan England, see Eldred Jones, *Othello's Countrymen* (London: Oxford University Press, 1965); Ruth Cowhig, 'Blacks in English Renaissance Drama and the Role of Shakespeare's Othello', in David Dabydeen (ed.), *The Black Presence in English Literature* (Manchester: Manchester University Press, 1985), pp. 4–7; and Ania Loomba, *Gender, Race, Renaissance Drama* (Manchester: Manchester University Press, 1989), pp. 42–5.

21 Martin Orkin, *Shakespeare against Apartheid* (Craighall, South Africa: Ad. Donker, 1987), pp. 88–96.

22 Jonathan Dollimore, 'Sexuality, Subjectivity and Transgression: the Jacobean Connection', *Renaissance Drama*, NS 7 (1986), pp. 53–82; and *Radical Tragedy: Religion, Ideology and Power in the Drama of Shakespeare and his Contemporaries*, 2nd edn (Hemel Hempstead: Harvester-Wheatsheaf, 1989), pp. xxxv–xi.

23 Sandor Feldman, 'On Homosexuality' in S. Lorand and M. Balint (eds), *Perversions: Psychodynamics and Therapy* (New York: Random House, 1956), pp. 74–5, 93–4 (my emphasis). (Incidentally, this volume also contains an essay co-written by Jacques Lacan.)

24 See, for example, Peter Stallybrass and Allon White, *The Politics and Poetics of Transgression* (London: Methuen, 1986).

25 John Rechy, *The Sexual Outlaw: A Documentary/A Non-Fiction Account, with Commentaries of Three Days and Three Nights in the Sexual Underground* (London: W.H. Allen, 1978), pp. 299, 301.

26 Dollimore, 'Different Desires: Subjectivity and Transgression in Wilde and Gide', *Textual Practice*, I: 1 (1987), pp. 48–67, and *Genders*, 2 (1988), pp. 24–41; 'The Dominant and the Deviant', in Colin MacCabe (ed.), *Futures for*

English (Manchester: Manchester University Press, 1988), pp. 179–92.
27 *The Letters of Oscar Wilde*, ed. Rupert Hart-Davis (New York: Harcourt, 1962),
p. 466.

3 'Poets and lovers evermore': the poetry and journals of Michael Field

This chapter owes much to the thought and care of Elaine Hobby, Simon
Shepherd, and Joseph Bristow, to whom thanks and love.
1 Lillian Faderman, *Surpassing the Love of Men: Romantic Friendship and Love
between Women from the Renaissance to the Present* (1981; London: The Women's
Press, 1985). Page references are included in the text.
2 These journals are held in British Library under the title 'Works and Days'
from 1870 on. All British Library manuscript reference numbers and folio
numbers indicate these texts. The published journals appeared as *Works and
Days*, ed. T. and D.C. Sturge Moore (London: John Murray, 1933) hereafter
referred to as *Works and Days*.
3 See Donna C. Stanton and Jeanine F. Plottel (eds), *The Female Autograph:
Theory and Practice from the Middle Ages to the Present* (Chicago: University of
Chicago Press, 1987); Liz Stanley and Sue Scott (eds), *Writing Feminist
Biography* (Manchester: Manchester University Press, 1986).
4 'Lesbian' is here and elsewhere used to refer to people and things pertaining
to Lesbos; 'lesbian' is used throughout to refer to sexual or emotional
relationships between women.
5 Arran and Isla Leigh, *Bellerophôn* (London: Kegan Paul, 1881), p. 159.
6 Examples of homosexual treatments of Greek literature and culture from the
nineteenth century include William Cory, 'Heraclitus' from *Ionica* (London:
Smith, Elder, 1858); Charles Kains-Jackson, 'Antinous' from *The Artist and
Journal of Home Culture*, 12 (October 1891); Walter Pater, *Greek Studies: A Series
of Lectures* (1894); John Addington Symonds, *A Problem in Greek Ethics* (1883).
7 William Mure, *Critical History of the Language and Literature of Ancient Greece*
(1850–7), cited in Richard Jenkyns, *Three Classical Poets: Sappho, Catullus,
Juvenal* (London: Duckworth, 1982), p. 2.
8 Gilbert Murray, *Ancient Greek Literature* (1897), cited in Jenkyns, op. cit., p. 2.
9 The version of Sappho as heterosexual lover appeared in ironized form as
early as 1848 in Christina Rossetti's suppressed poem 'What Sappho would
have said had her leap cured instead of killing her'.
10 Michael Field to Walter Pater, 11 June 1889, in Laurence Evans (ed.), *The
Letters of Walter Pater* (Oxford: Clarendon Press, 1970), p. 96.
11 See Walter Pater, *Greek Studies: A Series of Lectures* (New York: Chelsea House,
1983).
12 See John Addington Symonds, *A Problem in Greek Ethics*, the full edition
(1901), and *A Problem in Modern Ethics* (1896).
13 Michael Field, *Long Ago*, Poem XXXV (London: Bell, 1889), p. 56.
14 ibid., Poem V, 'Where with their boats the fishers land', p. 8.
15 ibid., Poem LXVI, 'We sat and chatted at our ease', p. 123.
16 Arran Leigh, *The New Minnesinger and Other Poems* (1875), p. 2.
17 For nineteenth-century British homosexual usages of Walt Whitman, see, for
example, Edward Dowden, *Studies in Literature 1789–1877* (1878), John
Addington Symonds, *Walt Whitman: A Study* (London: Routledge, Kegan
Paul, 1893), and John Addington Symonds, 'Democratic Art with Special
Reference to Walt Whitman', in *Essays Speculative and Suggestive* (1893).
18 *Long Ago*, Poem LII, 'Climbing the hill a coil of snakes', p. 89.
19 Preface to *Long Ago*, p. iii; translation from Poem 78 in Josephine Balmer,
Sappho: Poem and Fragments (unpaginated edition), [p. 58].

20 Mary Sturgeon, *Michael Field* (London: Harrap, 1922), p. 47.
21 British Library, Add. MS 46803, fo. 100ᵛ.
22 Sturgeon, op. cit., p. 47.
23 Faderman, op. cit., p. 210.
24 Edward Carpenter, *Homogenic Love, and Its Place in a Free Society* (Manchester: Manchester Labour Society, 1894).
25 Elizabeth Mavor, *The Ladies of Llangollen: A Study in Romantic Friendship* (1971; London: Penguin Books, 1973), p. xvii.
26 Case histories of female sexual inverts contained in H. Havelock Ellis, *Studies in the Psychology of Sex*, vol. 1, *Sexual Inversion* (1897) included Edith Ellis and Renée Vivien.
27 Sonja Ruehl, 'Sexual Theory and Practice: Another Double Standard', in Sue Cartledge and Joanna Ryan (eds), *Sex and Love: New Thoughts on Old Contradictions* (London: The Women's Press, 1983), p. 219.
28 Gayle Rubin, 'Thinking Sex: Notes for a Radical Theory of the Politics of Sexuality', in Carole S. Vance (ed.), *Pleasure and Danger: Exploring Female Sexuality* (London: Routledge & Kegan Paul, 1984), p. 301.
29 *Works and Days*, p. 63.
30 British Library MS, 46798 fo. 25ᵛ.
31 See E. Ann Kaplan, 'Is the Gaze Male?', in Ann Snitow *et al.* (eds), *Desire: The Politics of Sexuality* (London: Virago, 1984), pp. 321–38.
32 British Library MS, 46798, fo. 20ᵛ.
33 Wayne Koestenbaum, *Double Talk: The Erotics of Male Literary Collaboration* (London: Routledge, 1989), p. 173: he is citing Sturgeon, op. cit., p. 23.
34 British Library MS, 46797, fo. 52ᵛ.
35 ibid., fo. 77.
36 British Library MS, 46777, fo. 87.
37 Michael Field, *The Wattlefold: Unpublished Poems by Michael Field*, collected by Emily C. Fortey (Oxford: 1930), p. 191.
38 *Works and Days*, p. 326.
39 See, with reservation and suspicion, since he suppresses or refutes any suggestions of homosexuality, Brocard Sewell, *Footnote to the Nineties: A Memoir of John Gray and André Raffalovich* (London: C. & A. Woolf, 1968) and Brocard Sewell, *In the Dorian Mode: A Life of John Gray 1866–1934* (Padstow: Tabb House, 1983).
40 Sturgeon, op. cit., p. 47.
41 *Works and Days*, p. xix.

4 Wilde, Dorian Gray, and gross indecency

Thanks to Jonathan Dollimore and D.A. Miller for responses.

 1 *The Complete Works of Oscar Wilde*, ed. J.B. Foreman (London: Collins, 1966). All references to this unreliable but widely available edition are contained in the text. Wilde's textual revisions to the version of *Dorian Gray* that appeared in *Lippincott's* in 1890 do not form part of the present discussion; for further details of the salient changes to the 1890 text, see Richard Ellmann, *Oscar Wilde* (London: Hamish Hamilton, 1987), pp. 292–306. Wilde's collected writings are now being prepared for an edition to be published by Oxford University Press.
 2 Walter Pater, *The Renaissance: Studies in Art and Poetry*, ed. Donald L. Hill ([1873 and subsequent editions] Berkeley: University of California Press, 1980), p. 190.
 3 Eve Kosofsky Sedgwick, *Between Men: English Literature and Male Homosocial Desire* (New York: Columbia University Press, 1985), and 'The Beast in the

Closet: James and the Writing of Homosexual Panic', in Ruth Bernard Yeazell (ed.), *Sex, Politics, and Science in the Nineteenth Century Novel*, Selected Papers from the English Institute 1983–84, NS 10 (Baltimore: Johns Hopkins University Press, 1986), pp. 147–86. One reading of *Dorian Gray* which has emerged from Sedgwick's investigation of homosocial and homosexual bonds is Richard Dellamora, 'Representation and Homophobia in *The Picture of Dorian Gray*', *Victorian Newsletter*, 73 (1988), pp. 28–31. Sedgwick considers the 'sentimental relations of the male body' in the writings of Wilde and Friedrich Nietzsche in *Epistemology of the Closet* (Berkeley: University of California Press, 1990; Hemel Hempstead: Harvester-Wheatsheaf, 1991), pp. 31–81. Further significant gay readings of Wilde's works include Kevin Kopelson, 'Wilde, Barthes, and the Orgasmics of Truth', *Genders*, 7 (1990), pp. 22–31; Wayne Koestenbaum, 'Wilde's Hard Labour and the Birth of Gay Reading', in Joseph A. Boone and Michael Cadden (eds), *Engendering Men: The Question of Male Feminist Criticism* (New York: Routledge, 1990), pp. 176–89; and Christopher Craft, 'Alias Bunbury: Desire and Transgression in *The Importance of Being Earnest*', *Representations*, 31 (1990), pp. 19–46.

4 Michel Foucault, *The History of Sexuality: An Introduction*, trans. Robert Hurley (Harmondsworth, Middlesex: Penguin Books, 1981), p. 43; Jeffrey Weeks, *Sex, Politics, and Society: The Regulation of Sexuality since 1800*, 2nd edn (London: Longman, 1988), pp. 99–100. A fresh analysis of the emergence of 'homosexuality' is provided by Ed Cohen, 'Legislating the Norm: From Sodomy to Gross Indecency', *The South Atlantic Quarterly*, 88:1 (1989), pp. 181–217.

5 Linda Dowling, 'Ruskin's Pied Beauty and the Constitution of a "Homosexual" Code', *Victorian Newsletter*, 75 (1989), p. 7. For a related account of emerging nineteenth-century homosexual codings, see Michael Lynch, '"Here Is Adhesiveness": From Friendship to Homosexuality', *Victorian Studies*, 28 (1985–6), pp. 67–96.

6 Philip E. Smith II and Michael S. Helfand (eds), *Oscar Wilde's Oxford Notebooks* (New York: Oxford University Press, 1989), p. 91. A briefer but nevertheless useful account of Wilde's philosophical affiliations with progressive late Victorian thought – Tylor, Spencer, and Buckle, among others – can be found in Bruce Haley, 'Wilde's "Decadence" and the Positivist Tradition', *Victorian Studies*, 28 (1985–6), pp. 215–29.

7 John Stokes, *In the Nineties* (Hemel Hempstead: Harvester-Wheatsheaf; Chicago: University of Chicago Press, 1989), p. 22. Stokes's study explores the nineties' fascination with Max Nordau's polemic on 'degeneration'. The publication of the English translation of *Degeneration* roughly coincided with two events that year: first, the Wilde trials, and second, a heated debate in the periodicals about fiction and sexuality (especially in relation to 'New Woman' fiction): see, among other examples, James Ashcroft Noble, 'The Fiction of Sexuality', *The Contemporary Review*, 67 (1895), pp. 490–8; and Janet E. Hogarth, 'Literary Degenerates', *The Fortnightly Review*, NS 57 (1895), pp. 586–92. (My thanks to Kate Flint for pointing out these references to me.)

8 Smith and Helfand, op. cit., p. 101.

9 Neil Bartlett, *Who Was That Man? A Present for Mr Oscar Wilde* (London: Serpent's Tail, 1988), pp. 128–43. On Bartlett's gay historiography, see Joseph Bristow, 'Being Gay: Politics, Identity, Pleasure', *New Formations*, 9 (1989), pp. 61–81.

10 John Marshall, 'Pansies, Perverts and Macho Men: Changing Conceptions of Male Homosexuality', in Kenneth Plummer (ed.), *The Making of the Modern Homosexual* (London: Hutchinson, 1981), p. 139. Marshall adds: 'Judging from the written records (Parliamentary Debates 1885), Henry Labouchère, who introduced the amendment, was concerned essentially with indecent assaults involving males, which at that time had to be committed on persons

under 13 years of age to be punishable. His clause was designed to make any assault of this kind punishable whatever the age of the assailant. However, the actual amendment referred rather vaguely to "acts of gross indecency", and it was this undefined offence that was to be so widely interpreted in the years that followed. Apparently Labouchère did not intend his clause to penalize "grossly indecent" acts which involved the consent of both parties' (p. 139). Questions arising from the eleventh-hour appearance of this amendment to the 1885 Act are covered in F.B. Smith, 'Labouchère's Amendment to the Criminal Law Amendment Bill', *Historical Studies* [Melbourne], 67 (1976), pp. 165–75.

11 Wilde made this remark in his petition to the Home Secretary for some reading materials to alleviate the boredom of solitary confinement: 'To the Home Secretary', 2 July 1896, in *The Letters of Oscar Wilde*, ed. Rupert Hart-Davis (London: Rupert Hart-Davis, 1962), p. 402.

12 Judith Walkowitz, 'Male Vice and Female Virtue: Feminism and the Politics in Nineteenth-Century Britain', in Ann Snitow *et al.*, (eds), *Desire: The Politics of Sexuality* (London: Virago Press, 1984), p. 49.

13 H. Montgomery Hyde, *The Trials of Oscar Wilde* (London: William Hodge, 1948), p. 124.

14 ibid., p. 236.

15 Hesketh Pearson, *Oscar Wilde* (1946; Harmondsworth, Middlesex: Penguin Books, 1982), p. 157. Pearson's commentary here on this phase of the trials is especially valuable.

16 Hyde, *Oscar Wilde: A Biography* (London: Eyre Methuen, 1976), p. 118. The extract is taken from the *Scots Observer*, 5 July 1890.

17 Pearson, op. cit., p. 286.

18 Weeks, 'Discourse, Desire and Sexual Deviance: Some Problems in a History of Homosexuality', in Plummer, op. cit., p. 102.

19 Hyde, *Oscar Wilde: A Biography*, p. 118.

20 Walter Pater, 'A Novel by Mr Oscar Wilde', in Richard Ellmann (ed.), *Oscar Wilde: A Collection of Critical Essays* (Englewood Cliffs, NJ: Prentice-Hall, 1969), p. 37. Pater's review originally appeared in *The Bookman*, November 1891.

21 ibid.

22 Jonathan Dollimore, 'Different Desires: Subjectivity and Transgression in Wilde and Gide', *Textual Practice*, 1:1 (1987), pp. 48–67.

23 Rachel Bowlby, 'Promoting Dorian Gray', *Oxford Literary Review*, 9:1–2 (1987), p. 148. For a further analysis of how sexual desire is connected with the seductions of advertising and the organization of the consumerist gaze, see Bowlby, *Just Looking: Consumer Culture in Dreiser, Gissing and Zola* (London: Methuen, 1985), pp. 18–34. A parallel analysis of this culture of 'self-advertisement' to be found both in the text of, and the critical responses to, *Dorian Gray* is provided by Regenia Gagnier, *Idylls of the Marketplace: Oscar Wilde and the Victorian Public* (Aldershot, Hampshire: Scolar Press, 1987), pp. 51–66. Gagnier's study balances the homosexual interests of the novel against the 'real story behind the novel and the nature of British decadence' (p. 52), namely the longstanding nineteenth-century controversies surrounding the figure of the dandy from Beau Brummell onwards. Gagnier usefully points out that both Wilde and his critics 'were situated in the context of public images and self-advertisement: the journalists posing as the gentlemen guardians of public morality, Wilde advertising himself as the subtle dandy-artist of higher morality' (p. 57).

24 Ed Cohen, 'Writing Gone Wilde: Homoerotic Desire in the Closet of Representation', *PMLA*, 102 (1987), p. 806.

25 Elaine Showalter, 'Syphilis, Sexuality, and the Fiction of the Fin de Siècle', in Yeazell, op. cit., p. 103.

26 Pater, *The Renaissance*, p. 190.

27 ibid., p. 445. Colvin's remarks were first published in the *Pall Mall Gazette*, 1 March 1873, p. 12.

28 Hyde, *Trials of Oscar Wilde*, p. 359. Stead's article, 'The Progress of the World', appeared in *The Review of Reviews* in 1895.

29 'To Lord Alfred Douglas', *c.* 9 November 1894, *Letters*, ed. Hart-Davis, p. 377. Wilde adds that he 'hate[s] England'. It must be borne in mind that Wilde was in many respects an outsider to the elite and fashionable world in which he thrived, not least because he was an Irishman.

5 Forster's self-erasure: Maurice and the scene of masculine love

1 E.M. Forster, *Maurice* (London: Penguin Books, 1972), p. 207. All further references are included in the text.

2 Robert K. Martin, 'Edward Carpenter and the Double Structure of *Maurice*', in Stuart Kellogg (ed.), *Essays on Gay Literature* (New York: Harington Park Press, 1985), pp. 35–46.

3 Cynthia Ozick, 'Forster as Homosexual', *Commentary*, 52 (1971), pp. 81–5; Jeffrey Meyers, *Homosexuality and Literature 1890–1930* (London: Athlone Press, 1977).

4 Claude J. Summers, *Gay Fictions: Wilde to Stonewall: Studies in a Male Homosexual Literary Tradition* (New York: Continuum, 1990), pp. 78, 111.

5 Martin op. cit., pp. 37, 45, n.8.

6 John Addington Symonds, 'A Problem in Greek Ethics', in Symonds, *Sexual Inversion: A Classic Study of Homosexuality* (New York: Bell, 1984), pp. 9–97.

7 The broad outline of Symonds's description of Greek *paiderastia* as an institution has been confirmed by recent scholarship: K.J. Dover, *Greek Homosexuality* (London: Duckworth, 1978); and especially David M. Halperin, *One Hundred Years of Homosexuality and Other Essays on Greek Love* (New York: Routledge, 1990), writing in a Foucauldian constructionist framework very different from Symonds. Symonds nowhere discusses pederastic sexual practices in any detail, confining himself to embarrassed generalities about 'sensuality', 'indulgences', and 'carnal appetite', but it is clear that what he calls 'Greek love' includes sexual expression. Symonds also makes a useful distinction between Socratic and Platonic conceptions of love. The figure of Socrates in Plato's dialogues presents an idealized version of *paiderastia* as a transmitter not only of martial values but of a philosophical idea of the noble life and a metaphysics of the Good, the True, and the Beautiful, to be found in a number of Plato's dialogues, particularly *Phaedrus* and *The Symposium*. Plato's late dialogue *The Laws*, where the figure of Socrates is absent, declares sexual acts and pleasure between men to be against nature and fit to be criminalized. Here Plato assigns sexual activity to procreation and relations with women. Same-sex love (*philia* or friendship) is to be chastely directed towards the beloved's soul not his body. It is to this late Platonic but non-Socratic conception that Clive Durham's ideal of homosexual love in *Maurice* conforms. To confuse matters, however, the particular Platonic dialogues that Forster associates with Clive, i.e. *Phaedrus* and *The Symposium*, are the very ones that present the Socratic celebration of an ennobling *paiderastia*, beginning with sexual desire for male bodily beauty and ending in a sublimated love of Beauty as a philosophical vision. Consequently there can be no simple equation of the Platonic texts as a whole (with their different concep-

tions) with Symonds's conception of 'Greek love' nor of either with Clive Durham and his ideals, along the lines Martin proposes.

8 In Symonds, *Sexual Inversion*, op. cit.

9 Jonathan Katz, '1859–1924: Walt Whitman, John Addington Symonds and Edward Carpenter', in *Gay American History: Lesbians and Gay Men in the U.S.A.* (New York: Discus Books, 1978), pp. 508–51.

10 *Maurice* op. cit., p. 217.

11 Jean Laplanche and Jean-Bertrand Pontalis, 'Fantasy and the Origins of Sexuality' (1964), reprinted in Victor Burgin, James Donald, and Cora Kaplan, (eds), *Formations of Fantasy* (London: Methuen, 1986), pp. 5–34.

12 For a discussion of heterosexual difference and primal fantasy, see John Fletcher, 'Freud and his Uses: Psychoanalysis and Gay Theory', in Simon Shepherd and Mick Wallis (eds), *Coming On Strong: Essays in Gay Politics and Culture* (London: Unwin Hyman, 1989), pp. 90–118.

13 Maud Mannoni, *The Child, his 'Illness' and the Others* (1967; London: Penguin Books, 1973).

14 E.M. Forster, 'Edward Carpenter', in *Two Cheers for Democracy* (London; Edward Arnold, 1951), p. 218.

15 P.N. Furbank, *E.M. Forster: A Life*, vol. 1 (1977; reprinted London: Penguin, 1988), p. 257.

16 Edward Carpenter, 'Self-Analysis for Havelock Ellis', in David Fernbach and Noel Greig (eds), *Selected Writings: Volume One: Sex* (London: Gay Men's Press, 1984), p. 290.

17 Francis King, *E.M. Forster* (London: Thames & Hudson, 1978), p. 80.

18 Edward Carpenter, 'The Intermediate Sex' [1906], in Fernbach and Greig (eds), *Selected Writings*, op. cit., pp. 185–244.

19 ibid., p. 190.

20 ibid., p. 197.

21 ibid., p. 290.

22 Christine Battersby, *Gender and Genius* (London: The Women's Press, 1989), esp. chapters 11 and 12.

23 Carpenter, op. cit., p. 196.

24 For Gramsci's analysis of the intelligentsia, see Antonio Gramsci, 'The Intellectuals', *Problems of History and Culture*, in Quinton Hoare and Geoffrey Nowell Smith (eds), *Selections from the Prison Notebooks* (London: Lawrence & Wishart, 1971), pp. 3–23. For a 'Gramscian' mapping of the nineteenth-century British social formation, see Robert Gray, 'Bourgeois Hegemony in Victorian Britain', in Jon Bloomfield (ed.), *Class, Hegemony and Party* (London: Lawrence & Wishart, 1977), pp. 73–93.

25 Matthew Arnold, 'Democracy', in *The Popular Education of France* (1861); *Culture and Anarchy* (1866), in P.J. Keating (ed.), *Matthew Arnold: Selected Prose* (Harmondsworth: Penguin Books, 1970).

26 Raymond Williams, 'The Bloomsbury Fraction', in *Problems in Materialism and Culture* (London: Verso Books, 1980), pp. 148–69.

27 See Tennyson's *In Memoriam* (1850) sections LXXXVI and LXXXVIII.

28 King, op. cit., p. 10.

29 T.S. Eliot, 'Hamlet' (1919), in *Selected Essays* (London: Faber & Faber, 1932).

30 Cyril Connolly, 'Corydon in Croydon', *Sunday Times*, 10 October 1971, reprinted in Phillip Gardner (ed.), *E.M. Forster: The Critical Heritage* (London: Routledge & Kegan Paul, 1973), p. 460.

31 Sigmund Freud, 'The Uncanny' in *Art and Literature*, ed. Albert Dickson (Harmondsworth: Penguin Books, 1985); pp. 335–76.

32 E.M. Forster, *The Life to Come and Other Stories* (1972; London: Penguin Books, 1975).

6 What is not said: a study in textual inversion

An earlier version of this chapter, entitled 'What Is Not Said: Lesbian Texts and Contexts', was presented at the Conference of the Higher Education Teachers of English at the University of Kent in 1987. I am indebted to Kate McLuskie and Maggie Humm for that opportunity, and to Elaine Hobby and Chris White for subsequent discussions. I developed the essay while on research leave from the University of Durham, holding the Donald C. Gallup Fellowship in American Literature at the Beinecke Library, Yale University. I want to thank Wayne Koestenbaum and other participants in the eventful Conference on Lesbian and Gay Studies held at Yale in 1989, who have informed my thinking on this otherwise unthinkable subject. Above all, I am grateful to Sandi Russell for sharing African-American literature with me, and to Joseph Bristow for his patience and encouragement.

1 Havelock Ellis, *Sexual Inversion* (Philadelphia: F.A. Davis, 1901), p. v.
2 Eve Kosofsky Sedgwick, 'Denaturalizing Heterosexuality', Third Annual Conference, Lesbian and Gay Studies Center, Yale University, 1989.
3 Monique Wittig, 'Author's Note', in *The Lesbian Body*, trans. David Le Vay (New York: Avon Books, 1978), p. ix. Originally published in French as *Le Corps lesbien*, 1973.
4 Adrienne Rich, 'Women and Honour: Some Notes on Lying', in *On Lies, Secrets and Silence: Selected Prose, 1966–1978* (London: Virago, 1980), p. 190.
5 Audre Lorde, 'Uses of the Erotic: the Erotic as Power', in *Sister Outsider: Essays and Speeches* (Trumansburg, New York: Crossing Press, 1984), p. 57. Presented to the Fourth Berkshire Conference on the History of Women, 1978.
6 Wittig, op. cit., p. x.
7 Virginia Woolf, *A Room of One's Own* (Harmondsworth: Penguin Books, 1945), ch. 5, p. 84. Based on papers presented at Newnham and Girton Colleges, Cambridge, in 1928.
8 Adrienne Rich, 'It Is the Lesbian in Us . . .', in *On Lies, Secrets and Silence*, p. 201. Presented at the MLA Convention, 1976.
9 Virginia Woolf, 'Reminiscences', in *Moments of Being: Unpublished Autobiographical Writings*, ed. Jeanne Schulkind (St Albans: Triad/Panther Books, 1978), pp. 41–2. Subsequent quotation from the same passage. Schulkind says that 'Reminiscences' was begun in 1907.
10 James Merrill, *The Inner Room: Poems* (New York: Alfred A. Knopf, 1988), p. 92.
11 Alice Walker, title essay, *In Search of Our Mothers' Gardens: Womanist Prose* (London: The Women's Press, 1984), p. 235.
12 Ann Ferguson, 'Is There a Lesbian Culture?', Third Annual Conference, Lesbian and Gay Studies Center, Yale University, 1989.
13 Audre Lorde, *Zami: A New Spelling of My Name* (Trumansburg, New York: The Crossing Press, 1983), p. 179. Lorde identifies 'Zami' as 'a Carriacou name for women who work together as friends and lovers'.
14 ibid., p. 179.
15 ibid., p. 180.
16 Nella Larsen, *Quicksand & Passing*, ed. Deborah McDowell (New Brunswick, NJ: Rutgers University Press, 1986). *Passing* was originally published in 1929.
17 Audre Lorde, 'Scratching the Surface: Some Notes on Barriers to Women and Loving', in *Sister Outsider*, p. 48. Originally published 1978.
18 See Henry Louis Gates, Jr, *The Signifying Monkey: A Theory of African-American Literary Criticism* (New York and Oxford: Oxford University Press, 1988), pp. 51–60.

19 For Jordan's poem, see *Early Ripening: American Women's Poetry Now*, ed. Marge Piercy (New York/London: Pandora, 1987), pp.107–14.
20 *Zami*, p. 224.
21 ibid., p. 226.
22 ibid., p. 249.
23 ibid., p. 252.
24 Adrienne Rich, 'When We Dead Awaken: Writing as Re-vision', in *On Lies, Secrets and Silence*, p. 45. Presented at the MLA Convention in 1971.
25 Audre Lorde, 'The Transformation of Silence into Language and Action', in *Sister Outsider*, p. 41. Presented at the MLA Convention in 1977.
26 ibid., p. 40.
27 'An Interview: Audre Lorde and Adrienne Rich', ibid., p. 98. The interview was held in 1979 and first published in 1981.
28 ibid., p. 99. The publisher was the Black poet Don E. Lee of the Broadside Press.
29 See Gillian Hanscombe and Virginia Smyers, 'Amy Lowell's Garden', in *Writing For Their Lives: The Modernist Women, 1910–1940* (London: The Women's Press, 1987), pp. 63–75; also Lillian Faderman, *Surpassing the Love of Men* (New York: William Morrow, 1981), pp. 392–9.
30 Audre Lorde, *Chosen Poems – Old and New* (New York: W. W. Norton, 1982), p. 77. First published in *New York Headshop and Museum* (Chicago: Broadside Press, 1975).
31 Compare the spatial metaphors and bodily detail of Amy Lowell's 'In Excelsis', in *What's O'Clock* (Boston: Houghton Mifflin, 1925), pp. 54–7:

> I drink your lips,
> I eat the whiteness of your hands and feet.
> My mouth is open,
> As a new jar I am empty and open.
> Like white water are you who fill the cup of my mouth,
> Like a brook of water thronged with lilies. . . .

32 In the *Southern Review*, 18 (1982), pp. 344–7.
33 One of the typescripts of the poem is headed 'I Said/(Winter 1919)'. In a letter to John Cournos, believed to be dated November 1919, H.D. wrote of Bryher's 'suicidal madness' and her own efforts to secure medical help for her friend. She adds: 'The worst thing is that the girl is in love with me, so madly that it is terrible.' Bryn Mawr College Library; see Donna Hollenberg, 'Art and Ardor in World War One: Selected Letters from H.D. to John Cournos', *Iowa Review*, 16:3 (1986), pp. 145–7.
34 *Poetry*, 17:3 (1920), pp. 136–7. The poems – 'Blue Sleep', 'Eos', and 'Wild Rose' – were reprinted in Bryher's volume *Arrow Music* (London: J. & E. Bumpus, 1922). See my 'Images at the Crossroads: the H.D. Scrapbook', in Michael King (ed.), *H.D.: Woman and Poet* (Orono, Maine: National Poetry Foundation, 1986), pp. 366–7.
35 See Barbara Guest, *Herself Defined: The Poet H.D. and Her World* (New York: Doubleday, 1984), pp. 122–3; also Phyllis Grosskurth, *Havelock Ellis: A Biography* (London: Allen Lane, 1980), pp. 296–7.
36 This phrase occurs in an obituary of H.D. for the *Bryn Mawr Alumni Bulletin* (1961) by her friend Marianne Moore; summing up the earlier poetry, Moore writes: 'H.D. contrived in the short line to magnetize the reader by what is not said.' Reviewing H.D.'s *Collected Poems* (1925) for *The Dial*, Moore compared H.D. with Sappho. *The Complete Prose of Marianne Moore*, ed. Patricia Willis (New York: Viking Penguin, 1987), pp. 558, 114.
37 Pierre Macherey, 'The Spoken and the Unspoken', in *A Theory of Literary*

Production, trans. Geoffrey Wall (London: Routledge & Kegan Paul, 1978), pp. 87, 86 respectively.

38 Michael Riffaterre, 'Conclusion', in *Semiotics of Poetry* (Bloomington: Indiana University Press, 1978), p. 164. The definition of 'intertext' is from 'The Semiotic Approach to Literary Interpretation', a paper presented to the Georgetown Conference on Literary Criticism, 1984.

39 Julia Kristeva, 'Place Names', in *Desire in Language*, ed. Leon S. Roudiez (Oxford: Basil Blackwell, 1981), p. 291.

40 Catharine Stimpson, 'Zero Degree Deviancy: the Lesbian Novel in English', *Critical Inquiry*, 8:2 (1981), p. 364. The expression 'intertexts of relation and desire' was used by Rachel Blau Du Plessis in a paper presented at the MLA Convention, 1986.

41 Riffaterre, op. cit., pp. 164–5.

42 The correspondence between Bryher and H.D., Bryher and Ellis, and H.D. and Ellis is in the Beinecke Rare Book and Manuscript Library, Yale University. The unpublished Bryher material concerning her relationship with H.D. was, in 1986, reunited with the unpublished H.D. material in the same archive.

43 H.D., 'I Said', in *Collected Poems: 1912–1944*, ed. Louis L. Martz (New York: New Directions, 1983; Manchester: Carcanet, 1984), pp. 322–5.

44 Manuscript pages preserved by Bryher and bound in H.D., 'Poems II', Beinecke Library, Yale University.

45 Adrienne Rich, Poem IX of 'Twenty-One Love Poems' in *The Dream of a Common Language* (New York: W.W. Norton, 1978), p. 30; see also her 'Vesuvius at Home: the power of Emily Dickinson' (1975), in *On Lies, Secrets and Silence*, pp. 157–83.

46 H.D., 'The Master', in *Collected Poems: 1912–1944*, p. 453. In Bryher's unpublished 'Notes', this fragment seems to describe H.D.: 'A volcano that had fettered its own force.' Beinecke Library, Yale University.

47 Ros Carroll, 'Flower on Flower: H.D. and the Sapphic Tradition', unpublished essay, University of Cambridge, 1989.

48 Bion the Smyrnean, *The Lament for Adonis*, trans. Winifred Bryher (London: A.L. Humphreys, 1918), p. 13. This may have been the book that Bryher sent H.D. before their meeting in July 1918.

49 H.D., *Notes on Thought and Vision & The Wise Sappho* (London: Peter Owen, 1988), p. 57. Originally published by City Lights Books in 1982.

50 L.R. Farnell, *The Cults of the Greek States* (Oxford: Clarendon Press, 1896–1909), vol. 2, p. 126. The passage is marked in H.D.'s copy of this volume, inscribed 'Mullion Cove, 1919'.

51 H.D., 'The Mysteries', in *Collected Poems: 1912–1944*, p. 304.

52 H.D., *Tribute to Freud* (New York: New Directions, 1984), p. 56; during her analysis with Freud, he indicated his statuette of Nike with the words: 'She has lost her spear' (*Tribute to Freud*, p. 69). Bryher describes H.D., when they first met, as 'a spear flower if a spear could bloom', *Two Selves* (Paris: Contact Editions, 1923), pp. 124–5.

53 See my 'H.D.'s "Gift of Greek"/Bryher's "Eros of the Sea" ', in *H.D. Newsletter* 3:1 (1990), pp. 11–14. I quote there the version in which Nancy (Bryher) tells Helga (H.D.) of her intention to drown herself, adding in words close to those of 'I Said': 'I know it is not Greek but then I'm not a Greek.' Bryher's prose ends more positively than H.D.'s poem, climaxing wordlessly on a kiss, to which Nancy responds: 'Because of your lips I will live.' Bryher Papers, Beinecke Library, Yale University.

54 The holograph version of 'I Said' has this variant text: 'being a girl-heart, proud of her vast gest'. H.D., 'Poems II', Beinecke Library.

7 'If I saw you would you kiss me?': sapphism and the subversiveness of Virginia Woolf's Orlando

1 Nigel Nicolson, *Portrait of a Marriage* (New York: Athenaeum, 1973), p. 202.
2 Quentin Bell, *Virginia Woolf: A Biography*, vol. 2, *Mrs Woolf 1912–1941* (London: Hogarth, 1972), p. 116.
3 ibid., p. 119.
4 Nicolson, op. cit., p. 207.
5 Virginia Woolf, *The Letters of Virginia Woolf 1923–1928*, ed. Nigel Nicolson and Joanne Trautmann, vol. 3 (New York: Harcourt, 1978), pp. xix, xxi.
6 Vita Sackville-West, *The Letters of Vita Sackville-West to Virginia Woolf*, ed. Louise DeSalvo and Mitchell A. Leaska (New York: William Morrow, 1984), p. 11.
7 Woolf, *Letters*, vol. 3, pp. xxi, xxii.
8 ibid., pp. 131, 161, 164.
9 ibid., pp. 428–9, 430.
10 ibid., p. 443.
11 Charlotte Wolff, *Love between Women* (New York: Harper, 1971), pp. 17, 86, 119.
12 Joanne Trautmann, *The Jessamy Brides: The Friendship of Virginia Woolf and V. Sackville-West* (University Park: Pennsylvania State University Press, 1973), pp. 32, 33.
13 Jean O. Love, '*Orlando* and its Genesis: Venturing and Experimenting in Art, Love, and Sex', in Ralph Freedman (ed.), *Virginia Woolf: Revaluation and Continuity* (Berkeley: University of California Press, 1980), pp. 192, 218. An important exception to this trend is Blanche Wiesen Cook's spirited essay on the ways lesbian themes and lives are represented and misrepresented in standard literary criticism and biography: see ' "Women alone stir my imagination": Lesbianism and the Cultural Tradition', *Signs*, 4 (1979), pp. 718–39. Her penetrating remarks on Woolf complement and reinforce some of the arguments I develop in this chapter, though they are not part of a sustained thesis about Woolf and they touch on *Orlando* only in passing. Victoria Glendinning, *Vita: The Life of Vita Sackville-West* (New York: Knopf, 1983) is frank about including evidence for the sexual relationship between Virginia and Vita, but she is not interested in the cultural significance of lesbianism in general or in the relationship between Virginia and Vita in particular. Her brief discussion of *Orlando* emphasizes the importance of Orlando's marriage to Shelmerdine as an aspect of Vita that 'was important to the virginal, childless Virginia' (p. 204). Louise DeSalvo acknowledges the nature of the relationship between Virginia and Vita but emphasizes the literary productivity it engendered in both women rather than its explicit significance as a sapphic relationship: see 'Lighting the Cave: The Relationship between Vita Sackville-West and Virginia Woolf', *Signs*, 7 (1982), pp. 195–214.
14 Love, op. cit., p. 192.
15 Ellen Hawkes, 'Woolf's "Magical Garden of Women" ', in Jane Marcus (ed.), *New Feminist Essays on Virginia Woolf* (Lincoln: University of Nebraska Press, 1981), p. 49.
16 J.J. Wilson, 'Why is *Orlando* Difficult?' in Marcus, op. cit., p. 170. Wilson may well have in mind works such as Nancy Bazin, *Virginia Woolf and the Androgynous Vision* (New Brunswick: Rutgers University Press, 1973), and Herbert Marder, *Feminism and Art: A Study of Virginia Woolf* (Chicago: University of Chicago Press, 1968).
17 Mitchell Leaska, *The Novels of Virginia Woolf: From Beginning to End* (New York: Jay, 1977).

18 Howard Harper, *Between Language and Silence* (Baton Rouge: Louisiana State University Press, 1982).
19 Woolf, *The Diary of Virginia Woolf*, vol. 3, ed. Anne Olivier Bell and Andrew McNellie (New York: Harcourt, 1980), pp. 184–5.
20 Woolf, *Diary*, vol. 2, ed. Anne Olivier Bell and Andrew McNellie (New York: Harcourt, 1978), p. 235.
21 Woolf, *Letters*, vol. 3, pp. 155–6; my emphases.
22 Woolf, *Diary*, vol. 3, p. 48.
23 Bell, op. cit., p. 116.
24 Nicolson, op. cit., p. 206.
25 Quoted in Woolf, *Letters*, vol. 3, p. 223.
26 Woolf, *Diary*, vol. 3, p. 51.
27 Woolf, *Letters*, vol. 3, p. 224.
28 Sackville-West, *Letters*, p. 151.
29 ibid., p. 238.
30 Woolf, *Letters*, vol. 3, pp. 306–7.
31 Sackville-West, *Letters*, p. 209.
32 Woolf, *Letters*, vol. 3, pp. 391–2.
33 ibid., p. 395; my interpolation.
34 Woolf, *Diary*, vol. 3, p. 165.
35 Sackville-West, *Letters*, pp. 242–3.
36 Woolf, *Letters*, vol. 3, p. 435.
37 ibid., p. 429. Sibyl Colefax was one of the 'society women' who 'lionized' Woolf (*Letters*, vol. 3, pp. xviii–xix). Ozzie (Oswald) Dickinson was the brother of Violet Dickinson, to whom Virginia had been intimately attached since her childhood: *Letters*, vol. 1, *1915–1919*, ed. Anne Olivier Bell (New York: Harcourt, 1977), p. xviii. Vita used Heinemann as her publisher until she met Virginia and Leonard and began giving her works to their Hogarth Press.
38 *Letters*, vol. 3, p. 553.
39 Sackville-West, *Letters*, p. 238.
40 Martin Stevens, *Vita Sackville-West: A Critical Biography* (New York: Scribner's, 1973), p. 44. Nicolson 'decodes' the story in his foreword to *Challenge* (1924; New York: Avon, 1975).
41 Woolf, *Diary*, vol. 3, p. 162.
42 For Virginia, Vita, and the PEN club, see Sackville-West, *Letters*, pp. 47–9, and Woolf, *Letters*, vol. 3, pp. 24–5, 28. For Virginia and the Femina prize, see ibid., pp. 337–8. For Radclyffe Hall, see Michael Baker, *Our Three Selves: The Life of Radclyffe Hall* (New York: Morrow, 1985), pp. 144, 194.
43 Lady Una Troubridge, *The Life and Death of Radclyffe Hall* (London: Hammond, 1945), pp. 81–2.
44 For a detailed account of the proceedings against Hall, see Vera Brittain, *Radclyffe Hall: A Case of Obscenity?* (London: Femina, 1968).
45 Trautmann, op. cit., p. 17.
46 Brittain, op. cit., p. 57.
47 Woolf, *Letters*, vol. 3, pp. 525–6.
48 Sackville-West, *Letters*, pp. 279–80.
49 Woolf, *Letters*, vol. 3, p. 555.
50 Leonard Woolf, *Downhill All the Way: An Autobiography of the Years 1919–1939* (London: Hogarth, 1967), p. 143.
51 Bell, op. cit., p. 139.
52 Jeanette Foster, *Sex Variant Women in Literature* (1956; Baltimore: Diana, 1975), p. 287.
53 Dolores Klaich, *Woman + Woman: Attitudes Toward Lesbianism* (New York: Morrow, 1974), p. 189.

54 Lillian Faderman, *Surpassing the Love of Men: Romantic Friendship and Love between Women from the Renaissance to the Present* (New York: Morrow, 1981), p. 392.
55 Esther Newton offers a sympathetic and insightful discussion of Radclyffe Hall and the 'sexologists': see 'The Mythic Mannish Lesbian: Radclyffe Hall and the New Woman', *Signs*, 9 (1984), pp. 557–75. Barbara Fassler gives a detailed and compelling exploration of the influence of these 'sexologists' on the 'androgyny' of Bloomsbury: see 'Theories of Homosexuality as Sources of Bloomsbury's Androgyny', *Signs*, 5 (1979), pp. 237–51.
56 Radclyffe Hall, *The Well of Loneliness* (New York: Covici-Friede, 1928), p. 232.
57 Nicolson, op. cit., p. 106.
58 ibid., p. 5.
59 ibid., p. 12.
60 ibid., pp. 23–4, 29.
61 ibid., pp. 105–6.
62 A similar distinction lies behind Virginia's remark about Duncan Grant's androgynous nature in *Letters*, vol. 3, p. 381. Compare also the practices of critics who write about androgyny. Herbert Marder calls *Orlando* 'a kind of hymn to androgyny', and notices that it is the 'only book by Virginia Woolf that evokes the sensations of physical love', but his discussion has nothing to say about Orlando's erotic relationships: see *Feminism and Art*, op. cit., pp. 110, 111. Carolyn Heilbrun elaborates the benefits heterosexual relationships stand to gain from less rigid gender expectations, but she carefully distances homosexuality, when she mentions it, from the main issue she discusses: *Towards Androgyny: Aspects of Male and Female in Literature* (London: Gollancz, 1973). Barbara Fassler puts the emphasis back where it belongs (op. cit., p. 237).
63 Nicolson, op. cit., pp. 34–5.
64 ibid., p. 106.
65 Woolf, *Orlando: A Biography* (1928; New York: Harcourt, 1956), p. 138.
66 Woolf, *Letters*, vol. 3, pp. 134–5.
67 Woolf, *Orlando*, p. 139.
68 For lengthier discussions of the medical issues in their historical context, see Faderman, op. cit., pp. 314–33; Fassler, op. cit., and Newton, op. cit.
69 Nicolson, op. cit., pp. 30, 33.
70 Woolf, *Orlando*, p. 242.
71 ibid.
72 ibid., p. 250.
73 Nicolson, op. cit., pp. 31–2.
74 Woolf, *Orlando*, p. 252.
75 ibid., p. 258; my emphasis.
76 ibid., p. 161.
77 ibid., pp. 216–22.
78 ibid., p. 264.
79 ibid., pp. 265–6.
80 Woolf, *Letters*, vol. 3, p. 381.
81 Woolf, *Diary*, vol. 3, p. 164.
82 ibid., p. 161.
83 ibid., p. 168.
84 ibid., p. 34.
85 Woolf, *Letters*, vol. 3, p. 429.
86 Woolf, *Diary*, vol. 3, p. 118.
87 Woolf, *Letters*, vol. 3, p. 429.
88 My colleague John Limon made this point in stimulating conversations with me over this chapter.

89 Woolf, *Letters*, vol. 3, p. 548n.
90 Sackville-West, *Letters*, p. 298.
91 ibid., p. 288.
92 ibid., p. 289.

8 Sylvia Townsend Warner and the counterplot of lesbian fiction

1 To judge by how frequently it is repeated, the story of Queen Victoria's pronouncement has taken on, alas, the status of cultural myth – the 'truth' of which is that lesbians don't really exist. Whenever it is retold – even seemingly jokingly, by anti-homophobic historians and critics – it almost always prefigures the erasure of lesbianism from the discourse that is to follow, usually through some equation of homosexuality with male homosexuality only. For an example of this phenomenon see Richard Ellmann's *Oscar Wilde* (New York: Vintage Books, 1988), p. 409n., in which lesbianism – and Queen Victoria's views thereupon – are mentioned in a footnote, then never referred to again.

2 Theoretical writing on lesbian fiction remains sparse. Since Jane Rule's somewhat impressionistic *Lesbian Images* (New York: Doubleday, 1975), most of the criticism written on the subject has tended to be either biographically oriented or focused on lesbian readers, as in Judith Fetterley's 'Writes of Passing', *Gay Studies Newsletter*, 14 (March 1987). Several important exceptions must be noted, however: Monique Wittig's 'The Straight Mind', *Feminist Issues*, 1 (1980), pp. 103–11; Catherine Stimpson's 'Zero Degree Deviancy: the Lesbian Novel in English', *Critical Inquiry*, 8 (1980), pp. 363–80; Marilyn R. Farwell's 'Toward a Definition of the Lesbian Literary Imagination', *Signs*, 14 (1988), pp. 100–18; Sherron E. Knopp's '"If I Saw You Would You Kiss Me?": Sapphism and the Subversiveness of Virginia Woolf's *Orlando*', *PMLA* (1988), reprinted as chapter 7 in this volume; and most recently, Bonnie Zimmerman's *The Safe Sea of Women: Lesbian Fiction 1969–1988* (Boston: Beacon Press, 1990; London: Onlywomen Press, 1991). The most useful bibliographic study of lesbian fiction is still Jeannette Foster's classic *Sex Variant Women in Literature* (1955; New York: Diana Press, 1975).

3 Eve Kosofsky Sedgwick, *Between Men: English Literature and Male Homosocial Desire* (New York: Columbia University Press, 1985). Page numbers of citations are noted in parentheses. Since the publication of *Between Men*, it is true, Sedgwick has begun to explore the subject of lesbianism (and of lesbian authorship) more fruitfully, notably in relation to what she calls 'the epistemology of the closet' – the peculiar way in which the reality of homosexuality is at once affirmed and denied, elaborated and masked, in modern cultural discourse. Two of her recent essays are especially relevant here: 'Privilege of Unknowing' (on Diderot's *La Religieuse*), *Genders*, 1 (1988), pp. 102–24; and 'Across Gender, Across Sexuality: Willa Cather and Others', *The South Atlantic Quarterly*, 88 (1989), pp. 53–72. Even in these seemingly more encompassing pieces, however, Sedgwick's unwillingness to separate herself from the spectacle of male bonding is still in evidence. In the Diderot essay Sedgwick chooses a work which can be labelled 'lesbian' only problematically, if at all: as Sedgwick herself says at one point, 'because of the mid-eighteenth-century origin of the novella and because of its convential venue, the question of lesbian sexual desire – *is* what is happening sexual desire, and will it be recognized and named as such? – looks, there, less like the question of The Lesbian than the question of sexuality *tout court*'. This may be true, but Sedgwick's immediate

and seemingly reflexive transformation of the 'lesbian sexual desire' she admits to seeing in *La Religieuse* into a figure for 'sexuality *tout court*' – the site at which the 'privilege of unknowing' is manifest – might also be taken as a symptom of a certain 'unknowingness' regarding lesbianism itself: whatever *it* (lesbianism) is, Sedgwick implies, it is not worth bothering about in and of itself; it is simply a metaphor for other things that can't be talked about, such as (no surprise here) *male* homosexuality. Having disposed, at least theoretically, of any lesbian element in *La Religieuse*, Sedgwick then proceeds to slot the novel comfortably back into the framework of male homosocial desire. Citing approvingly Jay Caplan's observation that 'this novel has the form of a message addressed by one father to another about their symbolic (and hence, absent) daughter', Sedgwick concludes that *La Religieuse* displays the 'distinctively patriarchal triangular structure' of male homosocial bonding (p. 119) – thus foreclosing any more complex reading of its erotic relations. Tellingly, Sedgwick wonders at one point whether her own resistance to lesbian desire may perhaps have limited her understanding of the novel, but decides that this can't be so: 'it would not be enough,' she reassures her reader, 'to say that it is my fear of my own sexual desire for Suzanne [Diderot's heroine] that makes me propulsively individuate her as an "other" in my reading of this book' (p. 120). In the Cather piece, Sedgwick's resistance to lesbianism manifests itself less openly but is still palpable: she is interested in Cather, whom she refers to as 'the mannish lesbian author', primarily to the extent that Cather exemplifies a 'move toward a minority gay identity whose more effectual cleavage, whose more determining separatism, would be that of homo/ hetero*sexual* choice rather than that of male/female *gender*' (pp. 65–6). In choosing in the story 'Paul's Case' to depict a young homosexual man sympathetically, argues Sedgwick, Cather at once performed an act of symbolic contrition for writing a hostile editorial in her youth about Oscar Wilde ('cleansing,' in Sedgwick's lurid phrasing, 'her own sexual body of the carrion stench of Wilde's victimization') and provided a wholesome model of 'cross-gender liminality'. That Sedgwick prefers such 'liminality' to what she disdainfully labels 'gender separatism' (of which lesbian separatism is a sub-category) is obvious: Cather is praised, because like 'James, Proust, Yourcenar, Compton-Burnett, Renault' and others she is part of the 'rich tradition of cross gender inventions of homosexuality of the past century' (p. 66). Sedgwick concludes with a swooning paean to Cather's *The Professor's House*, that 'gorgeous homosocial romance of two men on a mesa in New Mexico' (p. 68). Lesbian authors, it seems, are valuable here exactly to the extent that they are able to imagine and represent – what else? – male homosocial bonding. Thus the elevation of Cather, Yourcenar, Compton-Burnett and Renault (significant choices all) to an all-new lesbian pantheon: of lesbians who enjoy writing about male–male eros, triangulated or otherwise, more than its female equivalent. What is missing here is any room for the lesbian writer who *doesn't* choose to celebrate men's 'gorgeous homosocial romances' – for whom indeed such romances are anathema, precisely because they get in the way, so damagingly, of women's homosocial romances.

4 Witness one of the findings of a survey conducted by lesbian sex therapist Joanne Loulan among 1,566 lesbians between 1985 and 1987. While 80 per cent of all lesbians surveyed reported that they liked to hold hands with their partners, only 27 per cent said they felt able to hold hands in public. This 'poignant' finding, writes Loulan, is 'a statement about the oppression of lesbians in our culture. Heterosexuals assume they have the

right to hold hands with their partner in public; most lesbians do not.' See Loulan, *Lesbian Passion: Loving Ourselves and Each Other* (San Francisco: Spinsters/Aunt Lute, 1987), p. 205.

5 The 'interlocking male homosocial triangles' at the end of *Shirley* can be visualized as follows:

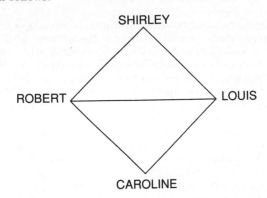

Here the line linking Robert and Louis separates Caroline and Shirley. One can imagine, of course, some hypothetical renewal of erotic bonding between the two women that would recross, so to speak, the line of male bonding; but one would be on the way then to writing a lesbian 'post-marital' sequel to Brontë's novel.

6 Townsend Warner's brilliant and varied writings, many of which touch on the theme of homosexuality, have been sorely neglected since her death in 1978 – not least by gay and lesbian readers and critics. Her most enthusiastic admirer, somewhat unexpectedly, remains George Steiner, who in the pages of the *TLS* (2–8 December 1988) pronounced *The Corner That Held Them* a 'masterpiece' of modern English fiction. Claire Harman's biography, *Sylvia Townsend Warner* (London: Chatto & Windus, 1989), will no doubt help to rectify this curious situation, as should Wendy Mulford's *This Narrow Place – Sylvia Townsend Warner and Valentine Ackland: Life, Letters and Politics, 1930–1951* (London: Pandora, 1988), a superb study of the relationship between Townsend Warner and the poet Valentine Ackland, her lover of thirty years. Also of great interest is Townsend Warner's correspondence, edited by William Maxwell (London: Chatto & Windus, 1982). Besides displaying Townsend Warner's matchless wit and unfailingly elegant style, the letters also demonstrate that she was capable of imagining Queen Victoria's sex life, even if Queen Victoria could not have imagined hers (see letter to Llewelyn Powys, 7 December 1933).

7 Townsend Warner, *Summer Will Show* (1936; London: Virago, 1987). All page numbers noted parenthetically refer to this edition.

8 George Eliot, *The Mill on the Floss*, book. 5, ch. 4.

9 Townsend Warner, *Letters*, p. 40. Townsend Warner seems to have had Berlioz in mind – and his despairing comment on the hardships suffered by artists and musicians during the 1848 revolution – when she created the character of Guitermann, the impoverished Jewish musician befriended by Sophia late in the novel. See *The Memoirs of Hector Berlioz*, ed. and trans. David Cairns (London: Victor Gollancz, 1969), pp. 44–5.

10 Frederick Willoughby is condemned by his name on two counts of course: if his first name recalls the stooge of Flaubert's *L'Education sentimentale*, his last he shares with the unprincipled villain of Austen's *Sense and Sensibility*. In

Austen's novel, we recall, the more hapless of the two heroines is abandoned by (John) Willoughby in favour of a rich heiress. To the extent that (Frederick) Willoughby – now married to his rich heiress – is himself abandoned by wife and mistress both, one might consider Townsend Warner's novel a displaced sequel to Austen's: a kind of comic postlude, or 'revenge of Marianne Dashwood'.

11 A very similar plot twist occurs, interestingly, in a novel that Townsend Warner certainly knew – and paid homage to in *Summer Will Show* – Colette's *L'Autre*, first published in 1929 and translated into English (as *The Other One*) in 1931. In Colette's novel as in Townsend Warner's, a wife and mistress discover to their mutual delight that they vastly prefer each other's company to that of the man they are supposedly competing for. Colette, it is true, does not eroticize the relationship between her two women characters as explicitly as Townsend Warner does, but her depiction of their alliance (scandalous to the husband) is exhilarating none the less. The Colettian 'wife–husband–other woman' configuration turns up again in Townsend Warner's writing, in the slyly comic short story 'An Act of Reparation' in *Stranger with a Bag* (London: Chatto & Windus 1961). Here a divorced woman named Lois accidentally meets the young, somewhat befuddled new wife of her former husband while out shopping. After the young woman confesses her anxiety about cooking, Lois goes home with her and shows her how to make oxtail stew. The husband, returning home, smugly concludes that Lois is trying to win him back by showing off her superior culinary skills; but Lois herself knows she is merely performing an 'act of reparation' to the young wife, whom she now pities, with unexpected tenderness, for being stuck with the boorish ex-husband.

12 That overtly lesbian and gay male characters often end up inhabiting the same fictional space makes a kind of theoretical as well as mimetic sense: if the imperative toward heterosexual bonding in a fictional work is weak enough to allow one kind of homosexual bonding, chances are it will also allow the other. Two lesbian novels lending support to this idea are May Sarton's *Mrs. Stevens Hears the Mermaids Singing* and Jane Rule's *Memory Board*, both of which include important male homosexual characters.

13 I borrow the euphoric/dysphoric distinction from Nancy K. Miller, who in *The Heroine's Text* (New York: Columbia University Press, 1980) uses the terms to refer to the two kinds of narrative 'destiny' stereotypically available to the heroines of eighteenth- and nineteenth-century fiction. A euphoric plot, Miller argues, ends with the heroine's marriage; a dysphoric plot with her death or alienation from society. That the terms undergo a dramatic reversal in meaning when applied to lesbian fiction should be obvious: from a lesbian viewpoint, marriage can only be dysphoric in its implications; even death or alienation – if only in a metaphoric sense – may seem preferable.

14 The reader may object, rightly, that the most famous lesbian novel of all, Radclyffe Hall's *The Well of Loneliness*, does not seem to fall clearly into either the euphoric or the dysphoric category. It may well be that we need to devise a new category – that of 'lesbian epic' – to contain Hall's manic-depressive extravaganza. True, in that it manages to work unhappy variations on both the pre-marital and the post-marital plot types (Stephen's first love, Angela, is a married woman who refuses to leave her husband; her second, Mary, leaves her in order to marry a male friend), *The Well of Loneliness* often leans in a dysphoric direction. Yet the introduction midway through the novel of the Natalie Barney character, Valérie Seymour, and Hall's tentative limnings of a larger lesbian society in Paris, also seem to promise an end to Stephen's

intolerable 'loneliness' – if only in some as yet ill-defined, unknown future. With its multiplying characters and sub-plots, constant shifts in setting and mood and powerfully 'ongoing' narrative structure, *The Well* seems more a kind of Homeric or Tennysonian quest-fiction – a lesbian *Odyssey* – than a novel in the ordinary sense.

15 Mulford, *This Narrow Place*, op. cit. pp. 121–2.
16 That lesbian novelists have been drawn to science fiction should come as no surprise; to the degree that science fiction itself is a form of utopian fantasy, one that posits a fictional world radically different from our own, it lends itself admirably to the representation of alternative sexual structures.

9 The African and the pagan in gay Black literature

1 W.J. Weatherby, *James Baldwin: Artist on Fire* (New York: Dell, 1989), p. 334.
2 Eldridge Cleaver, *Soul on Ice* (New York: McGraw-Hill, 1968), p. 97.
3 ibid.
4 ibid., p. 102.
5 ibid., p. 105.
6 ibid., p. 107.
7 ibid., p. 206.
8 ibid., p. 207.
9 ibid., pp. 107–8.
10 ibid., p. 106.
11 Robert A. Bone, 'The Novels of James Baldwin', in Seymour L. Gross and Joan E. Hardy (eds), *Images of the Negro in American Literature* (Chicago: University of Chicago Press, 1966), p. 283.
12 Cleaver, op. cit., p. 110.
13 James Baldwin, *Just Above My Head* (New York: Dell, 1979), pp. 36–7.
14 Samuel R. Delany and Joseph Beam, 'Samuel R. Delany: The Possibility of Possibilities', in Joseph Beam (ed.), *In the Life: A Black Gay Anthology* (Boston: Alyson Publications, 1986), p. 196.
15 Richard Goldstein, '"Go the Way Your Blood Beats": An Interview with James Baldwin', in Quincy Troupe (ed.), *James Baldwin: The Legacy* (New York: Simon & Schuster, 1989), p. 174.
16 ibid., p. 176.
17 Leslie A. Fiedler, 'A Homosexual Dilemma', in Fred L. Standley and Nancy V. Burt (eds), *Critical Essays on James Baldwin* (Boston: G.K. Hall, 1988), pp. 147–8.
18 Claude J. Summers, *Gay Fictions: Wilde to Stonewall: Studies in a Male Homosexual Literary Tradition* (New York: Continuum, 1990), p. 174.
19 Goldstein, op. cit., p. 180.
20 Weatherby, op. cit., p. 135.
21 Goldstein, op. cit., p. 177.
22 ibid., p. 179.
23 Bernard Branner, 'Blackberri: Singing for Our Lives', in *In the Life*, op. cit., p. 172.
24 Joseph Beam, 'Brother to Brother: Words from the Heart', ibid., p. 231; emphasis in original.
25 Cleaver, op. cit., p. 106.
26 ibid.
27 Max C. Smith, 'By the Year 2000', in *In the Life*, op. cit., p. 266.
28 ibid., p. 227.
29 A. Billy S. Jones, 'A Father's Need, A Parent's Desire', in *In the Life*, op. cit., p. 144.

30 ibid., p. 150.
31 Goldstein, op. cit., p. 178.
32 Baldwin, *The Price of the Ticket* (New York: St Martin's, 1985), p. 102.
33 Goldstein, op. cit., p. 183.
34 Baldwin, *The Evidence of Things Not Seen* (New York: Henry Holt, 1985), p. 72.
35 ibid., p. 109.
36 ibid., p. 75; emphasis in original.
37 Baldwin, *The Price of the Ticket*, p. 110.
38 'The Male Prison', ibid., p. 101.
39 ibid., p. 103.
40 ibid., p. 104.
41 ibid., p. 105.
42 ibid.
43 ibid.
44 Baldwin, *Another Country* (New York: Dell, 1962), p. 255.
45 Goldstein, op. cit., p. 182.
46 Baldwin, *Going to Meet the Man* (New York: Dell, 1965), p. 35.
47 ibid., p. 36.
48 ibid., pp. 25–6.
49 Goldstein, op. cit., pp. 174–7.
50 Baldwin, *Going to Meet the Man*, p. 38.
51 Baldwin. *Just Above My Head*, p. 47.
52 James S. Tinney, 'Struggles of a Black Pentecostal' in Michael J. Smith (ed.), *Black Men/White Men: A Gay Anthology* (San Francisco: Gay Sunshine Press, 1983), p. 169.
53 ibid., p. 170.
54 ibid., p. 169.
55 ibid., p. 120.
56 Leonard Patterson, 'At Ebenezer Baptist Church', in *Black Men/White Men*, op. cit., p. 164.
57 ibid., p. 165.
58 Amitai Avi-Ram, 'The Unreadable Black Body: "Conventional" Poetic Form in the Harlem Renaissance', *Genders*, 7 (1990), p. 37.
59 Tinney, op. cit., p. 169.
60 Tinney, 'Why a Black Gay Church', in *In the Life*, op. cit., p. 81.
61 Max C. Smith, 'By the Year 2000', ibid., p. 227.
62 Cleaver, op. cit., p. 105.
63 ibid., p. 103.
64 ibid., p. 109.
65 ibid., p. 99.
66 Gill Shepherd, 'Rank, Gender, and Homosexuality: Mombasa as a Key to Understanding Sexual Options', in Pat Caplan (ed.), *The Cultural Construction of Sexuality* (London: Tavistock, 1987), p. 241.
67 ibid., p. 250.
68 Quoted in *Outweek*, 11 July 1990, p. 62.
69 Henry Louis Gates, Jr, *The Signifying Monkey: A Theory of Afro-American Literary Criticism* (New York: Oxford University Press, 1988), p. 29.
70 Arnold Rampersad, *The Life of Langston Hughes: Vol 1: 1902–1941, I, Too, Sing America* (New York: Oxford University Press, 1986), pp. 66–93.
71 Rebecca T. Cureau, 'Toward an Aesthetic of Black Folk Expression', in Russell J. Linnemann (ed.), *Alain Locke: Reflections on a Modern Renaissance Man* (Baton Rouge: Louisiana State University Press, 1982), p. 77.
72 James B. Barnes, 'Alain Locke and the Sense of the African Legacy', ibid., p. 104.

73 David M. Halperin, *One Hundred Years of Homosexuality and Other Essays on Greek Love* (New York and London: Routledge, 1990), p. 1.
74 See my *Gaiety Transfigured: Gay Self-Representation in American Literature* (Madison: University of Wisconsin Press, 1991).
75 Halperin, op. cit., p. 2.
76 Rampersad, op. cit., p. 68.
77 ibid.
78 ibid.
79 Locke, *The New Negro: An Interpretation* (New York: Albert and Charles Boni, 1925; repr. New York: Arno, 1968), p. 256.
80 ibid., p. 267.
81 ibid., p. 254.
82 ibid., pp. 258–9.
83 ibid., p. 199.
84 ibid., p. 205.
85 ibid., pp. 243–5.
86 ibid., p. 250.
87 ibid.
88 ibid., pp. 251–2.
89 ibid., p. 252.
90 ibid., p. 253.
91 Langston Hughes, *The Big Sea: An Autobiography* (New York: Thunder's Mouth Press, 1986), p. 10.
92 ibid., p. 11.
93 ibid.
94 Rampersad, op. cit., p. 77.
95 ibid., p. 80.
96 Hughes, op. cit., p. 273.
97 ibid., p. 8.
98 ibid., p. 7.
99 Susan Vogel (ed.), *Perspectives: Angles on African Art* (New York: Center for African Art and Harry N. Abrams, 1987), p. 117.
100 ibid., p. 118.
101 ibid., p. 119.
102 ibid., p. 122.
103 ibid., p. 127.
104 ibid.
105 Baldwin, *The Price of the Ticket*, p. 50.
106 ibid.
107 ibid., p. 51.
108 ibid., p. 52.
109 ibid., p. 56.
110 ibid., p. 58.
111 ibid., p. 56.
112 ibid., p. 48.
113 ibid., p. 54.
114 ibid.

10 Who was afraid of Joe Orton?

1 Oscar Wilde, *The Picture of Dorian Gray* (Harmondsworth: Penguin Books, 1949), p. 10.
2 Joe Orton, *The Orton Diaries*, ed. John Lahr (London: Methuen, 1986), p. 219.

3 In 1962 Orton and Halliwell were sent to prison for stealing and damaging library books: they made cover pictures bizarre and typed in false blurbs. See John Lahr, *Prick Up Your Ears* (Harmondsworth: Penguin Books, 1980), pp. 93–105; Simon Shepherd, *Because We're Queers* (London: GMP, 1989), pp. 13–14.

4 See Alan Sinfield, 'Theatre and Politics', in Malcolm Kelsall, Martin Coyle, Peter Garside, and John Peck (eds), *Encyclopedia of Literature and Criticism* (London: Routledge, 1990), pp. 475–87; Alan Sinfield, 'Closet Dramas: Homosexual Representation in Postwar British Theatre', *Genders*, 9 (1990), pp. 112–31.

5 On the cross-class liaison, see Jeffrey Weeks, 'Discourse, Desire and Sexual Deviance: Some Problems in a History of Homosexuality', in Kenneth Plummer (ed.), *The Making of the Modern Homosexual* (London: Hutchinson, 1981), pp. 76–111, p. 105; Jeffrey Weeks, *Sex, Politics and Society* (London and New York: Longman, 1981), pp. 108–17; Alan Sinfield, *Literature, Politics and Culture in Postwar Britain* (Oxford: Basil Blackwell, 1989; Berkeley: California University Press, 1989), ch. 5; Sinfield, 'Closet Dramas'; Sinfield, 'Private Lives/Public Theatre: Noël Coward and the Politics of Homosexual Representation', *Representations*, 36 (Fall 1991), pp. 43–63.

6 J. R. Ackerley, *My Father and Myself* (London: Bodley Head, 1968), p. 120; Peter Wildeblood, *Against the Law* (London: Weidenfeld, 1955), p. 55. On the marginal, scarcely audible status of homosexuality, see Eve Kosofsky Sedgwick, 'Epistemology of the Closet (I)', *Raritan*, 7 (1988), pp. 39–69; Jonathan Dollimore, 'Homophobia and Sexual Difference', in *Sexual Difference*, ed. Robert Young (special issue of *Oxford Literary Review*, 8, nos 1–2; 1986), pp. 5–12; Jonathan Dollimore, 'The Dominant and the Deviant: a Violent Dialectic', *Critical Quarterly*, 28, nos 1–2 (1986), pp. 179–92.

7 Sigmund Freud, *The Interpretation of Dreams*, trans. James Strachey (New York: Avon Books, 1970), p. 545.

8 Martin Esslin, *The Peopled Wound* (London: Methuen, 1970), p. 129. John Marshall shows the persistence into the 1960s of the distinction between inverts (effeminate, anomalies in nature) and perverts (willfully debauched); see Marshall, 'Pansies, Perverts and Macho Men: Changing Conceptions of Male Homosexuality', in Plummer, op. cit., pp. 145–50.

9 James Broom Lynne, *The Trigon*, in John Russell Taylor (ed.), *New English Dramatists 8* (Harmondsworth: Penguin Books, 1965), p. 106. *The Creeper*, by Pauline McCauley (1964), was another 'Pinteresque'/homosexual play: as in *The Servant*, for which Pinter wrote the screenplay, a leisure-class man employs a mysteriously menacing, lower-class companion (*The Creeper* also resembles *The Green Bay Tree* by Mordaunt Shairp, on which see Sinfield, 'Private Lives/Public Theatres').

10 Lahr, *Prick Up Your Ears*, p. 178; for Sloane's awareness, see Joe Orton, *The Complete Plays* (London: Eyre Methuen, 1976), pp. 125, 135.

11 John D'Emilio, *Sexual Politics, Sexual Communities* (Chicago and London: University of Chicago Press, 1983), p. 52. On the situation in the US theatre see Kaier Curtin, *We Can Always Call Them Bulgarians* (Boston: Alyson Publications, 1987).

12 H. Montgomery Hyde, *The Other Love* (1970; London: Mayflower, 1972), p. 238; Gordon Westwood, *A Minority* (London: Longman, 1960), p. 93, referring back to Westwood's *Society and the Homosexual* (London: Gollancz, 1952). See D. J. West, *Homosexuality*, revised edn (Harmondsworth: Penguin Books, 1960), pp. 11, 71; Jeffrey Weeks, *Coming Out: Homosexual Politics in Britain, from the Nineteenth Century to the Present* (London: Quartet, 1977), ch. 14. Plays that figured in this process included *The Green Bay Tree* by Mordaunt Shairp

(1933, revived in London in 1950); *Third Person* by Andrew Rosenthal (1951); *The Immoralist* by Ruth and Augustus Goetz (1954); *South* by Julien Green (1954); *Serious Charge* by Philip King (1955); *The Prisoners of War* by J.R. Ackerley (1925, revived in 1955); *The Children's Hour* by Lillian Hellman (1934, produced in London in 1956); *The Lonesome Road* by Philip King and Robin Maugham (1957); *The Balcony* by Jean Genet (1957); *The Catalyst* by Ronald Duncan (1958); *Quaint Honour* by Roger Gellert (1958); *The Hostage* by Brendan Behan (1958); *Five Finger Exercise* by Peter Shaffer (1958). Some of these evaded censorship by being produced at the 'private' Arts theatre club (see Sinfield, 'Closet Dramas').

13 Orton, *Diaries*, p. 127.
14 Peter Burton, *Parallel Lives* (London: GMP, 1985), p. 42 and pp. 38–42; Weeks, *Coming Out*, pp. 41–2.
15 Barry Took, *Laughter in the Air* (London: Robson Books, 1981), pp. 153 and 146–55.
16 Orton, *Diaries*, pp. 78–9. On decoding and Coward, see Sinfield, 'Private Lives'.
17 Lahr, *Prick Up Your Ears*, pp. 250–1; see Orton, *Diaries*, p. 112.
18 Frank Parkin, *Middle Class Radicalism* (Manchester: Manchester University Press, 1968), p. 43. The figures were 94 per cent in social classes 1–2, 87 per cent in classes 3–4 and 75 per cent in classes 5–7. See Alan Sinfield, 'The Theatre and its Audiences', in Sinfield (ed.), *Society and Literature 1945–1970* (London: Methuen, 1983).
19 Lahr, *Prick Up Your Ears*, pp. 206–7; Shepherd, op. cit., pp. 119–20.
20 Richard Ellmann, *Oscar Wilde* (London: Hamish Hamilton, 1987), p. 430.
21 See Shepherd, op. cit., pp. 74–7, and his comments on the cult of The Boy, the fantasy answer to so many tensions of that time (pp. 60–4); this too was affronted by the character of Sloane. The US director had difficulty with Sloane's capricious murder of Kemp (Lahr, *Prick Up Your Ears*, p. 215).
22 Orton, *Complete Plays*, p. 200.
23 Lahr, *Prick Up Your Ears*, pp. 236–8, 255–6. Also it had been revealed shortly before that rhino whips were in use in a Sheffield police station. For another appreciation of the play from this point of view, see Albert Hunt, 'What Joe Orton Saw', *New Society*, 17 April 1975, pp. 148–50.
24 Orton, *Complete Plays*, pp. 245–6; and see pp. 248, 255, 266, 271–5.
25 ibid., p. 273; for the Lord Chamberlain's changes see Simon Trussler (ed.), *New English Dramatists 13* (Harmondsworth: Penguin Books, 1968), p. 84.
26 Trussler, introduction to *Loot*, in *New English Dramatists 13*, p. 11; Trussler, 'Farce', *Plays and Players* (June 1966), p. 72.
27 Orton, *Complete Plays*, p. 262.
28 Lahr, *Prick Up Your Ears*, p. 249; see also p. 227, and Orton, *Diaries*, pp. 75–6, 150.
29 Orton, *Diaries*, p. 91; Shepherd, op. cit., p. 126.
30 Lahr, *Prick Up Your Ears*, p. 175.
31 ibid., pp. 247, 258.
32 This account is indebted to Simon Shepherd's *Because We're Queers*, especially pp. 26–8, 31, 56–8, 89, 97–8, 111. Shepherd calls the standard view of Orton as hampered and ruined by Halliwell 'The Revenge of the Closet Queens' (p. 26). I have benefited also from William A. Cohen, 'Joe Orton and the Politics of Subversion' (unpublished paper, University of California, Berkeley, 1989), and from the comments of Joseph Bristow, Peter Burton, William A. Cohen, Jonathan Dollimore, and Simon Shepherd.
33 Lahr, *Prick Up Your Ears*, p. 204. Rattigan put money into *Sloane* – he thought it was about a society diminished by watching television (Lahr, *Prick Up Your*

Ears, p. 184). Like Rattigan, Orton was not straightforward about himself in interviews (ibid., p. 180; Shepherd, op. cit., p. 86).

34 Orton, *Diaries*, pp. 249–50.

35 ibid., p. 256. *Butler* was produced by Beaumont and Oscar Lewenstein at the Queen's Theatre in 1969.

36 Orton, *Diaries*, p. 256; Lahr, *Prick Up Your Ears*, pp. 330–3.

37 Hunt, op. cit., p. 149.

38 Orton, *Complete Plays*, p. 368.

39 Hunt, op. cit., p. 150.

40 Simon Trussler, 'Farce', *Plays and Players* (June 1966), pp. 58, 72. Orton also said: 'There's supposed to be a healthy shock, for instance, at those moments in *Loot* when an audience suddenly *stops* laughing. So if *Loot* is played as no more than farcical, it won't work' (p. 72). Orton seems to have abandoned this idea in *Butler*.

41 Shepherd, op. cit., p. 96.

42 Orton, *Diaries*, pp. 256–7. Stanley Baxter is quoted there saying that the barracking started ten minutes after the start of the second act. I'm grateful here for a personal communication from Colin Spencer, author of *Spitting Image* (on which see below).

43 Dollimore, 'The Dominant and the Deviant', p. 189; and Dollimore, 'The Challenge of Sexuality', in Sinfield (ed.), *Society and Literature*, p. 78.

44 Jonathan Dollimore, 'Different Desires: Subjectivity and Transgression in Wilde and Gide', *Textual Practice*, 1:1 (1987), p. 59; see also Dollimore's *Sexual Dissidence: Augustine to Wilde, Freud to Foucoult* (Oxford: Oxford University Press, 1991).

45 Dollimore, 'The Dominant and the Deviant', p. 189; Orton, *Complete Plays*, p. 416.

46 Dollimore, 'The Dominant and the Deviant', pp. 180, 182; see also Dollimore, 'Homophobia and Sexual Difference', p.8.

47 Weeks, *Coming Out*, chs 14, 15.

48 See Shepherd, op. cit., p. 111.

49 Sinfield, 'Private Lives'.

50 Lahr, *Prick Up Your Ears*, pp. 248, pp. 187, 189.

51 Orton, *Complete Plays*, p. 244.

52 Michael Billington, *The Times*, 25 October 1968, p.8. *Spitting Image* was favourably reviewed there and by Philip French in the *New Statesman* and Hilary Spurling in the *Spectator*. But Milton Shulman's review in the *Evening Standard* was headed 'Ugh!'

53 Colin Spencer, *Spitting Image*, printed in *Plays and Players*, 16 (November 1968), p. 28.

54 John Russell Taylor, review of *Spitting Image* in *Plays and Players*, 16 (November 1968), p. 64.

55 Colin Spencer, interview with Peter Burton, *Transalantic Review*, 35 (Spring 1970), p. 63. Spencer was moved partly by the attempt to gain access to his son, which was being opposed on the grounds of his homosexuality (personal communication).

56 Nancy K. Miller, 'Emphasis Added: Plots and Plausibilities', in Elaine Showalter (ed.), *The New Feminist Criticism* (London: Virago, 1986), pp. 357, 352. See Sinfield, *Literature, Politics and Culture*, pp. 25, 225–6, 300–4.

11 Constructing a lesbian poetic for survival: Broumas, Rukeyser, H.D., Rich, Lorde

1 Elly Bulkin, *Lesbian Poetry: An Anthology*, ed. Elly Bulkin and Joan Larkin

(Massachusetts: Persephone Press, 1981), p. xxi.

2 Diana Collecott, 'What Is Not Said: a Study in Textual Inversion', *Textual Practice* (1990); reprinted as Chapter 6 in this volume, p. 94.

3 ibid.

4 Adrienne Rich, 'It Is The Lesbian In Us . . .' (1976), in *On Lies, Secrets and Silence: Selected Prose 1966–1978* (London: Virago, 1980); p. 201.

5 Olga Broumas, untitled poem, in *Lesbian Poetry*, pp. 211–12.

6 Collecott, op. cit., p. 101. For further exploration of these issues see chapter 9, 'Mother, Daughter, Sister, Lover: Adrienne Rich's Dream of a Whole New Poetry', in Liz Yorke, *Impertinent Voices: Subversive Strategies in Contemporary Women's Poetry* (London: Routledge, 1991).

7 Rich, 'The Meaning of our Love for Women', op. cit., p. 224.

8 Bulkin, Introduction, 'A Look at Lesbian Poetry', in *Lesbian Poetry*, p. xxv.

9 Muriel Rukeyser, 'Looking at Each Other', in *The Collected Poems of Muriel Rukeyser* (New York: McGraw-Hill, 1982), p. 493.

10 I am grateful to Joseph Bristow for drawing attention to this figure.

11 Rukeyser, 'Despisals', op. cit., p. 491.

12 Bulkin, *Lesbian Poetry*, p. xxiv. Bulkin gives 1971, but 1968 is correct.

13 Rukeyser, 'What Do I Give You', op. cit., p. 435.

14 Collecott, op. cit., p. 104.

15 Mythopoetic = mythmaking. Mythopoet = a myth-maker. I use the term 'myth' to denote those messages emerging from patriarchal discourses, whether religious, historical, classical, or cultural, which have functioned to organize our perceptions of reality. An exploration of the re-visionary processes of transforming such 'myth' within poetic discourses is offered in my *Impertinent Voices*. See especially pp. 13–17. See also Rachel Blau DuPlessis, ' "Perceiving the Other-side of Everything": Tactics of Revisionary Mythopoesis', in *Writing Beyond the Ending: Narrative Strategies of Twentieth-Century Women Writers* (Bloomington: Indiana University Press, 1985).

16 Rukeyser, 'The Poem as Mask, *Orpheus*', op. cit., p. 435.

17 Jacob Korg, *Language in Modern Literature: Innovation and Experiment* (Brighton: Harvester Press, 1979), p. 90.

18 Susan Gubar, 'Sapphistries', *Signs: Journal of Women in Culture and Society*, 10:1 (1984), p. 47.

19 DuPlessis, *H.D. The Career of That Struggle*, (Brighton: Harvester Press, 1986), p. 23. DuPlessis's reference is to Norman Holmes Pearson, 'An Interview on H.D., with L.S. Dembo', *Contemporary Literature: Special Issue on H.D.*, 10:4 (1969), pp. 435–46.

20 ibid., pp. 3–4.

21 ibid., p. 14.

22 'Hymen (1921)', in *H.D.: Collected Poems, 1912–1944* (Manchester: Carcanet Press, 1984), p. 108.

23 ibid., pp. 109–10.

24 ibid., p. 110.

25 Judith Butler suggests that since ' "identity" is assured through the stabilising concepts of sex, gender, and sexuality, the very notion of "the person" is called into question by the cultural emergence of those "incoherent" or "discontinuous" gendered beings who appear to be persons but who fail to conform to the gendered norms of cultural intelligibility by which persons are defined. "Intelligible" genders are those which in some sense institute and maintain relations of coherence and continuity among sex, gender, sexual practice, and desire': *Gender Trouble: Feminism and the Subversion of Identity* (New York: Routledge, 1990), p. 17. Here the attempt is to claim for

lesbian identity a conceivable 'intelligibility' within discourse that affirms and celebrates the kaleidoscopic complexity of this matrix of desire.

26 Rich, 'Splittings', in *The Dream of a Common Language: Poems 1974–1977* (New York: W.W. Norton, 1978), p. 10.

27 Jane Gallop, *Feminism and Psychoanalysis: The Daughter's Seduction* (London: Macmillan, 1982), p. 30. Gallop draws on Lacan's use of the term 'contiguity' to explore the patterns of feminine sexuality. She quotes: 'feminine sexuality appears as the effort of a *jouissance* enveloped in its own *contiguité* [*Ecrits*]. Such *jouissance*, she adds, 'would be sparks of pleasure ignited by *contact* at any point, at any moment along the line, not waiting for closure, but enjoying the touching.' Following the logic of Kristeva, I link this *jouissance* to the eroticism which "is indissociable from the experience" of the m/other's body.' See 'Julia Kristeva Talks to Susan Sellers: "A Question of Subjectivity"', *Women's Review*, 12 (October 1986), p. 20.

28 See chapter 9, in *Impertinent Voices*, p. 126–9. How close Rich is to Irigaray may be seen in this passage which immediately precedes my quotation: 'Yet how do we stay alive when far from each other? That's the danger. How can I await your return if we don't remain close when you are far away? If something palpable, here and now, doesn't evoke the touch of our bodies? How can we continue to live as ourselves if we are open to the infinity of our separation, closed upon the intangible sensation of absence?': Luce Irigaray, 'When Our Lips Speak Together', trans. Carolyn Burke, *Signs: Journal of Women in Culture and Society*, 6:1 (1980), p. 77.

29 Gail Lewis, 'Audre Lorde: Vignettes and Mental Conversations', *Feminist Review*, 34 (1990), p. 100.

30 Audre Lorde, *A Burst of Light: Essays by Audre Lorde* (London: Sheba, 1988), p. 133.

31 ibid., p. 116.

32 ibid., pp. 122–3.

33 I should point to the contradiction that as well as being imposed by colonizing missionaries, the Christian faith was also more or less willingly adopted by Blacks in America. Many Black leaders have been willing to recognize the subversive potential inherent in the figure of Christ in his identification with suffering and oppression.

34 Lorde, 'Dahomey', in *The Black Unicorn: Poems* (New York: W.W. Norton, 1978), p. 10. See her glossary of African names used in the poems, p. 119.

35 Rich, 'The Phenomenology of Anger', in *Poems: Selected and New, 1950–1974* (New York: W.W. Norton, 1975), p. 201.

36 Lorde, *The Black Unicorn*, p. 121.

37 Mary K. DeShazer, *Inspiring Women: Reimagining the Muse* (New York: Pergamon Press, 1986), pp. 183–5.

38 Lorde, *The Black Unicorn*, p. 120.

39 Lorde, 'The Master's Tools Will Never Dismantle the Master's House', in *Sister Outsider: Essays and Speeches by Audre Lorde* (New York: Crossing Press, 1984), p. 111.

40 Lorde, *The Black Unicorn*, p. 119.

41 Lorde, 'Man Child: A Black Lesbian Feminist Response', in *Sister Outsider*, pp. 75–6.

42 Lorde, *The Black Unicorn*, pp. 119–20.

43 ibid., p. 121.

44 Lorde, *A Burst of Light*, p. 111.

45 Lorde, 'Poetry is Not a Luxury', in *Sister Outsider*, p. 38.

46 Lorde, *Zami: A New Spelling of My Name* (London: Sheba, 1982), pp. 11, 15, and 9.

47 Joanne M. Braxton and Andrée Nicola McLaughlin (eds), *Wild Women in the Whirlwind: Afra-American Culture and the Contemporary Literary Renaissance* (London: Serpent's Tail, 1990), p. xxv.
48 Chinosole, 'Audre Lorde and Matrilineal Diaspora: "Moving history beyond nightmare into structures for the future" ', ibid., p. 379.
49 Lorde, 'Age, Race, Class, and Sex: Women Redefining Difference', in Christian McEwen and Sue O'Sullivan (eds), *Out the Other Side: Contemporary Lesbian Writing* (London: Virago, 1988), p. 270.
50 Lorde, 'Call', in *Our Dead Behind Us: Poems by Audre Lorde* (London: Sheba, 1986), p. 75.
51 Lorde, 'Storybooks on a Kitchen Table', in *Chosen Poems – Old and New* (London: W.W. Norton, 1982), p. 35.
52 Lorde, *Zami*, p. 17.
53 ibid., p. 15.
54 ibid., p. 224. For a discussion of butch and femme roles, see Susan Ardrill and Sue O'Sullivan, 'Butch Femme Obsessions', and Inge Blackman and Kathryn Perry, who also discuss butch/femme style in dress, in 'Skirting the Issue: Lesbian Fashion for the 90s', both in *Feminist Review*, 34 (1990), pp. 79–85 and 67–78.
55 Lorde, *Zami*, pp. 224–5.
56 Lorde, 'A Litany for Survival', in *The Black Unicorn*, p. 31.
57 Lorde, 'Poetry is Not a Luxury', in *Sister Outsider*, p. 36.
58 Lorde, 'Age, Race, Class, and Sex: Women Redefining Difference', in *Out the Other Side*, pp. 269–70.
59 Lorde, 'Letter for Jan', in *The Black Unicorn*, p. 88.
60 Lorde, 'Uses of the Erotic: The Erotic as Power', in *Sister Outsider*, p. 53.
61 Lorde, 'Age, Race, Class, and Sex: Women Redefining Difference', in *Out the Other Side*, p. 270.
62 ibid., p. 275.

12 Reading awry: Joan Nestle and the recontextualization of heterosexuality

1 Elizabeth Wilson, 'I'll Climb the Stairway to Heaven: Lesbianism in the Seventies', in Sue Cartledge and Joanna Ryan (eds), *Sex and Love: New Thoughts on Old Contradictions* (London: Virago, 1983), p. 187.
2 See, for example, ibid., p. 186, and Margaret Hunt, 'Report on a Conference on Feminism, Sexuality and Power: The Elect Clash with the Perverse', in Samois (eds), *Coming to Power* (Boston: Alyson, 1987), pp. 88–9.
3 Joan Nestle, *A Restricted Country* (London: Sheba, 1987), p. 105.
4 Sidney Abbott and Barbara Love, *Sappho was a Right-on Woman* (New York: Stein & Day, 1972), p. 40.
5 ibid., pp. 96–7.
6 A reference to clause 28 of the 1988 Local Government Act which aims to prevent the promotion of homosexuality as a 'pretended' family relation.
7 Mary Daly, *Gyn/Ecology* (London: The Women's Press, 1984), p. 12.
8 The work of Jacques Derrida is particularly pertinent in this sense. See, for example, his approach to Lévi-Strauss, in Jacques Derrida, *Of Grammatology*, trans. Gayatri Spivak (Baltimore: Johns Hopkins University Press, 1976), Part II.
9 Nestle, *A Restricted Country*, p. 100.
10 ibid., p. 102.
11 ibid., p. 100.
12 Nestle, 'The Fem Question', in Ann Snitow *et al.* (eds), *Desire: The Politics of Sexuality* (London: Virago, 1984), pp. 232–3.

13 ibid., p. 235.
14 Toril Moi argues: 'If as a woman under patriarchy, Luce Irigaray has, according to her own analysis no language of her own but can only (at best) imitate male discourse, her own writing must inevitably be marked by this. She cannot pretend to be writing in some pure feminist realm outside patriarchy: if her discourse is to be received as anything other than incomprehensible chatter, she must copy male discourse': *Sexual/Textual Politics* (London: Methuen, 1985), p. 140. One option that is open to Irigaray, however, and that which Moi sees her as invoking, is the deployment of a mimicry which, as Moi puts it, 'intends to *undo* the effects of phallocentric discourse simply by *overdoing* them' (ibid.). The relation of this to the strategies I see at work in lesbian butch/femme should be clear.
15 Nestle, *A Restricted Country*, p. 103. This question was of particular importance, argues Nestle, because of the fear of police entrapment which was a continual danger within the heavily regulated bars. See for example, her remarks in *Gay Community News*, 15: 12 (1987), pp. 4–10.
16 Nestle, *A Restricted Country*, p. 103.
17 Privileged in the sense that few bar lesbians possessed the resources, later available to Nestle, with which to put pen to paper. On the subject of privilege and exclusion it might be pertinent to mention Audre Lorde's study of racism within the 1950s bar culture in Audre Lorde, *Zami: A New Spelling of My Name* (London: Sheba, 1984). Lorde's analysis of the exclusions operating within the 1950s lesbian bar communities around race and cultural difference present an interesting comparison with Nestle's work.
18 Madeline Davis and Elizabeth Lapovsky Kennedy, 'Oral History and the Study of Sexuality in the Lesbian Community: Buffalo, New York, 1940–1960', *Feminist Studies*, 12: 7 (Spring 1986).
19 Nestle, *A Restricted Country*, p. 104.
20 Such was the investment in dress that butches would frequently go to great lengths to maintain their butch iconography while barely managing to keep in line with US regulations on transvestism (which required that an individual at all times wear a minimum of three items of clothing designated as belonging to their own sex). As Nestle remembers, socks fringed with lace were one ingenious strategy for evading the vice squad.
21 Nestle, 'The Fem Question', p. 233.
22 Joan Riviere, 'Womanliness as Masquerade', in Victor Burgin *et al.* (eds), *Formations of Fantasy* (London: Methuen, 1986), p. 38.
23 Judith Butler notes: 'When it comes to the counterpart of the analogy that she herself sets up, the woman who "wishes for masculinity" is homosexual only in terms of sustaining a masculine identification, but not in terms of a sexual orientation or desire': *Gender Trouble: Feminism and the Subversion of Identity* (London: Routledge, 1990), p. 52.
24 Since theorizing this point I have come across Sue-Ellen Case's essay, 'Towards a Butch–Femme Aesthetic', in *Discourse: Journal for Theoretical Studies in Media and Culture*, 11: 1 (1988–9), pp. 55–73, which reaches a similar conclusion in its theorization of lesbian butch/femme.
25 Nestle, *A Restricted Country*, p. 108.
26 Butler, op. cit., p. x.
27 ibid., p. 30.
28 ibid., p. 31.
29 Nestle, *A Restricted Country*, p. 106.
30 I do not, of course, put any faith in the term erotica as a sufficient definition. It is intended here as a provisional description only.
31 Nestle, Interview with Gillian Rodgerson, *Gay Times* (October 1988), p. 45.

32 I am aware that this is a claim that has been made about writers from Sade to Bataille and is not in itself unproblematic. Unfortunately, here I can neither discuss the implications that arise from an appreciation of these writers, nor debate the relative merits of lesbian pornography in relation to them. My concern is primarily with an analysis of the exclusions which operate around Nestle as a sexually controversial figure within the women's movement, against whose norms she *can* certainly be said to react.

33 Nestle, *A Restricted Country*, p. 41.

34 ibid., p. 40.

35 ibid., p. 146.

36 ibid., p. 42.

37 ibid., p. 43.

38 ibid., p. 42.

39 Davis and Kennedy, 'Oral History and the Study of Sexuality in the Lesbian Community' pp. 14–15.

40 Nestle, *A Restricted Country*, p. 42.

41 Jane Gallop, 'Annie Leclerc: Writing a Letter with Vermeer', in Nancy Miller (ed.), *The Poetics of Gender* (New York: Columbia University Press, 1986), p. 144.

42 ibid., p. 146.

43 ibid., p. 147.

44 Gayatri Chakravorty Spivak, *In Other Worlds: Essays in Cultural Politics* (London: Routledge, 1988), p. 179.

45 Nestle, *A Restricted Country*, p. 127.

46 ibid., p. 131.

47 Nestle, *Gay Times*, p. 45.

48 Nestle, *A Restricted Country*, p. 155.

49 ibid.

50 ibid., p. 131.

51 ibid., p. 132.

52 ibid.

53 ibid.

54 The first paradigm being the belief that sex is always guilty, and that in order to save the vulnerable from its capacity to deprave and corrupt, sex must be policed extensively by the forces of moral law and order as instituted by the modern state. Its opposite argument, that sex, once released from its oppressive bonds of prudery and repression will act as an innately good and liberating force in the world is, however, equally suspect. For a further examination of these arguments see Michel Foucault, *The History of Sexuality: An Introduction*, trans. Robert Hurley (London: Pelican, 1978).

55 Jana Sawicki, 'Identity Politics and Sexual Freedom', in Irene Diamond and Lee Quinby (eds), *Foucault and Feminism* (Boston: Northeastern University Press, 1988), p. 189.

56 ibid.

57 We can see this in a particularly dramatic instance in Storme Webber's 'Like A Train', in Sheba Collective (eds), *Serious Pleasure* (London: Sheba, 1989), p. 68. This piece knowingly and wittily plays about with feminist injunctions against penetrative, phallic imagery, reshaping these to its own context. What it finally shows is that there is nothing intrinsically bad about trains. Where the problem does lie is with the institution that currently informs and runs them!

58 Nestle, *A Restricted Country*, p. 127 (my emphasis).

59 ibid., p. 133.

60 Wilson, Review of *A Restricted Country*, in *Feminist Review*, 30 (1988), p. 114.

61 The term 'sexual fix' is taken from Stephen Heath's book of that name: *The Sexual Fix* (London: Macmillan, 1982). This is a text whose intention is to debunk some of the more outrageous but none the less potent myths about the sexuality of our time. The state where sex is made the be all and end all of any encounter might be characterized by this term.

62 See, for instance, the preface to *A Restricted Country* where Nestle describes her sexuality as a 'hemp rope' (p. 11), binding her different identities together. The implication, that one's sexuality expresses some 'true' and deep seat of self, demanding immediate liberation is, as Foucault has argued in *The History of Sexuality*, an historical construction and not a 'natural' fact.

63 See, for instance, Susan Barrowclough's analysis of the feminist-identified anti-pornography film 'Not A Love Story': *Screen* 23: 5 (1982). In her analysis Barrowclough describes how the film, by its own terms and techniques, places the viewer in a more privileged position of voyeurism than would, ironically, be allowed by the commercial contract.

64 Sheba Collective (eds), op. cit., p. 10.

Index